**SCOTT, FORESMAN
SOCIAL STUDIES**

America Past and Present

About the Cover Art:

The cover art is one of ten works handcrafted in such traditional American art forms as quilting, needlepoint, embroidery, and appliqué. This art was specially commissioned for the covers of this series by Scott, Foresman and Company. Designed by Patricia Lenihan-Barbee, this 54″ × 54″ patchwork quilt was stitched by Carol Gorman of Glen Ellyn, Illinois. A quilt is a "sandwich" made of two layers of fabric on each side of a soft inner "filling." Simple stitches hold all three layers together and also form decorative lines. This makes a soft, warm fabric for clothing and bed covers. Patchwork quilts are a very American folk craft, originally made from scraps of fabric saved from clothing that was made at home.—Commentary by Barbara Lee Smith of Oak Park, Illinois.

SCOTT, FORESMAN
SOCIAL STUDIES

America Past and Present

Program Authors

Dr. Joan Schreiber
Professor of History
Social Studies Methods
Ball State University
Muncie, Indiana

William Stepien
Instructional Coordinator for Social Studies
School District No. 300
Dundee, Illinois

Dr. John Patrick
Professor of Education
Indiana University
Bloomington, Indiana

Dr. Richard Remy
Director of the Citizenship Development Program
Mershon Center
Ohio State University
Columbus, Ohio

Dr. Geneva Gay
Associate Professor of Education
Purdue University
West Lafayette, Indiana

Dr. Alan J. Hoffman
Professor of Education
Georgia State University
Atlanta, Georgia

Scott, Foresman and Company

Editorial Offices: Glenview, Illinois

Regional Offices: Palo Alto, California · Tucker, Georgia · Glenview, Illinois · Oakland, New Jersey · Dallas, Texas

Contributing Authors

Dr. Roger Berg
Associate Professor of
Elementary Education
The University of Nebraska
at Omaha
Omaha, Nebraska

Gary P. Capurro
Social Studies Department
Chairman
El Camino High School
South San Francisco, California

Dr. Gerald Danzer
Associate Professor of History
University of Illinois
at Chicago Circle
Chicago, Illinois

Sandra S. Deines
Former Teacher
Ridgewood High School
Norridge, Illinois

Joyce H. Frank
Haslett Public School
Haslett, Michigan

Dr. Richard K. Jantz
Associate Professor
Department of Early Childhood
Elementary Education
University of Maryland
College Park, Maryland

Mona Kahney
Glencoe Central School
Glencoe, Illinois

Lynn Klomfar
North Shore Elementary School
St. Petersburg, Florida

Dr. Bruce Kraig
Associate Professor of History
Roosevelt University
Chicago, Illinois

Frances Kaplan Moore
Anshe Emet Day School
Chicago, Illinois

Anne Pane
North Shore Elementary School
St. Petersburg, Florida

Dr. Barbara M. Parramore
Associate Professor and Head
Department of Curriculum
and Instruction
North Carolina State University
at Raleigh
Raleigh, North Carolina

Marian Payne
Reading Consultant
Shippensburg School District
Shippensburg, Pennsylvania

Dr. Richard E. Servey
Professor of Elementary
Education
San Diego State University
San Diego, California

William Smith
Beaver Acres School
Beaverton, Oregon

Special Area Consultants

Special Needs Activities
Judi Coffey
Former Learning Disabilities
Resource Teacher
Fox River Grove S.D. #3
Fox River Grove, Illinois

*Africa and
the Middle East*
Dr. Donna Maier
Associate Professor of History
University of Northern Iowa
Cedar Falls, Iowa

*Activities for
High-Potential Students*
Dr. James Payne
Professor, Department of
Elementary Education
Shippensburg State College
Shippensburg, Pennsylvania

Asia
Dr. Anthony Shaheen
Center for Chinese Studies
The University of Michigan
Ann Arbor, Michigan

Economics
Dr. John Sumansky
Director of Research
Joint Council on
Economic Education
New York, New York

Latin America
Dr. Antonio Vera
Chairman, Department of
Foreign Languages
William Jewell College
Liberty, Missouri

Teacher Consultants

Delores Bailey
Poston Road Elementary School
Martinsville, Indiana

Patricia Bailey
Fort Lowell Elementary School
Tucson, Arizona

James Bimes
Social Studies Consultant
Hazelwood Schools
Florissant, Missouri

Diane Cadei
Social Studies Chairman
Greenfield Union School
Greenfield, California

Sue Crow
Floydada Public Schools
Floydada, Texas

Momilani Dufault
Jackson Elementary School
Colorado Springs, Colorado

Frank Espinoza
Sierra Vista Elementary School
Clovis, California

Carol Lee Forsythe
R. E. Bennett Elementary School
Chelais, Washington

Charlie Mae Hutchings
Social Studies Specialist
Chattanooga Public Schools
Chattanooga, Tennessee

Helen Jenkins
Consultant
Nu-Ma-Ku Alternative School
Freeport, New York

Alyce Kaneshiro
Arleta Primary
Portland, Oregon

Daniel King
Assistant Principal
Mercy Mission Learning Center
Chicago, Illinois

Patricia Latimore
Bonillas Elementary School
Tucson, Arizona

David Luna
Cherrylee School
El Monte, California

Alan Mc Atee
Rattlesnake School
Missoula, Montana

José Martinez
Title IV Director
Illinois State Board
of Education
Chicago, Illinois

**Dr. Dorothy J.
Mugge-Johnson**
Former Professor, Early
Childhood Education
Shippensburg State College
Shippensburg, Pennsylvania

Barbara Okimoto
Burnett Jr. High School
San Jose, California

Earleen Parr
Social Studies Specialist
Midwest City-Del City Schools
Midwest City, Oklahoma

Sr. Marie de Porres, I.H.M.
St. Thomas Aquinas Convent
Philadelphia, Pennsylvania

Mary Ann Qualls
Haywood Elementary School
Nashville, Tennessee

Dr. Martha S. Rupert
Social Studies Coordinator
Greater Latrobe School District
Latrobe, Pennsylvania

Marie Strickland
Donald J. Richey School
Wilmington, Delaware

Serena Westbrook
William Paca Elementary School
Landover, Maryland

ISBN: 0-673-22005-2

Copyright © 1983, Scott, Foresman and Company, Glenview, Illinois. All Rights Reserved. Printed in the United States of America.

This publication is protected by Copyright and permission should be obtained from the publisher prior to any prohibited reproduction, storage in a retrieval system, or transmission in any form or by any means, electronic, mechanical, photocopying, recording, or otherwise. For information regarding permission, write to: Scott, Foresman and Company, 1900 East Lake Avenue, Glenview, Illinois 60025.

The Acknowledgments section on page 479 is an extension of the copyright page.

12345678910-RRW-91908988878685848382

4

Contents

List of Maps and Globes

List of Charts and Graphs

SCOTT, FORESMAN
SOCIAL STUDIES

America Past and Present

Unit ①

These United States

Chapter 1
One Nation, Many People

Chapter 2
North America: Land of Diversity

Chapter 3
The People and the Land

The people of the United States come from many different backgrounds. Working together or alone, they do many different jobs. The people, though different, have much in common. They share beliefs. They share experiences. And, they share the land. They work, live, and play on a land as different as they are. From mountains to deserts to rolling farmlands, it changes again and again.

This is a peaceful protest demonstration in Washington, D.C. It shows how different people can share the same beliefs. It also shows that Americans enjoy the right to openly express their opinions.

Chapter

1

Lesson 1 Americans: People of Every Description
Lesson 2 Americans at Work
Lesson 3 Americans Are a Free People

One Nation, Many People

America—
Cent[er] of equal daughters, equal sons,
All, all alike endear'd [loved], grown, ungrown, young
    or old . . .

                                —Walt Whitman

Lesson 1 Americans: People of Every Description

Who are the sons and daughters in Walt Whitman's poem? They are people like you, your family, and your friends. They are also people from hundreds of different backgrounds. They are like the people shown on these pages.

They are all Americans. They may be tall, short, thin, heavy, women, men, young, or old. They may be rich or poor, famous or unknown to all but a few. They may live in Miami, Arizona, or Miami, Florida. Americans are white, black, Spanish-speaking, of Asian **descent**, or American Indian. Together they form the nation of the United States.

descent, family line; ancestors; parentage; heritage.

More than 228 million people are citizens of the United States. No two of these people are exactly alike. Though every person is different, no one is more or less American than any other person.

16

One way to see what the American people are like is to study population statistics. Population statistics are number facts about people. Here are a few statistics about Americans.

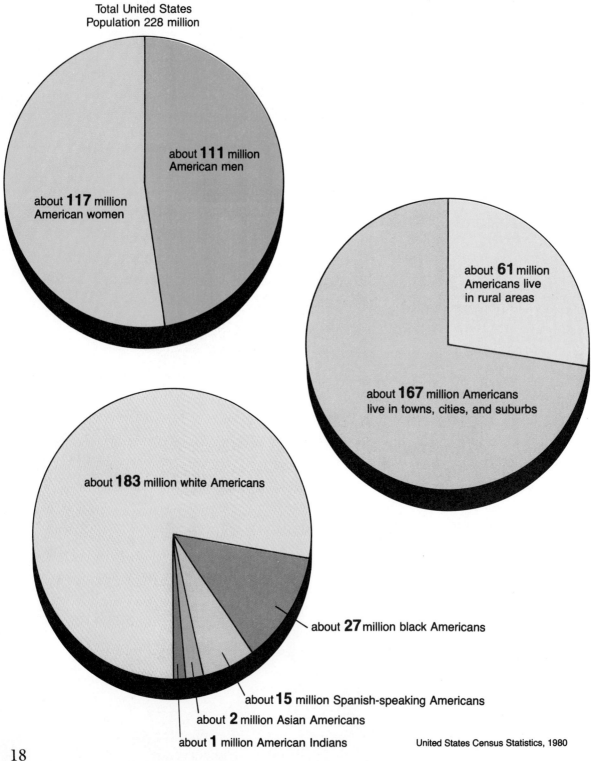

Total United States Population 228 million

about **111** million American men

about **117** million American women

about **61** million Americans live in rural areas

about **167** million Americans live in towns, cities, and suburbs

about **183** million white Americans

about **27** million black Americans

about **15** million Spanish-speaking Americans

about **2** million Asian Americans

about **1** million American Indians

United States Census Statistics, 1980

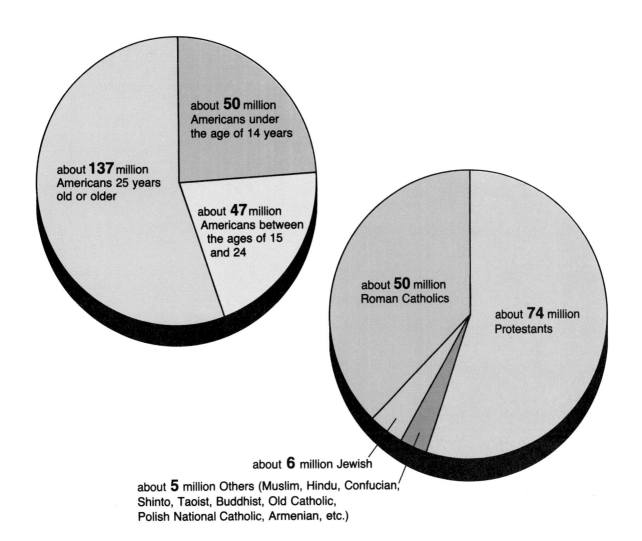

about **50** million
Americans under
the age of 14 years

about **137** million
Americans 25 years
old or older

about **47** million
Americans between
the ages of 15
and 24

about **50** million
Roman Catholics

about **74** million
Protestants

about **6** million Jewish

about **5** million Others (Muslim, Hindu, Confucian,
Shinto, Taoist, Buddhist, Old Catholic,
Polish National Catholic, Armenian, etc.)

One fact seems clear from these population statistics. The people of the United States are diverse, or different. They show their diversity in the color of their skin, their age, whether they are men or women, where they live, and in what they believe. How else do they show diversity?

Checking Up

1. What kinds of groups make up the American nation?

2. What does the United States mean to you?

3. How can you use population statistics to describe the people of the United States?

Lesson 2 Americans at Work

The People, Yes

Without the daily chores of the people
The milk trucks would have no milk
The markets neither meat nor potatoes
The railroad and bus timetables
Would be on the fritz
And the shippers would say "Phooey!"
And daily the chores are done
With heavy toil here, light laughter there,
The chores of the people, yes.

—*Carl Sandburg*

Carl Sandburg wrote *The People, Yes* almost fifty years ago. What do you think he was saying in the poem? He might have been saying that each worker depends on other workers. He might have been thanking the American people for helping each other get their daily jobs done.

Many people would agree with Carl Sandburg. They feel good about working because they know they are helping others. They know that other workers need them and that they need other workers.

A hardware store clerk can put products on the shelves because a truck driver delivered them. Factory workers made the delivery truck. A power plant supplied the factory with electricity. Construction workers built the power plant. Those workers bought their tools at the hardware store. Each job has different responsibilities. Each worker helps other workers get jobs done.

Why else do people work? The clerk, truck driver, and construction worker feel good about working. But they also need to earn a living. The workers *need* food, clothing, and housing to live. They also *want* certain things to make their lives enjoyable: a TV set, a vacation, an air conditioner. People work to earn money to take care of their needs and wants.

Americans work at thousands of jobs. They work on farms, in factories, in offices, on roads, in the air, underwater, and underground. A few have even worked on the moon.

Shown at the left are two of about eighteen thousand women who work as carpenters in the United States.

Kinds of Workers

goods, personal property, belongings; thing or things for sale. **services**, a performance of duties; work done in the service of others.

There are two kinds of workers in the United States. There are producers of manufactured **goods** or farm products and producers of **services**.

Go to any store in the United States. American workers manufactured, made by hand or with a machine, many of the products for sale. Go to a grocery store. Fill your cart with good things to eat such as apples, cereal, and milk. American workers tended the plants and animals that these foods came from.

Go to your doctor or dentist. Ask a police officer for help. Call a plumber to repair a drainpipe. These people do not make products. They do not grow anything that can be used or eaten. Instead, they produce a service. They do things for you and get paid for doing them.

Today there are more workers producing services than there are producing products. Why is this so? Most goods in the United States are made by machine. Fewer workers are needed to make goods this way than if goods were made by hand.

Workers in the United States

Each Figure = 2,500,000 Workers

Producers of Manufactured Goods   25,500,000

Producers of Services   66,500,000

Producers of Farm Products   3,200,000

22

Look carefully at the photos on this page and on page 24. Which workers are producing goods? Which are producing a service? How do the workers differ in terms of:
- where they work? (inside or outside)
- the conditions under which they work? (noisy or quiet)
- the people they would meet on the job?
- whether they work more with their hands or their minds?
- whether they work with people or machines?

23

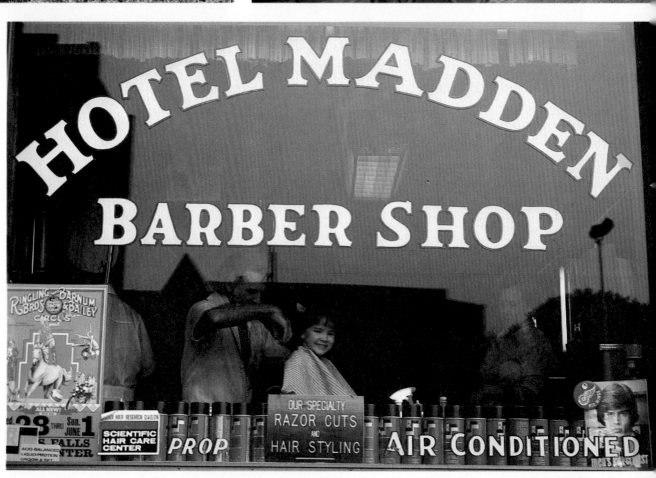

24

Number of Men and Women Workers in the United States 1950–1980

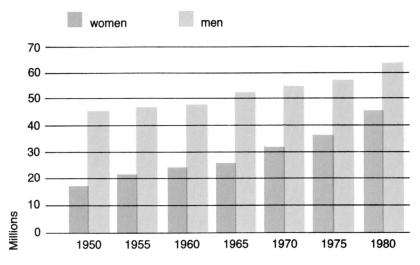

women   men

```
Millions
70 ────────────────────────────
60 ────────────────────────────
50 ────────────────────────────
40 ────────────────────────────
30 ────────────────────────────
20 ────────────────────────────
10 ────────────────────────────
 0
      1950  1955  1960  1965  1970  1975  1980
```

Source: Handbook of Labor Statistics Dec. 1980

But workers who do not produce goods must also make a living. They do so by producing a service. Today, most people cannot or do not want to do everything for themselves. They want to use free time for other things. They are willing to pay for a variety of services. What are some services that you and your family pay for?

Today, there are more women producing goods and services than in the past. They work as police officers, telephone line workers, bus drivers, doctors, farmers, computer programmers, and government officials. Look at the graph on this page and see how the number of women working outside the home grew between 1950 and 1980. Today, almost half of all Americans working outside the home are women.

Checking Up

1. What is the difference between a producer of goods and a producer of services?

2. What are the most important services you and your family pay for?

3. If a man and woman have the same amount of experience and do the same job, should they be paid the same?

Facts and Figures

As the following facts show, millions of women are now working outside the home.

Doctors	56,000
Lawyers	67,000
Musicians	41,000
Photographers	23,000
Carpenters	18,000
Aircraft Mechanics	3,000
Truck drivers	41,000
Firefighters	3,000
Police—Detectives	28,000

Source: U.S. Gov't Statistics, 1980.

Finding the Right Job For You

In some jobs, people work in large groups. The groups are led by managers who help the workers plan their daily chores. Read what one man has to say about his job as a factory manager:

"My job seems to grow and grow. I'm the general manager at a big plastics company. I have to know about every machine and every worker here. The owner, about fifty workers, and thousands of customers depend on me to plan what our company will make and how we will make it. Sometimes, it seems like there's too much to do and too many people to please. How can you please everyone?

"My job isn't only problems, though. I feel good when the problems get solved. I also feel good when a project is finished. There's something special about starting off with an idea drawn on paper and watching it grow into something real.

"Last week I took my kids to a shopping center. As we walked through the stores, I could show them something in almost every store that my workers and I helped make. I like the feeling that all the little jobs I do every day add up to something I can be proud of."

Not all workers deal with large groups of people or machines. Some people work

(above) The factory manager and an assistant plan the development of a new product. (right) The social worker proposes solutions to a senior citizen's problems.

with only one other person at a time. Read what a young social worker has to say about her job:

"A lot of people wonder wny I'd take a job like this. I mean, it seems like my whole job is to listen to people's problems. Not all their problems can be solved. And I don't really make much money, so people wonder why I bother.

"Mostly I like being a social worker because I really like people. Their problems aren't just problems. They are real day-to-day events that the people need help to solve. I help children with family problems. I meet with adults with job problems. I speak to teenagers having trouble with school. I help the elderly meet their basic needs. It doesn't matter if they're rich or poor or in-between. I work with anyone who asks for help.

"I like helping people learn how to help themselves. By showing people choices they can make to help themselves, I help them learn to solve their own problems. When that happens, the clients feel good and I feel proud."

Most Americans work about fifty years after they leave high school. Many will spend those years doing jobs they do not like. Some people might make better choices if they thought about their likes and dislikes *before* taking a job.

You have just read how two people feel about their work. How can you know your likes and dislikes about work? You might try to list your feelings about work. Here are some questions to ask yourself:

Do I like to work with my hands?
Do I like to work with machines?
Do I like to work with people?
Do I like to work alone?
Do I like to work with mathematics?
Do I like to read and write?
Do I like to solve problems?
Do I like to talk before large groups?
Do I like to be indoors?
Do I like the out-of-doors?
Do I like to work with plants?
Do I like to work with animals?
Do I like to help others?
Does the approval of others mean a lot to me?
Do I need lots of money to live the way I like?
Does it matter where I live while I work?
Do I like to travel?
Do I like to stay at home?

Answer questions like these and you may have an idea of the kind of work you would be happy doing over a long period of time. But be careful. You have one set of feelings now. Your feelings about some things may change. If your feelings change, so might your ideas about jobs.

Lesson 3 Americans Are a Free People

She heard the jet engines slow down as the plane prepared to land. It turned and made a final approach to the runway through a low layer of clouds. Suddenly, Yolanda Mariño saw her new home in the United States. It was night. Millions of lights in the city of Chicago reflected in Yolanda's eyes.

Chicago stretched for miles beneath her. She could see the outline of very tall buildings and the headlamps of thousands of cars. The people might have been on their way home from work, she thought. Perhaps they were on their way to a play, a museum, or a movie. Maybe they were going to visit friends, or shop, or eat at their favorite restaurant. "The important thing," Yolanda later told a friend, "was that they were probably doing what they wanted to do. Not what someone told them they should be doing."

It was a city and a way of life that was very different from the one she was used to in Cuba. But Yolanda knew that the real differences between the United States and Cuba could not be seen from the air. The real differences could only be seen and felt on the ground.

Yolanda enjoys one of her many new freedoms in the United States.

The plane stopped when it reached the terminal. Inside the waiting area, Yolanda saw smiling faces. She knew she had a smile on her face, too.

Soon she had found a new apartment and a new job. Her new friends could see that she was happy to be living in the United States. They wanted to know why she had left her home in Cuba.

"Life in Cuba is very difficult. The government decides where you can live. It says where and when you can travel. It controls the radio and television stations. You hear and see what the government wants you to hear and see. All the newspapers and books are approved or written by the government. The government even decides who can go to school and what subjects they can take.

"In the United States I can eat, work, travel, and go to school where I want. I can shop where I want, too. If the prices are too high in one store, I can go to another. In Cuba, the government sets all the prices.

What do you think would be a good title for this cartoon?

a. People don't listen very well.
b. As stamp prices get fatter, our pocketbooks get thinner.
c. The Post Office is holding down costs.

The cartoonist is saying that stamp prices are going up so fast that people can't keep up with them. Since the Post Office is a department in the government, the cartoonist is really poking fun at the government, too. This would never be allowed in many countries around the world. What freedom do Americans have that allows them to openly give their opinion like the cartoonist did?

"It was both hard and easy to leave Cuba," said Yolanda. "Hard because my family and some friends were not coming with me. Easy because I hoped I would have a better life in the United States."

"Most important, I can speak what is on my mind. I can go to a bookstore or a newsstand and buy something that I want to read. I can form my own beliefs and give people my own opinions."

Yolanda is studying to become a **naturalized** United States citizen. To become citizens, people who are not born in the United States must pass a test and take an oath of allegiance to the country. The test shows if they understand how the United States government works. It also shows if they know the rights, freedoms, and responsibilities of citizenship. By taking the oath, they are saying they will be loyal to the United States.

Yolanda is excited about her new country. "America is a land of opportunity. You can decide your own future. Some Americans take this for granted. But when you have not had the freedoms and rights Americans enjoy, you appreciate them very much."

Checking Up

1. How did Yolanda explain the differences between Cuba and the United States?

2. What did Yolanda mean when she said that some Americans take their rights and freedoms "for granted"?

3. What is the most important freedom you feel you have?

4. How do people from other countries become citizens?

30

SOMEONE YOU SHOULD KNOW

General Daniel "Chappie" James, Jr.

In 1974, Chappie James became the first black, four-star general in the United States military. He served as the Commander in Chief of the North American Air Defense Command in Colorado until he retired in 1978. He commanded more than sixty-three thousand soldiers who were to protect the United States and Canada from attack.

James worked hard to reach this position. His mother taught him that there was no such thing as giving up. She told him that there was an eleventh commandment: "Thou shalt not quit."

He wanted to become a navy pilot. But in the 1930s, the navy did not want black pilots. He was finally accepted in the Army Air Corps, but was only allowed to fly with other black pilots. After World War II, he was not allowed to enter certain buildings because he was black.

Chappie James succeeded by believing in himself. He also believed deeply enough in his country to fight for it in two wars. Because of his wartime work, he was made commander of the biggest American air base outside the United States.

When he returned to the United States, he began to speak to people about patriotism. The best weapon the United States could have is "a weapon called unity," said James.

Most of all, his talks were about individual opportunity. He believed in what he called the "power of excellence." Everyone has enough knowledge and willpower to make their own excellence grow. "But, you have to be willing to work."

General James speaking on the "power of excellence."

Write your answers on paper. Do not write in the book.

Using Key Words

goods   **descent**
services   **naturalize**

Write a short meaning for each of the key words listed above.

Reviewing Main Ideas

Some of the sentences below are true and some are false. Number your paper from 1 to 5 and write either *true* or *false* by each number. If you believe a sentence is false, write it so it will be true.

1. Americans all look alike.

2. Different people have different religious beliefs.

3. People's wants and needs are the same.

4. Today, in the United States there are more workers who produce a product than provide a service.

5. There are now fewer women working outside the home than in 1950.

Thinking Things Over

1. Look at the job want ads in a newspaper. Select three ads for jobs that interest you. Place them on a sheet of paper. Next to the ads write the things that would attract you to those jobs. Next, select the ads for three jobs that you would not want to have. Next to the ads write those things which you did not like about the jobs.

2. Imagine that you met a person who had just come to the United States from another country. What would you tell the person about the freedoms that you have?

Practicing Skills

This chart shows the number of men and women who came from another country to become United States citizens. Use the chart to answer the questions.

Year	New Citizens	Men	Women
1970	111,000	53,000	58,000
1972	116,000	55,500	60,500
1974	134,000	62,000	72,000
1976	142,000	66,000	76,000
1978	174,000	79,000	95,000

1. In which of these five years did the most people become citizens?

2. Seventy-two thousand women became citizens in _____.

3. More men became citizens during these five years than women. Is that idea true or false?

4. In 1978, _____ more women became citizens than men.

TIME OUT for Map and Globe Review

What Maps Can Do

On the way to the zoo, Mr. Martin made a wrong turn. The Martins got lost and arrived late.

"We haven't much time," Mr. Martin said. "We can't see everything. What do you want to see most?"

"Snakes!" Jenny cried.

"Lions and tigers!" Brian said.

"Dolphins!" Carol shouted.

What would help the Martins find the animals they want to see?

If you answered, "a map," you're right. Maps show us where things are. They can help us get where we want to go. We can get a lot of information from them at a glance.

Exploring with Maps. Study the map of the zoo below. Answer the following questions.

1. How do you know this is a map of the zoo? What tells you?

2. What would help the Martins find a refreshment stand?

3. How would you tell someone to get from the ape house to the elephant exhibit? from the bird house to the zebras? What would help you give directions?

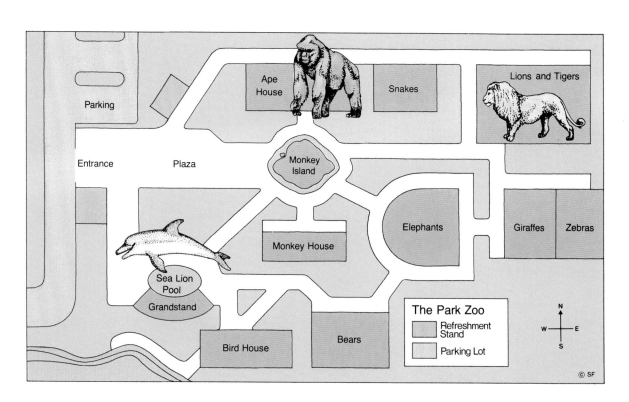

The Park Zoo
- Refreshment Stand
- Parking Lot

© SF

What Kind of Map?

There are many different kinds of maps. One kind you'll use often in this book is a political map. Political maps show boundaries between political areas, such as cities, states, and countries. The map on pages 34 and 35 is a political map. Look for the map title. Find your state on the map. What states border yours?

Another kind of map is a physical map. Physical maps show the landforms of a particular place. Landforms are the kinds of land a place has. Some places, for example, have low, flat land called plains. Other places have high mountains.

The United States has many different landforms. These are shown on the physical map on page 36. What do the colors on this map mean? (If you need to, refer to the geography glossary on page 458 for descriptions of the landforms shown on the map.)

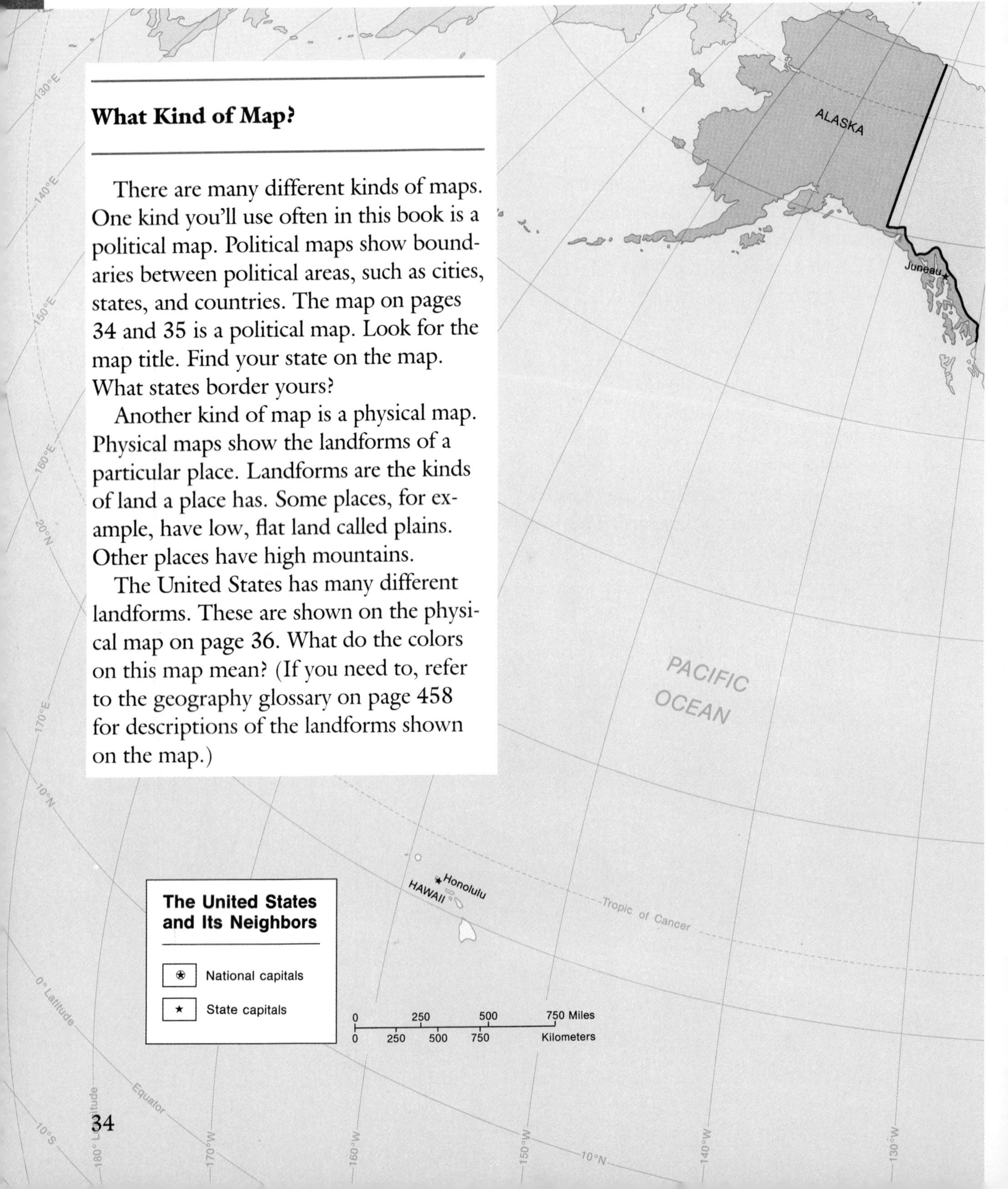

ALASKA

Juneau

PACIFIC OCEAN

*Honolulu
HAWAII

Tropic of Cancer

The United States and Its Neighbors

⊛ National capitals

★ State capitals

| 0 | 250 | 500 | 750 Miles |
| 0 | 250 | 500 | 750 | Kilometers |

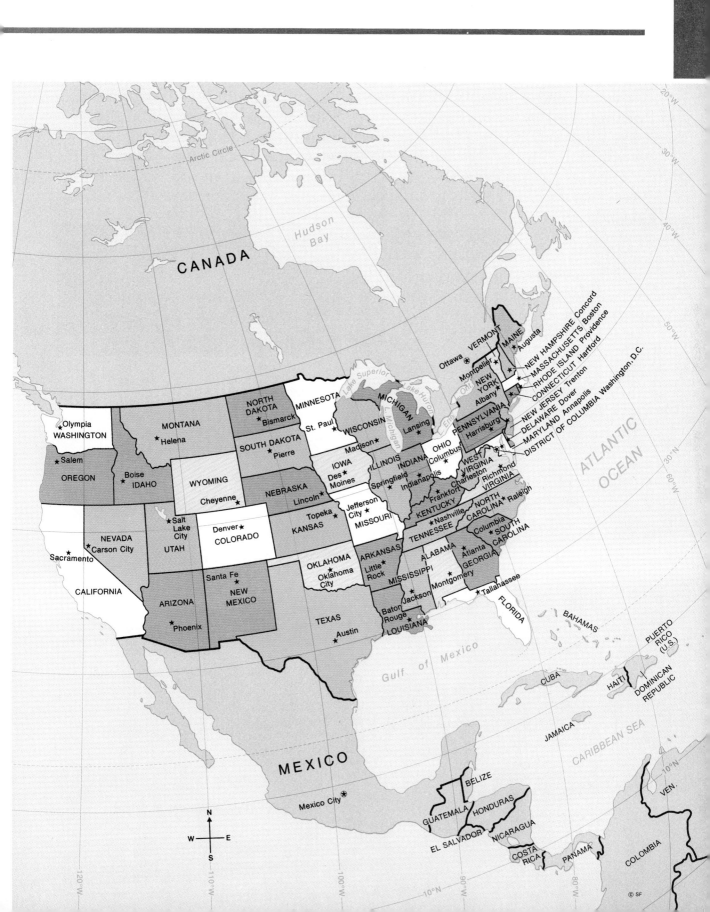

TIME OUT for Map and Globe Review

Another kind of physical map is shown on pages 456-457. It shows land elevation, which is the height of land above sea level.

Maps can give you information about many subjects. What kinds of information do the maps on pages 52 and 65 give? An easy way to answer this question is by reading the map titles. It also helps to read the key to find out what the map shows. Not all maps have keys but if special symbols are used, there will be a key to explain them.

Exploring with Maps. Copy the chart below on a sheet of paper. Using the maps on pages 34 and 35 and the map below, write one landform of each type on the chart. List the state or states where the landform is located.

Landform	Name	Location
Mountains		
Hills		
Plateaus		
Plains		

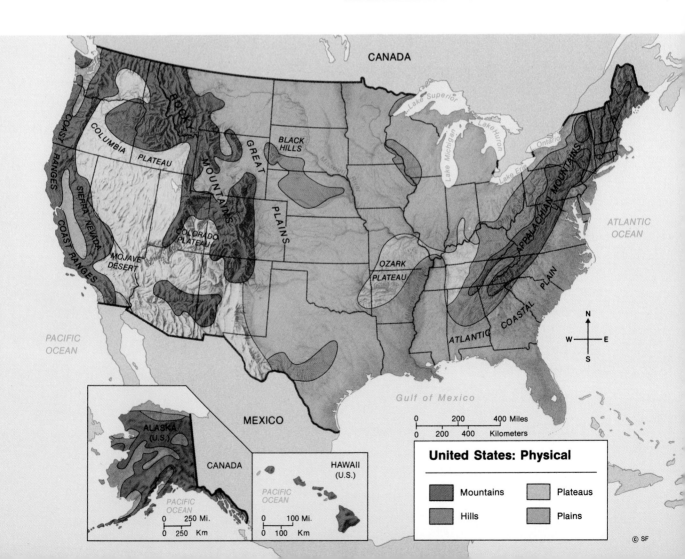

United States: Physical

Mountains / Plateaus / Hills / Plains

Where Is It?

Places on earth have exact locations. Mapmakers have drawn a system of imaginary lines around the earth. Some lines go around the globe from east to west. These are lines of latitude, or parallels. See Globe A. These lines do not touch at any point as they circle the earth. Imagine you walked along one of them. You would walk around the earth and end where you began.

The Equator is the 0 east-west line. The North Pole and South Pole are each numbered 90. All east-west lines, or lines of latitude, are numbered in degrees (°) from 0° to 90°, north and south from the Equator.

The other lines that mapmakers have drawn run north and south between the North Pole and the South Pole. These are lines of longitude, or meridians. These lines do not go all the way around the earth. Meridians only make up half circles on the globe. Find the meridians on Globe B.

The Prime Meridian is a special name for the 0 north-south line. All other north-south lines, or lines of longitude, are numbered in degrees (°) from the Prime Meridian. They are numbered from 0° east to 180°, and from 0° west to 180° around the globe.

Together, lines of latitude and longitude form a grid on the globe. This grid is shown on Globe C. The location of any place on the globe is the point where the latitude and longitude lines cross.

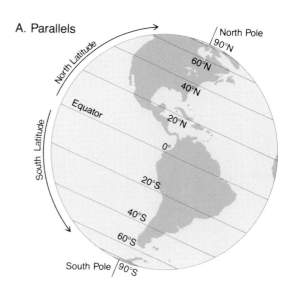

A. Parallels

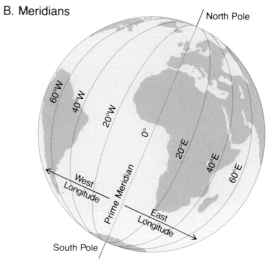

B. Meridians

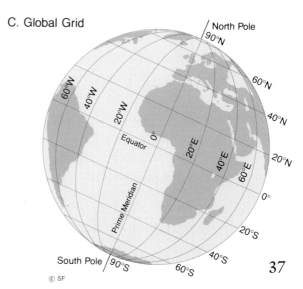

C. Global Grid

© SF

37

TIME OUT for Map and Globe Review

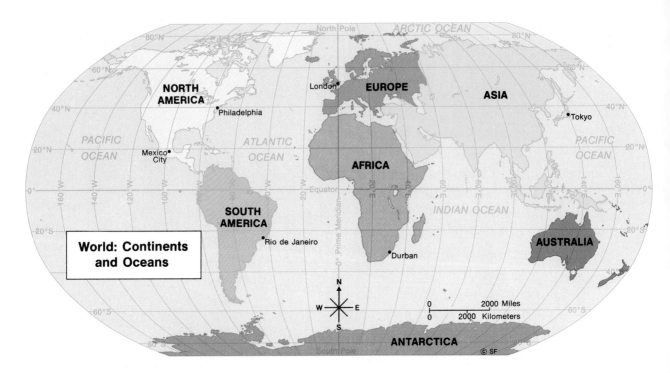

World: Continents and Oceans

Another way to locate places is to tell what hemisphere they're in. Hemisphere means half a sphere (hemi = half). The earth is a sphere. The Equator divides the earth in half. The two equal parts of the earth are the Northern and Southern hemispheres. Which of these hemispheres do you live in?

A line passing through the North and South poles divides the earth in half the other way. This form the Western and Eastern hemispheres. Which of these hemispheres do you live in?

Exploring with Maps. The world map above shows latitude and longitude lines. Using these lines, you can tell the earth location for the places shown.

1. Find the 60°W meridian. It is one-third of the way around the world from the Prime Meridian. Which continents does it cross?

2. Find the 20°N parallel on the map above. It is between the Equator and the North Pole. Which continents does it cross?

3. The numbers below are earth locations for three cities. What cities are they?
   40°N and 75°W
   30°S and 31°E
   20°N and 100°W

4. Give the earth locations for
   London: _____ and _____
   Tokyo: _____ and _____
   Rio de Janeiro: _____ and _____

North Pole

Northern
Hemisphere

Equator

Southern
Hemisphere

South Pole

North Pole

Western
Hemisphere

Eastern
Hemisphere

South Pole

Northern Hemisphere

ASIA

AFRICA

EUROPE

ARCTIC OCEAN

• North Pole

PACIFIC
OCEAN

ATLANTIC
OCEAN

NORTH
AMERICA

Equator

Western Hemisphere

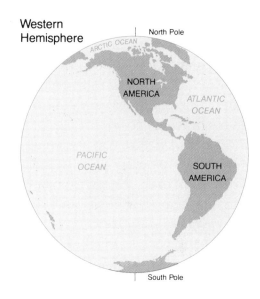

North Pole

ARCTIC OCEAN

NORTH
AMERICA

ATLANTIC
OCEAN

PACIFIC
OCEAN

SOUTH
AMERICA

South Pole

Southern Hemisphere

PACIFIC
OCEAN

SOUTH
AMERICA

• South Pole

ATLANTIC
OCEAN

ANTARCTICA

AUSTRALIA

AFRICA

INDIAN
OCEAN

Equator

© SF

Eastern Hemisphere

North Pole

ARCTIC OCEAN

EUROPE

ASIA

ATLANTIC
OCEAN

AFRICA

INDIAN
OCEAN

PACIFIC
OCEAN

AUSTRALIA

© SF

South Pole

Which Way?

When we use lines of latitude and longitude, we are using directions—north, south, east, and west. These are the four cardinal directions. North is toward the North Pole; south is toward the South Pole. East is to the right as you face north; west is to the left as you face north.

Many maps show directions with an arrow pointing north and lines pointing to the other directions. Maps can be made with north in any position. Check the direction arrows before you use a map.

Of course, not every place is directly north, south, east, or west. Some places are in between—northeast, southeast, southwest, and northwest.

Exploring with Maps. Look at the map on pages 34 and 35. Find your state. What state or ocean is west of your state? Find Iowa on the map. Which direction is

Minnesota from Iowa? Which direction is it from Washington to Oregon? What is the most northeastern state? Which way would you go to get from Denver, Colorado, to Richmond, Virginia?

How Far?

The map on page 41 is a road map. It shows part of the state of Texas.

The map key tells what the symbols on the map mean. The key shows the different sizes of cities and kinds of roads. Highway 10 heading west from Houston is an interstate highway. Highway 290 northwest from Houston to Austin is a U.S. highway.

The U.S. and interstate highways connect major cities of the country. They are national highways. What national highways are near where you live? On the Texas map, find Route 35 heading south from Houston. What kind of highway is this? Do you have state highways near your home?

The map shows two ways to figure distance. One way is by the bar scale of miles. It is easy to see why maps must have a bar scale to show distance. Could you carry a map which was the *real* size of Texas?

People who make maps draw them to scale. Mapmakers take the real distance on earth and draw it smaller on the map. The scale on this map shows that thirty real miles on the earth are equal to one unit on the map. Using a ruler, you can see

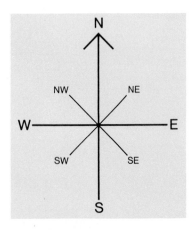

that the center of Houston is about thirty miles from Rosenberg. About how far is Houston from Austin?

The other way to figure distance with this map is by adding the numbers shown between places on a highway. Black dots are often placed where roads meet. The numbers between the dots tell the number of miles between two places. Find Galveston, southeast of Houston. Use the black dots to find how far it is from Galveston to Houston. According to the bar scale,

what is the distance? Why is there a difference between these two measurements?

To find how far it is between two places, add up the numbers between the dots or use the bar scale. Which way do you like better?

Exploring with Maps. What is the shortest route from Elgin (twenty-five miles east of Austin) to Edna (about eighty-nine miles southwest of Houston). What direction would you go, and how far would you travel?

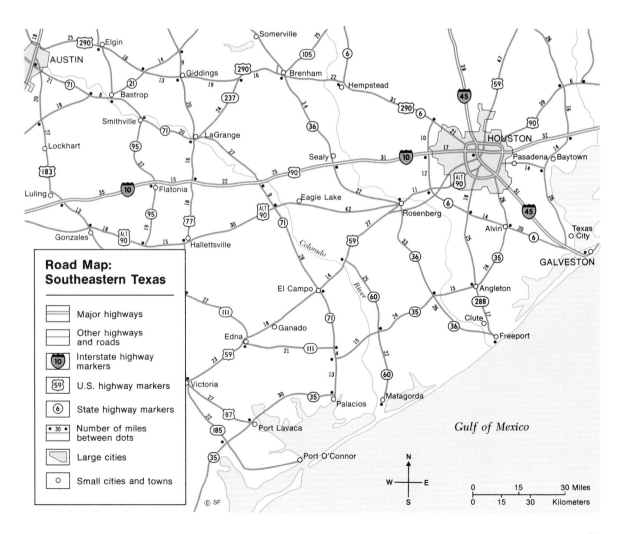

Day, Night, and Seasons

You often hear about sunrise and sunset. Does the sun really rise and set or only seem to?

Actually, it is the earth that moves. If you imagine yourself over the North Pole looking down on the globe, the earth turns the opposite direction from the way the hands of a clock move. The earth spins, or rotates, around an imaginary line that runs through the center of the earth. This line is called an axis. One end of the earth's axis is the North Pole. The other end is the South Pole.

The earth makes one complete turn every twenty-four hours. As the earth rotates, different parts of the world face toward or away from the sun. At 12:00 noon where you live, you are facing the

sun and it is day. By 9:00 in the evening, the spinning earth has turned you away from the sun, and it is night. What is another way of saying "the sun has set"?

As the earth spins, it also moves around the sun. Each trip around the sun, or revolution, takes a whole year (365¼ days).

As the earth moves around the sun, the seasons change. How does this happen? The earth's axis is tilted at an angle of 23½°. This makes different parts of the earth's surface get different amounts of sunlight at different times as the earth revolves around the sun.

When a part of the earth is pointing most directly at the sun, it gets the strongest sunlight. The strong sunlight brings a warm season. At a different time in the year, when that same part points away from the sun more, it gets weaker sunlight. This brings a cold season. Look

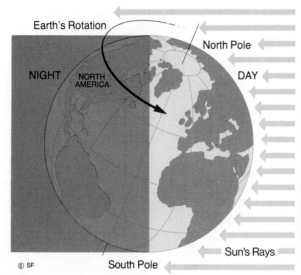

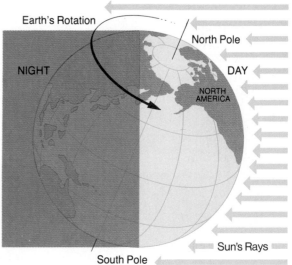

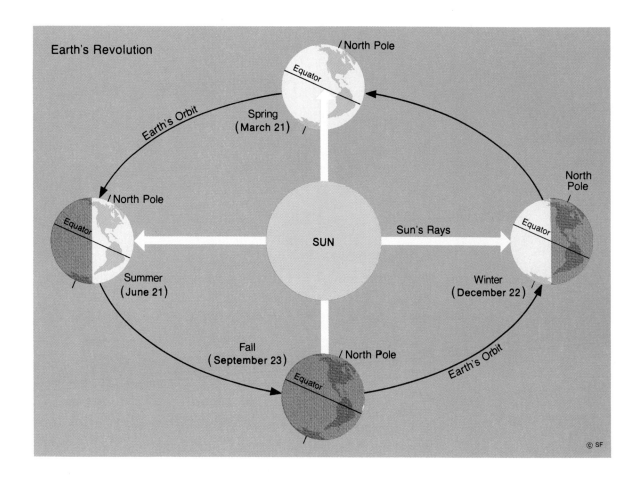

Earth's Revolution

North Pole

Equator

Earth's Orbit

Spring
(March 21)

North Pole

Equator

SUN

Sun's Rays

North
Pole

Equator

Summer
(June 21)

Winter
(December 22)

Fall
(September 23)

North Pole

Equator

Earth's Orbit

© SF

at the drawing on this page. Describe the two ways the earth is moving in this drawing.

Exploring with Maps. Stand four or five feet away from a lamp. Your left shoulder should face the lamp. Look straight ahead. Slowly rotate or turn to your left. Do you always have the same view of the lamp? How is this similar to the movement of the earth rotating on its axis?

North America: Land of Diversity

Pleasant it looked,
this newly created world.
Along the entire length and breadth
of the earth, our grandmother,
extended the green reflection
of her covering
and the escaping odors
were pleasant to inhale.*

—*Winnebago*

The Winnebago are American Indians who live in eastern Wisconsin. The poem tells of their love of the land. Others have grown to love their home, their land, in North America. One of the reasons for this love is the land's diversity.

Lesson 1 Landform Regions

The land of the United States, like its people, is very diverse. It is made up of many parts, or **regions**. A region is an area that has some common feature that makes it different from other areas. One type of region in the United States is **landform**. The common feature in one landform region might be mountains. In another, it might be plains or plateaus.

When you look at the map on page 46, you will see that landform regions are divided by color. You should also notice that landform regions do not stop at the United States political **boundaries**, or borders. Some are found in other parts of North America such as Canada and Mexico.

Look at the landform map of North America. You will see that most of the land near the Atlantic Ocean and the Gulf of Mexico is a plain. This region is called the Atlantic Coastal Plain Region. It is rocky in the north and sandy in the south. In some places, great swamps stretch for hundreds of miles. Away from the coast, the soil is rich and red.

This land and water is in Wisconsin. How does the photo compare with the ideas in the poem of the Winnebago?

landform, one of the many physical shapes that cover the earth's surface.

*"This Newly Created World," taken from *The Medicine Rite* as recorded in Paul Radin *The Road of Life and Death: A Ritual Drama of the American Indians* (p. 254), Bollingen Series V. Copyright © 1945 by Princeton University Press; copyright © renewed 1972 by Princeton University Press. Reprinted by permission.

The peaceful harbor town of Gloucester, Massachusetts, on the Atlantic Coastal Plain.

An early morning fog rises above the fall colors that blanket the Appalachian Highlands.

45

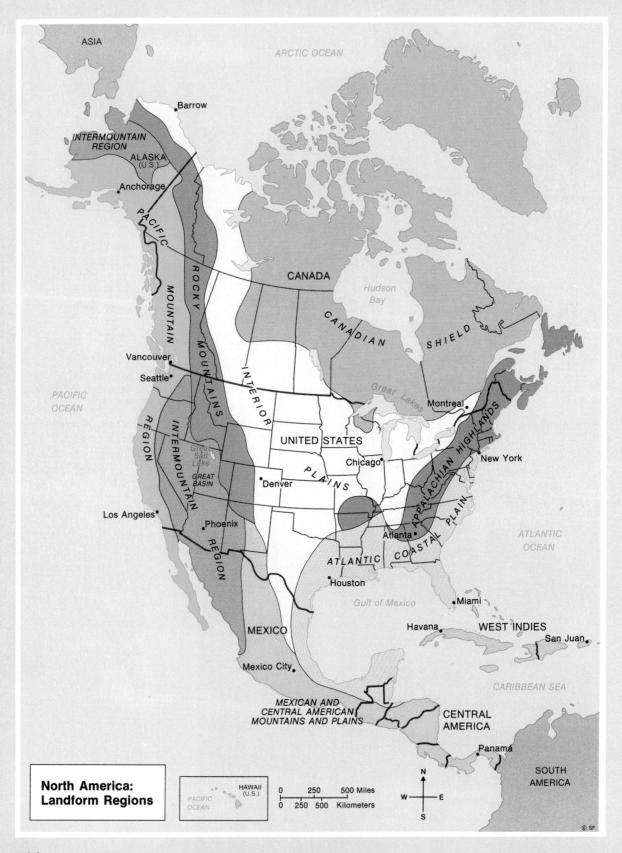

ASIA

ARCTIC OCEAN

Barrow

INTERMOUNTAIN REGION

ALASKA (U.S.)

Anchorage

PACIFIC

ROCKY MOUNTAINS

MOUNTAIN

CANADA

Hudson Bay

C A N A D I A N   S H I E L D

PACIFIC OCEAN

Vancouver

Seattle

INTERIOR

Great Lakes

Montreal

REGION

INTERMOUNTAIN

UNITED STATES

Great Salt Lake

APPALACHIAN HIGHLANDS

New York

Chicago

GREAT BASIN

Denver

P L A I N S

Los Angeles

REGION

Phoenix

COASTAL PLAIN

ATLANTIC OCEAN

Atlanta

A T L A N T I C

Houston

Gulf of Mexico

Miami

MEXICO

Havana

WEST INDIES

San Juan

Mexico City

CARIBBEAN SEA

MEXICAN AND CENTRAL AMERICAN MOUNTAINS AND PLAINS

CENTRAL AMERICA

Panamá

SOUTH AMERICA

North America: Landform Regions

HAWAII (U.S.)

PACIFIC OCEAN

0   250   500 Miles

0   250   500   Kilometers

N
W   E
S

© SF

West of the coastal plain is the Appalachian Highlands Region. You can see from the photograph of this region that it has high hills, valleys, and rounded mountains. The region extends from the southern United States to southeastern Canada.

Located in the middle of the continent is the region called the Interior Plains. It stretches from northern Canada to the center of Mexico. It is made up of plains and gently rolling hills. This is a major crop-growing area in Canada and the United States.

North of this region lies the Canadian Shield. This huge area covers almost half of Canada. It reaches south to include parts of the north central United States. The rocks of the Canadian Shield are among the oldest on earth. Glaciers, or giant sheets of ice, passed over this land thousands of years ago. They carved the mountains and plains of this large region.

West of the Interior Plains is the region of the Rocky Mountains. The Rocky Mountains are really a series of ranges that extend from Alaska down to New Mexico. These ranges have some of the roughest and highest peaks in the world.

(top left) Buffaloes graze peacefully on the Interior Plains of Nebraska. (above) Glaciers have clearly done their work on these rocks of the Canadian Shield.

Winter's first snow dusts the sharp peaks of the Rocky Mountains.

To the west of the Rocky Mountains is the Intermountain Region. It is called that since it lies between the Rocky Mountains and the Sierra Nevada. This large region extends from northern Washington to Mexico. It is made up of a number of high plateaus. Some of these have been carved by wind and water into beautiful rock forms and canyons. The most famous feature in the area is the Grand Canyon.

Also in this region is an area called the Great Basin. It is called this because it is shaped like a huge bowl. The bowl is almost five hundred miles wide. Much of the water in this region drains toward the center and forms the Great Salt Lake.

Along the coast of the Pacific Ocean is the Pacific Mountain Region. This region has two major landforms. Next to the plateaus of the Intermountain Region is a line of mountain ranges. They include the Alaska Range, the Coast Mountains in Canada, the Cascades in Washington and Oregon, and the Sierra Nevada in California. These ranges contain many high peaks and active volcanoes. Further west is another, but shorter, line of mountain ranges.

Between these two groups of mountain ranges is the second major landform. Here lie the rich, green valleys of Oregon and California. Fruits and vegetables are grown in these valleys all year around.

48

Wind-weathered buttes (isolated hills with flat tops) greet the early evening shadows in Monument Valley, Utah. This huge valley of sandstone-rock formations lies within the Intermountain Plateau.

(left) Spring is welcomed in the Santa Ynez Valley of California along the Pacific Mountain Region.

The contrast of rugged mountains and deep valleys is seen in the photo of Mexico.

Also part of this region is Hawaii. The islands of Hawaii are really the tips of giant mountains. Their bottoms are on the floor of the Pacific Ocean, more than six thousand feet below sea level.

The last landform region shown on your map is the Mexican and Central American Mountain and Plains Region. It is an area of high, rugged mountains, deep, green valleys, and a central plateau. The central plateau is the location of Mexico City and other large cities. It is an ideal place for crop growing because of its rich soil.

Look again at the landform map. North America gives a good example of how two kinds of borders, landform and political, are not always the same.

Checking Up

1. In what landform region of the United States do you live?

2. Explain how any two of the landforms are different.

3. How might people living in different landform regions lead different lives?

Lesson 2 Climate Regions

Why is the map on page 52 called a "Climate Regions" map? Why isn't it called a "weather" map? To answer that, look at the map key.

A **climate** region is formed, in part, by the temperature of an area. The words cold, cool, mild, warm, and hot are used. A climate region is also formed by the **precipitation** in an area. This is the water that falls to the land in the form of rain or snow. But weather deals with temperature and precipitation, too. What is the difference between weather and climate?

The wonder of a rare desert snowstorm. It means water in a dry land. And it means life will continue. The Joshua trees seen here, like most desert plants, can live quite well during short periods of cold weather. Seen in the background are the San Gabriel Mountains of southern California.

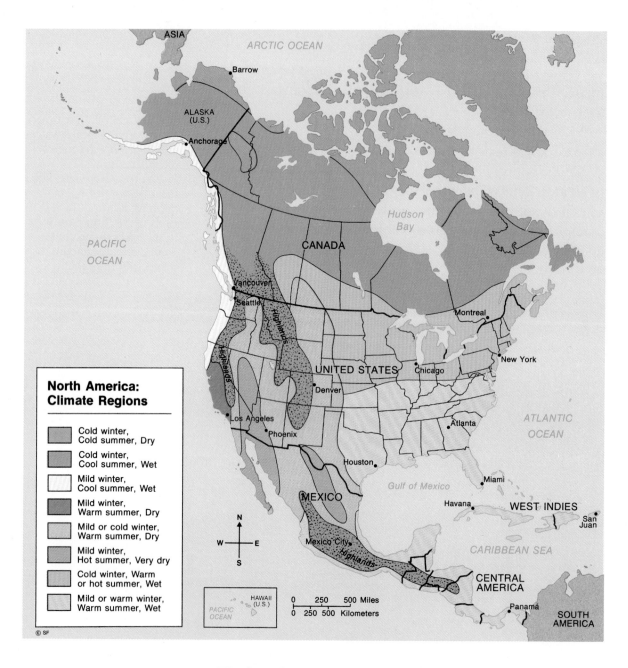

The key also uses the words "winter" and "summer." That means that a region's climate is the temperature and precipitation over a long period of time. In fact, climate is the temperature and precipitation in an area for the entire year.

Weather is the *daily* temperature and precipitation of a region. Knowing the weather of a place is useful. It tells you what to wear and helps plan what to do. But weather tells you little about what a region is like over a long period of time.

What Influences Climate?

The map on page 52 shows the different climate regions in North America. Look at the map key that describes the climate for any other region. Why does one region have a climate different from another region? What things influence, or affect climate?

The sun. As the earth revolves around the sun, some areas receive more direct sunlight than others. Areas closer to the Equator receive more direct sunlight. Areas closer to the poles receive less direct sunlight. The chart below shows how the sun affects climate. Cities that are close to the Equator are usually warmer than those farther away. Acapulco, Mexico, is about twelve hundred miles from the Equator. Compare its average temperatures to Winnipeg, Canada. How far is Winnipeg from the Equator?

The elevation of a place. As air is warmed by the sun's rays, it rises above the surface of the earth. As it rises, it cools. Places that are located at high elevations have cooler temperatures than places at lower elevations. Phoenix, Arizona, and Albuquerque, New Mexico, are good examples.

You can see from the small thermometer on page 54 that the two cities have different average temperatures. They are about the same distance from the Equator. But they are not at the same elevation. As the drawing on page 54 shows,

The Influence of the Sun on Climate

Country/ City	Average Temperature in F°		Miles From The Equator
	January	July	
Canada			
Edmonton	9	62	3800
Winnipeg	10	67	2500
Montreal	14	70	3200
United States			
Philadelphia	33	76	2800
Dallas	46	85	2300
Portland	39	66	3200
Mexico			
Mexico City	54	64	1400
Acapulco	77	82	1200
Veracruz	72	80	1300

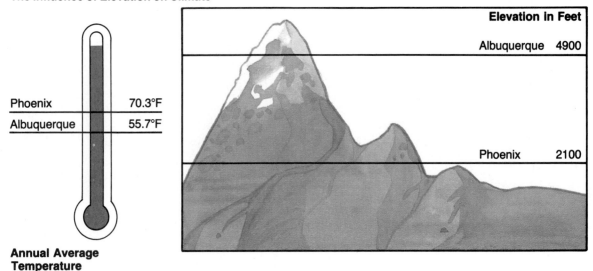

Phoenix — 70.3°F
Albuquerque — 55.7°F

Annual Average Temperature

Elevation in Feet

Albuquerque 4900

Phoenix 2100

Albuquerque is much higher. How does that affect Albuquerque's temperature?

Landforms. Seattle and Spokane, Washington, are only about two hundred miles apart. Yet, they have very different climates. Spokane is usually about ten degrees colder than Seattle during the winter months. Seattle usually gets about thirty-nine inches of precipitation while Spokane gets only seventeen. Why are there differences?

The small map on page 55 helps explain the temperature difference. The Cascade Range stops the warm winter winds off the Pacific Ocean from reaching Spokane. Therefore, Spokane will be colder.

The small drawing on page 55 helps explain the difference in precipitation. The mountains stop many storms from reaching Spokane. Therefore, Seattle will be wetter. In both cases, the Cascade Range has affected the climate of these cities.

Bodies of water. The sun heats both land and water. But it does not heat them both in the same way. Water holds heat longer than land. It also loses heat slower.

During the summer months, land heats up quickly. A body of water, such as a lake or ocean, still holds some of its winter chill. Because of this, water acts like an air conditioner. It cools the nearby land.

During the winter months, land cools down quickly. A body of water still holds some of its summer heat. Because of this, water acts like a heater. It warms the nearby land.

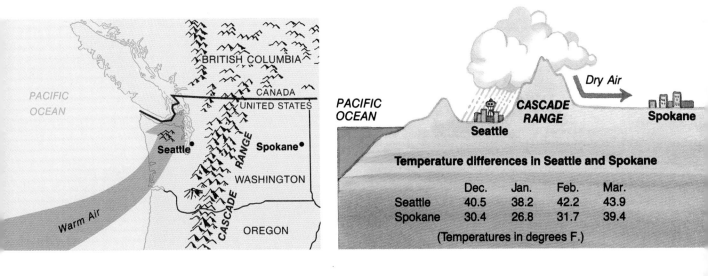

Temperature differences in Seattle and Spokane

	Dec.	Jan.	Feb.	Mar.
Seattle	40.5	38.2	42.2	43.9
Spokane	30.4	26.8	31.7	39.4

(Temperatures in degrees F.)

The area around Chicago is a good example of these effects. Chicago is located next to Lake Michigan. Land next to Lake Michigan is usually ten degrees warmer during the winter months than the land only ten miles away. During the summer months, land next to the lake is about ten degrees cooler than land ten miles away.

You can see that climate is influenced by many things. Look at your climate region. What is the climate like in your region? What different things affect it?

Checking Up

1. What is the difference between weather and climate?

2. Briefly explain how the following influence climate:
   - The sun
   - The elevation of a place
   - Landforms
   - Bodies of water

3. What is your weather like today?

4. Locate a city in a climate region different from your own. What is the climate like in that region? What things might be influencing it?

Lesson 3   Natural Vegetation Regions

In Lessons 1 and 2, you read that North America has different landform and climate regions. North America also has **natural vegetation** regions. These regions are set up according to the main kinds of plants that grow there. Some plants grow better in some areas than in others. Why is this so?

natural vegetation, plants that grow in an area without the help of people.

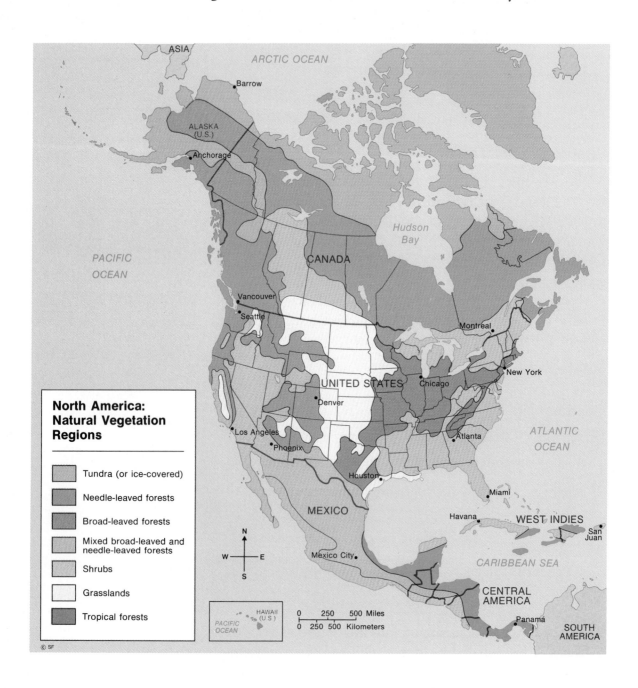

North America: Natural Vegetation Regions

- Tundra (or ice-covered)
- Needle-leaved forests
- Broad-leaved forests
- Mixed broad-leaved and needle-leaved forests
- Shrubs
- Grasslands
- Tropical forests

© SF

0   250   500 Miles
0   250 500 Kilometers

If you could look at all three region maps at the same time, you would begin to get an answer to that question. The maps are not the same, but there are some similarities. One reason for this is because the vegetation of a region is, in part, determined by landform and climate.

Different landforms have different types of soil. Certain plants grow well in one type of soil, but not in another. Some plants grow well in one type of climate, but not in another. It takes the right combination of soil and climate for certain plants to grow. The following two examples will show how this is true.

The saguaro (sə gwär′ō) is a cactus, a plant with spines instead of leaves, that grows well in a small area of the southwestern United States and Mexico. It is well suited to the sandy, rocky soil, and the dry, hot, desert climate.

The giant redwood and sequoia (si kwoi′ə) trees would not do well in that region. They grow naturally only in a small area of the Pacific Mountain Region of the United States. They require a wetter and cooler climate. They grow well in a different type of soil than that needed by the saguaro.

Redwood giants stand a silent guard in Sequoia National Park, California.

(above right) Shown here are the broad leaves of a maple tree. (above) The needles on a variety of pine trees reach for the late afternoon sun.

The natural vegetation region map on page 56 can help show other examples of where vegetation changes as soil and climate change. In the Atlantic Coastal Plain Region, where the climate is hot in the summer and mild in the winter, needle-leaved trees like the pine often mix with broad-leaved trees like the maple and oak. These trees also grow well in the Appalachian Highlands, and in parts of the Canadian Shield and Interior Plains.

The western half of the Interior Plains, the Great Plains, is mainly a grassland region. The Intermountain Region, which has a hot and dry climate, has a variety of bushes, shrubs, and cacti. The cool and moist Rocky Mountain and Pacific Mountain regions have great needle-leaved forests.

In parts of Mexico and Central America, where the climate is moist and warm all year, there are tropical forests of mahogany, coconut, and palm. A completely different type of vegetation is found in the frozen, northern plains of Alaska. This area is called the tundra vegetation region. Grasses, shrubs, and mosses, or small nonflowering plants, grow here.

The vegetation map shows the diversity of plant life in North America. Because of differences in soil and climate, certain plants grow better in one area than in another. The plants you have read about are only the main kinds that grow in a region. There are many types of bushes, flowers, and grasses that grow throughout the regions of North America.

Checking Up

1. What is a vegetation region? Describe four different types.

2. What is the main vegetation in the area in which you live?

3. How do climate and soil affect the vegetation of a region?

Learning Geography Terms About Rivers

Over a million people come to see it each year. They hurry up to the guardrail and stare in silence. Below them is the Grand Canyon. It stretches for over two hundred miles. At one point, it is almost eighteen miles wide. Most of the visitors wonder, "How was it made?"

Part of the answer lies almost a mile below the guardrail. There, in a twisting line, is the Colorado River. Over thousands of years, this fast-flowing river has cut through rock and soil to carve the canyon. The canyon is one of the world's natural wonders, but it is only one part of the river. To fully understand this river, we must look at some questions.

Where is the water coming from?

To answer this question, look at the map on page 62. In the Rocky Mountains of Colorado, melting snow and rainwater form streams. As these streams join together, they form the headwaters or **source** of the river. This is where the Colorado River is born.

If you follow the river south, you can see other rivers of rain water and melted snow join the Colorado. These are called **tributaries**. The place where a tributary joins the main river is called a **fork**. When the tributaries join the main river, they make it stronger. The sound of the river, as it rushes over rocks and through canyons, can be deafening.

The All-American Canal brings the Colorado River to the fields of southern California.

But if you were to stand at the **mouth**, the place where the river ends, you would notice something very strange. When the Colorado empties into the Gulf of California, there is not much water left. It has lost almost all of its power. In fact, the river is little more than a creek.

Where is the water going?

Much of the water has been taken from the river by man-made canals, irrigation ditches, and pipelines. One pipeline is 250 miles long. It takes almost one million gallons of water to California every day.

Some of the water is being held by dams. A dam stops the flow of water and creates a holding area called a **reservoir** (rez′ər vwär). As you look at the map, you notice that many of the reservoirs behind the dams are lakes.

How is the river used by people?

The water has many uses. As you might think, much of the water is used by people in cities and towns for drinking and cleaning. Much of the water is used by farmers to irrigate their fields.

Water is also used to make electricity for these cities, towns, and farms. This is how it is made. Some of the water in the reservoir is allowed to pass through the dam. As it does this, the water turns huge wheels. The wheels are attached to machines called generators. The generators make the electricity.

60

Shown here is Hoover Dam in Nevada. The Lake Mead reservoir is to the left.

Another use of the Colorado River is recreation. Millions of people come to the river each year just to look at it. Some camp in the many beautiful canyons. Others raft through the fast water or take pleasure-boat rides. A few find a quiet tributary and fish.

You can see that a river is more than just a twisting line in a deep canyon or on a map. It is water that comes from many places, goes to many places, and is used by many people in many ways.

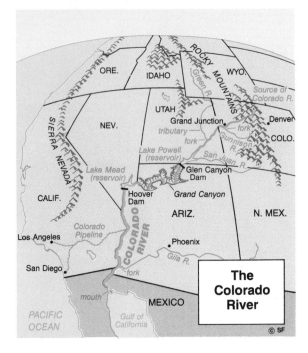

Exploring with Maps

Answer the following questions on a separate sheet of paper.

1. The start of a river is called its headwaters or _____.

2. A tributary joining the Colorado River in Utah is the _____ River.

3. _____ is a city at a major fork where the Colorado and the Gunnison rivers join.

4. The mouth of the Colorado River is in the country of _____.

5. The reservoir behind Glen Canyon Dam is Lake _____.

6. Two cities in California that have water from the Colorado piped to them are _____ and _____.

Reviewing Chapter 2

Write your answers on paper. Do not write in the book.

Using Key Words

region
climate
weather
mouth
tributary
source

natural vegetation
precipitation
boundary
fork
reservoir
landform

Write a short meaning for each of the key words listed above.

Reviewing Main Ideas

Number your paper from 1 to 4. Choose the word or phrase that best ends the sentence. Write the correct letter next to the number on your paper.

1. Areas closer to the Equator receive **a.** less direct sunlight than other areas. **b.** more direct sunlight than other areas. **c.** the same amount of sunlight as other areas.

2. An example of a broad-leaf tree is **a.** moss. **b.** cactus. **c.** oak.

3. "High hills, valleys, and rounded mountains" would be a description of the _____ Region. **a.** Atlantic Coastal Plain **b.** Appalachian Highlands **c.** Interior Plains

4. The landform regions of the United States **a.** stop at its political borders. **b.** are all the same size. **c.** sometimes extend into other areas of North America.

Thinking Things Over

Write two paragraphs. One should describe what weather is; the other should describe what climate is. Then, explain how knowing each of these can help you in your daily life.

Practicing Skills

Lightly trace a map of North America from the one on page 46. Draw in the boundaries of the main landform regions. Label each of the regions in large letters. Trace another map of North America over the first with a second sheet of paper. Draw the boundaries for the climate region. Label each climate region in large letters. Do the same thing for the natural vegetation map. Tape the maps together like the diagram below shows. You will be able to tell the landform, climate, and vegetation for any area in North America.

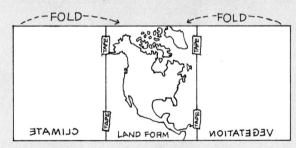

The People and the Land

Night Journey

Now as the train bears west,
Its rhythm rocks the earth,
And from my Pullman berth
I stare into the night
While others take their rest.

Wheels shake the roadbed stone,
The pistons jerk and shove,
I stay up half the night
To see the land I love.

—*Theodore Roethke*

Take an imaginary train ride from New York to California
or from Minnesota to Texas. You would pass through cities,
towns, and villages. You would see different people living in
different homes and using the land in different ways.

Lesson 1   Where Do People Live?

Over two hundred million people live in the United
States. The map below shows where they have settled. This
settling of people over an area is known as **population
distribution**. You can see from the map that more people
have settled in certain areas than in others. This makes the
population distribution of the United States uneven. Why
have people settled this way?

North America:
Population Distribution

· 300,000 people

In the past, people settled in different places because they were looking for different things in life. Some people wanted to farm. They looked for an area with good soil. Others wanted to get rich quick. They looked for land that held minerals, such as gold and silver. The promise of a factory job attracted people to other areas. Some people settled in an area because the land was exciting compared to where they had lived.

Today, people live in certain areas for these and other reasons. Some people live in an area because it offers a special job or school. Some people live where they can attend museums, concerts, or sporting events. Others live where they can shop in a special store. Some choose an area because of the climate it offers. Some select an area because of its beautiful scenery.

The population distribution map shows that a large part of the population is found in or around **urban**, or city, areas like Los Angeles, Houston, and Chicago. These cities can also be called central cities. Central because they are surrounded by smaller cities and towns called **suburbs**. The map below gives a good example of this.

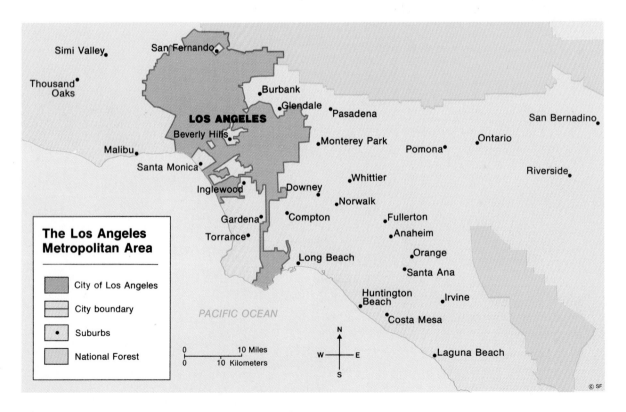

The heavy population density of New York City is seen in this photo.

Population density is the average number of people living in a square mile or square kilometer. As you can see, density varies from city to city. It depends on how many people live in a given area. Use an encyclopedia to find the population and square miles of these major United States cities.

City	Density
New York	6,661
Chicago	1,890
Los Angeles	1,740
Philadelphia	1,342
San Francisco	1,284
Detroit	1,130
Washington, D.C.	1,071
Pittsburgh	747
Miami	710
Memphis	389
Houston	382

Source: U.S. Gov't Statistics, 1980

Together, the central city, like Los Angeles, and the surrounding suburbs form a **metropolitan area**. The people move freely about to enjoy the businesses, shops, and entertainment of the entire area. Someone who lives in the city may work in the suburbs. Someone who lives in the suburbs may see a baseball game in the city. Many people live in a metropolitan area because of all the opportunities it offers.

Many other people live in rural settings. These are farm, country, or small-town communities. The surrounding land may be rich for growing vegetables, fruits, or raising livestock. People may also live in such areas for the clean air and open spaces.

The number of people living in a certain area is called **population density.** Metropolitan areas are usually crowded places to live. They have a heavy population density. Rural areas are less crowded. They have a lighter population density. The pictures on pages 67 and 68 show how urban and rural areas have different population densities.

67

By the Way

Why would these fast growing areas attract people?

The lowest population densities were once found in regions where it was hard to live. People stayed out of regions with a poor climate or a lack of such things as minerals, trees, and water. Now that is changing.

For example, in the last twenty years, Arizona has become one of the five fastest growing states in the country. Yet, much of the state is a hot and dry desert. Why are so many people moving there?

Arizona offers health benefits to many because of its clean, dry air. It has become a major recreation area for skiers, boaters, and campers. It has beautiful scenery in areas like the Grand Canyon and the Painted Desert. But there is another reason.

People move to Arizona because it is now easier and more enjoyable to live there. Modern building methods make homes, offices, and factories attractive and comfortable to live and work in. Air conditioning makes them livable! Transportation brings in a variety of foods and products. Irrigation of fields with water piped in from hundreds of miles

(near left) People usually change their surroundings to fit their wants and needs. But it is also important that people protect the natural environment against too much change. Tucson, Arizona, is a good example. The surrounding desert, and animal and plant life are protected by laws. Buildings are designed to fit into the natural desert beauty and not replace it. (far left) Small towns, like Franklin, New Hampshire, usually have lighter population densities than large metropolitan areas.

away has added farming to the natural desert beauty. It also helps farmers earn a good living. Arizona is an example of people changing their surroundings to fit their wants and needs.

Checking Up

1. What is the difference between population distribution and population density?

2. What reasons could people give for choosing to live in a certain area?

3. Which do you think is truer? People control their surroundings, or their surroundings control them?

4. What is the difference between an urban and a suburban area? Do you live in an urban, suburban, or rural area?

Lesson 2   Natural Resources and Land Use

These newspaper headlines have something in common. They remind us that the United States is rich in **natural resources**. Some resources, such as the sun and air are plentiful. Others are renewable. Trees, for example, can be replanted. Polluted lakes and rivers can be cleaned. Other resources can be used up. Once oil, coal, and natural gas are gone, they are gone forever. Whatever the type of resource, the headlines could also tell of disaster.

People's lives would change greatly without natural resources. They help produce things that meet the needs and wants of people in three ways.

Food

Much of the land in the United States is used for **agriculture**, or farming. The climate and rich soil help produce large harvests of many crops. The nation is the world's leading producer of farm products. What it does not need is often sold or traded to other nations.

Energy

Today, one of the nation's biggest needs is energy. Energy powers the machines that make life easier, safer, and more enjoyable. Energy is used to heat, cool, and light schools, homes, and factories. It powers cars, trucks, trains, and airplanes. It powers machines that cook, clean, or entertain. The United States uses more energy than any other nation.

Our energy needs are met by natural resources. Coal, oil, and natural gas have been common sources of energy. But

Facts and Figures

This is how the United States compares to other nations in the production of certain resources and manufactured products.

1st	corn
1st	meat
1st	coal
1st	copper
1st	natural gas
1st	automobiles
2nd	lumber
2nd	paper
2nd	gasoline
2nd	steel
3rd	sugar
3rd	crude oil
3rd	wheat

Source: U.S. Gov't Statistics 1980

these resources are being used up quickly. People are now trying to test other resources. Someday you may be using solar, thermal, hydroelectric, wind, or atomic energy.

Finished Goods

Natural resources are also used as **raw materials** in the making of finished goods. They are taken from in or on the earth, brought to a factory, and manufactured into a finished product. Often, the finished product does not look or feel like the raw material. Sand, for example, is used to make glass. Oil is used to make plastics. Lumber is used to make paper.

The map below shows that the land in the United States is used in many ways. It has many purposes because it is rich in natural resources. Yet, without one natural resource, the land could not be used in all these ways.

raw materials, anything that can be manufactured, treated, or prepared to make it more useful or to increase its value.

Land use maps show the different ways land is used in an area. What are some ways the land is used in the United States? Check the map key to find out. Then answer these questions:
1. In which states is the land used for drilling oil, for growing crops?
2. How is the land used in your state?

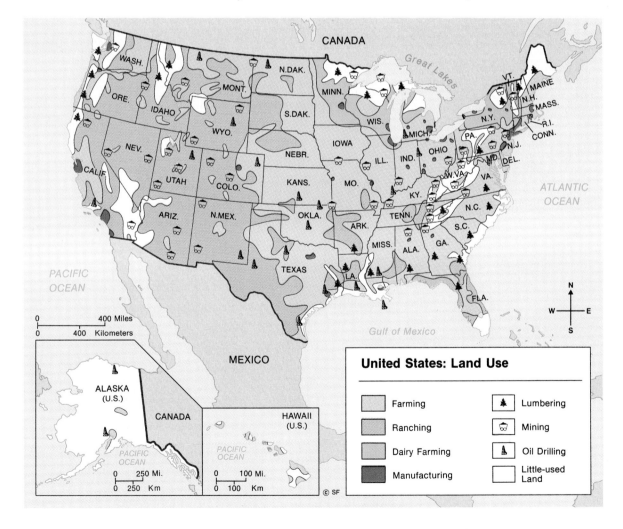

United States: Land Use

- ▢ Farming
- ▢ Ranching
- ▢ Dairy Farming
- ▢ Manufacturing
- ♠ Lumbering
- ⛏ Mining
- ⚑ Oil Drilling
- ▢ Little-used Land

"Oh, beautiful for spacious skies and amber waves of grain . . ." are shown in abundance in this photo of a Kansas wheat field.

The people of the United States are a natural resource, too. Their labor, knowledge, and skills turn other natural resources into tools that serve millions of people. The people thought of ways to improve the soil so that it produces more food. The people thought of ways to use natural resources to power machines. The people built machines that make finished products from raw materials.

The people have the power to use the resources wisely. They also have the power to abuse the resources. Pollution, over-use, and careless use of natural resources are problems the nation faces. The people also have the power to solve those problems.

Checking Up

1. What are the three types of natural resources?

2. How do natural resources help produce food, energy, and finished products?

3. What is the major way land is used where you live?

72

Reviewing Chapter 3

Write your answers on paper. Do not write in the book.

Using Key Words

natural resource

metropolitan area

population distribution

population density

agriculture

urban

raw material

suburb

Write a short meaning for each of the key words listed above.

Reviewing Main Ideas

Number your paper from 1 to 5. Write the word or phrase that best completes the idea in the sentence.

1. People have settled (evenly, unevenly) across the United States.

2. Most of the population has settled in (urban, rural) areas.

3. Oil, coal, and natural gas are resources that can be (renewed, used up).

4. The United States (keeps, sells or trades) the farm products that it does not need.

5. Once coal, oil, and natural gas are used up, the nation (does, does not) have other sources.

Thinking Things Over

1. How do natural resources help people take care of their needs and wants? Why are people resources, too?

2. Write a paragraph describing how people use the land where you live. Remember, they may use it many ways.

Practicing Skills

1. Look at the population distribution map on page 65. First, explain where people live and do not live. Next, explain why population distribution and density are not even across the United States or North America. You may wish to look back at your climate, vegetation, and landform maps.

2. Draw a flat plan of your house like the one shown below. Measure the major rooms to figure out the number of square feet in your house. Divide the number of people in your family into the total number of square feet to find out how much room each family member has. Do the same for your classroom. Do you have more space at home or school?

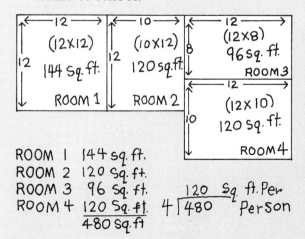

ROOM 1   144 sq. ft.
ROOM 2   120 sq. ft.
ROOM 3   96 sq. ft.
ROOM 4   120 sq. ft.
         480 sq. ft.

120 sq. ft. per
4) 480   person

What Do You Know?

Write your answers on paper. Do not write in the book.

Words to Know

metropolitan area	precipitation
landform	naturalize
climate	reservoir
natural resource	boundary
goods	tributary

Number your paper from 1 to 10. Write the key words next to the number of their definition.

Definitions

1. a type of land throughout an area

2. a place where water is collected and stored

3. a person who has become a citizen by passing a test and taking an oath of allegiance

4. a stream or river that flows into another river

5. things that help satisfy the basic needs and wants that people have

6. borders between cities, states, and countries

7. a central city surrounded by suburbs

8. water that falls to the earth in the form of rains, snow, sleet, hail

9. the weather of a place over a long time

10. items that are manufactured by hand or machine

Ideas to Know

Number your paper from 1 to 4. Choose the word or phrase that best ends the sentence. Write the letter next to the number on your paper.

1. America is a diverse land because
   a. some people are better than others.
   b. not all people are alike.   c. everyone has the same habits and beliefs.

2. A doctor would be an example of a worker that   a. provides a service.
   b. grows useful plants and animals.
   c. produces a product.

3. Televisions, vacations, and movies are _____ make life easier.   a. things that people need to   b. things that people want to   c. natural resources that

4. Natural resources   a. can always be renewed.   b. do not include people.
   c. help in the production of food.

Number your paper from 5 to 9. Match the examples of regions in List 1 to the type of region in List 2.

List 1

5. hot summer, mild winter, very dry

6. broad leaf

7. Intermountain Region

8. tropical forests

9. Canadian Shield

List 2

a. Landform

b. Climate

c. Vegetation

Using What You Know

1. Below is a drawing of a river much like the Colorado that you read about. Certain areas on the river are numbered. Match the number to one of the following parts of a river. Number your paper from 1 to 4.

   a. tributary   c. source
   b. mouth   d. reservoir

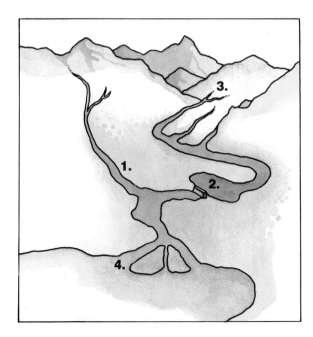

2. You may look back to Chapter 2, "North America: Land of Diversity" to do this activity. Below is a map of North America. A few major cities have been included on the map. On your paper write the names of the cities you see on the map. Then give information that describes each city's region.
Example:
   1. Houston
      a. landform—
      b. climate—
      c. natural vegetation—

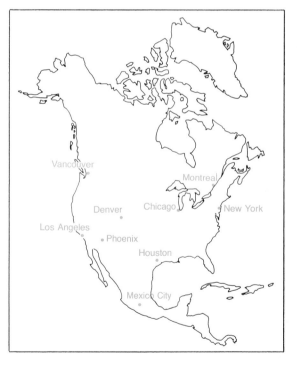

75

Unit 2

Settling North America

Chapter 4
American Indians

Chapter 5
Explorations of North America

Chapter 6
Settlement of North America

Chapter 7
Life in the English Colonies

Who settled this New World, this land named America? Indian hunters found a New World more than thirty thousand years ago when they came from Asia. European explorers rediscovered the New World around 1500. Africans found a New World, too, when they were brought in 1619. Each group brought with them a **culture**, or way of life. Each had a way of looking at the world around them. As their cultures touched each other and the land, a new American culture was born.

The cliff-overhang protects Square Tower House and other Anasazi ruins from a light winter snowfall at Mesa Verde National Park in Colorado.

76

American Indians

Archaeologists try to explain how ancient people lived. In doing this, they anger some people today. By digging in places they think early people lived, the archaeologist sometimes destroys ancient burial sites. Many Indians feel this is disrespectful to their religion and ancestors. They have fought back by taking the archaeologists to court. It is not an easy question to answer. Do we try to understand the people of the past or protect them?

"They invite you to share anything that they possess, and show as much love as if their hearts went with it . . ." This is what Christopher Columbus wrote about the first people he saw after landing on a tiny island in the Caribbean in October of 1492. The people of the island called it Guanahani (gwä′nä hä′nē). Columbus named the island San Salvador—Holy Savior. The people called themselves Arawaks. Columbus named them Indians. He thought he had reached the East Indies, a group of islands near the continent of Asia.

Columbus did not know it, but he had discovered a New World for the people of Europe. But to the people of Guanahani, it was an old world. These people had lived there for thousands of years before Columbus came.

Lesson 1   The First People of North America

There is a Loucheaux (lü shō′) Indian village near the Old Crow River in the northwest corner of Canada. One of the villagers, Peter Lord, often walked along the river. One day, in 1966, Lord found a piece of bone from a large animal. It seemed to be very, very old and strange. The end appeared to be carved, not broken.

Lord showed his find to some **archaeologists**. Archaeologists study **artifacts**. These are objects that were made and used by early people. For example, pieces of pottery, remains of a building, and bone-tools are artifacts. All these things help archaeologists describe the people who lived at a place.

The archaeologists told Lord that the bone was probably used as a tool. The end had been carved to form a cutting edge. They thought it might have been used to scrape animal flesh away from bones and skin.

Archaeologists found many other tools and weapons along the Old Crow River. They believe these things were left by

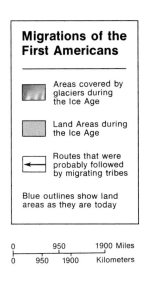

Migrations of the First Americans

Areas covered by glaciers during the Ice Age

Land Areas during the Ice Age

Routes that were probably followed by migrating tribes

Blue outlines show land areas as they are today

0	950	1900 Miles
0	950 1900	Kilometers

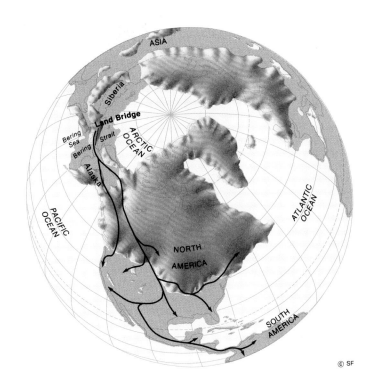

Indians who lived there about twenty-seven thousand years ago! Where did these people come from?

The First Americans

Many thousands of years ago, North and South America were very different from the way they are today. Thick forests stood in some places where there are now deserts. Huge lakes covered some spots where there are now grassy plains. Glaciers spread across much of North America.

For thousands of years only animals roamed the lands of the Americas. Then, about thirty thousand years ago the first people arrived. They probably **migrated** from Siberia, an area in Asia. Archaeologists believe that these men, women, and children were hunters following the tracks of animals.

Today, animals and people cannot simply walk on land from Siberia to North America. A strip of water, fifty-five miles wide, called the Bering Strait, separates Asia and North America. But more than thirty thousand years ago, archaeologists say, the waters of the Bering Sea were lower than they are now. A strip of land stood above the water like a bridge. Animals crossed freely from Asia to North America on this

Find the Bering Strait on this map. During the Ice Age this strait was a land bridge connecting the continents of Asia and North America. Most of present-day Canada was covered by glaciers during the Ice Age.

migrate, move from one place to another

79

A bone-tool artifact found along the Old Crow River in Canada. What might this tool have been used for?

land bridge. Wherever the animals went, the hunters followed closely behind.

The animals roamed south out of Alaska. They came through a narrow, ice-free strip of Canada into the Great Plains Region of what is now the United States. Here the plains were warmer than those of Alaska or Canada. Many animals liked to eat the plentiful grass of the Great Plains. So, they stopped their roaming. Many of the hunters decided to stay also.

Over the years, some of the hunters of the Great Plains went west to live in the Pacific Mountain Region. Others went to live in the woodlands of the Atlantic Coastal Plain and the Appalachian Highlands. Archaeologists have uncovered many bones and spear points in caves near Pittsburgh.

Some bands of hunters kept moving south. Spear tips and cutting tools made from stone have been found in areas of Mexico and South America. Some archaeologists believe these could be twenty-two thousand years old.

Then climates and natural vegetation slowly began to change. About six thousand years ago, the regions we know today came about. Some kinds of animals, like the mammoths, the giant beavers, and the North American camel, could not live with the changes. They died out. The people, however, could.

We know these people as the Indians of North America. But it is wrong to think that all Indians were or are alike. Indian groups settled in different regions. They had their own **customs**, or ways of doing things. They had their own type of home, clothing, food, and ways to make a living.

Checking Up

1. What objects do you have in your home that an archaeologist two hundred years from now might be interested in?

2. Why was it once possible for early hunters to walk between the two continents of North America and Asia?

3. Describe what you think would be the day-to-day life of the early hunters of North America.

Lesson 2   Cliff-dwellers of the Southwest

A great tower stands here. But no one stands guard in it. There are no laughing children at play. No one plows the fields. It is quiet as the light winter snow falls.

This is what you would see at Mesa Verde National Park in Colorado. Here stand the ruins of very old dwellings. They were built more than fifteen hundred years ago by the Anasazi (ä nə sä′zē), which means "the old people."

These dwellings were made of stone and sun-dried brick called adobe (a dō′bē). They are called **pueblos** (pweb′lōz). This is the Spanish word for village.

As the photograph on pages 76 and 77 shows, the dwellings were built along the sides of steep cliffs. The photograph below shows that pueblos were also built on mesas. Mesas are high hills with steep sides and flat tops. Why would the Anasazi have built their pueblos along cliffs or on mesas?

What's in a Name?

There were other groups of Indians living in the Southwest at about the same time as the Anasazi. They also have interesting names. The Sinagua people lived in northern Arizona. They succeeded in farming in a very hot and dry area. Their name is Spanish for "without water."

The Hohokam people lived in central Arizona. They, too were farmers. Like the Anasazi, they made beautiful pottery and baskets. And, like the Anasazi, they disappeared. The name given to them tells the story. It means "the ones who are no more," or "worn out."

The Acoma pueblo was built high atop a mesa over eight hundred years ago in what is today the state of New Mexico.

81

The pueblos were like apartments. They could be two, three, or even eight stories high. Hundreds of people usually lived in each pueblo. Most rooms were used as living areas. Some rooms were used to store grain or hold meetings in. Others were used as places to worship gods and spirits.

Our knowlege of the Anasazi culture comes from archaeologists. The Anasazi left no written records. They did, however, leave other traces of their way of life. Archaeologists have studied many Anasazi artifacts in Arizona, Utah, Colorado, and New Mexico. They have found dried seeds, pieces of jewelry, pottery, tools, cloth, and weapons. These remains helped archaeologists describe the Anasazi culture.

Archaeologists believe the Anasazi were once hunters and gatherers. They had no real home, but moved from place to place in search of food. Later, the Anasazi found that they could also plant seeds to produce food. They grew corn, beans, squash, and other foods. They also trapped game such as rabbit and deer.

The Anasazi were a skilled people. They used sharpened sticks to turn over the soil before planting. They buried seeds so they would not dry up or blow away. Since there was little rainfall, they dug ditches to bring water from nearby streams. This way of watering crops is called irrigation.

(below) These paintings were found near the Anasazi ruins in Colorado. What do you think the artist was trying to say in the paintings?

The Anasazi made fine pottery and jewelry. They also made sturdy grass baskets and sandals. They were weavers of colorful blankets and clothing made from cotton cloth. Some of their clothing was made from the hides of animals. Tools and weapons were carved from wood and stone.

By A.D. 1200, the Anasazi began to leave many of their pueblos. They might have left to find a safer place to live. They were a peaceful people, but they did have enemies. The Anasazi might also have gone to find a better climate. Some archaeologists think the area had a long period of dryness.

The Anasazi left, but their culture was not lost. The Hopi and Zuni people have carried on much of the Anasazi culture. They still lead simple farming lives. Clothing, baskets, and pottery are crafted with the same care and skill.

These Hopi and Zuni were living in pueblos when the Spanish explored this part of North America in the 1540s. Some pueblos are still lived in today. The pueblo of Oraibi, Arizona, has been occupied for over eight hundred years. These Indians were part of the Southwest Indian group. Find the Southwest Indian group on the map on page 86.

(left) These are examples of grass sandals and pottery (above) that were found at Anasazi ruins in Arizona.

A.D. and B.C., the letters A.D. stand for *anno domini* in Latin. They are used to indicate the years on a calendar after the birth of Jesus, almost 2,000 years ago. B.C. stands for the years before Jesus' birth.

Checking Up

1. Where and when did the Anasazi live in North America?

2. How did archaeologists help you learn about the Anasazi culture, or way of life?

3. Describe the Anasazi culture. Hint: What did they do for a living? What were their homes like? How did they dress?

To the Europeans, the land was something to own. To the American Indians, the land was something for everyone to share. Here is a poem about the Papago Indians and their land, the desert of the American Southwest. The poem tells why the Indians believed as they did.

CHILDREN OF THE DESERT

Talk to Papago Indians.
They're
Desert People.
They know
desert secrets
that no one else
knows.
Ask
how they live
in a place
so harsh and dry. . . .

They never say,
"This is my land
to do with as I please."
They say,
"We share . . .
we only share."
And they *do* share. . . .
Women weave grass
into their baskets
and birds weave it
into their nests.
Men dig
in the earth
for soil
to make houses—
little square adobe houses
the color of the hills.
And lizards
dig burrows
in the same
safe earth. . . .

They share in other ways too.
They share
the feeling
of being
brothers
in the desert,
of being
desert creatures
together. . . .

Desert People
are patient too.
You don't see them rushing.
You don't hear them shouting.

They say you plant happier corn
if you take your time
and that squash tastes best
if you've sung it
slow songs
while it's growing.
They do.

Anyway,
the desert has
its own kind of time
(that doesn't need clocks).
That's
the kind of time
snakes go by
and rains go by
and rocks go by
and Desert People
go by too.

That's why
every desert thing
knows
when the time comes
to celebrate.

Suddenly . . .
All together.
It happens.

Cactus blooms
yellow and pink and purple.
The Papagos begin
their ceremonies
to pull down
rain.
Every plant joins in.
Even the dry earth
makes a sound of joy
when the rain touches.

Hawks call across the canyons.
Children laugh for nothing.
Coyotes dance in the moonlight.

Where else
would
Desert People
want to be?

—Byrd Baylor

Lesson 3   Hunters of the Great Plains

66We were several hundred feet above the plain . . . and in every direction, as far as we could see, there were buffalo, buffalo, and still more buffalo. They were a grand sight. Nature had been good to these Indians . . .99

Who were these Indians the writer spoke of? They were the Indians of the Great Plains. Their culture was very different from that of the Anasazi.

The Plains Indians lived on the flat, grassy land that stretches from the Mississippi River in the east to the Rocky Mountains in the west. Using the map on page 86 find the names of some Indians who lived on the Great Plains.

Until about one hundred years ago, most Indians on the Great Plains were hunters. They did not usually build long-lasting villages. They followed the great herds of buffalo that roamed across the plains.

The Plains Indian used the buffalo as a natural resource. A visitor to an Indian camp once described how the buffalo helped the Indians meet their needs.

Indians on swift ponies take part in a buffalo hunt on the Great Plains.

"The Buffalo Hunt" by C. M. Russell, courtesy of The Thomas Gilcrease Institute of American History and Art, Tulsa, Oklahoma.

ASIA

ARCTIC OCEAN

Eskimo

Ingalik

Aleut

Tlingit

Kaska

ARCTIC

Eskimo

Eskimo

Slave

Hudson Bay

Chipewyan

NORTHWEST COAST

FAR NORTH

Cree

Nootka

Chippewa

Great Lakes

Algonquin

Abanaki

PLATEAU

Blackfoot

Flathead

Missouri R.

Iroquois

Massachusetts

Chinook

Coos

Nez Percé

Crow

Mandan

Sioux

Sauk

Fox

Mohawk

Mohegan

PACIFIC OCEAN

Cheyenne

PLAINS

EASTERN WOODLAND

Delaware

Modoc

Pomo

Arapaho

Omaha

Miami

Powhatan

Shoshone

Pawnee

Illinois

Ohio R.

Shawnee

GREAT BASIN

Ute

Cherokee

CALIFORNIA

Paiute

Navajo

Hopi

Zuni

Pueblo

Kiowa

Chickasaw

Creek

Chumash

Apache

Wichita

Comanche

Choctaw

Yuma

Papago

ATLANTIC OCEAN

Coahuiltec

Seminole

SOUTHWEST

Gulf of Mexico

Arawak

ROCKY MOUNTAINS

Mississippi R.

Major Indian Cultures and Tribes, about A.D. 1400

Otomi

Aztec

Maya

CARIBBEAN SEA

Area where the Anasazi lived in an earlier period

0	300	600 Miles
0	300	600

Kilometers

N
W — E
S

© SF

SOUTH AMERICA

Indians temporarily set up their tepees at Fort Laramie in Wyoming.

66With the skins they build their houses and make their clothes. With the sinews [strong tissue like muscle] they make threads with which they sew their clothes and tents. From the bones they shape awls [a tool used to make holes in leather or wood]. The dung [waste matter from animal intestines] is burned as firewood since there is no other fuel in that land. The bladders are used as jugs and drinking containers.99

The buffalo was very important to the Indians. Yet, without one other thing, the Indians could not easily hunt the buffalo. And that was the horse.

Before they hunted with horses, Indians had driven whole herds over cliffs. This wasted thousands of animals. Horses helped the Indians take only the buffalo that they needed.

Horses served in other ways. They helped the Indians move their possessions and trade goods. The Indians' skin houses, the tepees, could be taken down and used as a carrying sled. By helping the Indian with work, horses gave the Indian more free time. Horses were also used in play. The Indians loved to race and have contests to see who could shoot arrows or throw a lance the best from horseback.

Warfare was sometimes acted out as a game or contest, too. The Indians kept score during battles to show who was the best warrior. One way to score points was to capture enemy horses and weapons. But scoring a coup (kü) was the best way to win points in battle. A coup was the act of

We, the People

Indian culture differed from people to people. But, it is interesting that their tribal names often had similar meanings.

Illinois
  men or people
Winnebago
  people of the real speech
Pawnee
  men of men
Navajo
  the people
Hopi
  the peaceful people
Yavapai
  the sun people
Delaware
  true men
Zuni
  the flesh
Cherokee
  real people

touching or hitting an enemy with a special stick or lance. The best warriors were the ones with the most coup.

The Indians of the Great Plains loved to sit around their camp fires and tell **legends** about great warriors, battles, and coup. A legend is a story with special meaning passed from parent to child. It might or might not be exactly true. The people and places mentioned in a legend were probably true. But the story could be changed to make a special point. Parents told their children the legends to teach the ways and beliefs of the people. Here is a legend of the Cheyenne.

The Legend of Standing Bear

Big Eagle was a mighty Pawnee warrior. His people often fought the Cheyenne. The Cheyenne warriors feared Big Eagle. They hoped that one of them might score a coup on him. They agreed that whoever counted a coup on Big Eagle should be made war chief.

Soon, the Cheyenne met the Pawnee in a hard battle. The Cheyenne came back to their camp with several horses and many coup. A victory celebration was held to honor the best warriors. Standing Bear, a young warrior, told how he scored a great coup on Big Eagle by sticking him with a lance. Standing Bear was made war chief of his people.

A few years later Big Eagle made a friendly visit to the Cheyenne camp. The Cheyenne teased him about the coup their war chief had scored on him. Big Eagle said this was a lie. To prove it, he threw aside his robe. There was no scar.

Everyone knew that Standing Bear had lied. He felt great shame. He could no longer be war chief. He had lost all honor among his people.

An Indian coup stick. Why do you think it was more important for Plains Indians to touch rather than kill an enemy?

Checking Up

1. Why were legends important to the Plains Indian?

2. How did the Plains Indians get the things they needed to live?

3. How were the Plains Indians like and unlike the American Indians of the Southwest?

Lesson 4   Algonquins of the Eastern Woodland

Their name meant "to live at the place for spearing fish." They were the Algonquin (al gong'kən) people. Their name makes us think of rivers, lakes, and oceans. Their land, the Eastern Woodland, makes us think of pine, oak, and birch trees. Together, these two ideas tell us much about their region. It was a land of dense forests, winding rivers, and shimmering lakes.

The map on page 86 shows that the Eastern Woodland stretched from the Mississippi River to the Atlantic Ocean. The map also shows that the woodland was the home of many groups with a common way of life. What are the names of other groups in this region besides the Algonquins?

The Algonquins, like the Cheyenne and Anasazi, used the resources of the land to meet their needs. They hunted the animals of the forest with bows and arrows. They fished the waters with spears, nets, and traps. Their boats were made from a carved-out log, or the strong bark of the birch tree. The Algonquins cleared large patches of the forest for gardens of corn, squash, beans, and potatoes. The people gathered berries, nuts, and roots that grew wild in the forest.

By the Way

Like other Indians, the tribes of the Eastern Woodlands often traded for things that they needed. But, they also used money. It was strings of beads made from shells. The money was called wampum.

Algonquin Indians are shown here in one of John White's famous paintings. How many different methods of fishing do you see? Look carefully at the Algonquin's boat. What word did White use to identify the boat? What word is it like in our language today?

Their rype corne.

Their greene corne.

Corne newly sprong.

The place of solemne prayer.

Their sitting at meate.

The house wherin the Tombe of their Herounds standeth.

SECOTON.

A Ceremony in their prayers with strange iestures and songs dansinge abowt posts carued on the topps lyke mens faces.

(far left) Another type of Algonquin home is shown here. It is called the long house. How did it differ from the wigwam (at near left)? How do John White's paintings on pages 89 and 90 show differences between the Plains and Eastern Woodland Indians' cultures?

The forest also supplied materials used for building homes. The wigwam was one type of home in the Algonquin village. It was built with wood, bark, and grass. The ends of wood poles were placed in the ground in a circle. The other ends were tied together to form a dome roof. The bark and grass were tied to the wood poles to form walls.

The Algonquins made clothing from the skins and furs of animals. Their moccasins were made of deerskins. Wood, stone, and the bones of animals were shaped into tools and weapons. The Algonquins also carved bowls and utensils from wood blocks.

Explorers from Europe met the Algonquins about five hundred years ago. Artists sometimes came on the explorations to draw pictures of people, land, animals, and plants. One artist, John White, visited the Algonquin village of Secoton in 1585. His pictures are like the Cheyenne legends and the Anasazi artifacts. They can tell us much about a culture. What do they show you about the Algonquin culture?

What's in a Name?

Of the fifty United States, at least half have names that come from Indian words. See if you can find the Indian meanings for the following state names in an almanac or encyclopedia.

Alabama	Mississippi
Alaska	Missouri
Arizona	Nebraska
Arkansas	North Dakota
Connecticut	Ohio
Idaho	Oklahoma
Illinois	Oregon
Iowa	South Dakota
Kansas	Tennessee
Kentucky	Texas
Massachusetts	Utah
Michigan	Wisconsin
Minnesota	Wyoming

Checking Up

1. Where did the Algonquins live in North America?

2. Compare the way the Algonquins used the land to the way the Cheyenne and Anasazi used it.

3. How was the homeland of the Algonquins unlike the land of the Cheyenne and the Anasazi?

Building Social Studies Skills

Using Time Lines

Is it possible that John Cabot saw blacks working in Virginia? How many years passed between the time Columbus landed at San Salvador and colonists settled Jamestown? You could find the answers to these questions by looking in your book. You could also use a **time line**.

A time line shows a certain length of time. Vertical time lines are read from top to bottom. The earliest dates are at the top. Horizontal time lines, like the one on this page, are read from left to right. The earliest dates are at the left. What is the length of time shown on this time line?

The small marks divide the two hundred years into smaller units of time. Years are the most common unit used on a time line. The smallest unit of time on this line is five years. What are other units of time that could be used on a time line?

Time lines show events in the order they occurred. Find the line that marks John Cabot's explorations. Now find the line that marks when blacks were brought to America. Could Cabot have seen blacks in Virginia?

Time lines also show the amount of time between events. Find the date when Columbus landed at San Salvador. Find the date when colonists settled Jamestown. Subtract the earlier date from the later date. The number is the amount of time between the two events.

Copy the following time line on a sheet of paper. Use your index to help you add these events to the line.
- John White visits the Algonquins
- Champlain settles Quebec
- Cartier first tries to find a passage to China
- Vespucci explores the New World
- Cortez sails to Mexico

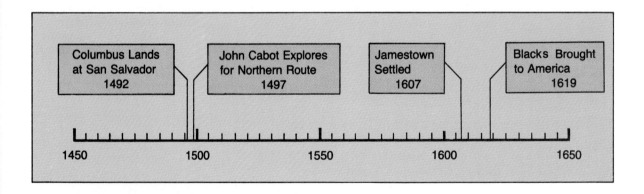

| Columbus Lands at San Salvador 1492 | John Cabot Explores for Northern Route 1497 | Jamestown Settled 1607 | Blacks Brought to America 1619 |

1450   1500   1550   1600   1650

Reviewing Chapter 4

Write your answers on paper. Do not write in the book.

Using Key Words

artifact   culture   A.D. and B.C.
legend   migrate
pueblo   archaeologist
time line   custom

Write a short meaning for each key word listed above.

Reviewing Main Ideas

Number your paper from 1 to 4. Pick the word or phrase that best completes the following sentences.

1. The first Americans came to North America   **a.** about 2,000 years ago.   **b.** on ships from Europe.   **c.** across an ice-bridge from Asia.

2. The _____ people lived in adobe homes made of sun-dried bricks.
   a. Anasazi   **b.** Cheyenne
   c. Algonquin

3. The main natural resource used by the Cheyenne was   **a.** water for irrigation of crops.   **b.** the buffalo for food.   **c.** good soil for raising crops.

4. All the Indians described in the readings   **a.** left legends to help the people of today understand them.   **b.** had the same culture.   **c.** were different because of where they lived.

Thinking Things Over

Archaeologists explain how people lived in the past by looking at the artifacts, drawings, and legends they left behind. What artifacts, drawings (or photographs), and legends (family stories) does your family have that an archaeologist of the future might use to explain your family's culture?

Practicing Skills

Copy the chart below onto your paper. Fill it in with information from the lessons.

Indian Cultures of North America

Name of Culture	Housing	Foods	Clothing	Indian Culture Region
Anasazi				
Cheyenne				
Algonquin				
Papago				

Explorations of North America

"The pirates will rob you!"

"You will fall off the edge of the earth!"

"Sea monsters will have you for supper!"

"A tiny ship like that will break up in the ocean!"

"If you lose sight of land, you will be lost forever!"

Sailors in Europe might have listened to these warnings a thousand years ago. They would not have known of the Indians already living in America. Soon all this would begin to change.

Around A.D. 1000, Vikings from Norway sailed from Greenland and landed on the eastern shore of North America. The Vikings built a number of dwellings, but did not remain.

About five hundred years later, other European sailors began to use bigger and stronger ships. Tools were invented to help sailors find their way across the oceans. They could now begin to **explore**, or search in hopes of discovering something new. What did they hope to find?

Monsters such as this were once believed to have lived in the sea. Do we have similar fears of the unknown today?

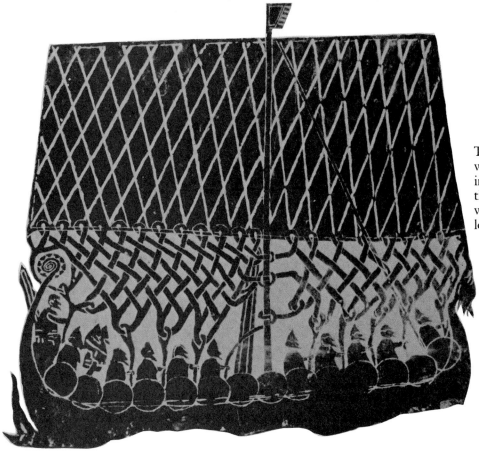

This picture of a Viking warship was actually carved into a gravestone. Do you think this type of ship would have been good on long ocean trips?

Lesson 1 The Vikings

About a thousand years ago, a group of people lived in Denmark, Sweden, and Norway. They were the Vikings, or Norse. They were the best sailors in Europe. The Vikings traveled in sturdy wooden ships. During their voyages, the Vikings found the two large islands of Iceland and Greenland shown on the map on page 96. Thousands of Vikings went to live in Iceland. A few Vikings settled in Greenland.

In the year A.D. 986, a Norseman by the name of Bjarni Herjulfson (byär′nē hər yōl′sən) sailed from Iceland to Greenland to see his father. Bjarni lost his way, and he sailed past Greenland. Finally, he sighted a strange land with many trees. Bjarni did not know it, but he had seen the coast of North America. He told other Vikings about the strange land he had seen.

About fifteen years later, another Norseman, Leif Eriksson, decided to see if Bjarni's story was true. Eriksson sailed with his crew west and south of Greenland. This old Viking story tells what happened when they sighted land:

95

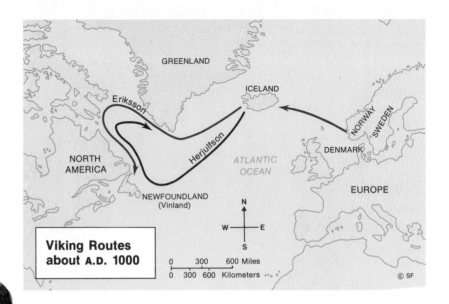

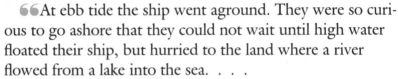

Viking Routes about A.D. 1000

66At ebb tide the ship went aground. They were so curious to go ashore that they could not wait until high water floated their ship, but hurried to the land where a river flowed from a lake into the sea. . . .

They decided to stay for the winter and they built a large house. . . . The qualities of the surrounding country were so good that they believed there would be no shortage of cattle fodder [food] in the wintertime. No frost came in winter and the grass withered only a little. . . .

When they had built their house Leif said to his followers: "Now I will divide the company into two parts so that the land can be explored. One half of the company shall remain at home while the other half goes exploring; but not farther away than they can return in the evening; and they are not to separate." . . .

One evening word came that a man was missing from one of the [exploration] parties. This was Tyrker (tir′kər), the southerner. . . .

Leif gave Tyrker's companions a tongue-lashing and ordered an expedition to be made in search of him by twelve men, and went along himself. They had gone only a short way from the hall when Tyrker came to meet them and was warmly greeted. . . .

[Tyrker said,] "I have walked not much farther than here but I have something interesting to relate. I found vines and grapes." . . .

Then they all went to bed, but in the morning Leif said to his crew: "Hereafter we shall have two tasks. Every day we will either gather grapes and cut vines, or fell timber to make a cargo for my ship."

They cut a full cargo for the ship. When spring came they sailed away. And Leif gave a name to the land, in keeping with its products, and called it Vinland. 99

For a long time, people thought this story was a legend. Archaeologists have now studied the land of Newfoundland. That is the place where many believe Eriksson landed. On the northern tip of Newfoundland, archaeologists found the remains of houses from a thousand years ago. The houses looked much like the ones in old Norway.

Archaeologists cannot prove that Leif Eriksson's crew built the houses they found in Newfoundland. But they think they have found evidence of European exploration and settlement at about the year 1000.

Among the remains, archaeologists found several tools and a tiny whorl. A whorl is a round piece of stone or baked clay with a hole in its center. People used whorls as parts of tools to spin wool into yarn. Viking men are not known to have done the job of spinning yarn from wool. Archaeologists guess that Viking women were in Newfoundland with the men. If that was so, the Norse houses may have been more than a stopover for Viking explorers. The houses may have been part of a European settlement in North America.

(far left) This 5-inch carving was found by archaeologists in a Viking burial. It looks like the much larger carvings that Vikings put on the front of their ships. Why would Viking sailors want such carvings on their ships? (below) A Viking whorl found by archaeologists.

Checking Up

1. Why did the Vikings probably come to America?

2. What are two kinds of evidence that show the Vikings might have been the first Europeans to come to North America?

3. What did Leif Eriksson want to do in the land he visited?

Lesson 2   Columbus and the New World

Hundreds of years ago, Europeans placed great value on the gold, silk, and spices of the Indies. These lands include China, Japan, India, and other areas shown on the map on page 99. People in the Indies wanted wool, grain, and salt from Europe.

Trading went on with the help of **merchants** who bought and sold goods. The trade routes were long and dangerous. They went through thousands of miles of mountains and deserts. Trading parties were often attacked by thieves. Some people believed there had to be a better way to trade.

In 1492, Christopher Columbus, an Italian mapmaker and sailor, tried to prove a point. He wanted to show the people of Europe that they could trade with the Indies in a quick and easy way. Columbus thought the world was round.

He thought he could reach the Indies by sailing west across the Atlantic Ocean. He felt he would eventually reach the Indies in the East. Many Europeans still believed that the world was flat. Columbus, they thought, would fall off the earth. Others felt that horrible sea monsters would destroy Columbus's ships.

Queen Isabella and King Ferdinand of Spain finally gave Columbus his chance. They gave him three ships, the *Santa María,* the *Pinta,* and the *Niña.* After two months at sea,

Mystery in History

Is Columbus buried in two places? His remains had been put into a small casket in a chapel in Santo Domingo. In 1795, the French took this land over. It was decided that his remains should be sent to Cuba and then to Seville, Spain. Later, in 1877, while the chapel in Santo Domingo was being enlarged, a casket with Columbus's initials on it was found. For many years, no one could agree on where Columbus was really buried. Was it in Spain or Santo Domingo? The mystery has been solved. See if you can find out where he is buried.

The *Pinta,* and *Niña,* and the *Santa María* sail into a sunset in 1492.

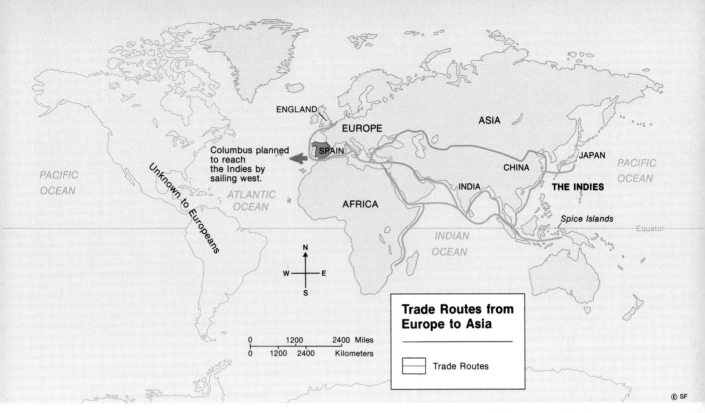

Map labels:
ENGLAND
EUROPE
ASIA
SPAIN
JAPAN
CHINA
PACIFIC OCEAN
Columbus planned to reach the Indies by sailing west.
THE INDIES
Unknown to Europeans
PACIFIC OCEAN
ATLANTIC OCEAN
INDIA
AFRICA
Spice Islands
Equator
INDIAN OCEAN

N
W — E
S

0   1200   2400 Miles
0   1200   2400   Kilometers

Trade Routes from Europe to Asia

Trade Routes

© SF

What stopped Columbus from reaching the Indies by sailing west? Turn to the map on page 102. Follow Columbus's route from Europe to the island of San Salvador.

Columbus's crew was frightened and ready to quit. Land was discovered just in time. Read what a sailor wrote in his record book:

66THURSDAY, IITH OF OCTOBER They saw sandpipers, and a green reed near the ship. Those on the *Pinta* saw a cane and a pole, and they took up another small pole which appeared to have been worked with iron; also another bit of cane, a landplant, and a small board. The crew of the *Niña* also saw signs of land, and a small branch covered with berries. Every one breathed afresh and rejoiced at these signs. . . .

As the *Pinta* was a better sailer, and went ahead of the Admiral, she found the land, and made the signals ordered by the Admiral. The land was first seen by a sailor named Rodrigo de Triana (rô drē′gō ᴛнā trē ä′nä). . . .99

Columbus named the island on which he landed San Salvador. He called the people he met Indians, thinking he was in the East Indies islands off Asia. Then Columbus returned to Spain. He was disappointed that he had not found the big cities in China and Japan. He believed he would find them on a later trip.

99

Shown here is the busy port of Lisbon, Portugal, in the late 1400s. The artist drew both the old and the new in sailing at this time. On the ship in the center is a carved head. It is much like the ones that appeared on Viking ships almost five hundred years before. The ship in the upper left corner, however, shows something new. The improved rudder at the end of the ship helped keep the ship on course in rough ocean seas. The sail, also at the end, allowed sailors to sail *into* the wind instead of just *with* the wind.

Columbus made three other trips to the same area. Each time he thought he was visiting Asia. He still hoped to return to Spain with a shipload of gold, silks, and spices. Instead he returned with Indians he had taken as slaves, new kinds of animals and birds, and tobacco.

After Columbus's fourth trip, the king and queen of Spain became angry. Where were the riches he had promised them?

On May 20, 1506, Columbus died still thinking he had reached Asia. He still wondered why he could not find China and Japan. But just a few years before, in 1501, Amerigo Vespucci (ve spü′chē), another Italian sailor who worked for Spain, understood what Columbus never did. The Americas were a New World. This New World was really two giant pieces of land called continents. In honor of Amerigo Vespucci, people began calling this New World North and South America.

Checking Up

1. Explain how Columbus thought he could get to Asia in the East by heading west across the Atlantic Ocean.

2. Why did Columbus fail to reach the Indies?

3. How was Columbus both a success and a failure?

Lesson 3   Cabot and Cartier

Other Europeans began explorations after Columbus's first voyage. They, too, hoped to find a passage to the riches of the Indies. John Cabot, a visiting Italian merchant, might have been standing in the crowd that welcomed Columbus home to Spain.

Cabot felt that a shorter route than Columbus's was possible. But the rulers of Spain and Portugal would not listen to his request for ships. It then occurred to him that England could benefit from a shorter route to the Indies. If you look on the map on page 99 you will see what Cabot realized.

England was farthest from the Indies if one went east across Europe to get there. This forced the English to pay the highest price for their goods. But, thought Cabot, England might be closest to Asia if one sailed west around the world. Henry VII, king of England, agreed.

The *Mathew,* with Cabot as captain, set sail on May 22, 1497. Heading west for what he thought was China, Cabot reached land on June 24, 1497. It was not China, Japan, or India. It was, according to Henry VII, a "newe founde lande." Today, it is Newfoundland, Canada.

Henry VII was pleased enough to send Cabot on a second voyage. Again, he was to find "spices and jewels." When Cabot left England in May of 1498, this was the last anyone saw of him, his crews, and four ships. Were their ships lost at sea in a storm? Did they crash into icebergs? No one knows. Cabot never reached his goal. His journey, however, excited explorers from England and other nations.

One such explorer was Jacques Cartier (zhäk kär tyā′) of France. Cartier made three voyages for France to the New World between 1534 and 1543. Yet, these were not his only trips to the unexplored lands of North America. He had, as a boy in 1507, gone with his father to fish in the cod-rich waters off Newfoundland. He often dreamed of finding what no other explorer had found: a sea road to the Indies.

After many years as a sea captain, Cartier got the chance to see his dream come true. The king of France ordered him to explore the lands beyond Newfoundland in hopes of locating a passage to the Indies. On his first voyage, Cartier saw a swimming bear "as big as a cow and white as a swan," and

Facts and Figures

In 1519, Ferdinand Magellan set out to sail around the world for Spain. No one had done it before, so no one knew what to expect.

Magellan did not know if he would have enough food to last for the entire voyage. Below is a list of some of the items he took.

15 tons of biscuits
6,100 pounds of beans and peas
5,700 pounds of dried pork
1,512 pounds of honey
3,200 pounds of raisins
322 pounds of rice
100 pounds of mustard
500 gallons of flour
5,600 pounds of vinegar
450 strings of onions and garlic

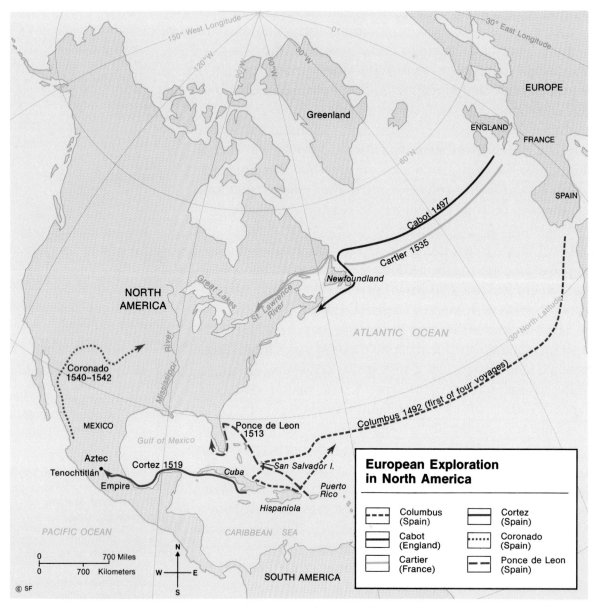

European Exploration in North America
Columbus (Spain)
Cabot (England)
Cartier (France)
Cortez (Spain)
Coronado (Spain)
Ponce de Leon (Spain)
150° West Longitude
120°W
90°W
60°W
30°W
0°
30° East Longitude
60°N
30° North Latitude
Greenland
EUROPE
ENGLAND
FRANCE
SPAIN
Cabot 1497
Cartier 1535
Newfoundland
Great Lakes
St. Lawrence River
NORTH AMERICA
ATLANTIC OCEAN
Mississippi River
Coronado 1540–1542
Columbus 1492 (first of four voyages)
MEXICO
Gulf of Mexico
Ponce de Leon 1513
Aztec
Tenochtitlán
Empire
Cortez 1519
Cuba
San Salvador I.
Puerto Rico
Hispaniola
PACIFIC OCEAN
CARIBBEAN SEA
SOUTH AMERICA
0 700 Miles
0 700 Kilometers
N
S
E
W
© SF

Use the map's scale to help you answer these questions.

1. How far did Cabot travel from England to Newfoundland?
2. Coronado's journey brought him within ______ miles of the Mississippi.

"beasts as big as oxen, with two teeth in their mouth like the elephant, and which live in the sea." The polar bear and walruses were interesting, but they were not the riches he had hoped for.

Cartier took a second voyage. As the above map shows, he followed what is today the St. Lawrence Seaway. The Indians he found were friendly. They showed him many unusual customs such as how to smoke sun-dried leaves of tobacco. They made him bread from the dried, yellow kernels of the

The modern city of Montreal; what do you think Cartier would say if he saw it today?

corn plant. When his men got scurvy, a disease from a lack of vitamin C, the Indians showed him how to make a curing drink from boiled pine bark and pine needles. Cartier explored as far as present-day Montreal. But he found no route to the Indies.

On his last voyage, Cartier failed to produce the gold and diamonds he had promised the king. The treasures turned out to be iron pieces and quartz. Cartier, however, was not a failure. His trip turned his nation's interests away from exploration and more to settlement in North America.

Checking Up

1. What goal did Columbus, Cabot, and Cartier all have in common? What stopped them from reaching it?

2. From what you have read, what dangers did early explorers face?

3. What kind of person would have made a good explorer in the 1500s? How would they compare to astronauts of today?

taxes (taks′ez), money paid to support the government to pay for public works and services.

(above) An Aztec warrior.
(right)
Most of the Aztecs' buildings no longer stand. But this artist has probably created an accurate picture of life in Tenochtitlán. How is this possible? Think back to your study of the Anasazi people. How have we learned about them? For an up-to-date story about the archaeology of ancient Mexico, look at *National Geographic*, Dec., 1980.

Lesson 4   Cortez and Coronado

Even before Cartier began his explorations of Canada, Spanish colonists had settlements in the New World. They built settlements on the islands of Puerto Rico, Cuba, and Hispaniola (his′pə nyō′lə).

The Indians who lived there told stories to the Spanish about a great city of gold to the west in a land called Mexico. One who heard the stories was Hernando Cortez (er nän′dō kôr tez′), a soldier and trader. He wanted to find this city of gold and claim the land for Spain. In 1519, he sailed with eleven ships and about six hundred soldiers from Cuba to Mexico. Find his route on the map on page 102.

When Cortez landed, he met a friendly group of Indians. They quickly agreed to join him. They had been **conquered**, or taken over by force, by another Indian group, the powerful Aztecs. The Aztecs were hated rulers. They took food and prisoners and forced the people to pay **taxes**. Cortez thought the Aztecs controlled the city of gold.

To reach the Aztec capital city of Tenochtitlán (te nôch′tē tlän′), Cortez and his forces marched for more than two hundred miles. Much of the land was jungle. It took almost two months to reach the city.

Tenochtitlán was a fabulous place. It was built on an island in Lake Texcoco and connected to land by rock roadways. It had more people and riches than any city in Spain. About 250,000 people lived in the city. Sixty thousand people traded goods in its market every day. There were beautifully painted buildings and palaces, statues, and parks.

One of Cortez's men later wrote:

66We were amazed . . . on account of the great towers and temples and buildings rising from the water, and all built of masonry or brick. And some of our soldiers even asked whether the things that we saw were not a dream.99

Cortez thought the Indian stories he had heard were true. The city had more gold than he had ever seen.

Cortez found that the leader of the Aztecs, Montezuma (mon′tə zü′mə), was friendly to the Spanish. Montezuma believed in an old legend that said a god would return from

104

the sea. Montezuma thought Cortez was the god. The Aztecs also thought the Spanish horses were gods. One of the Aztecs said that the running horses made noises, "as if stones were raining on the earth." Soldiers on horseback with steel weapons must have terrified the Aztecs.

The Spanish war dogs also scared the Aztecs. They had never seen fierce animals that obeyed the commands of people. One of them reported: "Their dogs are enormous . . . their eyes flash fire and shoot off sparks . . ."

The Spanish guns seemed strange and horrible. Cortez had fourteen pieces of artillery. These cannons were often fired to frighten the Aztecs.

Cortez decided to conquer the Aztecs and take their gold and jewels. Cortez attacked with four hundred of his own soldiers, and 100,000 Indians. After eighty-five days, Tenochtitlán lay in ruins. The Spanish soon began to build a new city out of the ruins. Many people from Spain came to live there. By 1521 the Spanish had begun to take the place of the Aztecs as rulers of Mexico.

Coronado and his troops crossing the hot, dusty, plains of present-day Kansas in 1541. He and his soldiers were searching for the Seven Cities of Gold.

After their conquest of Mexico, the Spanish were eager to claim more land in North America. One Spanish explorer who succeeded at this was Francisco Coronado (fran sis'kō kôr'ə nä'dō). His two-year journey took him north from Mexico into land that is now part of the southwestern United States. Coronado was looking for the legendary "Seven Cities of Gold." He never found the gold. He did, however, claim large areas of land, including parts of Texas, New Mexico, Arizona, and Colorado. You can follow his journey and the journeys of other Spanish explorers by looking at the map on page 102.

Checking Up

1. Why did Cortez lead the Spanish into Mexico?

2. Both Montezuma and Cortez believed in stories or legends. How did this affect their actions?

3. How were Cortez and Coronado similar in their reasons for exploration?

Write your answers on paper. Do not write in the book.

Using Key Words

merchant   explore
conquer   tax

Write a short meaning for each of the key words listed above.

Reviewing Main Ideas

Number your paper from 1 to 4. Pick the word or phrase that best completes the following sentences.

1. Archaeologists believe that the Vikings **a**. settled in Newfoundland around A.D. 1000. **b**. never settled in North America. **c**. settled in North America long before Indians migrated there.

2. Columbus was trying to **a**. discover a New World. **b**. get to the Indies by sailing west on the Atlantic Ocean. **c**. find a new trade route across land.

3. Cabot and Cartier were **a**. looking for a water passage through the continent of North America. **b**. satisfied with their explorations when they found strange animals. **c**. trying to set up Christian settlements in the New World.

4. Cortez wanted to **a**. help the Aztecs build their capital city. **b**. conquer the Aztecs. **c**. claim the Aztecs' land for France.

Thinking Things Over

Write a paragraph explaining whether you think that the Europeans discovered America or not.

Practicing Skills

Number your paper from 1 to 5. Match the explorer with the land he explored.
Eriksson   Cartier
Columbus   Cortez
Coronado

Chapter
6
Lesson 1   Spanish Colonies
Lesson 2   French, Dutch, and Swedish Colonies
Lesson 3   The English Colony at Jamestown

Settlement of North America

By the Way

Some explorers became famous and some became rich. Some died trying. Magellan, who was trying to sail around the world, was killed in the Philippine Islands in 1521. Juan Ponce de León, who had failed to find the Fountain of Youth, also failed to make friends with the Indians in Florida. He was killed. Sir Walter Raleigh, who had set up a colony in Virginia, but disobeyed the orders of his king, had his head cut off. Robert de La Salle, who had claimed the area of present-day Louisiana was killed by his men in Texas in 1687. Hernando de Soto died of a fever while exploring in present-day Arkansas. His men buried him in the Mississippi River.

"We came here to serve God, and also to get rich." This was one Spanish explorer's reason for coming to the New World. Many who came from France, England, and other countries to explore or settle would have agreed. Some settlers wanted to teach the Indians the Christian way of life. Some wanted to find gold and silver. Others felt they could become rich by owning their own land. These settlers from different countries had their own customs and culture.

Lesson 1   Spanish Colonies

The lands claimed in North America by Spanish explorers were called New Spain. These lands were colonies of Spain. A **colony** is a settlement made by people who leave their own country and settle in another land. The colony is ruled by the country from which the settlers came.

One of the lands claimed by Spain was present-day Florida. Juan Ponce de León (pons′ də lē′ən) had explored Florida in 1513. Like other Spanish explorers, he searched for gold. He also tried to find the "Fountain of Youth." Its waters were supposed to make old people young. But he failed to find either gold or a fountain and did not set up a colony.

A colony was set up in Florida in 1564. But it belonged to France, not Spain. A group of French settlers came to the New World to find a place where they could live and worship in freedom. Their colony was named Fort Caroline.

Spain did not want to lose Florida. In 1565, Pedro Menendez (mā nān′dāth) led Spanish soldiers in an attack on Fort Caroline. After destroying the settlement, they built their own fort nearby. This was the start of the city of St. Augustine. This is the oldest city in what is now the United States.

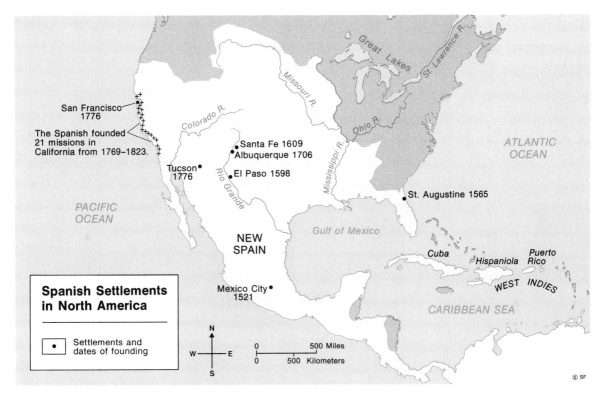

Spanish Settlements in North America

- San Francisco 1776
- The Spanish founded 21 missions in California from 1769–1823.
- Tucson 1776
- Santa Fe 1609
- Albuquerque 1706
- El Paso 1598
- Mexico City 1521
- St. Augustine 1565

NEW SPAIN

Colorado R., Missouri R., Ohio R., Mississippi R., Rio Grande, St. Lawrence R., Great Lakes

ATLANTIC OCEAN, PACIFIC OCEAN, Gulf of Mexico, Cuba, Hispaniola, Puerto Rico, WEST INDIES, CARIBBEAN SEA

Settlements and dates of founding

500 Miles
500 Kilometers

© SF

Notice how far north Spanish territory extended into the present-day United States. Locate the Spanish colonies of Cuba, Puerto Rico, and Hispaniola

Spain became interested in starting other colonies. It decided to move into the land explored by Coronado. In 1609, New Mexico's present capital city, Santa Fe, was founded. The following description of Santa Fe gives us an idea how Spain ruled the colony. It was written by Alonso de Benavides (bä′nä vē′ҒHas), a church leader of New Mexico.

❝[In Santa Fe,] live the governing leaders and the Spaniards. They must number as many as two hundred and fifty. Only some fifty can arm themselves, they have so few weapons. . . . But God has allowed that they always win. He has caused among the Indians so great a fear of them and their guns that they only need to hear that a Spaniard is coming to their pueblos. Then they flee. In order to keep up this fear the Spaniards act very harshly towards the Indians.

The Indians pay taxes in cotton cloth and corn. With this the needy Spaniards keep alive. The Spaniards must have some seven hundred servants. There must be a thousand people in all at Santa Fe. Priests attended first to building churches for the Indians they were converting and with whom they were working and living.❞

Located nine miles southwest of Tucson, Arizona, is Mission San Xavier del Bac. It has long been called the "White Dove of the Desert." It is one of the oldest Spanish missions, having been built around 1700.

By 1770, other permanent, or lasting, Spanish settlements were also started in California. Father Junipero Serra (hü′nē pe′rō se′rä) and a group of priests and soldiers built twenty-one churches, called **missions.** Their locations are shown on the map on page 109. The priests came to teach the Indians how to farm, but mostly how to lead a Christian way of life. The soldiers made sure the Indians obeyed rules. Indians were also forced to work on large farms called haciendas (hä′sē en′dəz).

Spanish settlers built towns that have grown into large American cities. But El Paso, Texas; Albuquerque, New Mexico; Tucson, Arizona; and San Francisco, California, have more than just Spanish names. They still have much of the culture brought by the Spanish settlers.

Checking Up

1. What part of North America was claimed by Spain?

2. Why did Spain want to set up colonies in America?

3. How might you have acted toward the Spanish at Santa Fe if you had been an Indian?

Lesson 2 French, Dutch, and Swedish Colonies

Spain was joined by other countries looking for colonies. France began a colony called New France in the land explored by Cartier. The first lasting settlement was made in 1608 by the explorer Samuel de Champlain. It was the village of Quebec (kwi bek′).

Like Spain, France sent explorers to the New World to find riches. To France, however, riches meant animal furs, not gold. Furs were collected from French trappers. They were also collected from Indians in trade for goods. Trappers and Indians sold the furs to merchants in such villages as Quebec. The merchants then sent the furs to France to be made into clothing.

Priests also went to New France. They wanted to teach Indians the Christian way of life. Sometimes they became explorers when trying to set up missions. One priest, Father Jacques Marquette (zhäk mär ket′), explored much of the Mississippi River.

Two trappers wade into an icy pond to set their fur traps.

The InterNorth Art Foundation, Joslyn Art Museum, Omaha, Nebraska

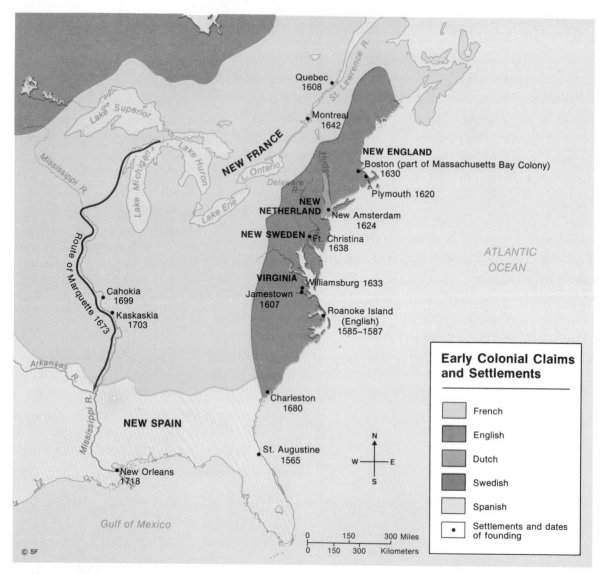

Map labels:

Quebec 1608
Montreal 1642
NEW FRANCE
Lake Superior
Lake Michigan
Lake Huron
L. Ontario
Lake Erie
Mississippi R.
St. Lawrence R.
NEW ENGLAND
Boston (part of Massachusetts Bay Colony) 1630
Plymouth 1620
Hudson R.
Delaware R.
NEW NETHERLAND
New Amsterdam 1624
NEW SWEDEN
Ft. Christina 1638
VIRGINIA
Williamsburg 1633
Jamestown 1607
Roanoke Island (English) 1585–1587
ATLANTIC OCEAN
Route of Marquette 1673
Cahokia 1699
Kaskaskia 1703
Arkansas R.
Mississippi R.
NEW SPAIN
Charleston 1680
St. Augustine 1565
New Orleans 1718
Gulf of Mexico
© SF

N
W — E
S

0   150   300 Miles
0   150   300   Kilometers

Early Colonial Claims and Settlements

- French
- English
- Dutch
- Swedish
- Spanish
- • Settlements and dates of founding

Use the map key to locate the early colonial settlements. Find the cities of Quebec, Plymouth, Jamestown, New Amsterdam, Charleston, and Kaskaskia. The location of these settlements all have something in common. What is it.?

Wherever French explorers went, they claimed large areas of land. The above map shows the boundaries of New France. However, there were few French settlers in most of this land.

Small towns such as Kaskaskia and Cahokia in Illinois were built as trading posts and missions. The trappers, traders, priests, and soldiers came and went. Most French settlers lived in the growing towns of Quebec, Montreal, and New Orleans.

At about the same time the French settled in Canada, people from the Netherlands came to America. In 1624, these

New York City in 1644. The man is posting a notice that explains how a wall will be built around part of the city. The wall was to keep Indians from killing the settlers' cattle. From that time on, this area of New York was called "Wall Street." Today, Wall Street is the home for many large banks, the New York Stock Exchange, and other trading centers. It is considered to be the money center of the United States.

Dutch families built forts and trading posts along the Hudson and Delaware rivers. One settlement was built on Manhattan Island at the mouth of the Hudson River. It was named New Amsterdam. The island, which was bought from Indians, is today part of New York City. The Dutch colony was named New Netherland.

In 1638, settlers from Sweden came to America. They built a town on the banks of the Delaware River, south of New Netherland, in what is now New Jersey. New Sweden did not last very long. It was taken over by Dutch settlers.

Most of the Dutch and Swedes lived by trading and farming. There were not many Dutch and Swedish settlers. But even that was too many for the English colonists. The English settlers wanted to farm and trade in the same area. The Dutch were outnumbered. They gave in to the English by 1664. New Netherland was no longer a colony.

Checking Up

1. How were French explorers and settlers like and unlike the Spanish?

2. Compare the Dutch way of getting land from the Indians with the Spanish way.

113

Lesson 3   The English Colony at Jamestown

One hundred forty-four Englishmen crowded aboard three ships in December of 1606. The three ships were the *Godspeed,* the *Susan Constant,* and the *Discovery*. The passengers were headed for the English part of America called Virginia. Yet, they were not the first English to see Virginia.

In 1587, a small settlement was built on Roanoke Island, off the coast of what today is North Carolina. By 1590 the one hundred seventeen settlers had disappeared. No one knew what happened to them. The passengers on the three ships in 1606 had good reason to be afraid.

On board were carpenters, doctors, poor farmers, millers (people who make flour from grain), and criminals. Some wanted to go to Virginia to have land of their own. Some wanted to teach the Indians about Christianity. Some went just to find adventure. Many were looking for gold. A few were even looking for a passage to the riches of India.

After four months at sea, the passengers sighted land. On May 14, 1607, they decided to settle on the banks of a river. They named the river James and their settlement Jamestown after their king, James I.

Jamestown was built close to the river and near a swamp. The spot, however, gave them some safety from attack. The settlers quickly built a church, a trading post, houses, and, of course, a fort.

During the first seven months at Jamestown many settlers died. Disease-carrying mosquitoes from the nearby swamps killed many. Others died when the settlement was attacked by a group of Algonquin Indians. Other settlers died of hunger. It had been too late to plant crops when the settlers first arrived so they had no harvest. They had also eaten most of the food brought from England. By Christmas of 1607, only thirty-two settlers were left alive.

The settlers needed a strong leader to guide them. They elected John Smith and he quickly took charge. The people agreed to Smith's law of survival: "He who will not work shall not eat . . ." Smith ordered the people to stop looking for gold. Instead, he ordered them to plant crops and repair their homes.

In December, 1607, John Smith went exploring for food and other supplies. On the trip the Algonquins captured him and took him to their chief, Powhatan (pou′ə tan′). Here is how Smith described what happened:

(far left) The camera recreates the landing at Jamestown in 1607. (above) An artist recreates what the Jamestown settlement might have looked like. What are three ways your life is different from the settlers' at Jamestown?

❝❝Two great stones were brought before Powhatan; then as many as could laid hands on him [Smith], dragged him to them, and thereon laid his head, and being ready with their clubs to beat out his brains. Pocahontas, the king's dearest daughter, when no entreaty could prevail, got his head in her arms, and laid her own upon his to save his from death . . . Powhatan came unto him and told him now they were friends . . .❞❞

No one knows if the story is true. Yet, after Smith's trip, the settlers had peace for a time with the Indians. The Indians even taught the settlers how to plant corn.

But Jamestown soon became a village of death. First, a group of Indians became angry after over four hundred settlers arrived and took more land. The Indians attacked and killed thirty people and much of the livestock. The frightened colonists crowded into the fort. These crowded conditions brought on deadly diseases. Hunger killed many. One colonist remembered eating "dogges, catts, ratts, and myce." After a terrible winter in 1609, only sixty-five colonists were alive.

One of the colonists, John Rolfe, looked for a way to improve life in the colony. Rolfe found a crop for which people might pay money. That crop was tobacco. In 1613, Rolfe sent the first shipment of tobacco to England. People bought the tobacco and wanted more of it. Year after year, the amount of tobacco shipped to England grew. This brought wealth to Jamestown.

Archaeologists have helped rebuild the fort at Jamestown. Why do you think such a fort was needed?

In 1619, three important events took place in the colony. First, a Dutch ship brought twenty blacks from Africa. These first blacks might have been **indentured servants**. An indentured servant had to work for a set time to pay off a debt. Usually, such a person was working off the cost of their passage to America.

These first blacks might also have been **slaves**. Slaves were owned and forced to work for someone else. Unlike indentured servants, slaves rarely got their freedom. By the 1640s, most blacks were brought to America as slaves.

Second, the settlers chose a General Assembly. This group of people was elected to make laws and act as judges for everyone in the colony. It was the first assembly in North America. This had not happened in the French or Spanish colonies.

Third, a ship arrived at Jamestown with ninety women aboard. These were not the first women in the colony. But most of the others had died. Jamestown for a time became a settlement of families.

Jamestown grew during the next eighty years. But fires burnt it to the ground a number of times. Each time the town was rebuilt, more Indian land was taken. The Indians attacked for revenge. Once they killed a third of the settlers. Finally, the settlers felt they had had enough of fires, attacks, and mosquitoes. In 1699 they decided to move their capital to Williamsburg, Virginia. Jamestown became almost a ghost town.

Checking Up

1. Why did English settlers come to Jamestown?

2. How did John Smith and John Rolfe help the Jamestown colony survive?

3. How was the way of life in Jamestown like and unlike life in the French and Spanish colonies?

Reviewing Chapter 6

Write your answers on paper. Do not write in the book.

Using Key Words

colony   mission
slave   indentured servant

Write a short meaning for each key word listed above.

Reviewing Main Ideas

Number your paper from 1 to 5. Pick the word or phrase that best completes the following sentences.

1. The main interest of the French in New France was **a.** fur. **b.** silk. **c.** gold.

2. The first lasting English settlement in North America was **a.** Jamestown. **b.** Williamsburg. **c.** St. Augustine.

3. The Dutch settled in present-day **a.** Canada. **b.** Florida. **c.** New York.

4. Missions were started in California by Spanish settlers to **a.** find gold. **b.** teach the Indians about Christianity. **c.** locate the "Fountain of Youth."

5. Life in Jamestown was **a.** always easy. **b.** never enjoyable. **c.** better after the settlers started to grow tobacco.

Thinking Things Over

Write down reasons for agreeing or disagreeing with the following statement. The American Indians in many regions helped European settlers stay alive in the New World.

Practicing Skills

Match the location of a settlement in the New World with the name of that settlement below.

St. Augustine   Santa Fe
Jamestown   New Amsterdam
Quebec

Life in the English Colonies

In 1619, Virginia was the only English colony in America. About one thousand settlers were trying to make a new life in this new land. By 1760, there were thirteen English colonies with more than one and a half million settlers. There were colonists from France, the Netherlands, Ireland, Germany, and other nations. They were people with their own identity. They shared an identity, too. They were Americans.

Lesson 1 The New England Colonies

One hundred forty-nine men, women, and children sailed from England for Virginia in 1620. About forty of them were traveling to the New World to find religious freedom that they did not have in England. Today we call these people Pilgrims. A **pilgrim** is someone who takes a religious journey.

The Pilgrims had taken religious journeys before. They left England in 1608 and tried to make their home in the Netherlands. But soon they grew unhappy. They may have disagreed with other English people about religion, but they still wanted to keep their English culture. In the Netherlands, the Pilgrims saw their children acting and speaking like Dutch children instead of English. Slowly, the Pilgrims came to believe they needed to settle in a brand-new land to be happy.

In 1620, the Pilgrims got their chance. With William and Mary Brewster as their leaders, they set out for Virginia on a tiny ship called the *Mayflower*. A storm drove the *Mayflower* far north of the colony of Virginia. The Pilgrims liked the spot where they landed, so they decided to stay. The place had been named Plymouth by earlier explorers. It had a clean stream nearby and flat fields ready to be planted.

What's in a Name?

Why were the founders of Boston called Puritans? Their name gives us a clue. Purify means to clean or to free. While in England, this group wanted to purify the services of the Church of England. They wanted to do away with the fancy and complicated church ceremonies. They wanted to worship God in a simple way. These ideas made the rulers of England angry. The Puritans were often punished. Many Puritans decided to go to the New World. There, they felt, they would have the freedom to worship as they pleased.

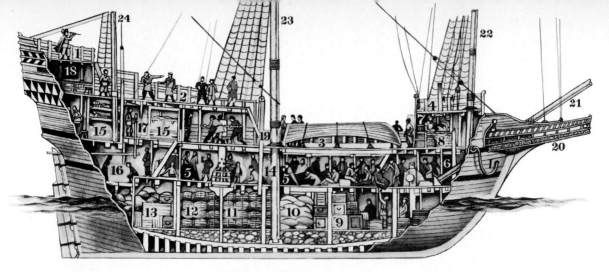

1. Stern deck
2. Quarter deck
3. Upper deck
4. Forecastle
5. Main deck (The Pilgrims lived here with most of their possessions. There were no bunks or hammocks to sleep on, so beds had to be made here or on the upper deck)
6. Crew's quarters
7. Boatswain's store
8. Galley, with cooking range
9. Main hold (containing cargo and supplies including barrels of beer, dried meat, and vegetables)
10. Cargo
11. General stores
12. Barrels of water
13. Barrels of biscuit and flour
14. Temporary cabin
15. Special cabins
16. Tiller room
17. Helmsman with whipstaff connected to the tiller (ship is steered from here)
18. Captain's Great Room or Great Cabin (in the sterncastle)
19. Pens for livestock
20. Beak
21. Bowsprit
22. Foremast
23. Mainmast
24. Mizzenmast

This cross section of the Mayflower shows where the 101 passengers lived during their voyage across the Atlantic. The living areas were cramped and poorly ventilated. The passengers were usually cold, wet, and sick. This was "home" for over 2 months.

Life was hard during the first year of the settlement. Without the help of nearby Indians, the colony might have failed. The Indians taught the colonists to plant corn, to fish, and to make homes with natural resources. Still, over half the settlers died of disease during the first winter.

The Pilgrims harvested a good crop in the fall of 1621. They wanted to give thanks for their good harvest. They invited their Indian friends to a feast of wild turkey, duck, goose, squash, and corn. Today, on Thanksgiving Day, Americans honor this Pilgrim celebration.

Another group of English people came to the area in 1630. This group, called Puritans, also wanted religious freedom. They settled a few miles north of Plymouth and called their colony Massachusetts Bay. The first group numbered about one thousand men, women, and children.

John Winthrop was the leader at Massachusetts Bay. He and other Puritans quickly built the towns of Boston, Salem, and Watertown. By 1640, about twenty thousand people lived in the area.

The Puritan leaders put many of their religious beliefs into their laws. They made a law that forced people to attend church. They allowed only church members to vote on who should lead the people. The Puritans also set up schools to teach their children the Puritan beliefs.

Not everyone agreed with those laws. Roger Williams, a religious teacher living in Salem, began teaching that the churches of the Puritans were too strict. He taught that people should have the right to vote without being members of the churches. The government, he thought, should not force people to go to church. He also felt that the settlers should not take land from Indians without paying for it.

(above) The first Thanksgiving: the Pilgrims give thanks for a good harvest in the year 1621. (left) The snow-swept colony at Plymouth huddles against winter along the Atlantic coast.

Which color in the map key is used to represent the New England Colonies? You will read about the Middle and Southern Colonies later in this chapter. Which colors are used to show these two groups of colonies?

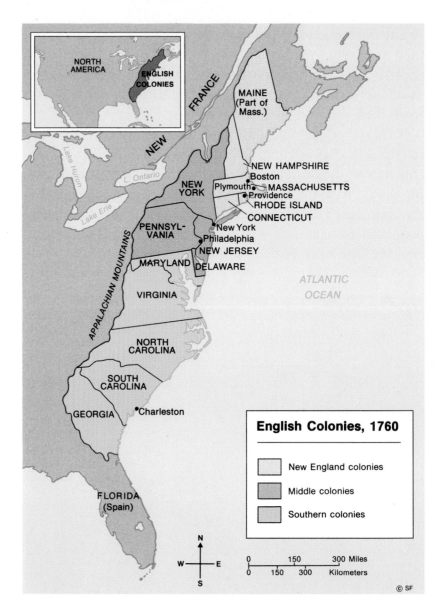

NORTH AMERICA

ENGLISH COLONIES

FRANCE

NEW

MAINE (Part of Mass.)

Lake Huron

L. Ontario

Lake Erie

NEW YORK

NEW HAMPSHIRE
Boston
Plymouth MASSACHUSETTS
Providence
RHODE ISLAND
CONNECTICUT

PENNSYL-VANIA

New York
Philadelphia
NEW JERSEY

MARYLAND DELAWARE

ATLANTIC OCEAN

APPALACHIAN MOUNTAINS

VIRGINIA

NORTH CAROLINA

SOUTH CAROLINA

GEORGIA Charleston

FLORIDA (Spain)

English Colonies, 1760

New England colonies

Middle colonies

Southern colonies

N
W — E
S

0   150   300 Miles
0   150   300   Kilometers

© SF

Williams angered the leaders of Massachusetts Bay. John Winthrop, governor of the colony, warned Williams to leave or be arrested. In 1635, Williams and a few followers left. They went to an area south of Massachusetts where the Narragansett Indians lived. Williams bought land from the Indians and built a town on it. He called the town Providence and the colony Rhode Island. There, he and his followers practiced their beliefs.

Disagreements in Massachusetts Bay did not end when Roger Williams left the colony. Another colonist, Anne Hutchinson, held meetings in her home. At the meetings, she discussed the sermons of the Puritan ministers. She sometimes disagreed with the ministers' teachings. This disturbed the Puritan ministers. They wanted to be the only ones to preach. They made Anne Hutchinson and her family leave Massachusetts Bay Colony.

Common Beginnings

Many people of Plymouth, Massachusetts Bay, Rhode Island, and New Hampshire argued with each other about religion. In spite of this, they had much in common. Most people believed in the idea of hard work. A popular saying was, "To work is to pray." The people meant that one way to serve God was to do the best job you could when working.

The settlers had something else in common. It was the ocean. The map on page 122 shows that most of the early settlements stayed near the ocean. People did farm, but it was mostly for their own use. The soil in this area was too rocky and the weather too harsh to earn a living by farming. Many people, however, did make a living from the ocean.

The ocean was filled with whales, cod, and other fish. There were ships to be built from the strong trees of the forests. There were goods to be loaded and unloaded from the ships. Many people chose to earn a living by whaling, fishing, building ships, or trading goods.

People in this area also had a common past. Either they or their **ancestors** had come to America from England. (An ancestor is a person from whom one is descended; a grandparent, or great-grandparent.) They had the same language and the same customs. Many people started to call the area New England.

During the 1700s, sailors from Massachusetts began going to sea to hunt whales. Whales supplied the raw materials for many products. Whale oil was used to light lamps in homes and on the streets. It was also used in soap making. Bones from the whale were used to make whip handles and corset stays. Other parts of the whale were used to make perfume and candles.

Whaling became a big business for colonial merchants. They not only sold products in America, but overseas as well. The business came to an end, however, in the 1860s. People started to use another fuel called kerosene for their lamps.

It ended just in time for the whales. Many types of whales had almost been killed off. Today, the United States has laws that protect whales from being hunted.

Checking Up

1. How did the settlers from England depend on the Indians?

2. How were Roger Williams's and Anne Hutchinson's ideas different from those of most Puritans?

3. What did New Englanders have in common?

4. How did land influence the way of life in New England?

CITIZENSHIP

The New England Town Meeting

> City Council meets on Tuesday night at 8:00 P.M. All are welcome to attend. The following ideas will be discussed . . .

This is a common notice that appears in the newspapers of small towns and cities all across America, today. The notice is saying that all citizens of a community can help govern themselves. And, notices like it have been appearing for more than two hundred years. The practice began in small New England towns like Plymouth.

At the early town meetings, the people elected officers to do a certain job. The job might be to serve as sheriff, tax collector, or even collector of stray hogs.

Decisions at town meetings were made by majority rule of those present. People who had not voted with the majority had to obey the decision, but were allowed to openly disagree. All citizens had the right to speak and write freely. They also had the responsibility to vote carefully.

What kinds of decisions were made at town meetings? Here are some examples from the records of Plymouth, Massachusetts.

March 1, 1725 Town officers were chosen by majority vote. It was decided to keep the Grammar School in the middle of the town near the Court House. A committee was chosen to find a schoolmaster. The schoolmaster would be hired to teach "writing, reading & arethmetick."

November 13, 1727 The people voted to build an Alms House to care for the poor. It was also decided to give one of the town's citizens enough money to buy a strong winter coat.

December 25, 1727 A committee was chosen to stop the townspeople from capturing a certain fish in the harbor.

Lesson 2   The Middle Colonies

As you have seen, the English sent their navy to the harbor of New Amsterdam in 1664. The English ordered the Dutch to turn the whole colony over to them. The Dutch had no strong army or navy with which to fight. So, they gave up the colony to the English.

The king of England gave New Netherland to the Duke of York. The Duke changed the colony's name and the name of its main city to New York. Then he gave part of the land to two of his friends. These two men formed a new colony and called it New Jersey.

In 1681, the king of England gave another large piece of land to an Englishman named William Penn. Penn's land was located south of New York and west of New Jersey. He called it Pennsylvania, or Penn's woods.

Penn wanted his land and its main city, Philadelphia, to be a "free colony for the benefit of all mankind." All people were to have the same rights and responsibilities. People who were not welcome in their own country came to Pennsylvania for a new beginning.

New York City. Nearby are the busy shipping docks. After reading the lesson, decide what goods are possibly being loaded and unloaded.

125

BREAD IN AMERICA

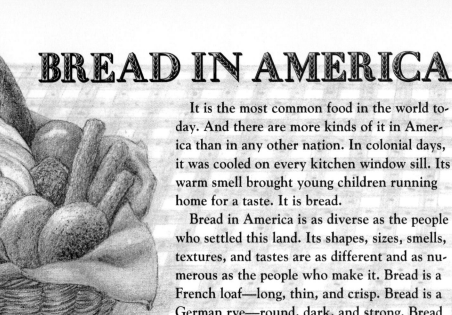

It is the most common food in the world today. And there are more kinds of it in America than in any other nation. In colonial days, it was cooled on every kitchen window sill. Its warm smell brought young children running home for a taste. It is bread.

Bread in America is as diverse as the people who settled this land. Its shapes, sizes, smells, textures, and tastes are as different and as numerous as the people who make it. Bread is a French loaf—long, thin, and crisp. Bread is a German rye—round, dark, and strong. Bread is an English muffin—crusty, chewy, and tangy. Bread is an African coriander—tall,

The Quakers are a good example. This religious group could not get along with the English government. They would not give money to the English church. They also refused to fight in England's wars. Penn, himself, was a Quaker.

In 1682, Penn received another piece of land. The Duke of York gave Penn the land that had once been known as New Sweden. In time, it became known as the colony of Delaware.

The colonists of New York, New Jersey, Delaware, and Pennsylvania had much in common. They lived on land with deep, rich soil. Farmers here, unlike those in New England, could make a good living. They produced large crops of grains such as wheat, corn, rye, and barley. These colonies became known as the breadbasket colonies. They were also called the Middle Colonies as shown on the map on page 122.

These farmers of the Middle Colonies grew crops for sale. Their farm products were shipped to New York and Philadelphia. From here, these and other products were shipped to other colonies or England. The docks at these two seaports were always busy with the loading and unloading of ships. But there were other jobs to be done, too.

Small shops quickly opened. The Middle Colonies became famous for beautiful pottery and glassware. Some people carved furniture, clocks, or cabinets that could be used in the tender, and spicy. Bread is a Mexican tortilla—thin, round, and light.

Bread is American, too. It is Vermont Johnnycakes and Boston Brown. It is Southern Corn and Indian Fry. It is Virginia Sally Lunn and San Franciso Sourdough.

In America it is made with bananas, tomatoes, squash, buttermilk, buckwheat, whole wheat, wheat germ, honey, cheese, potatoes, cider, sour cream, and a thousand other ingredients.

Yet with all this diversity, with all this variety, America has a favorite bread. Ninety-five out of one hundred Americans prefer it to all others. It is basic, simple, sometimes plain and everyday, white bread.

Best-Ever Bread

This dough is easy to handle!

2c. milk
2 tblsp. sugar
2 tsp. salt
1 tblsp. lard

1 pkg. yeast
1/4c. warm water
6c. flour

* Scald milk. Stir in sugar, salt, and lard. Cool to lukewarm. Dissolve yeast in warm water. Add yeast and 3c. flour to milk mixture. Beat until batter is smooth and sheets off spoon.

* Slowly add enough flour to make a dough that leaves the sides of the bowl. Turn onto lightly floured board; cover and let rest 10 minutes.

* Knead until smooth and elastic. Round up into a ball and put into lightly greased bowl; turn dough over to grease top. Cover and let rise in warm place until doubled, about 1-1/2 hours. Punch down, cover and let rise again until almost doubled.

* Turn onto board, shape into ball. Divide in half. Shape into loaves and place in 2 greased loaf pans. Cover and let rise until doubled.

* Bake in hot oven (400°) 35 min. or until deep golden brown. Cool on wire racks away from drafts.

richest homes in the world. Others made fine cloth from cotton or hats from animal fur.

Unlike the settlers of New England, the people of New York, New Jersey, Delaware, and Pennsylvania came from many different places. They came from England, Sweden, Finland, the Netherlands, France, Ireland, Germany, and many other places. And they worshiped in many ways. They were Catholics, Protestants, and Jews. The streets must have been filled with the sounds of many languages. Eighteen were spoken in New York alone. And through open windows came the smell of different foods made by people who had traveled across an ocean to find a new home.

Checking Up

1. How were the Middle Colonies different from the New England Colonies?

2. How did the kind of land of the Middle Colonies differ from that of New England? How did this make a difference in the kind of work people did there?

3. Why did small religious groups like living in the Middle Colonies rather than in New England?

Asher Levy

Twenty-three Jews came to New Amsterdam in 1654. They hoped to find freedom in the Dutch colony to worship as they pleased. But, Asher Levy, their leader, was worried.

They had not been lucky elsewhere. Portuguese soldiers had forced them to

Asher Levy: " . . . the same rights and duties as others."

leave their homes in Brazil. Before that, their ancestors had been pushed out of Portugal. All this happened because the Jews refused to give up their religion. Would it be the same in New Amsterdam?

Mayor Peter Stuyvesant said he did not want them to live in New Amsterdam, either. The Dutch began to pass laws to keep the Jews from having the same responsibilities and rights as others in the colony. All adult males were supposed to share the duty of helping defend the colony. But the Jews were not allowed to join the local defense forces. All citizens were supposed to pay a fair share of taxes to support the colony. But the Jews were made to pay more than anyone else. The Jews were not even allowed to build a house of worship.

Asher Levy became very angry. He wanted freedom to live as a Jew. Asher insisted that Jews should give to the community as others did. In return, they should have the same rights. He demanded that the Jews have guard duties, and not pay higher taxes than the Dutch.

The leaders of New Amsterdam tried to ignore Levy, but he kept after them. Finally, they gave in. Jews were allowed to share the duties of defending the colony. They worked hard at it. Asher Levy and other Jews won the respect of other citizens. Soon they had the same rights as anyone else.

128

Lesson 3   The Southern Colonies

In the South, Maryland became the second important English colony after Virginia. Some Roman Catholics, led by an English nobleman, Lord Baltimore, were unhappy in England. They came to North America in 1634 and settled north of Virginia. They called their colony Maryland. In time, other church groups came to Maryland. Because people of different church groups lived in Maryland, the colony became known as a place of religious freedom.

South of Virginia were the Carolinas and Georgia. North Carolina was first settled by Virginians who wanted more land for their tobacco farms. Then in 1680, a group from England built a village we now call Charleston. Charleston, South Carolina, became the only city in all of the Southern Colonies that could be compared in size with the cities of New England and the Middle Colonies.

Georgia, the last of the thirteen English colonies, was settled in 1733. James Oglethorpe, the colony's leader, wanted Georgia to be a place where the poor people of England could come to live. Some of those who settled in Georgia were poor. But most newcomers were neither richer nor poorer than settlers of other colonies.

The colonies of Maryland, Virginia, the Carolinas, and Georgia were known as the Southern Colonies. Locate these on the map on page 122. The climate was warm and wet. The land was flat and the soil rich. It was ideal land to farm.

One group of farmers in the Southern Colonies was called the planters. They came to the colonies for one reason. They hoped to make money from the sale of their crops. Two crops grown for **export** were tobacco and rice. Export means to send a product from one country to another for sale. The statistics to the right show the amounts sold to England.

Cotton was another crop grown in the Southern Colonies. For many years, though, it was not a very important one. It was a slow and costly job to separate the cotton fiber from the seeds. For this reason, it was not a good export crop.

The crops were grown on large farms called **plantations**. Many of the plantations were built near rivers along the Atlantic Coastal Plain. This made it easy to ship the crops to the big seaports and then to England.

Exports to England

Tobacco Exported to England From Virginia and Maryland

Year	Amount
1700	23
1710	34
1720	37
1730	35
1740	35
1750	51

(in millions of pounds)

Rice Exported to England From the Carolinas

Year	Amount
1700	304
1710	1,200
1720	4,500
1730	13,600
1740	16,400
1750	26,100

(in thousands of pounds)

The plantations had many fields. Some were used to grow the sale crops. The other fields were used to grow food for the workers.

In order to grow a lot of one crop, the planter needed many workers. Most plantation workers were blacks taken from their homes in Africa. They were owned as slaves. Some large plantations had over one hundred slaves. Most had fewer than ten.

Look at the map on page 131. The thickness of the arrows shows that most blacks were taken to places other than the United States. But wherever the blacks were taken, the trip into slavery was a terrible one. Read how one black described life aboard a slave ship.

66 The [smell inside of the ship] while we were on the coast was so [bad], that it was dangerous to remain there for any time, . . . but now that the ship's cargo were confined together, it became [deadly]. The closeness of the place, and

Plantations differed in terms of size. But most had the buildings that are shown here. How did southern communities differ from New England towns? From the farms and towns in the Middle Colonies?

Slave Cabins

Storehouses

Tobacco Field

Kitchen

Barn

Garden

Blacksmith   Stable

Main House

Orchard

Storage Barn   Dock

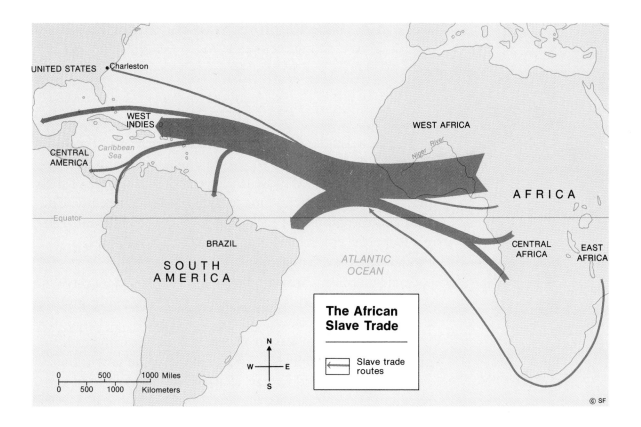

UNITED STATES •Charleston

WEST INDIES

CENTRAL AMERICA

Caribbean Sea

Equator

BRAZIL

SOUTH AMERICA

ATLANTIC OCEAN

WEST AFRICA

Niger River

AFRICA

CENTRAL AFRICA

EAST AFRICA

The African Slave Trade

Slave trade routes

N
W   E
S

0   500   1000 Miles
0 500 1000   Kilometers

© SF

the heat of the climate, added to the number in the ship, which was so crowded that each had scarcely room to turn himself, almost suffocated us. 99

Most of the southern farmers had no need for slaves. They cleared small patches of land and grew only enough to feed themselves. They lived in the backwoods country, far from the plantations.

Checking Up

1. Why did the planters feel they needed slaves?

2. How did the people of the Southern Colonies use the land to make a living?

3. How were the Southern Colonies like and unlike the New England and Middle Colonies?

131

Lesson 4   The Beginnings of the American People

We shall be one person

—Pueblo Indian

The New England Colonies differed much from the Southern Colonies. And the Middle Colonies were not like those to the north or those to the south. The people of these places often believed and made their livings differently. The land and the climate of each region were also different. People from one colony visiting another colony probably thought they were in a different world.

Some colonists, however, slowly began to feel a unity with other colonists. A look at one family's history might give us a clue about that feeling.

John Washington was an English sailor. He came to Virginia from London in 1657. He liked what he saw in the colonies and decided to stay. Washington worked hard and became a wealthy farmer. He loved his new home in Virginia. But he never forgot about England. He always thought of himself as an Englishman.

John Washington's grandson, George, had a very different identity. He was born and raised in Virginia. He had never seen England. As a young man, George Washington thought of himself as a Virginian. Later, he also began to say that he was an American.

As the English colonists became more and more American, they changed a wilderness land into towns and cities. What do you think the next few frames of this picture would look like?

The grandchildren of the first colonists probably thought the same way. They were becoming Americans. But what was an American? Did the colonists start running through the streets of their towns shouting "I'm an American, I'm an American!"? No, the change was very slow. Most of the colonists probably did not think too much about it at first.

There is no exact date when the colonists began to think of themselves as Americans. They did realize that the men and women who had settled in the English colonies had much in common. The colonists or their ancestors had come to a new and frightening world. Yet, they had turned wilderness into farms, towns, and cities. They had started schools, businesses, and their own religions. They had seen some of their dreams come true. Many had died trying.

All this work done by the settlers and by their children made them feel proud. And whether right or wrong, many of the colonists began to feel something else. It was they, not the king of England or the Indians who owned the land. This gave them a feeling of unity.

Most people did not travel from one colony to another to talk about these ideas. Travel was difficult in colonial times. The roads were rough and few. Most people and the mail traveled along the coast or the rivers. Even with these difficulties, people in the colonies were more in touch with each other than with people in their ancestors' homeland. Like George Washington, many had never seen that homeland and had no desire to.

The Many Identities in the English Colonies

Look at the circle graph to the right. Another name for this type of graph is a pie graph. Like a pie, a circle graph is divided into parts. Each part represents a different thing. In this pie graph, each part represents a different group of people living in the English colonies around 1760. Some pie graphs have numbers to help you compare the different parts. Such pie graphs appear on pages 18 and 19. This pie graph does not have numbers. But its message is still clear: The English colonies included people from many different places. And, more people came from certain places than from other places. Which group of people was most heavily represented in the colonies? Which was second?

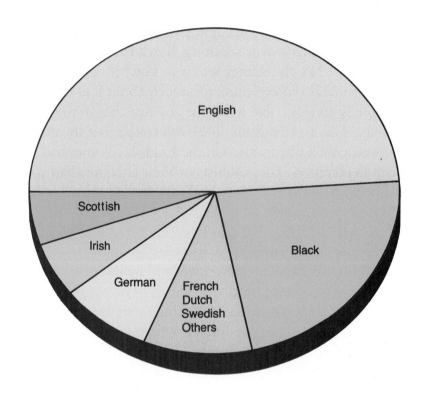

In 1760, America was still a colony of England. The population was a little over one and a half million people. Yet, less than half of the colonists or their ancestors were from England. America was no longer just the land of the English. It was a land made up of the ideas and customs of Europeans, Africans, and the American Indians. Most of these people probably felt little loyalty to England. America was, as one visitor said, becoming a land of new people.

Checking Up

1. How would you describe yourself if you had been a farmer in Massachusetts, Pennsylvania, or Virginia?

2. Why did the colonists start to feel like Americans?

3. Why weren't all the colonists loyal to England?

Reviewing Chapter 7

Write your answers on paper. Do not write in the book.

Using Key Words

ancestor   export
plantation   pilgrim

Write a short meaning for each key word listed above.

Reviewing Main Ideas

Number your paper from 1 to 10. Some of the sentences below are true and some are false. Write either *true* or *false* by each number.

1. Unlike the Virginians at Jamestown, few Pilgrims died during the first year at Plymouth.

2. The Puritans often made people who disagreed with them about religion leave Massachusetts.

3. Roger Williams believed in buying land from the Indians.

4. The Southern Colonies had more large cities than either New England or the Middle Colonies.

5. New England had the best soil for raising sale crops.

6. England hoped to sell the colonists raw materials.

7. Anne Hutchinson became well known because she gave in to the wishes of Puritan church leaders.

8. The Middle Colonies had large farms called plantations.

9. Pennsylvania was started as a colony for people who were not welcome in their own land.

10. Cotton was the most important crop grown in the Southern Colonies.

Thinking Things Over

Write a paragraph explaining why the colonists were starting to feel like Americans.

Practicing Skills

Use the following population statistics to help you describe the way of life in the three colonial groups. You may look back into your book for more information.

Estimated Population in 1750	
White	
New England	349,000
Middle Colonies	276,000
Southern Colonies	310,000
Black	
New England	11,000
Middle Colonies	21,000
Southern Colonies	205,000
Total White	935,000
Total Black	237,000

What Do You Know?

Write your answers on paper. Do not write in the book.

Words to Know

conquer	plantation
artifact	tax
explorer	ancestor
legend	indentured servant

Copy the small crossword puzzle on your paper. Use the clues at the right and the above words to fill in the puzzle.

Down

1. an object that can be used to describe the early people that lived at a place.

2. a story with a meaning that is passed down from parent to child.

3. large farms in the Southern Colonies that produced crops for sale.

4. one who searches trying to find something new.

Across

1. a type of servant that must work off a debt for a period of years.

2. one's parent or grandparent

3. an amount of money collected by a government which is used to support the government and the people.

4. to take over by force.

Ideas to Know

Use the following list of words to fill in the blanks on page 137. No words can be used twice. Some will not be used. Number your paper from 1 to 10.

Asher Levy	town meeting
Junipero Serra	archaeologists
breadbasket	natural resources
Pilgrims	Indies
Montezuma	colonies
pueblos	Puritans
culture	bridge
merchants	

136

1. _____ and 2. _____ tried to find religious freedom in New England.

3. The different _____ in an area helped Indians to have their own 4. _____.

5. People in New England could take part in their own government by going to a _____.

6. Because of their large harvests of grains, the Middle Colonies were called the _____ colonies.

7. _____ help people trade by buying and selling goods.

8. Cortez had to defeat _____ in order to conquer the Aztecs.

9. _____ fought for equal rights and responsibilities in colonial New Amsterdam.

10. Columbus hoped to find a quick route to the _____ by traveling west on the Atlantic Ocean.

Number your paper from 1 to 9. For each of the dwellings shown, give the name of the Indians that used it (1–3), the name of the dwelling (4–6), and the main natural resources used to build it (7–9).

Using What You Know

Copy the time line shown below onto your paper. Place the following events on the time line in the appropriate spot.

- Cartier Explores the St. Lawrence–1543
- Columbus Lands at San Salvador–1492
- Jamestown Established–1607
- John White Draws the Algonquins–1585
- City of Quebec Started–1608
- Vikings Settle in North America–1100

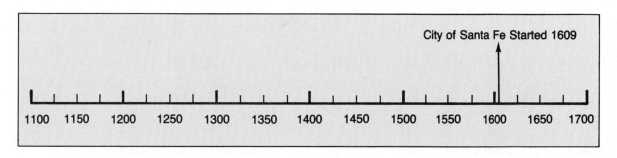

City of Santa Fe Started 1609

1100 1150 1200 1250 1300 1350 1400 1450 1500 1550 1600 1650 1700

Unit ③

Winning Independence

By 1754, many American colonists felt closer to their colonial friends than to their English rulers. They lived and worked with other colonists. They shared their good times and their problems. It bothered them, sometimes, that they were controlled by a government over two thousand miles away. But they were still loyal to England. They probably ended their conversations with "God save the King!"

By 1775 England was the enemy. The colonists were facing English soldiers in battle. Their angry fists were raised. Their words are lost to us, but not their message. "We are Americans!" What made them change?

The American colonists stand against the English at Lexington.

Chapter

8

Lesson 1   Why England Wanted Colonies
Lesson 2   Laws That Angered the Colonists
Lesson 3   The Colonists Protest English
          Laws

Problems Between England and the Colonies

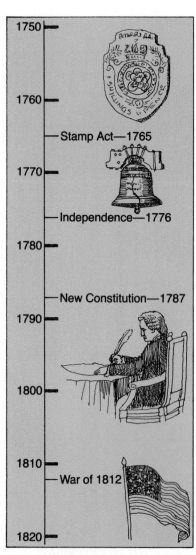

1750

1760

Stamp Act—1765

1770

Independence—1776

1780

New Constitution—1787

1790

1800

1810

War of 1812

1820

In Unit 2, you learned that a time line can be read from left to right or from top to bottom. This time line shows you some of the important events covered in Unit 3. How many years are covered in this unit?

Henry Adams left England for America in 1640. He was proud to be from England. England, he thought, was one of the strongest nations in Europe. Its laws seemed to be the fairest in the world. In America, he would have the same rights and freedoms as people in England.

One hundred and twenty years later, his great-great-grandson, John Adams, disagreed with those ideas. The young lawyer saw that colonists no longer had the same rights or freedoms as people in England. He thought that people in the colonies might be better off breaking away from England.

Lesson 1   Why England Wanted Colonies

Why did England, France, Spain, and other nations in Europe want colonies? There are at least two reasons. These nations believed that colonies would make them rich through trade. And having colonies would increase the land and people under their control. Each of these nations wanted to be the richest and most powerful nation in Europe.

The English government passed laws to force the colonists to do business in the English way. These laws said that the colonists had to export their raw materials to England. English workers would take such raw materials as lumber, fur, whale oil, tobacco, and iron and make them into finished products. The finished products would then be sold in Europe or in the colonies. The map on page 141 shows how this was done.

The colonies were only allowed to **import**, or bring in, finished products from England. Products could be bought from other nations. But they first had to be sold to England. Then they could be resold to the colonists at a higher price.

140

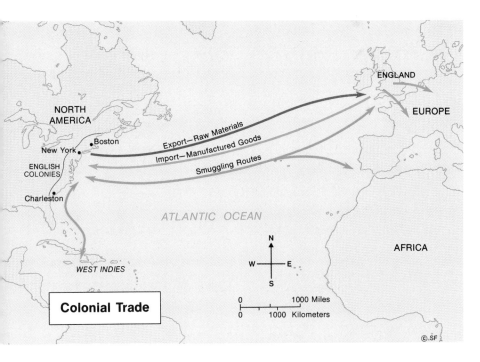

Colonial Trade

Export—Raw Materials
Import—Manufactured Goods
Smuggling Routes

ENGLAND
EUROPE
NORTH AMERICA
Boston
New York
ENGLISH COLONIES
Charleston
ATLANTIC OCEAN
AFRICA
WEST INDIES
N / W—E / S
0 1000 Miles
0 1000 Kilometers

Notice how far it is from England to the colonies. Measure this distance. How did this distance help make the colonists independent?

We, the People

Early to bed and Early to rise; makes a man Healthy, Wealthy and Wise.

Benjamin Franklin wrote and printed *Poor Richard's Almanack* every year from 1732 to 1757. An almanac has interesting facts about people, weather, places, government, and many other things. Franklin's almanac also gave wise and witty sayings. Here are a few examples.

- Well done is better than well said.
- Wish not so much to live long, as to live well.
- A true friend is the best possession.
- If you have something to do tomorrow, do it today.
- Haste makes waste.

Which of these ideas can you agree with most? Why? Just for fun, go to your school or neighborhood library and find a current almanac. What kind of information does it have that you might need someday?

Imports and exports were supposed to be carried on English ships. This would help England build a strong navy. By having a strong navy, England could be one of the most powerful nations in Europe.

Some Americans disobeyed these laws. They built their own factories. Others **smuggled** goods. They secretly brought goods made outside England into North America. They also took American goods to other countries in Europe and to islands in the West Indies.

The colonists who broke these laws were sometimes punished. Other times they were only warned by officials. Generally, England was not too concerned since most colonists obeyed the business laws. And by 1750, England's eyes were not on the colonists. They were on France.

The French and Indian War

England and France gained wealth and power from their colonies. Both thought they could become richer and more powerful if they had more land. The land they wanted was south of Lakes Erie and Huron in the Ohio River valley. Explorers from both nations claimed this land. So, in 1755, England and France fought for control of the area. They knew the winner would control North America east of the

141

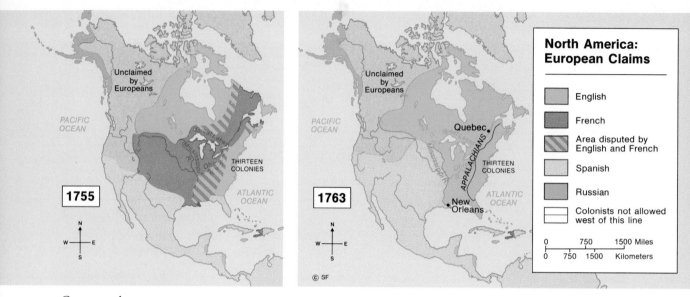

North America: European Claims

English

French

Area disputed by English and French

Spanish

Russian

Colonists not allowed west of this line

0   750   1500 Miles
0 750 1500   Kilometers

© SF

Compare these two maps. One shows North America before the French and Indian War. The other shows North America after that war. Which two countries gained the most land from the war? Which country lost the most land?

treaty, a written agreement between two or more nations.

Mississippi River. The first map above shows the area they fought over.

Americans call this conflict the French and Indian War. It was named this because many Indians joined the French. The Indians did not really like either the French or English colonists. But the French trappers did not settle on the Indians' land. The English farmers did. Both sides won battles in the French and Indian War. The English, however, won the deciding battle at the Canadian city of Quebec.

In 1763, a peace **treaty** was signed in Paris, France. This was an agreement to end the war. As the second map shows, France lost almost all its land in North America. The war was over between England and France. But troubles were just beginning between England and the colonists.

Checking Up

1. Why did England and other nations in Europe want colonies?

2. How did England control the way the colonists did business?

3. Why did the English and French fight in North America?

142

Lesson 2 Laws That Angered the Colonists

England's war with France ended in 1763. But it left England with bigger problems. Colonists moved onto the new land taken from France. Some of the Indians' lands were ruined by farmers who cut down trees to make room for fields. The Indians tried to protect their hunting grounds by attacking the settlers.

England could not pay to send more troops to America to protect these settlers. In 1763, England tried to stop settlers from moving onto the new land. See the map on page 142. This angered the settlers.

England soon had another problem. The war with France cost England a lot of money. The English government felt that the colonists should pay their share. England tried to raise money by making Americans obey the old trading laws. They also passed a few new ones. Here are some of the laws passed between 1764 and 1773.

- **The Sugar Act of 1764**: This was a tax on all sugar, cloth, coffee, and iron shipped to North America. The tax raised the prices Americans had to pay for all these goods.
- **The Stamp Act of 1765**: This called for American businesses to buy a stamp for certain products. The stamp was to be placed on all newspapers, law papers, playing cards, and dice. The cost of the stamps would be passed on to the buyers.
- **The Quartering Act of 1767**: Americans had to pay for the food and housing of English soldiers serving in America.
- **The Townshend Acts of 1767**: These were taxes on tea, paper, lead, and glass.
- **The Tea Act of 1773**: This law allowed an English tea company to sell tea for less than American tea companies. The Tea Act was not a tax, but it drove colonial business people out of business. So, many Americans hated the law.

Stamps like this were glued onto colonial paper goods.

Making the Colonists Pay

Unlike some of the earlier laws, England decided to enforce these. English soldiers and officials would make the colonists obey. Many Americans felt that doing business according to the English laws was unfair.

143

In the South, planters had to sell their crops to English merchants. The planters believed they could make more money by selling their goods themselves. In the Middle Colonies, people could not run their own factories to make hats, woolen clothes, and iron goods. Only English workers could make these things. In New England, shipbuilders saw that only English ships carried goods to Europe and Asia.

Many Americans felt they were being stopped from making a good living. The English laws limited the amount of money they could earn. They felt English taxes reduced their **incomes** even more.

Many colonists became angry. They felt they had worked hard to make a living. They asked serious questions. "Why can't we sell our products to any country?" "Why can't we

income, money earned for providing labor or a service, from the selling or renting of property, or from investments.

(top) The colonists protested the Stamp Act by placing this drawing on their paper goods. Why do you think they used a "skull and crossbones"? (right) Another way to protest the Stamp Act was by burning the stamps.

What is the cartoonist saying is the problem with the way the colonists must export and import goods? What is a good title for this cartoon?

buy products from any country?" "Why do our workers have to go without jobs?" "Why do we have to pay such taxes?" They did not like the answers the English gave them.

"The laws were fair," said the English. The colonists had been protected from the Indians and French. Colonial trade was protected by the large English navy. The colonists should help pay for that protection. And besides, the people in England were paying higher taxes than the colonists.

The English also believed that they had the right to control trade with their colonies. The colonies were not independent. They had to listen and obey. After all, thought the English, the main reason for having colonies was to increase the wealth and power of England.

Checking Up

1. Why did England try to enforce trade and tax laws *after* the French and Indian War?

2. For what reasons did the colonists think they were being treated unfairly?

3. How did the English think they were being fair?

Lesson 3   The Colonists Protest English Laws

The English soldiers had torn open and overturned crates for an hour. They did this to look for evidence, or proof, that the merchants were smuggling goods or not paying enough taxes. An English tax official stood quietly nearby, making a list.

The colonial merchant looked on with both sadness and anger. His house and storeroom were a mess. Tomorrow, he promised, he would speak to James Otis.

James Otis was a Boston lawyer. Merchants came to him because he spoke out against unfair English laws. The merchants asked him to defend their rights in a court of law.

On a cold day in February, 1761, Otis spoke before five English judges. He reminded them of one of the most important English freedoms. "A man's house is his castle." Otis asked the judges to stop the English soldiers and officials from breaking into the merchants' homes and stores.

The judges agreed. English law protected the property rights of the colonial merchants. Yet they still refused to stop the soldiers and officials. Many Americans were angry with the English over cases like this. One of them was John Adams. After listening to Otis in the courtroom, Adams felt that more Americans would begin to disobey English laws.

James Otis argues his case.

146

Different Ways of Protesting

John Adams was proven right. In 1765, his cousin, Samuel Adams, helped start a secret protest group. It was called the Sons of Liberty. The Sons of Liberty sometimes protested with physical force. They often beat up tax collectors or broke into their homes and offices.

The group also used peaceful methods of protest. They asked Americans to not buy English-made goods. That way England would make little money from the colonists.

Women all over New England set up groups called Daughters of Liberty. These women protested by refusing to buy cloth made in England. They made their own cloth from American linen and wool.

Read what John Adams wrote about another protest in 1766. It concerned the collectors of the stamp tax.

66At Philadelphia, the Heart-and-Hand Fire Company has expelled Mr. Hughes, the stamp man for that colony. In Maryland, they have built a gibbet [post] in front of the door of the court house and have hanged on it effigies [likenesses] of people in favor of the stamp tax.99

WILLIAM JACKSON,

an *IMPORTER*; at the

BRAZEN HEAD,

North Side of the TOWN-HOUSE,

and *Oppofite the Town-Pump, in*

Corn-hill, BOSTON.

It is defired that the Sons and Daughters of *LIBERTY,* would not buy any one thing of him, for in fo doing they will bring Difgrace upon *themfelves,* and their *Pofterity,* for *ever* and *ever,* AMEN.

(above) This is a poster asking colonists not to buy from a merchant who imports goods from England. What is the importer's name? Who is asking the colonists not to buy English goods? (left) Another way to protest English taxes was by "tarring and feathering" the tax collector. The picture, drawn by an artist loyal to England, shows the Americans to be ugly, mean, and lawbreakers.

147

Some of the protests worked. In 1766, the English government ended the stamp tax. In its place, though, the government started a new tax on tea, paper, lead, and glass. More English soldiers were sent to the colonies to enforce the new taxes. This only made matters worse. In New York, people refused to pay the tax or to give food and housing to the English soldiers.

To calm the colonists, England removed all the taxes except the one on tea. The colonists knew what was really meant by this. England was saying it still had the power to tax the colonists. England didn't want to be pushed around by the colonies.

In 1773, a ship carrying a load of tea came to Boston Harbor. The Sons of Liberty saw this as a good chance to let England know how they felt about taxes. One night they dressed up as Indians. They boarded the ship and poured over three hundred crates of tea into the harbor.

The Boston Tea Party, as this event was called, delighted Americans who wanted to break away from England. The English government saw things differently. In 1774, England passed laws meant to punish the colonists in Massachusetts. More soldiers were sent to keep the peace. The colonists were ordered to feed and house them. Abigail Adams described what life was like in Boston.

66We are invaded with fleets and armies. Our businesses have been ruined. The courts of justice have been closed. Many people have been driven out from Boston. Thousands need the charity of their neighbors for a daily supply of food. A civil war threatens us on one hand, and the chains of slavery are ready for us on the other.99

A growing number of Americans believed in the words, "No taxation without **representation**! Taxes may be needed. But can't Americans elect someone in the colonies to make tax laws? What do people two thousand miles away in England know about us and what we can pay?" Many Americans believed that they had the right to elect their own officials and to make laws for themselves.

In 1774, a group of Americans met in Philadelphia. Among those present were Patrick Henry, Richard Henry

Abigail Adams

representation, electing or appointing someone to speak and act for others.

Lee, Peyton Randolph, Sam and John Adams, and George Washington. This was the meeting of the First Continental Congress. The **Congress** met to discuss the important questions of the day. The Congress voted to continue the protests and to form a citizens' army. It was a warning to the king of England.

King George III replied, "The colonies must submit [give in] or triumph." Patrick Henry of Virginia spoke the feelings of many Americans: "Give me liberty or give me death!" England and the American colonies were ready to fight to see who had the right to make and enforce laws.

The colonists throw **342** chests of English tea in Boston Harbor. Why do you think the colonists dressed up as Mohawk Indians? Did they want England to blame the Indians? Or did they not want to be identified? At the time of the Boston Tea Party, tea actually cost less in the colonies than it did in England.

congress, a group that meets to discuss ideas and make decisions.

Checking Up

1. Why were some of the colonists' homes and offices searched?

2. What are some of the ways the colonists protested against England's laws and taxes?

3. Why did many of the colonists want their own representatives?

149

Samuel Gray, . . . a black man named Crispus Attucks, . . . (and) Mr. James Caldwell. . .99

Word of the fight spread through the colonies. Americans grew angrier than ever before. Soon, the event was known as the Boston Massacre. But, was it really the brutal killing people said it was?

Captain Preston and his soldiers were arrested. Most of the people of Boston quickly decided that the English were

The Right to a Fair Trial

On March 5, 1770, a fight broke out in Boston between colonists and English soldiers. Here is how a Boston newspaper described what happened.

66Thirty or forty persons, mostly lads . . . gathered in Kingstreet. Capt. Preston, with a party of men with charged bayonets, came to the commissioner's house. The soldiers pushed with their bayonets, crying, "Make way!" They took place by the custom house, and continued to drive the people off. The Americans were in an uproar and it is said, threw snow-balls.

On this, the Captain ordered them to fire. . . . One soldier then fired, and a townsman with a stick hit him over the hands. He dropped his gun. The townsman rushed forward and aimed a blow at the Captain's head, which hit his hat and fell pretty heavy upon his arm. However, the soldiers kept on firing till seven or eight or, as some say, eleven guns were fired.

After the firing was over, three men were laid dead on the spot, and two more struggling for life. . . The dead are Mr.

guilty of murder. They demanded the death penalty.

The English soldiers could not find a lawyer until John Adams agreed to defend them. Many of John Adams's friends turned against him. His cousin, Sam Adams, said that no loyal American should try to help the "guilty" soldiers.

John Adams disagreed. To him the main question was not the soldiers' guilt or innocence. The main question was

John Adams

whether or not they received a fair trial. He believed that it was better for a guilty person to go free than for an innocent person to be punished.

The Boston newspapers said that Captain Preston told his men to fire at the crowd. As he spoke to witnesses in the case, however, John Adams began to think the newspaper reports were wrong.

One citizen who saw the event said the crowd had yelled "Kill them! Kill them!" *before* the English fired. Another witness saw a soldier clubbed before he fired. A third witness said that ice had been thrown, not just snow-balls.

John Adams was able to prove in court that Preston had not told his men to fire on the crowd. Rather, the soldiers fired because they were frightened. Preston's men were just trying to protect themselves. The jury decided that two of the accused were guilty of manslaughter [killing without intending to], not murder.

But John Adams had really proven much more. He had shown how important rights and freedoms were to Americans.

Kids Have Power, Too!

Being able to protest peacefully is a right that many Americans will always value. Some Americans might protest high prices at the grocery store. Others might protest that they can't charge people enough. Some Americans might protest against something the government *has* done. Others might protest because the government *hasn't* done something.

And it isn't just adults who protest. The following true story about eleven-year-old Amaryllis Beirne-Keyt is proof of that! While you read, ask yourself what you would have done if you were Amaryllis.

By the time Amaryllis was eight, she had saved a little more than $30. She decided to put her money in a bank. In a bank, she thought, her money would earn interest. Interest is the money a bank pays you for saving at that bank.

Three and a half years later, Amaryllis went to the bank. She wanted to see how much her $30 had grown. The $30 had changed, all right. It had become $28.90! Amaryllis found that she had lost money!

Amaryllis first asked a bank teller why she had lost money. The teller explained a rule that the bank had made two years earlier. The rule was that the bank could subtract twenty-five cents a month from any savings under $100. The bank had taken about $7 from her savings. This was more than the $5.74 she earned in interest.

Amaryllis explained the problem to her mother. Together, they went and spoke to the bank manager. This talk didn't do any good, though.

Then her mother came up with another idea. If you can't get results on your own, go to someone who might be able to help. Amaryllis sat down and wrote two letters. One was to *Penny Power*, a consumer magazine for young people. The second letter went to Betty Furness, a TV consumer reporter.

Both *Penny Power* and the TV station called the bank. Soon the bank wrote to Amaryllis. They asked her to come in for a talk.

The bank apologized for a big mistake. Amaryllis was given all her money back, plus interest.

But Amaryllis got much more than just money. She now knows that kids have power, too!

Reviewing Chapter 8

Write your answers on paper. Do not write in the book.

Using Key Words

smuggle   congress
income   import
treaty   representation

Number your paper from 1 to 6. Write the definition for each of the above words.

Reviewing Main Ideas

Number your paper from 1 to 6. If the sentence is true write *true* next to the number. If it is false write *false* next to the number.

1. Before workers can make finished products they must have raw materials.

2. English merchants used physical force against colonial tax collectors.

3. England, France, and Spain felt that colonies could make them powerful.

4. English soldiers had planned to shoot the colonists in Boston in 1770.

5. The English trade laws caused problems between England and the colonies.

6. France lost most of its land in North America as a result of the French and Indian War.

Thinking Things Over

The colonists protested against what they felt were unfair laws. What are some ways they protested? Should people be allowed to protest today if they disagree with the government? If you answer "yes," explain how they should be allowed to protest. If you answer "no," explain why people should not be allowed to protest.

Practicing Skills

The bar graphs below show the value of exports and imports between England and the colonies. Who seemed to make more money in the English way of doing business?

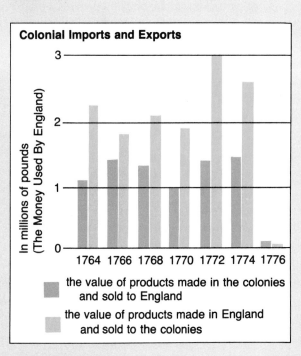

Colonial Imports and Exports

In millions of pounds (The Money Used By England)

1764 1766 1768 1770 1772 1774 1776

■ the value of products made in the colonies and sold to England

■ the value of products made in England and sold to the colonies

America's War for Independence

And when to Boston we did come,
We thought by the aid of our British guns,
To drive the rebels from that place,
And fill their hearts with sore disgrace.
But to our sorrow and surprise,
We saw men like grass-hoppers rise;
They fought like heroes much enraged,
Which did affright old General Gage.

The verse to the left is from a popular song of the 1770s. The words tell how an English soldier might have felt in late 1774. By then English soldiers knew that Americans had prepared for war against them. Some Americans secretly stored guns and ammunition. One of the storehouses was in Concord, Massachusetts, just outside of Boston.

The English retreat from Concord.

Lesson 1   Lexington and Concord

The day was April 19, 1775. General Gage, the English military leader in New England, sent a lieutenant and other soldiers to Concord. They were to destroy the ammunitions and guns stored there. Here is how Lieutenant John Barker described the day.

66We waited at Lexington a long time, and then went on our way to Concord . . . . [At Concord we destroyed] three pieces of cannon, several gun carriages, and about one hundred barrels of flour . . . . Three companies of soldiers were sent across the river to search some of the houses there.

During this time the people were gathering together in great numbers . . . . Across the river, the rebels were about one thousand strong, on the hill above, covered by a wall . . . .

The rebels marched into the road and were coming down upon us. The rebels when they got near the bridge halted and faced us. The fire soon began from a shot on our side . . . .

A minuteman prepares to go to war in 1776.

After taking care of our wounded as well as we could, we set upon our return . . . . We were fired on from houses and behind trees, and before we had gone half a mile we were fired on from all sides, but mostly from the rear, where people had hid themselves in houses till we had passed . . . . "

The Americans planned well for that day in April, 1775. They had formed an army of farmers and shopkeepers. They were called **minutemen**. The minutemen could be ready to fight at a minute's notice.

Americans secretly watched the English army. Two people who watched were Paul Revere and William Dawes. They spread the word that the English were coming hours before they arrived.

More than four thousand Americans fought the English at Lexington and Concord and on the march back to Charlestown. Both sides lost soldiers. Ninety-three Americans were dead, wounded, or missing. But the British lost almost 275 men. Find these battles on the map on page 161.

After the fight at Lexington and Concord, more than twenty thousand Americans went to Charlestown and made camp for almost a year. They wouldn't let the English out of town without a fight.

Nation or Colony?

In Philadelphia, in May of 1775, the Second Continental Congress met. Some of those at the meeting were Benjamin Franklin of Pennsylvania, John Adams of Massachusetts, and Thomas Jefferson of Virginia. The Congress chose a Virginian named George Washington to lead the American army.

Members of the Continental Congress also discussed another question. Should the thirteen colonies become **independent**? That would mean breaking away from England's control and becoming a free nation. It was not an easy question to answer.

Independence would mean that the new nation would have to protect itself. The English army would no longer protect it from Indians or other nations. It would have to elect its own citizens to make laws and decisions. It would also have to learn how to trade with other nations.

Many Americans felt that this was too much responsibility. America had always been a part of England and they liked it that way. They felt America should fight, but only until the English agreed to treat them fairly. Then they would again be loyal to England.

Other Americans felt that the colonies should no longer be a part of England. England had mistreated them long enough. Yes, independence would mean other problems. But, they asked, would not freedom be worth it?

George Washington. The country's gratitude is shown in the number of things it named after him.

1	state
7	mountains
8	streams
9	colleges
10	lakes
33	counties

121 towns and villages
How many can you find on a map of the United States?

Checking Up

1. How did fighting start between England and the colonies?

2. What were the arguments for and against independence?

3. What had the colonists done to prepare for a fight?

Lesson 2   A Declaration of Independence

It was very hot in Philadelphia in that summer of 1776. The arguments in the Continental Congress over independence seemed to make it even hotter. During one argument, someone warned that England would have to be told if independence was agreed upon. That job was given to a young, thirty-three-year-old lawyer named Thomas Jefferson.

In a small, stuffy room above a stable, Jefferson sat down to write a letter to King George III of England. The letter had three major points. One listed twenty-seven wrongs done to the colonists by George III. Among them were:

By the Way

July 4, 1826, should always be remembered as a historic day. It was the fiftieth anniversary of the Declaration of Independence. It was also the day our second and third Presidents died: John Adams and Thomas Jefferson.

But should we really celebrate Independence Day on July 4? It is true that the Declaration was dated July 4, 1776. Yet independence had been declared *two* days earlier. The document was not even officially signed on July 4. That did not happen until August 2.

You have cut off our trade with the rest of the world!

You have taxed us without our approval!

You have forced us to give food and shelter to English soldiers!

You have not allowed us to elect our own Congress!

The second point in Jefferson's letter explained how the new nation would be governed. Jefferson wrote that Americans did not want a king to rule them. This was a shocking idea in 1776. For hundreds of years, the English believed that God gave kings and queens the right to rule. People asked, "If Americans refused to obey the king were they not disobeying God, too?" No, said Jefferson. He wrote that all people are given certain rights by "their creator." They have the right to live, be free, and seek happiness. Since these rights were given by God, no person could take them away, not even a king or queen.

Jefferson went on to explain other American beliefs about how people should be governed.

Fair laws are made by people, not by kings or armies.

Fair laws help people get what they need to live freely.

The government is suppose to put fair laws to work.

If a government does not do its job well, the people may change it.

If a government does not do its job at all, the people may do away with it and set up a new one.

People have the duty to obey fair laws.

JOIN, or DIE.

Jefferson ended the Declaration of Independence the only way he could. He knew George III would be furious after reading that America was breaking away from England. So, Jefferson wrote that the colonists were willing to stand together against England. It was a declaration of war.

Those who approved the declaration in July of 1776 knew what a dangerous thing it was to do. They were traitors to the king and to England. If caught they could be put to death. But as Benjamin Franklin said to a friend, "We must all hang together, else we will all hang separately."

Benjamin Franklin's cartoon about unity first appeared in 1754. He also worked for independence as a member of the 2nd Continental Congress. Franklin helped write, and later signed the Declaration of Independence.

Franklin had other interests, too. He published Poor Richard's Almanack (see page 141), was Governor of Pennsylvania, invented the lightning rod, the Franklin stove, and bifocal glasses. Franklin served as a delegate to the Constitutional Convention in 1787, and signed the Constitution.

Checking Up

1. What do you think Benjamin Franklin meant by his statement?

2. What does a good government agree to give its people? What should the people give in return?

3. Would you have voted for or against independence? Explain your answer.

159

(above) The Americans pictured themselves as a coiled snake, ready to strike. It was a simple, clear message to England. (below) George Washington and his soldiers suffer through a winter at Valley Forge.

Lesson 3 Americans Fight for Their Freedom

By 1777 independence was agreed upon and the declaration was signed. America's problems were only just beginning. First, the cold and snowy winter of 1777 almost broke up the army. Only a few hundred soldiers stayed with General Washington at Valley Forge, Pennsylvania.

Second, Washington had a hard time keeping soldiers in camp even in good weather. Every spring and fall, some soldiers left the army to plant and harvest crops. Washington probably never led any more than fifteen thousand soldiers at one time. The English army usually numbered about forty thousand soldiers.

Third, the Congress had little money. It did not have enough to pay soldiers, buy them food and clothing, and get guns and ammunition.

These were serious problems. They were made worse because the young nation was divided over independence. Those for independence were called **Patriots**. Those who wanted to stay loyal to England were called **Loyalists**. This division made it hard to raise and keep an army.

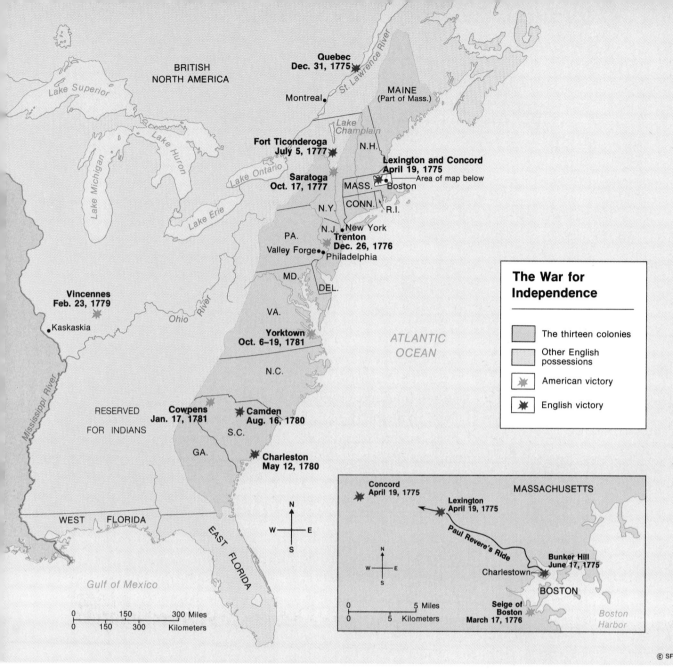

The War for Independence

- The thirteen colonies
- Other English possessions
- ✦ American victory
- ✸ English victory

Quebec Dec. 31, 1775

Fort Ticonderoga July 5, 1777

Saratoga Oct. 17, 1777

Lexington and Concord April 19, 1775
← Area of map below

Trenton Dec. 26, 1776

Vincennes Feb. 23, 1779

Yorktown Oct. 6–19, 1781

Cowpens Jan. 17, 1781

Camden Aug. 16, 1780

Charleston May 12, 1780

BRITISH NORTH AMERICA

MAINE (Part of Mass.)

N.H.

MASS.

CONN.

R.I.

N.Y.

N.J.

PA.

MD.

DEL.

VA.

N.C.

S.C.

GA.

RESERVED FOR INDIANS

WEST FLORIDA

EAST FLORIDA

ATLANTIC OCEAN

Gulf of Mexico

Montreal

Boston

New York

Valley Forge

Philadelphia

Kaskaskia

0 150 300 Miles
0 150 300 Kilometers

Concord April 19, 1775

Lexington April 19, 1775

Paul Revere's Ride

Bunker Hill June 17, 1775

Charlestown

BOSTON

Seige of Boston March 17, 1776

MASSACHUSETTS

Boston Harbor

0 5 Miles
0 5 Kilometers

© SF

Yet, six years after the first shots were fired, the fighting stopped. The English gave up at a place in Virginia called Yorktown. The above map gives a brief history of the war. A peace treaty was signed in 1783. The thirteen colonies, now called the United States of America, were free.

How the Colonists Defeated England

The American army was outnumbered, poorly trained, and poorly cared for. It did have some advantages, though. The American soldiers knew the land. They knew where to

The two maps on this page show the location of some of the important battles during the War for Independence. You can figure out how long the war lasted by comparing the battle dates of Lexington and Concord with the battle date of Yorktown. What are two English victories? What are two American victories?

161

American men, women, and children fight the English. How were the English and Americans' way of fighting different as seen in this painting?

Many blacks felt that the words "all men are created equal," were worth fighting for. They were not only fighting for America's independence, but their own.

fight and where not to fight. Since there were so few of them, the Americans often chose not to fight in the open. They would have been quickly defeated. They sometimes chose to attack the English from behind trees and bridges. They tried to surprise the English by attacking at unusual times of day or night and in bad weather. Their surprises succeeded for another reason, too.

Many American soldiers used a new rifle called the Pennsylvania rifle. The rifle was able to fire a bullet 150 yards directly at a target. The English became easy targets as they marched in rows through open fields.

The Americans also did not have to fight the English alone. England's long-time enemy, France, joined the Americans in 1778. The French sent money, soldiers, and ships to America.

America's real advantage, however, was its spirit. The army was led by a man of great courage and skill, George Washington. He always reminded his soldiers that they were not just fighting against the English. They were fighting for their freedom.

Most of the soldiers who fought on the American side were white males of English background. But others fought as well. About six thousand blacks fought in the army and navy. One soldier who fought on the side of the English wrote, "No regiment [group of soldiers] is to be seen in which there are not Negroes in abundance and among them are able-bodied, strong and brave fellows."

Americans from other backgrounds also fought against the English. Many Jews, like Haym Saloman, helped their country win independence. Saloman served the United States by secretly watching the enemy. He was eventually caught by the English. After Saloman gained his freedom, he raised money to pay the soldiers and to buy supplies.

A nineteen-year-old nobleman, the Marquis de Lafayette (lä′fē et′), came from France. He became a trusted adviser and friend of General Washington. A German, Baron von Steuben (stü′ben), also came to America. He became the first teacher of the American army. Two leaders came from Poland. Casmir Pulaski (kaz′ə mir pù las′kē) died leading a group of soldiers into battle at Savannah, Georgia. Tadeusz Kosciuszko (tä dä′us kos′ē us′kō) planned the fort at Saratoga in New York. Without his work, Americans would not have won an important battle there.

Women also helped America win independence. Many wives of American soldiers stayed at home to run the farms. Without them, many men would have had to stay at home.

Other women went to war with their husbands. They followed the army wherever it went. The army needed doctors and nurses. It needed people to carry water to thirsty soldiers or cool down the red-hot barrels of cannon. Soldiers needed their uniforms mended after battle. Women did all of these jobs.

Some women, like Margaret Corbin and Mary Hays, fought in the battles. They took up their husbands' fighting duties when the men died. Other women, such as Sally St. Clair and Deborah Sampson, disguised themselves as men and joined the army.

Checking Up

1. Name at least three problems America had at the beginning of the war.

2. What advantages did Americans have in fighting the war?

3. Why do you think it was important to have many different groups fight for independence?

We, the People

During the War for Independence, most of the fighting took place in the East. There were also battles fought as far west as Indiana and Illinois.

In one such battle was a twenty-one-year-old American colonel named George Rogers Clark. He led his 175 men across 180 miles of wilderness from Kaskaskia, Illinois, to Fort Vincennes, Indiana. (See the map on page 161.) It was February in 1779.

The soldiers waded and swam across icy rivers and creeks. They slept on cold, damp ground. Several times they seemed ready to quit. But George Rogers Clark would not let them. He told them to believe in themselves.

The English never believed that the Americans would try a long, wilderness march in winter. The Americans won an easy victory.

163

Mercy Otis Warren

In 1754, Mercy Otis and James Warren were married. James Warren was a lawmaker in Massachusetts. Because of this, other colonial leaders, such as John Adams, Sam Adams, and Thomas Jefferson often visited the Warren home. There, they talked about freedom and American independence.

Mercy listened to the men. She knew she could use her education to help the colonies break away from England. It wasn't strange that Mercy Otis Warren wanted to help. It *was* strange that she was educated.

Mercy Otis Warren lived during a time when it was rare for women to receive an education. And most women probably didn't want to. It was important to organize and run the household.

But Mercy was one of thirteen children. Sometimes it was easy to study along with her brothers. And as they went off to college, Mercy continued to educate herself.

Mercy soon developed a talent for writing. And so, Mercy wrote plays that poked fun at England. Her plays helped unite the colonists against England.

At first, few people knew that Mercy was the author of the plays. No one expected that a woman would be able to write them. Because of this, Mercy's works did not have her name on them. After a while, people discovered that she was the author of the plays. She was praised throughout the colonies.

Mercy's largest work was a three-book history of the war for American independence. In it, she explained the causes of the war. She also wrote about some famous colonial leaders.

One of those she wrote about was John Adams. He didn't care for the way he was presented in the book. He said, "History is not the province of the ladies." He meant: women should not write history.

Mercy Otis Warren disagreed. She strongly believed that women should be good wives and mothers. She also felt that women should receive educations if they wanted them. And, as Mercy proved, if a woman was good at something, she should be allowed to use that talent.

Reviewing Chapter 9

JOIN, or DIE.

Write your answers on paper. Do not write in the book.

Using Key Words

minutemen   independent
patriot   loyalist

Number your paper from 1 to 4. Write the meaning for each of the above words.

Reviewing Main Ideas

Number your paper from 1 to 5. Fill in the blank with a word or phrase that completes the idea.

1. The colonists had stored _____ at the storehouse in Concord.

2. The _____ Congress discussed the idea of independence.

3. _____ wrote most of the Declaration of Independence.

4. Without help from the nation of _____, it would have been harder for the American colonists to win the war.

5. The declaration said that laws should be made by _____, not by kings.

Thinking Things Over

Pretend that you are a colonist living in 1776. Explain to your family why you must leave them to fight as a Patriot or a Loyalist.

Look again at the verse on page 154. Then write a song that American soldiers might have sung. You might want your song to explain why Americans are fighting the English. Your song could also explain what it was like to be a soldier and fight in the War for Independence.

Practicing Skills

Copy the time line on your paper. Do not write in the book. Arrange the following events in their correct order of time. You may look back in your book to find the correct dates. Then write the events on the time line.

- Declaration of Independence
- Battle of Yorktown
- Peace Treaty with England
- Battles of Lexington and Concord
- Second Continental Congress Meets

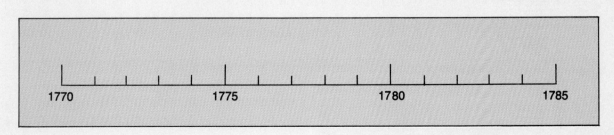

1770   1775   1780   1785

Chapter

10

Lesson 1 The Articles of Confederation
Lesson 2 A New Constitution
Lesson 3 Unfinished Business

The United States Constitution

Americans showed they had the power to win a war. They needed to prove they could live together in peace. By breaking away from England, they were telling the rest of the world "We can build a better government!" It was not an easy job to build a new government. Americans made mistakes. But they learned from their mistakes, and they did succeed.

Lesson 1   The Articles of Confederation

During the war, Americans put their ideas about government to work. The Second Continental Congress wrote a plan of government for the new nation. This **constitution** was called the Articles of Confederation. A **confederation** is a joining together of people, states, or nations.

The Articles said that each of the thirteen states would have its own government. That government would make laws for the people of that state. The Articles also said that the states would be *loosely* joined together by a central government.

The central government would make laws for all the people in the nation. This is how it would be done. Each state was asked to send a representative to Philadelphia to meet in a congress. Each representative was to speak and give the opinions of the people of that state. The representatives would also choose a leader.

A Weak or Strong Government?

This central government had many powers. It could decide on going to war or making peace. It could send people to speak for the United States in other nations. It could set up a post office. It could try to settle troubles between states.

The Massachusetts state army stops Shays' Rebellion.

166

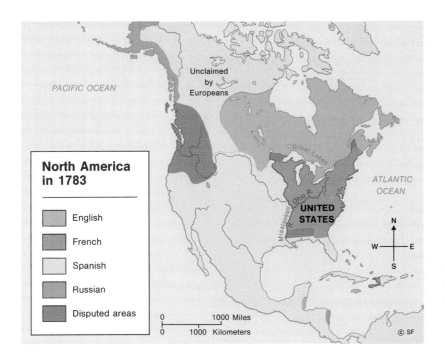

North America in 1783

- English
- French
- Spanish
- Russian
- Disputed areas

PACIFIC OCEAN

Unclaimed by Europeans

Great Lakes

Ohio R.

Mississippi R.

UNITED STATES

ATLANTIC OCEAN

0   1000 Miles
0   1000 Kilometers

© SF

Compare this map to the one on page 142. What change was brought about by the Americans' winning their independence in 1783?

This list of powers may seem to make a government strong. The first central government of the United States, however, was really very weak. Many Americans wanted the central government to be weak. They believed the king of England had been too powerful. So, they did not give any one person too much power to make decisions. They felt the English government made unfair tax laws. So, they did not give the central government the power to tax. They believed that the English had kept each colony weak. So, they wanted the new state governments to be strong.

Shays' Rebellion

For a time, Americans believed their central government served them well. Soon, some realized that the government had trouble solving problems. Here is an example.

In 1786, hundreds of Massachusetts farmers had so little money that they could not pay their bills. Many lost their land and homes. They told the Massachusetts state government about their problem. The state government did nothing to help them.

Some of the angry farmers decided to start a **rebellion**. A rebellion is a fight against one's own government. They were led by a man named Daniel Shays. Armed with guns, they

During Shays' Rebellion, angry farmers who had many debts fought with bill collectors.

tried to make the state government pass certain laws to help them.

Since the central government could not tax the people, it had no money. Without money it could not help the farmers. It also could not pay soldiers to stop Shays' Rebellion.

Shays and his followers were finally stopped by the Massachusetts state army. Americans had learned a lesson. The weak central government could not protect itself or one of the states. Daniel Shays had been defeated. But what if an enemy nation attacked the United States? This was a question Americans had to answer.

It was not the only question. To raise money, states taxed the goods coming from other states. The states then became angry at one another. There were no national courts set up to solve this problem.

Many of the states also had their own money. Some states accepted another state's money. Others did not. Some people carried several types of money.

Many Americans felt that the central government was not serving them well. It needed to be changed, and changed quickly. Americans needed another plan of government. Americans needed a new constitution that would protect them and their right to live freely and happily.

Checking Up

1. What are some things the central government could not do under the Articles of Confederation?

2. Why had some Americans wanted a weak central government?

3. When Americans saw the problems they were having, what did they decide they must do?

4. If you were living in 1785, how many governments could make laws for you? What are the governments?

5. What lesson did Americans learn because of Shays' Rebellion?

Lesson 2   A New Constitution

The War for American Independence has also been called a **revolution**. And it was. America had gone through a big change. It no longer was an English colony. In 1776 it became an independent nation. Americans also made changes in their thoughts about government. These changes began in May of 1787 in Philadelphia.

Fifty-five men traveled to that city to hold a convention, or series of meetings. They came from each state except Rhode Island. Most of them were young. Most were educated. Most were landowners. All of them were white.

They came with one goal in mind: They wanted to improve the Articles of Confederation. That was not an easy job. They did not all agree on how to do it. The heat of summer did not make it any easier.

The Constitutional Convention

They started by asking a very important question about government. *"Who gave power to governments?"* They did not want to make the same mistakes made by the king of England or in the Articles of Confederation.

revolution, a big change that makes a difference in the lives of many people.

The Constitutional Convention. People such as Benjamin Franklin, George Washington, James Madison, and Alexander Hamilton were present. Four important people were absent: John Adams, Thomas Jefferson, Sam Adams, and Patrick Henry. See if you can find out why.

democracy, a government that is run by the people who live under it.

republic, a nation or state in which the citizens elect representatives to manage the government.

Representation in Congress

Population: California 23,668,562
Arizona 2,777,866

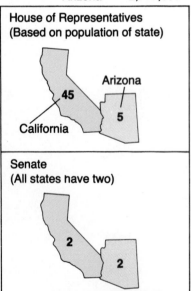

House of Representatives
(Based on population of state)

Arizona

California 45

5

Senate
(All states have two)

2

2

How does the United States method of representing the people in Congress satisfy the states with big populations and the states with small populations?

The king of England seemed to say "I have all the power! The people must listen to me! I am the government!" The Articles of Confederation seemed to say "We don't know who has power, the state governments or the central government."

The question was answered in the opening sentence of the new constitution. "We the people . . . do ordain and establish this Constitution for the United States of America." The writers said that the people had the power to govern themselves. They would not be governed by a king, an army, or any one state. The United States would be a **democracy**. People would have the right to take part in running the government. *"But with almost four million citizens, how could everyone be heard?"*

Big States, Little States

The writers answered by saying that the United States would be a special type of democracy. It would be a **republic**. The voters of each state would elect representatives. Each representative would speak and act for about thirty thousand people. They would meet in one building called the House of Representatives. Then, people could be heard in an organized way.

The states with big populations liked the idea. They would have more representatives than states with smaller populations. It was also agreed to start a second law-making body called the Senate. Each state could send two representatives. The states with smaller populations liked the idea. In the Senate, at least, they were equal to the states with large populations. Together, the House and the Senate are called the Congress of the United States.

The writers knew that having representatives could be dangerous. It meant the people were giving up some of their power. The writers asked, *"How do we limit the power we give up?"* They answered the question in two ways.

The power the people gave up would be divided into three branches, or parts, of government. It was divided so one person or group would not have too much power. As the chart on the next page shows, each branch would have a specific job. The **Legislative Branch**, or Congress, would make the nation's laws. It would be made up of the House of Repre-

170

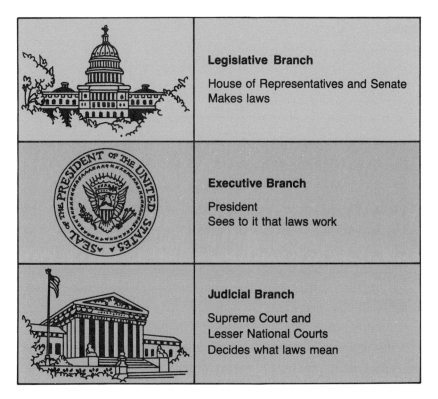

	Legislative Branch House of Representatives and Senate Makes laws
	Executive Branch President Sees to it that laws work
	Judicial Branch Supreme Court and Lesser National Courts Decides what laws mean

sentatives and the Senate. The **Executive Branch** would make sure that all laws were carried out. It would be led by a President. The **Judicial Branch** would make sure that the laws were fair for everyone. It would be made up of judges and their courts. The Supreme Court would be the highest court in the land.

A second way to limit power was by a system of **checks and balances**. This meant that each branch would need the help of another branch to do its job. For example, the Legislative Branch would make laws. But the President would have to sign the laws to put them to work. The President was made commander of the army. Only the Legislative Branch, however, could spend money to build an army. The judges could say what laws were fair. They only became judges, though, if the President appointed them and the Senate approved them.

It was clear to many people that this was a stronger plan of government than the Articles of Confederation. Some were worried that the central government was too strong. They wondered *"How will the state governments be protected?"* The writers answered by saying that the national government

"WELL, IT'S ABOUT TIME"

Copyright 1981 by Herblock in *The Washington Post*

171

How the Powers of Government are Divided

Central Government (Washington, D.C.)	Powers Shared by the Central and State Governments	Powers of the State Governments
To regulate foreign trade and commerce between the states	To collect taxes	To regulate trade within the state
To coin and print money	To borrow money	To conduct elections
To conduct foreign relations with other nations	To enforce laws and punish lawbreakers	To establish and support public schools
To establish post offices and roads	To provide for the health and welfare of the people	To license professional workers
To raise and support armed forces		To establish local governments
To declare war and make peace		To determine qualifications of voters
To pass naturalization laws and regulate immigration		To license business firms

federalism, a system of government where a central or national government handles affairs common to all citizens of a country while state governments handle local affairs.

would not have certain powers. Some powers would be kept by the states. This division of power between state and central government is called **federalism**. It is shown in the above chart.

The convention ended after seventeen weeks. The writers left the hall for the last time. They left with many questions answered and many remaining. But they left without the Articles of Confederation. They had written a new Constitution. It has lasted for almost two hundred years. It still governs our nation today.

Checking Up

1. Why was the writing of the Constitution an important change?

2. What were four major questions answered at the convention?

3. Name the three branches of government. What job do they do?

4. Why did the writers want each branch to check and balance the other two?

Fireworks displays were part of the country's celebration of its 200th birthday in 1976.

172

Lesson 3 Unfinished Business

Copies of the new Constitution were sent to each state's government. Between September, 1787, and August, 1788, nine states voted in favor of the new United States Constitution. That was enough votes to put it to work.

Why had it taken almost a year to get approval from the nine states? Some states were worried that the Constitution told only of the rights of government. They asked questions like, "What about the people? What rights do they have?" The leaders in some states would only vote for the Constitution if a list of people's rights was added. In 1791, the Bill of Rights was added to the Constitution. Below is the list of rights Americans still enjoy.

The Bill of Rights

1 Basic Freedoms and Rights	The government cannot make laws that stop people from speaking, writing, or believing what they wish as long as it does not hurt others. The government cannot stop people from meeting in groups or asking the government to correct problems in the country.
2 Right to Bear Arms	The people have the right to protect themselves by serving as armed citizens, subject to laws of the states.
3 Quartering of Soldiers	In peacetime, citizens cannot be forced to give soldiers a place to sleep or meals in their homes.
4 Searches and Arrests	A person cannot be arrested, and his or her house cannot be searched except in ways that follow the law.
5 Life, Liberty, and Property	People accused of a crime must be given a fair trial, and if necessary, a fair punishment. The government cannot take away a person's life, freedoms, or property except in ways that follow the law.
6 Rights of the Accused	An accused person has the right to a quick, public trial by jury. The accused has the right to a lawyer, and to hear witnesses that speak for or against him or her.
7 Right to a Jury Trial	In a disagreement that involves more than twenty dollars, either side in the disagreement can ask to have a jury trial.
8 Bail and Punishment	Bails, fines, and punishments should fit the nature of the crime.
9 All Other Rights	People have other rights that are not listed or explained in the Constitution.
10 Rights of the States and the People	The states or the people have all powers that have not been given to the central government. These are known as reserved powers.

There were other pieces of unfinished business. One point is explained in this letter from Abigail Adams to her husband John.

66In the new laws which I suppose you will make, I desire that you would remember the ladies. . . Do not put such unlimited power into the hands of the husbands. Remember, all men would be tyrants [harsh rulers] if they could. If attention is not paid to the ladies, we will start a rebellion. We will not hold ourselves to any laws in which we have no voice or representation.99

Members of other groups might also have written words like these. Women, blacks, and some American Indians took part in the fight against the English. Yet, they had not been asked to help write the Constitution. Many felt unhappy when they read the new Constitution.

They saw that the central government did not have one important power. It could not say who could vote. Each state government had this power. Because of this, the laws differed from state to state. In some states only white men who earned money from their own land could vote. In other states only white men who paid certain taxes could vote. In most states women, blacks, American Indians, and poor people could not vote.

This right was still a long way off for the American Indian and most blacks. In 1788, they were not considered citizens. In a land where the people are supposed to hold power, the right to vote is very important. These facts showed that Americans needed to change the way they ran their country.

Getting the Right to Vote

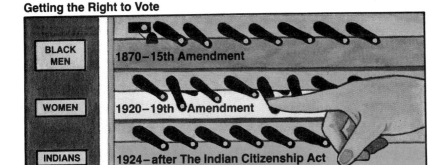

BLACK MEN — 1870–15th Amendment

WOMEN — 1920–19th Amendment

INDIANS — 1924–after The Indian Citizenship Act

We, the People
When did blacks, women, and American Indians get the right to vote?

175

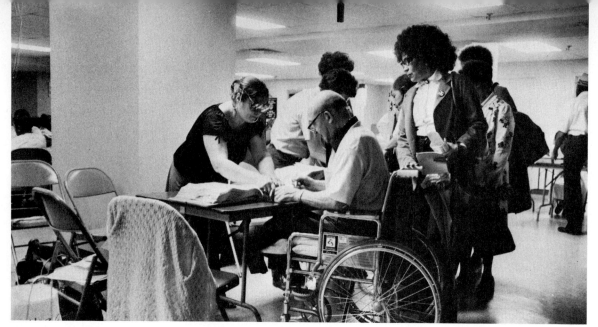

Americans practice one of their most important rights; the right to vote.

Many Americans were trying. They were unhappy that blacks were forced to be slaves. It seemed wrong for one person to own another. It seemed wrong for a nation that spoke of freedom to also allow slavery.

Some of the writers of the Constitution tried to outlaw the slave trade in 1787. But representatives from the southern states would not allow that. Slaves were a large part of the southern work force. In 1790, southern states had about 657,000 slaves. The southern representatives, however, did agree to end the slave trade by 1808.

Many northern states acted on their own. In 1790, northern states still had about forty thousand slaves. They did, however, pass laws to end slavery. Doing away with slavery remained unfinished business for many years.

Checking Up

1. Why were some women, blacks, and American Indians disappointed with the new Constitution?

2. Imagine that you were living in another country in 1790. What would you think about the United States saying one thing about freedom, yet allowing slavery to go on?

3. Which of the rights added to the Constitution in 1791 is most important to you? Why?

Reading Beyond the Encyclopedias!

Your teacher has asked the class to close their textbooks. The class has just finished reading about the War for American Independence and the writing of the Constitution. A hush falls over the room. You hear the word "report." The excitement builds. Everyone is leaning out of their seats to . . . get to the encyclopedias first!

But, wait! There is another way! Come with us now, as THE SUPER-SLEUTHS take you

THE SUPER-SLEUTHS are hungry detectives. They are looking for the juiciest tidbits of information. Textbooks and encyclopedias are good starting places to look for information. But, THE SUPER-SLEUTHS will take you on a "station-to-station" tour of their other favorite spots for finding and digesting facts and ideas.

Station A Books, Glorious Books! (also called **nonfiction** books)

THE SUPER-SLEUTHS KNOW: Some of the best places to gobble up facts and ideas about United States history are in nonfiction books.

THE SUPER-SLEUTHS GO: To the card catalog to find nonfiction books. This type of book tells about real people and events.

One type of nonfiction book is a biography. A biography is a book about a person's life. Maybe you want to find more information about Paul Revere, Abigail Adams, or other famous Americans in the Revolutionary War. Check your library's card catalog for biographies on these people.

Suppose you want more information on the War for American Independence or on the writing of the Constitution. Chances are that the card catalog lists some nonfiction books under these subjects.

The Library

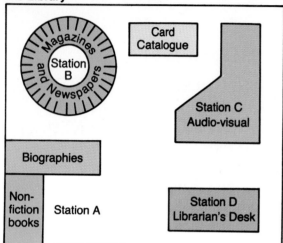

Station B — Magazines and Newspapers

Card Catalogue

Station C
Audio-visual

Biographies

Non-fiction books

Station A

Station D
Librarian's Desk

Station B Munchy Magazines! (also called periodicals)

THE SUPER-SLEUTHS KNOW: Magazines are sometimes the best places to find the freshest, munchiest, up-to-the-minute facts and ideas.

THE SUPER-SLEUTHS GO: To the newspaper and magazine area in the library. A magazine such as *American History Illustrated* might have the latest information about the War for American Independence. Magazines might also show how the people of today use their right of free speech.

Station C Audio-Visual Treats! (also called records, cassettes, filmstrips, and films)

THE SUPER-SLEUTHS KNOW: There is more to a library than books or magazines.

THE SUPER-SLEUTHS GO: To view filmstrips and films, or to listen to records and cassettes. Does your library have a recording of the famous poem, "The Midnight Ride of Paul Revere"? If not, maybe your librarian can get one. Does your library have the movie *Johnny Tremain?* This is a film about a young hero in the War for American Independence.

The events and people of the past can come alive with these interesting side dishes. **Station D** The Librarian's Desk (also called the reference desk)

THE SUPER-SLEUTHS KNOW: That many of the library's delights are known only to your librarian.

THE SUPER-SLEUTHS GO: To the librarian's desk whenever they need extra help. Your librarian can lead you on many new and exciting journeys . . . beyond the encyclopedias!

Reviewing Chapter 10

Write your answers on paper. Do not write in the book.

Using Key Words

constitution	federalism
revolution	rebellion
democracy	republic
legislative branch	judicial branch
executive branch	checks and balances
confederation	nonfiction

Number your paper from 1 to 12. Write a short definition for each of the above key words.

Reviewing Main Ideas

Some of the sentences below are true and some are false. Number your paper from 1 to 4 and write *true* or *false* by each. If the sentence is false, explain why.

1. The Articles of Confederation gave Americans a strong central government.

2. Shays' Rebellion showed how weak the nation was under the Articles.

3. The Bill of Rights was included in the Constitution when it was first written.

4. One of the main weaknesses of the United States government under the Articles was that it could not tax the people.

Thinking Things Over

Pretend that you are a newspaper reporter living in 1787. Make a list of five questions that you would ask the writers of the Constitution in an interview. You might ask why they wrote about certain things and not about others. For example, "Why did you include the idea about checks and balances?" "Why didn't you say anything about the rights that people have?" Write down answers you think they would have given you.

Practicing Skills

Copy on your paper a chart like the one below. Fill in the needed information about the three branches of government.

Branch of Government	Specific Job	Made up of or led by
1.	4.	7. Senate and House of Representatives
2.	5. makes sure that the laws are carried out	8.
3. Judicial	6.	9.

A New Nation Grows

On April 23, 1789, George Washington stood on a boat that entered New York Harbor. Thirteen men, one for each state in the new nation, rowed. Speedy sailboats darted around it. Washington stepped ashore to the sounds of ringing bells, booming cannons, and cheering crowds. All this was part of the greeting Americans gave Washington. He had been chosen as the first President of the United States.

Seven days later, Washington took the oath of office. *"I do solemnly swear that I will faithfully execute the office of President of the United States, and will to the best of my ability, preserve, protect and defend the Constitution of the United States."* The crowd cheered wildly. Washington looked at the smiling faces. He remembered the challenges the young nation had already met. When the cheering stopped, he knew the nation would face even harder challenges.

An artist's idea of George Washington's arrival in New York City on April 23, 1789.

Lesson 1   A New Nation and New Problems

George Washington and the new nation were faced with many problems. Perhaps the most serious problem involved the new Constitution. Most people did not feel that it would work. The Constitution was only a plan for government. It explained what powers the government had. It did not explain how people should use them.

A nation's problems are solved by its people, not by its important papers. In 1789, the President and the Congress would have to begin to show that the government and the Constitution could work.

One of the first acts of Congress was to set up the court system. Judges were selected. They were given the power to settle conflicts and set punishments. This was an important step. It showed the people that Congress could make laws. It showed that courts would deal with people that broke the laws.

The First Cabinet

The President selected advisers to help him carry out new laws. This group came to be known as the **Cabinet**. Thomas Jefferson was selected as Secretary of State. His job was to set up and keep good relations with other nations. Henry Knox was selected as Secretary of War. He had to build and train an army and navy. Alexander Hamilton was picked as Secretary of the Treasury. His job was, perhaps, the hardest. He had to help solve the nation's money problems.

One of the money problems was the nation's debt. Foreign countries had loaned the United States over 12 million dollars. The United States owed 43 million dollars to individuals. It had also borrowed over 25 million dollars from the state governments. Hamilton wanted the nation to pay off its debt. It would then gain respect from its citizens and other nations.

Hamilton also wanted to help American businesses. He asked Congress to tax certain imported goods. If Americans wanted foreign products, they would pay the taxes on the product. The tax money would go into the United States Treasury. The money would be used to help run the government. If Americans did not want to pay the taxes, they could

Washington's first cabinet meets. Why does the President need a cabinet? What are some of the cabinet jobs that were added since Washington's time?

Examples of the money printed by the Continental Congress.

buy American made products. This would help American manufacturers.

Hamilton wanted to raise money by taxing certain goods made in the United States. He asked Congress to place a tax on such products as whiskey and tobacco. Many farmers said this was an unfair tax. They raised corn and rye in order to make whiskey. If whiskey was taxed, people would not buy as much of it. The farmers felt they would lose money.

One group of Pennsylvania farmers rebelled. They beat up tax collectors and refused to pay the tax. This is known as the Whiskey Rebellion of 1794. President Washington did not ignore the law breakers. If he had, the people would not have respected the central government. They might have stopped obeying other laws. Washington sent soldiers to Pennsylvania. The rebellion quickly ended.

Hamilton also asked Congress to set up a National Bank. The bank would loan money to the government and to individuals. It would also make sure that only one **currency**, or money, was used.

But how could Congress set up a bank when the treasury had so little money? Hamilton suggested that the people supply most of the money. They could become part owners by buying shares in the bank. Each share would be worth about four hundred dollars. When all the shares were sold, the bank would have ten million dollars.

Everyone in Congress did not agree with Hamilton's ideas. Enough did to get the laws passed. Americans showed that they could solve their problems. They showed that their government worked.

Checking Up

---

1. What problems did the nation face in 1789?

2. How was money raised for the new government?

3. Why is it important for a nation to have the respect of its people and other nations?

Lesson 2 Federalists Versus Republicans

From almost his first day in office, Washington watched two groups of people argue about what was best for the United States. One group was led by Alexander Hamilton. The other group was led by Thomas Jefferson.

Alexander Hamilton and his followers believed that the United States government had to be strong. A strong central government could keep law and order. It would also be respected by other nations. Hamilton and his followers favored the National Bank and paying off the country's debt.

Jefferson and his followers did not want a strong central government. They believed a strong central government would take too much power away from the state governments. Jefferson and his followers disliked the idea of a National Bank. Only the rich could buy the shares. They also disliked the idea of paying off the debt. Much of the money was owed only to wealthy people.

Hamilton felt that the wealthy people should be the leaders in government. They had the most education. They could think out the problems clearly.

Jefferson disagreed. The common people were smart enough to make their own decisions, he said. They were usually closer to the problems than the few wealthy people.

Hamilton wanted American businesses to grow. He thought strong businesses would make a strong nation. Strong businesses would provide many jobs. They would also produce goods for people to buy.

Jefferson knew that most Americans were farmers. Farmers were close to sunshine, rich earth, and pure air. These were the best things in life, he felt, not the overcrowded cities. He did not like the tax on imported goods. Other nations would be angry when they could not sell their products in America. They might refuse to buy American farm products.

(top) Alexander Hamilton
(bottom) Thomas Jefferson

Hamilton and Jefferson could not agree on another matter. Hamilton wanted the United States to be friendly with England. Jefferson did not trust the English. He felt the nation owed France its friendship. After all, France had helped the colonies gain their freedom from England. Americans could not be friends with both the French and English.

The Birth of Political Parties

In time, people who disagreed over ideas about power and government split into two groups. Those who followed Hamilton were called Federalists. Those who followed Jefferson were called Democratic-Republicans. These two groups were the first **political parties**. A political party is a group of people who share ideas on how to improve their government and country. Political parties try to get their members elected to office. If elected, they lead the government and the country.

From 1797–1801 President John Adams and the Federalists were in office. Jefferson and his followers spoke out against the way the Federalists led the nation. In 1800, Jefferson defeated Adams in the presidential election. The Democratic-Republicans now had the power to lead the nation. The Federalists then spoke out against Jefferson and his party.

When Jefferson became President, he said that people from both parties could often agree on goals for the nation.

President Jimmy Carter explains an idea during a presidential debate with Ronald Reagan in 1980. Why is it important for Americans to hear the ideas and opinions of those people who are trying to be elected to office?

They sometimes would disagree, however, on how to reach those goals. Jefferson was speaking about an important idea in American government. Goals could be reached only if the parties disagreed peacefully.

Jefferson understood that no party should expect to have all of its ideas accepted all the time. That would not be fair to those with different opinions. Parties would have to learn to give and take ideas. They would have to **compromise**. Without compromise, the new government would fail. As the photograph on page 184 shows, political parties remained a part of the American way of government.

The candidates running for President in 1980 are shown here with the symbols of their political party. Ronald Reagan, a Republican, is riding an elephant. Jimmy Carter, a Democrat, is being pulled by donkeys. What message is the cartoonist trying to give us?

Checking Up

1. Why did political parties form in the United States?

2. What did the Federalists and Republicans disagree on?

3. Which party would you have favored if you lived in 1790?

4. Why is it important to let people disagree peacefully?

Lesson 3   The War of 1812

In 1796, George Washington said he would not run for President again. He had been elected to two, four-year terms. It was time for someone else to take the job. He had learned many things as President. He shared one of his thoughts in a farewell speech.

"Don't get too involved with other nations!" was his advice. As President he had seen that other nations could cause problems for the United States. For example, in 1793, France and England were at war. The United States was trading with both at the time. Soon, France began searching American ships that might be carrying weapons to England. England began searching American ships that might be carrying weapons to France.

Washington could have asked Congress to declare war. But he knew America was not strong enough to fight England and France. Instead, he said America would stay **neutral**. It would not take sides in the war between France and England. He also arranged a treaty with England. It was not a popular treaty with many Americans. Yet, Washington kept the young nation out of war.

France became angry when America made the treaty. It continued to stop American ships headed for England. John Adams, the nation's second President, could have asked Congress to declare war on France. Instead, he followed Washington's advice. He arranged a treaty with France. Again the treaty was not popular with many Americans. But Adams kept the nation out of war.

England became angry when it learned of the new treaty. In 1807, England tried to make it illegal for American ships to enter French ports. They also took American sailors and forced them to serve in the English navy. France announced that it was illegal for American ships to enter English ports. Again America was in the middle.

The nation's third President, Thomas Jefferson, tried to follow Washington's advice. He had Congress pass an **embargo** law. This stopped American ships from sailing. Jefferson thought, American ships cannot be searched if they are not allowed on the oceans to trade. This angered American merchants. If there is no trade, they said, no one makes money. In 1809, the embargo ended.

neutral, on neither side in a quarrel or war.

embargo, an order by a government forbidding ships to enter or leave its ports.

During the War of 1812, the English marched into Washington, D.C. and burned many of the public buildings. Among the buildings set afire were the Capitol and the White House.

The nation's fourth President, James Madison, also tried to keep America out of a war. He helped the merchants by allowing them to trade. They could trade, but not with England or France. Again the merchants complained.

The War Begins

Madison then made a costly mistake. He said America would trade with either England or France if that nation would stop searching American ships. France quickly agreed to this. Madison announced that America would not trade with England. He had taken sides in their fight. He had forgotten Washington's advice.

In June of 1812, Madison asked Congress to declare war on England. He said the nation was fighting for "freedom of the seas." Other Americans secretly wanted war with England for another reason. England controlled Canada. If America defeated England, Canada might become a part of the United States.

The war dragged on for over two years. Neither the United States nor England was a clear victor. Finally, a peace treaty was signed in 1814. It said nothing, though, about "freedom of the seas." Had anything been proven by this war?

Americans felt the war taught them two lessons. A nation's real power is not always shown on the battlefield. Sometimes it is shown by how it keeps the peace. And, as Washington advised, maybe it was best to stay out of Europe's problems. Americans tried to follow that advice for almost one hundred years.

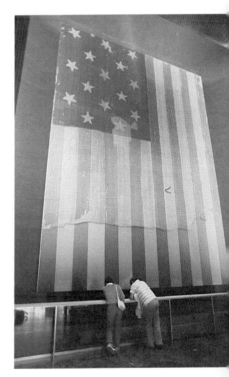

The "Star Spangled Banner" which flew over Ft. McHenry during the English attack in 1814.

187

Europe learned something, too. America was a young nation. It was not afraid to defend itself. It was not afraid to show its spirit and strength, too.

A young poet, Francis Scott Key, witnessed a battle in the War of 1812. He found the right words to show the American spirit and strength.

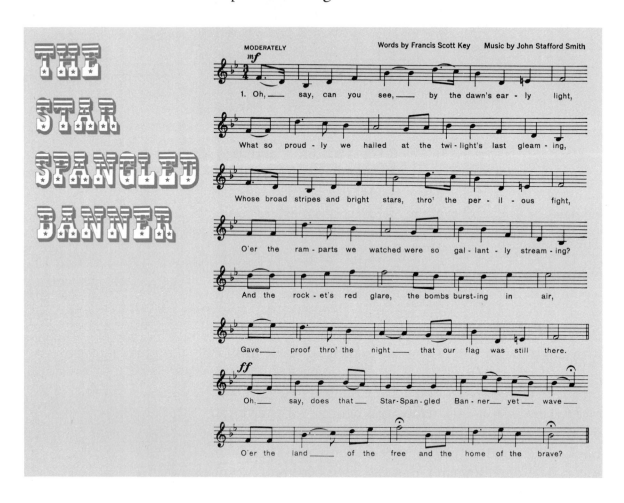

THE STAR SPANGLED BANNER

MODERATELY
Words by Francis Scott Key   Music by John Stafford Smith

1. Oh, say, can you see, by the dawn's ear-ly light,
What so proud-ly we hailed at the twi-light's last gleam-ing,
Whose broad stripes and bright stars, thro' the per-il-ous fight,
O'er the ram-parts we watched were so gal-lant-ly stream-ing?
And the rock-et's red glare, the bombs burst-ing in air,
Gave proof thro' the night that our flag was still there.
Oh, say, does that Star-Span-gled Ban-ner yet wave
O'er the land of the free and the home of the brave?

Checking Up

1. Why do you think England and France were stopping and searching American ships?

2. Why did Washington feel the United States should not get too involved with other nations?

3. How else can a country use its power besides going to war?

Write your answers on paper. Do not write in the book.

Using Key Words

cabinet	political parties
compromise	neutral
embargo	currency

Number your paper from 1 to 6. Write a short definition for each of the above words.

Reviewing Main Ideas

Number your paper from 1 to 5. Write the letter on your paper that best completes each sentence.

1. Alexander Hamilton wanted to **a.** stop taxing imports. **b.** pay off the national debt. **c.** have large state banks instead of a national bank.

2. The Federalists were **a.** loyal to France. **b.** taking American ships during the War of 1812. **c.** one of the first political parties.

3. In his farewell speech, Washington advised the country to **a.** stay out of other nation's problems. **b.** go to war as of-ten as possible. **c.** take sides in other nations' problems.

4. The Whiskey Rebellion of 1794 showed that **a.** states had to obey federal laws. **b.** Washington did not have the respect of the people. **c.** farmers and manufacturers paid the same amount of taxes.

5. Thomas Jefferson believed that the **a.** wealthy people should not have to pay a lot of taxes. **b.** manufacturers should be taxed. **c.** central government should not be too strong.

Thinking Things Over

Imagine that you are the first president of a new nation. Who is in your cabinet and what jobs will they do?

What are some peaceful and not so peaceful ways two countries can settle their differences?

Practicing Skills

Copy the small chart below on your paper. Fill in the blanks to show how the first political parties felt about certain ideas.

Political Party	Leader	Strong Central Government	Paying off the National Debt	Tax on Imported Goods
Federalists	Alexander Hamilton			
Democratic—Republicans	Thomas Jefferson			

What Do You Know?

Write your answers on paper. Do not write in the book.

Words to Know

treaty republic
Congress federalism
Constitution neutral
democracy embargo
rebellion compromise
cabinet import

Number your paper from 1 to 12. Write the definition of each key word.

Ideas to Know

Some of the sentences below are true and some are false. Number your paper 1 to 15 and write either *true* or *false* by each number. If you think an answer is false, explain why on your paper.

1. The English government wanted the colonies to be sources of finished goods.

2. England felt the colonists should pay part of the bill for the war with France.

3. Colonial protests forced England to end the Stamp Act.

4. The British army went to Concord to collect taxes.

5. The Articles of Confederation is the same government we have today.

6. In the Senate, all states are represented by two senators.

7. The Constitution ended slavery in America in 1787.

8. The Bill of Rights is a list of freedoms Americans are guaranteed.

9. Hamilton wanted to make America strong by passing laws to help businessmen.

10. Jefferson wanted America to stay a country of small farms instead of big cities.

11. John Adams refused to defend the English soldiers after the Boston Massacre.

12. The American colonists were only allowed to import raw materials and export finished goods.

13. Loyalists were people who didn't want to break away from England.

14. One cause of the War of 1812 was "freedom of the seas."

15. Mercy Otis Warren is famous for writing a history of the War for American Independence.

Using What You Know

1. You have learned that our government is divided into three branches. Number your paper 1 to 6. Match the correct branch with the statements written below.
   a. Legislative Branch
   b. Executive Branch
   c. Judicial Branch

   _____ makes sure laws are put to work
   _____ looks over laws to make sure they are fair
   _____ is made up of courts and judges
   _____ writes new laws
   _____ is made up of the House of Representatives and Senate
   _____ the President is the most important person in this branch

2. Pretend you are a member of the "Patriots' Club." Select one of the persons listed below. Write a speech explaining why your choice should receive the "Patriot of the Year" award.

   George Washington   John Adams
   Alexander Hamilton   James Otis
   Thomas Jefferson   James Madison
   Mercy Otis Warren   Abigail Adams

3. Draw the time line below on your paper. Place the following events on the time line in their correct position. Draw a symbol for each of the events. Your symbol should be a picture that helps you remember something about the event.

   • Declaration of Independence—1776
   • Stamp Act—1765
   • Constitution written—1787
   • Lexington and Concord—1775
   • War of Independence ends—1783
   • Boston Tea Party—1773

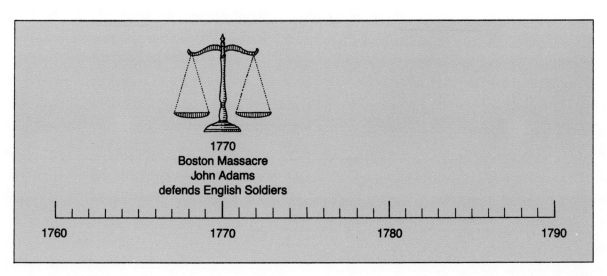

1770
Boston Massacre
John Adams
defends English Soldiers

1760   1770   1780   1790

Unit ④

The Nation Changes

Telegraph.
Factory.
Civil War.
California.
Steamboat.
Oregon.
Reservation.
Railroad.
Few of these words meant much to Americans in 1800. By 1860, they were everyday words. Together, they tell what happened to the United States in those sixty years. What happened can be summed up in a single word–*change*.

Heading toward "the promised land" on the Oregon Trail.

192

Chapter

12

Lesson 1 Moving West of the Appalachians
Lesson 2 New Lands Across the Mississippi
Lesson 3 Trails West of the Mississippi

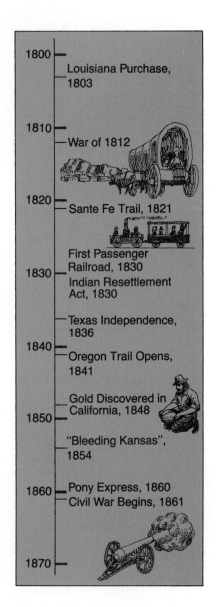

1800
Louisiana Purchase, 1803

1810
War of 1812

1820
Sante Fe Trail, 1821

First Passenger Railroad, 1830
1830
Indian Resettlement Act, 1830

Texas Independence, 1836
1840
Oregon Trail Opens, 1841

Gold Discovered in California, 1848
1850
"Bleeding Kansas", 1854

1860
Pony Express, 1860
Civil War Begins, 1861

1870

pioneer, someone who is among the first to do something.

The Growing West

"We're bound for the Promised Land!"

—*from a popular pioneer song
of the 1800s*

Americans seemed to have a restless feeling in the 1800s. They wished to see the "promised lands" in the West. In the early 1800s, the West was the land on the other side of the Appalachian Mountains. Later, in the 1840s and 1850s, the West was the land west of the Mississippi River. It was the new, faraway lands of Utah, Oregon, and California.

Thousands of men, women, and children headed west in the first half of the nineteenth century. They carried their hopes and dreams with them along the trails. They braved heat, cold, droughts, and floods. They stood against insects, diseases, and prairie fires. They crossed deserts, rivers, and mountains. They traveled along rough roads, bad roads, or no roads at all.

Lesson 1   Moving West of the Appalachians

In 1783, the United States and England signed a peace treaty ending the War of Independence. England gave up more than 400,000 square miles of land to the United States. The map on page 201 shows this large area of land.

Soon, settlers began to move onto the lands west of the Appalachian Mountains. These were lands few white people had ever seen. As these **pioneers** moved west, so did the **frontier**. The frontier was an imaginary dividing line between settled and unsettled land.

Most pioneers were under twenty-five, white, and poor. They had many reasons for leaving the East. But their reasons all seemed to mean the same thing: "We have a chance to change our lives in this new land!"

194

Who Moved West and Why

One reason for moving was the land itself. People hoped to find good, cheap farmland. By 1783, most of the good farmland in the original thirteen states was taken. The remaining land was costly because so many people wanted it.

Others moved to find jobs in the growing settlements. Workers were needed to build frontier towns. And the services of doctors, lawyers, merchants, and teachers were always needed.

A few moved west because they wanted to get rich. They bought large amounts of land. Then they sold it to farmers for more than they paid for it.

Other pioneers simply wanted to improve their lives. Back east, some of them had been slaves or indentured servants. To these people, life on the frontier could only be better.

Some pioneers moved west because the East was overcrowded. Sometimes it was hard to find good housing. These pioneers longed for the open spaces of the frontier.

Many people probably headed west just for adventure. The land was different than in the East. It was an unexplored, exciting wilderness. It was a promised land.

To dream of a promised land in the wilderness was one thing. To find it was another. Read how one pioneer, Moses Austin, described the trip west for some people.

❝I cannot [stop] noticing the many [suffering] families I passed . . . traveling a wilderness through ice and snow; passing large rivers and creeks without shoe or stocking and barely as many rags as cover their [bodies]; without money or [supplies], except what the wilderness [gives them].

Ask these pilgrims what they expect when they get to Kentucky. The answer is land. "Have you got any?" "No, but I expect I can git it." "Have you anything to pay for land?" "No." "Did you ever see the country?" "No, but everybody says it's good land."

Here are hundreds, traveling hundreds of miles—they know not for what . . . except it's to Kentucky—passing land almost as good . . . . But it will not do. It's not Kentucky. It's not the Promised Land. It's not . . . the Land of Milk and Honey.❞

Many pioneers settled in Kentucky. Some went to Tennessee, Alabama, or Mississippi. Others went to Ohio, Michigan, Indiana, Illinois, or Wisconsin.

They traveled by raft along the Ohio and Mississippi rivers. Others took mule or wagon trains along the Wilderness Road. This really wasn't a road like we know today. It was a rough Indian trail that passed through the Appalachian Mountains.

The Wilderness Road was about three hundred miles long. It joined Hillsboro, North Carolina, and Louisville, Kentucky. Find the Wilderness Road on the map on page 207. Part of the road was cleared by the explorer Daniel Boone and thirty friends.

Daniel Boone was a true pioneer. He explored the Kentucky area as early as 1769. As a hunter and trapper, he loved to be alone in the wilderness. But he also saw the frontier as a promised land for others.

New States in the New England, Ohio Valley, and Great Lakes Regions
(1791 to 1860)

State	Year entered the Union
Vermont	1791
Kentucky	1792
Tennessee	1796
Ohio	1803
Indiana	1816
Illinois	1818
Maine	1820
Michigan	1837
Iowa	1846
Wisconsin	1848
Minnesota	1858

The old fort at Boonesborough, 1775.

Conflict with the Indians

Whites were not the only people who thought the West was a promised land. The Indians who lived there did, too. The Indians saw the land as a living thing. The land's children were the soil, the trees, and animals. These were things that all people could share. These were not things, the Indians felt, that anyone could own.

Most white people could not understand the Indians' ideas about land. White settlers felt it was natural to chop down trees and make room for fields. They felt it was natural to put up lasting homes and fences. White settlers felt that people could own the land.

By 1800, over 700,000 white settlers had moved onto land west of the Appalachian Mountains. Tecumseh (tə kum′sə), chief of the Shawnees, told the white settlers: "You have taken our land from us and I do not see how we can remain at peace with you if you continue to do so." He asked many Indians to stand against the white settlers.

66Where today are the . . . once powerful tribes of our people? They have vanished [gone] . . . as snow before a summer sun . . . Shall we, without a struggle, give up our homes, our country . . . and everything that is dear and sacred to us? I know you will cry with me, never! Never!99

In 1811, Tecumseh's forces battled an army led by William Henry Harrison at Tippecanoe Creek in Indiana. See the map at right. Neither side won a victory. But Indians and white settlers were pulled further apart.

When the War of 1812 started, many Indians helped England fight the Americans. The Indians thought the English would help them keep out other white settlers. During this war, Tecumseh fought as an English general. He was killed at the Battle of the Thames (temz) in Canada. The hope of uniting all Indians against white settlers died with him.

Other battles between whites and Indians followed. Major General Andrew Jackson defeated the Creeks in 1814. Later, in 1818, he fought the Seminole (sem′ə nōl) Indians in Florida. His victories helped him get elected as the nation's seventh President.

In the early 1800s, this part of the United States was the West. Today, it is the Midwest.

197

Andrew Jackson had been a pioneer in Tennessee. He agreed with most white settlers of the time. White settlers had a right to the land.

Moved onto the Reservations

As President, he asked Congress to pass the Indian Resettlement Act of 1830. This act forced the Indians to move west of the Mississippi River. Moving the Indians, Jackson said, would help whites settle the land "occupied by a few savage hunters."

By 1840, about ninety thousand Indians had been moved west. As the map on page 199 shows, they were placed on **reservations**. For some tribes, moving was harder than any battle. The Cherokees lost over four thousand people along their thousand-mile walk to Oklahoma.

Other Indians, such as the Sauk and Fox, did not give up without a fight. Black Hawk, their leader, was captured in 1832. He explained how most Indians felt.

reservations, land set aside for use by a group of people.

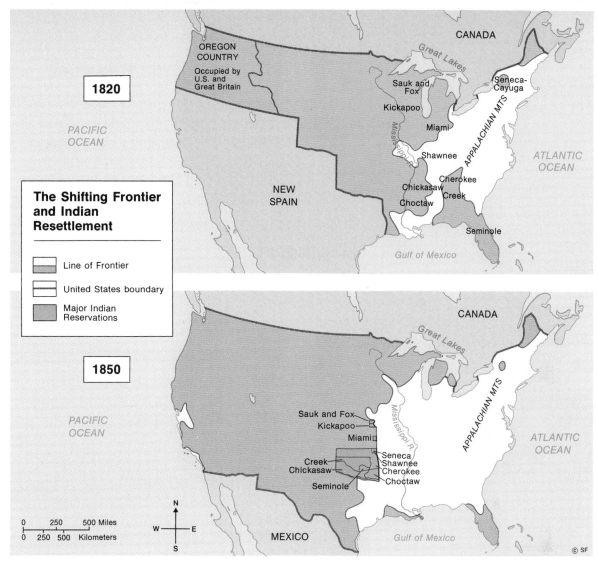

The Shifting Frontier and Indian Resettlement

1820

OREGON COUNTRY
Occupied by U.S. and Great Britain

PACIFIC OCEAN

NEW SPAIN

CANADA

Great Lakes

Sauk and Fox

Kickapoo

Miami

Shawnee

Mississippi R.

APPALACHIAN MTS.

Seneca-Cayuga

ATLANTIC OCEAN

Cherokee
Chickasaw
Choctaw
Creek

Seminole

Gulf of Mexico

Line of Frontier

United States boundary

Major Indian Reservations

1850

PACIFIC OCEAN

CANADA

Great Lakes

Sauk and Fox
Kickapoo
Miami

Creek
Chickasaw

Seminole

Mississippi R.

Seneca
Shawnee
Cherokee
Choctaw

APPALACHIAN MTS.

ATLANTIC OCEAN

0 250 500 Miles
0 250 500 Kilometers

N
W E
S

MEXICO

Gulf of Mexico

© SF

❝He [the Indian] has done nothing for which an Indian [can] be ashamed. He has fought for his countrymen . . . against white men, who came year after year, to cheat [him] and take [his] lands.❞

The map above shows some of the Indian tribes that were moved west of the Mississippi River. Note that by 1850 the line of the frontier had reached the Pacific Ocean.

Checking Up

1. What was the frontier?

2. How did white settlers and Indians disagree about the land?

3. How did the movement west change the life of the Indian?

(opposite)
The Cherokee call their journey to Oklahoma the "Trail of Tears."

199

Lesson 2   New Lands Across the Mississippi

In 1802, the western border of the United States stopped at the Mississippi River. The country was made up of about 889,000 square miles of land. By 1860, the western border was at the Pacific Ocean. The country had grown over three times larger than it was in 1802. The United States gained the new lands between the Mississippi River and the Pacific Ocean from different nations and in different ways.

The Louisiana Purchase

In 1803, President Thomas Jefferson offered to buy the city of New Orleans from the French. New Orleans is located at the mouth of the Mississippi River. The river empties into the Gulf of Mexico.

Having New Orleans would help American trade, thought Jefferson. Americans could ship their goods down the Mississippi River to New Orleans. From there, the goods could be sent to other countries. President Jefferson offered the French $8 million for the city.

The French government, however, was in need of more money. They offered to sell all of Louisiana for $15 million. Jefferson quickly accepted. The size of the United States had suddenly doubled. The map on page 201 shows you this large area of land.

President Jefferson wanted to learn about Louisiana's land, people, plants, animals, and climate. He asked Meriwether Lewis and William Clark to explore the area. In 1804, they left St. Louis with forty-three other men.

Lewis and Clark followed the Missouri River to its source. They crossed the Rocky Mountains into what is today the state of Oregon. Then, after eighteen months and almost four thousand miles, they reached the Pacific. Follow their route on the map on page 201.

During the trip, a French fur trader named Toussaint Charbonneau (tü san′ shär′bo nō′) joined the group. He helped Lewis and Clark speak to the Indians of Louisiana in their own languages. More importantly, Charbonneau brought his sixteen-year-old Shoshoni (shō shō′nē) Indian wife. Her name was Sacajawea (sak′ə jə wē′ə). She served as their guide during much of the trip. As Lewis explained in his diary, she helped in another way, too.

Sacajawea; her name meant "the Bird Woman."

200

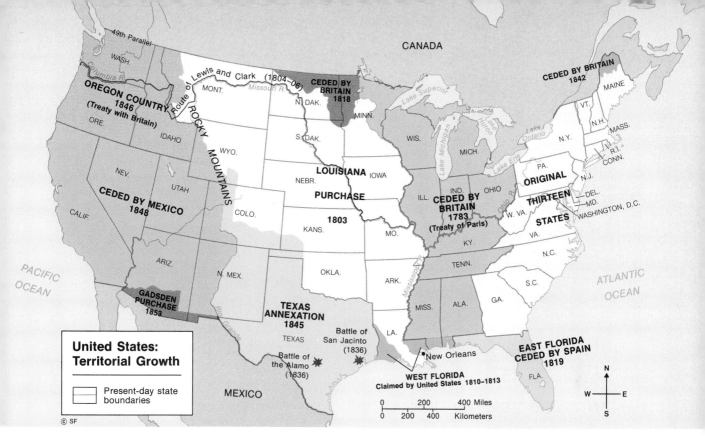

United States:
Territorial Growth

Present-day state
boundaries

© SF

The map above shows how
and when land was added
to the United States before
1860. What small territory
in the west was added in
1853?

❝Lewis/August 13, 1805

We had marched about 2 miles when we met a party of
about sixty warriors mounted on horses. They came at nearly
full speed. When they arrived, I went towards them with the
flag, leaving my gun with the party about fifty paces behind
me. The chief and two others who were a little in advance of
the main body spoke to Sacajawea. She told them who we
were. . . . These men then came to me and hugged me in
their way which is by putting their left arm over your right
shoulder. Then they apply their left cheek to yours and say
"Ah-hi-e! Ah-hi-e!" that is, "I am much pleased! I am much
rejoiced!"

Lewis/August 17, 1805

The Indian woman, Sacajawea, proved to be a sister of the
chief of these Indians, Chief Cameahwait.❞

Annexation of Texas

The purchase of Louisiana brought the American frontier
close to the boundaries of New Spain. In 1821, the people of
New Spain won their independence from Spain. The nation

of Mexico was born. At that time, Mexico held lands that today make up the states of Texas, New Mexico, California, Arizona, Nevada, Utah, Wyoming, and Colorado.

In the early 1820s, Mexico urged people from the United States to make their homes in Texas. By 1835, more than 30,000 people from the United States lived in Texas. This was far more than the number of Mexicans in Texas.

The Texans from the United States differed somewhat from their neighbors. Most of them were Protestants. The Mexicans were Roman Catholics. The Texans spoke English. The Mexicans spoke Spanish.

Many Texans came from the southern part of the United States. They wanted to grow cotton and sugar crops as they had in their old homeland. To do this, they believed they needed slaves. But the Mexican government did not want slavery in its country.

The differences between the Texans and the Mexican government caused much unhappiness on both sides. Finally, Texans from the United States decided to become independent of Mexico. Sam Houston and Stephen Austin led Texans in setting up their own government.

The Mexican government wasn't going to allow Texas to become independent without a fight. In 1835, General Antonio López de Santa Anna (san′tə an′ə), and his army marched against the Texans.

In one battle, 200 Texans tried to hold an old mission in San Antonio against 3,000 Mexican soldiers. The mission was called the Alamo. Among the Texans were William Travis, the leader of the Alamo, Davy Crockett, a Tennessee pioneer, and Jim Bowie, a pioneer from Louisiana.

Santa Anna demanded that the Texans give up. Travis replied, "I shall never surrender or retreat. . . . Victory or death!" For twelve days, the two sides fought. Finally, Santa Anna's army defeated the Texans. All of the Texans who fought at the Alamo died.

This struggle gave other Texans courage and time to prepare to fight. On April 21, 1836, Santa Anna's army met another group of Texans at San Jacinto (san hə sin′tō), Texas. The Texans' leader was Sam Houston. As they fought, Texan soldiers shouted, "Remember the Alamo!" Locate these two battles on the map on page 201.

Sam Houston (top).
Santa Anna (bottom).

According to some military leaders in the Mexican army, the battle at the Alamo should never have taken place. It had no real military importance. Instead, it seems, General Santa Anna wanted to win a big victory to make himself look good. Before the attack, Santa Anna warned that no survivors would be taken. Even his own men protested such useless slaughter. While the main force attacked, Santa Anna placed himself in command of the reserve forces. Later, Santa Anna claimed that his forces had killed over 600 Texans. This was to cover up the fact that his forces had over 1600 dead or wounded.

The Texas flag.

The Texans won the battle at San Jacinto and the war. The Texans declared themselves an independent state. It was called the Republic of Texas. Sam Houston was elected the first president. Less than ten years later, however, Texas gave up its independence. It was **annexed** by the United States. This meant Texas joined the United States as a state. Another 390,000 square miles of territory had been added to the United States. See the map on page 201.

War with Mexico

Shortly after Texas was annexed in 1845, the United States and Mexico went to war. The two countries had argued about the border of Texas for almost ten years. The United States said the border of Texas was the Rio Grande. Mexico said it was the Nueces (nü ā′sās) River.

Mexico surrendered in 1847. In 1848, the two nations signed the Treaty of Guadalupe-Hidalgo (gwad′ə lüp′ hi däl′gō). In the treaty, the two nations agreed that the Rio Grande was the southern boundary of Texas. Mexico also agreed to **cede**, or give up, 529,000 square miles of land. This land makes up all or part of present-day Nevada, Utah, Arizona, Colorado, New Mexico, Wyoming, and California. Find this area on the map on page 201.

This cartoon shows the border dispute between Mexico and the United States.

203

The Bear Flag of the California Rebellion of 1846.

Settlers in California played an important part in the war. In 1846, a group of Californians declared themselves independent of Mexico. They flew a flag with a bear on it. Their rebellion has been called the Bear Flag Rebellion of 1846. The Bear Flag rebels and the United States army joined forces and defeated the Mexican army in California.

Compromise over the Oregon Country

In 1846, as the Mexican War was starting, the United States and England were arguing about Oregon. Both nations claimed this land.

Some Americans wanted to go to war with England. They felt enough Americans had settled the land to make it more American than English. England pointed out that it had had fur traders there for over fifty years.

England did not look forward to another war with the United States. The United States did not want to fight England again, either. Many Americans felt that the nation should not fight two wars at once. The war with Mexico was enough.

President James Polk decided to accept England's compromise offer. A treaty was signed that divided Oregon at the 49th parallel of latitude. Find this line on the map on page 201. The United States received 285,000 square miles of land south of this line. The states of Washington, Oregon, and Idaho were later formed from this area. England received land north of this line. It became the Canadian province of British Columbia.

These were years of growth for the new nation. These were years of war and peace. These were years of change.

Checking Up

1. Make a list of the nations the United States had obtained land from by 1860. Next to each name, briefly explain *how* the United States obtained the land.

2. Find your home state on the map on page 201. When and how was the land of your home state obtained?

SOMEONE YOU SHOULD KNOW

Joseph Reddeford Walker

They were most at home in the wilderness lands of the West. There, they could trap for furs, find adventure, or just be alone. We call them trailblazers. As they searched for furs or adventure, they often made new trails. Later, pioneer settlers followed those trails.

One such trailblazer was Joseph Reddeford Walker. In 1833, he set out to do what few whites had ever done. Walker wanted to find a new route from the Rocky Mountains into California.

The trip had been made before. The other trailblazers, though, had followed a long and unsafe path. Walker's goal was to find a safer and shorter path west. Walker slowly led his group along the thousand mile route. He carefully studied the land. Walker also asked Indians for advice on the best route west.

The three-month trip led the group across the deserts and plateaus of the Great Basin. It also led them up to fourteen thousand feet in the Sierra Nevada.

Walker and his group survived the desert heat, the mountain cold, and even an earthquake. And they saw things that made all the hardships worthwhile. They were the first whites to enter Yosemite Valley. Today this area is known as Yosemite National Park. Walker and his party were also the first whites to see the giant redwoods in California.

Walker was a true trailblazer. In 1850, migrants followed his route to the California gold fields. In the late 1860s, the first train that ran from coast to coast followed part of his route. As one mountain man said, Joe Walker "didn't follow trails, but rather made them."

Yosemite Valley.

Part of the Oregon Trail as seen today.

They were about four feet wide and ten feet long. Most were about eight feet tall. They were called covered wagons, or prairie schooners. The prairie schooner is not to be confused with the Conestoga wagon. The Conestoga was used by pioneers who crossed the Appalachians. It was much heavier and could hold more.

For two thousand miles, the wagons were the pioneers' homes. The average covered wagon carried about 2,000 pounds of goods. Part of the weight were things the pioneer needed to start a new life on the frontier. The rest were supplies needed on the long trip west. The pioneers usually walked or rode next to the wagon.

Lesson 3   Trails West of the Mississippi

They looked like ships moving silently in single file across an ocean. Because of this, they were called prairie schooners, or prairie ships. But they were not ships. They were covered wagons. And it wasn't the wind that powered them. Mules or oxen pulled the wagons in slow motion toward new lands.

"New Mexico . . . Oregon . . . Utah . . . California." These were dream lands on the pioneers' lips. And how many pioneers moved west in covered wagons? No one knows for sure. So many moved west, though, that their wagons cut deep trails into the earth. Those trails can still be seen today.

The Santa Fe Trail

Beginning in the 1820s, people began to travel west on what was called the Santa Fe Trail. The Santa Fe Trail ran for about eight hundred miles from Independence, Missouri, to Santa Fe, New Mexico. It began as a trade route.

In 1821, Santa Fe was part of Mexico. The people who lived there needed such things as mules, guns, cloth, iron tools, and coffee. They could have bought these things from Mexico. But the trading centers in Missouri were closer. In return for their goods, American merchants received furs and silver. Follow the Santa Fe Trail on the map on page 207.

The Oregon Trail

Pioneers moved to Oregon long before it became a part of the United States. The land was ideal for farming or fur trapping. By 1845, over three thousand people had moved there.

The Oregon Trail was the longest and hardest trail that headed west. It was two thousand miles and eight months of bumps, ruts, and trail dust. Pioneers could also expect Indian attacks. But such attacks were not common.

Far more of a worry along the Oregon Trail was disease. And the worst disease was cholera. Cholera is an illness in the stomach and intestines. The disease was carried aboard trading ships from China and India. Many of these ships docked at New Orleans. From there, the disease was carried along the Mississippi and Missouri rivers. The Oregon Trail began at Independence, Missouri, on the Missouri River. It is believed that as many as thirty thousand pioneers died of cholera on the Oregon Trail. "Died of Cholera" was a very common grave marker.

Many of the pioneers kept a diary of their experiences. One such diary belonged to Jesse Applegate. He was part of a group of one thousand pioneers who traveled to Oregon in 1843. Here is what he wrote about the start of one day on the Oregon Trail.

Did any of the routes shown on the map pass through your home state?

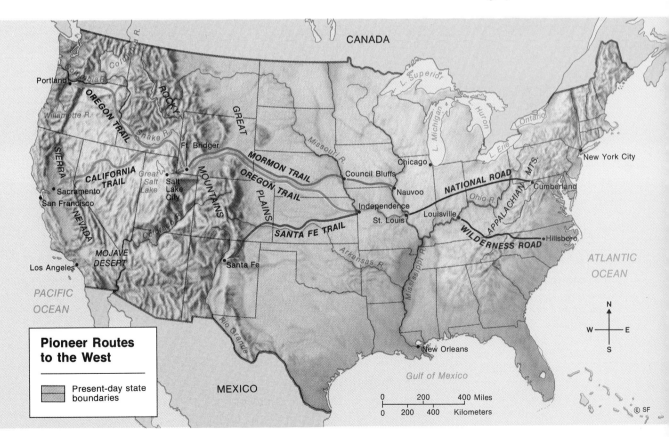

Pioneer Routes to the West

▨ Present-day state boundaries

0   200   400 Miles
0 200 400 Kilometers

© SF

207

> 66It is 4 a.m.; the [guards] on duty have [shot] their rifles—the signal that the hours of sleep are over; and every wagon and tent is pouring forth its night tenants . . . .
>
> From 6 to 7 o'clock is a busy time; breakfast is to be eaten, the tents [taken down], the wagons loaded, and the teams . . . attached to their wagons . . . .
>
> The wagons form a line three quarters of a mile in length; some of the [drivers] ride upon the front of their wagons, some walk beside their teams; scattered along the line are companies of women and children . . .99

Usually, the pioneers headed for the Willamette River. See map on page 207. Along the river was a valley of rich soil.

Many of those who went to Oregon, or nearby Utah, wanted to farm, ranch, or build communities. Others migrated for religious reasons as had the Pilgrims and Puritans in the 1600s. Marcus and Narcissa Whitman were two of the first to travel the Oregon Trail. They were missionaries. They wanted to teach the Indians of Oregon the Christian way of life.

The Mormon Trail

Another group called the Church of Jesus Christ of Latter-day Saints also traveled west. They were also called Mormons. They had known much unhappiness in the East.

First, they lived in New York, then in Ohio, and later in western Illinois. In each place, some Americans disliked them for their beliefs. The Mormons moved from each place in hopes of finding peace and safety.

Finally, the Mormons, led by Brigham Young, left Illinois in search of a frontier home. They traveled the Oregon Trail as far as Fort Bridger in the Rocky Mountains. Instead of going on to Oregon, however, they went south to a place on the western slope of the Rocky Mountains. They made their home near the Great Salt Lake in what is today Utah.

The California Trail

It was a cold, January morning in 1848. Fifty miles north of Sacramento, California, a man walked ankle-deep in a cold mountain stream. The man was the manager of a small sawmill that sat near the stream. It was his job to inspect the

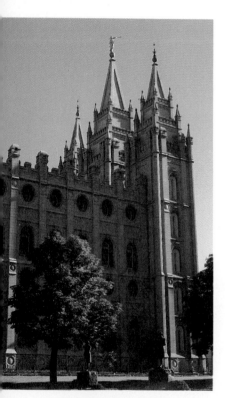

The Mormons' Temple in Salt Lake City, Utah. The building of the Temple took almost forty years. Much of it was built with granite blocks that weighed almost five tons each. The blocks were brought from a quarry twenty miles outside the city.

stream every Monday. If too many small rocks built up in the stream, the water would not flow fast enough to turn the saw blades in the mill.

Small rocks did not catch his eye that Monday, though. What he saw would change California and the United States forever. James Marshall saw something shimmering in the water. He slowly reached in and pulled out a small piece of gold.

Marshall and his boss, John Sutter, tried to keep the discovery a secret. Within a few months, however, a California newspaper headline read "GOLD MINE FOUND." Shortly after that, thousands of people began migrating to California. By 1852, over 100,000 people had made the trip.

Not everyone "struck it rich" after gold was discovered in California. One who never did was the man who first discovered gold, James Marshall.

No one knows what happened to the first nugget. But, as Marshall said, discovering it was not of "much benefit to me." Marshall never found enough gold to live on.

Even his sawmill didn't help him earn a living. It was torn down by miners. They were looking for wood to use in their mines.

Marshall died in 1885, a very poor man. But California was grateful to him. They built a ten-foot statue of him. It looks down on the spot where he found the gold on that cold January morning in 1848.

Sutter's Mill along the American River in California.

209

An original drawing by a miner on his way to California.

Facts and Figures

Many of the people who went to look for gold in California never walked a step across the country.

The small map below shows two other popular routes. One took gold seekers by ship around South America. It was a thirteen-thousand-mile trip. Most ships made the trip in six months. For some ships, the trip took as long as a year. People could expect to pay at least $500.

The second route took gold seekers through Panama in Central America. One ship dropped them on the Atlantic side of Panama. Another picked them up on the Pacific side.

Both routes had hardships. Travelers put up with poor food, bad water, sea sickness, and disease.

Water Routes to California

Most followed the Oregon Trail as far as Fort Bridger. Then they went across Utah, Nevada, and over the Sierra Nevada. Find this route on the map on page 207. One traveler, John Clark, kept a diary of his trip in 1852. Here is what he wrote as they approached the Sierra Nevada.

66Aug. 18—Today we make the last . . . effort of this wearisome trip; this is considered the hardest bit of travel on the route. About ten miles out the dead teams of '49 and '50 were seen scattered here and there upon the road. Very soon, however, they became more frequent and in a little while filled the entire roadside; mostly oxen, here and there a horse and once in a while a mule. Wagons . . . ox chains, harness, rifles . . . lay scattered along this . . . route.99

Checking Up

1. What trails did pioneers use during their migration west?

2. How do you think California and the United States were changed by the discovery of gold in 1848?

3. What are some of the hardships that the pioneers faced?

"Wilderness to West-town"

As Americans settled on the frontier, they changed the land to meet their needs and wants. The changes were small at first. A trapper might build a trading post to do business with Indians. A farmer might clear the land of trees and rocks.

These pioneers were often joined on the frontier by other people. Storekeepers, blacksmiths, miners, and ministers were just a few such people. These people needed churches, schools, and other buildings where they could work and live.

Could you have lived in the wilderness of the frontier? The game "Wilderness to West-town" will give you some idea. Pretend that you are a pioneer heading west. Like the pioneers, you will have to make some decisions along the trail. You'll know when you're supposed to decide. The trail will be marked like this:

To make the *best* decision, ask yourself "What do I know about the West and pioneers?" And, "What did *most* pioneers probably do?" Try the sample on this page. "Pack your grandma's grand piano in the wagon." Or, "Listen to the wagon master and leave much behind." On the game board, you will follow the trail marked by the sign. If you come to "Wagon wheel broke on the first rough road" you'll know you took the wrong trail. If you come to another decision, you'll know you made the *best* decision about grandma's piano!

Each time you make the best decision, give yourself a point. Your score below will tell you what kind of pioneer you would have made.

Pioneer Score

12–14
Great! Sew a "Trailblazer" award onto your deerskin coat.

9–11
Good job! You're alive and well in a growing community.

6–8
Ooops! You must have spent too much time digging for gold.

5
Forget it! Go back East!

Reviewing Chapter 12

Write your answers on paper. Do not write in the book.

Using Key Words

pioneer   frontier
reservation   annex
cede

Number your paper 1 to 5. Write a short meaning for each of the above key words.

Reviewing Main Ideas

Number your paper 1 to 6. Match the correct identification from List 2 with the proper term in List 1. Write the letter of the identification next to the proper number.

List 1

1. War with Mexico
2. Indian Resettlement Act
3. Lewis and Clark
4. Tecumseh
5. Marshall and Sutter
6. Annexation of Texas

List 2

a. tried to unite Indians against white settlers

b. forced Indians to move west of Mississippi River

c. became part of United States after it fought its own war of independence

d. discovery began a great migration to California

e. after this the United States gained the land that later became the states of New Mexico and Arizona

f. sent by Jefferson to explore land purchased in 1803

Thinking Things Over

Your family has just decided to move westward across the Mississippi River. Write a farewell letter to your best friend. Carefully explain the reasons why your family wants to move west. Explain how you feel about leaving the city and moving to the frontier.

Practicing Skills

Below is a map of the United States with three trails drawn on it. Match the trail name below with the trail on the map.

1. Santa Fe   2. Oregon   3. California

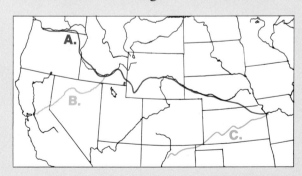

Chapter

13

Lesson 1 The Industrial Revolution
Lesson 2 That Funny Machine: A Play

Changing Ways of Life in the East

Between 1800 and 1860, the United States changed in many ways. You have already read about some important changes in the West. Large areas of land there were added to the United States. People moved from settled areas in the East to these western lands.

During these sixty years, there were also important changes in the East. **Factories** opened in New England. In the factories, people started to use machines to produce goods. Cities grew up around the factories because people wanted to be closer to their place of work.

Few factories opened in the South. And the cities of the South were smaller than those in New England. Yet, life also changed in the South. With a new machine called the cotton gin, the South produced more and more cotton. This increased the southerners' need for slaves. By 1860, the South had five times more slaves than in 1800.

Lesson 1 The Industrial Revolution

The ship moved steadily through the ocean waves. Its sails were filled with the wind. All three masts creaked under the strain. Salt spray misted against the twenty-one-year-old Englishman. He held onto a railing and watched the sun rise over the land that was going to be his new home: the United States.

The year was 1789. And it was a year of change for the United States. A new Constitution had been completed. A new government was trying to provide leadership.

The man at the rail was Samuel Slater. In his mind he carried a secret. His secret, like the Constitution, would change the United States forever.

factory, a building, or group of buildings where things are made by machines, or by hand.

Slater had memorized plans for making machines that could spin thread from raw cotton. He had to leave England in a disguise. It was illegal for the plans, or the people who knew of them, to leave England. England did not want to share its machines with the rest of the world.

In the 1750s, England had started to go through a big change. The change was in the nation's **technology**. Technology is the tools and knowledge that people use to make things that help them meet their needs and wants. England had started to become an **industrial** nation. It began to use machines to do work that used to be done by people or animals. Many of the machines were powered by water or steam.

Here is an example of the change. Before the 1750s, most of the cotton cloth in England was made by thousands of women working in their homes. After the 1750s, factory workers made cotton cloth with machines.

This new way of manufacturing cost a lot of money. Money that is used to build factories, machines, and tools is called **capital**. The capital for England's factories was provided by wealthy business people. These people joined together to form companies. Companies could afford to spend more money than individuals.

Workers in an early steel-making factory. Judging from the picture, how would you explain the working conditions?

The company idea worked. The machines made much more cloth than people could working in their homes. The cloth was sold in England and in other countries.

This big change in England's technology was called the Industrial Revolution. Slater brought some of the ideas of that revolution with him to the United States. In 1790, he and a partner started a cotton mill, or factory, in Pawtucket, Rhode Island. They made a lot of money from their mill. Soon, Slater started his own company. Other people copied his ideas.

The Factories at Lowell

By 1840, there were over twelve hundred clothing mills in the United States. Several companies built cotton and wool-making factories near each other on the banks of the Merrimack River in Massachusetts. Soon, there was a town there, then a city. The city was named Lowell, after Francis Cabot Lowell. He was the owner of one of the largest companies.

The Massachusetts countryside around Lowell had everything the factories needed: space, water power, and workers. Most of the workers at Lowell were young women. They were called the Lowell Girls.

The Lowell Girls and the men who worked with them spent twelve to fourteen hours each day, except Sundays, at the factories. The women stayed in boarding houses, often run by widows. They lived under strict rules both at the boarding houses and at the mills.

Not all the Lowell Girls loved their work. They believed they worked too long and hard for too little pay. Many of the women formed a group called the Female Labor Reform Association. The group tried to get the Massachusetts lawmakers to change conditions in the mills. The Lowell Girls did not succeed. But their efforts were important. They were the first group of women who tried to improve their working conditions.

In 1845, there were over fourteen thousand workers in the Lowell factories. Many other cities, like Lowell, grew up around factories. In 1800, only six out of every one hundred Americans lived in cities. By 1860, twenty out of every one hundred lived in cities. The graph at the right shows how the number of cities increased during those years.

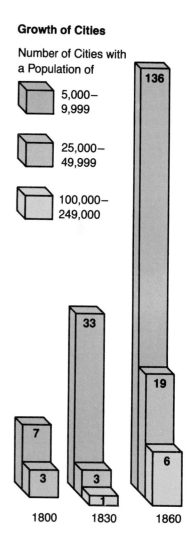

Growth of Cities

Number of Cities with a Population of

5,000–9,999

25,000–49,999

100,000–249,000

136

33

19

7

6

3

3

1

1800   1830   1860

People watching one of the first reapers in action. Reapers were machines that cut wheat much faster than people could do it by hand.

Machines Come to the Farm

The Industrial Revolution changed life on farms, too. Americans made new machines that helped farmers do their work quickly and easily. In 1834, Cyrus McCormick made a machine that cut wheat. Three years later, John Deere made a steel plow. These all helped farmers produce twice as much wheat and corn in 1859 as they did in 1839.

The Industrial Revolution changed the United States. At first, most of the changes took place in the northern states. Most of the factories and cities developed there. Farming remained the main way southerners made their living. These differences between the North and South caused two ways of living to develop in the country.

Checking Up

1. What was the Industrial Revolution?

2. What are some ways people's lives were changed by this revolution?

3. How did Samuel Slater bring the Industrial Revolution to the United States?

Lesson 2   That Funny Machine: A Play

The following play is based on the memory of Eliza F. Andrews of Georgia. Andrews knew members of the Greene family of Mulberry Grove and wrote in the 1870s about the invention of the cotton gin.

"That Funny Machine"

Characters:
Phineas Miller, manager of Mulberry Grove
Eli Whitney, a college graduate visiting in the South
Mrs. Catherine Greene, owner of Mulberry Grove
George Greene, a servant
A salesman

Scene one: place, Mulberry Grove, near Savannah, Georgia; time, 1793; stage is set up as a sitting room in the mansion at Mulberry Grove.

CATHERINE (*from off stage*): See Eli into the sitting room, Phineas.

(*Enter* PHINEAS MILLER *and* ELI WHITNEY.)

PHINEAS: How do you like Mulberry Grove, Eli?

ELI: I love it! This big house, the cotton fields—everything is beautiful.

PHINEAS: I hope you'll have the peace and quiet here you'll need to read the law.

ELI: It'll be perfect. Thanks again for letting me stay here while I study.

PHINEAS: It's nothing. We have all the room you'd ever need.

ELI: Only one thing bothers me. I love to tinker. You know, get things working right again. If you see me doing too much tinkering, stop me. If you don't, I'll never be a lawyer.

(*Enter* CATHERINE *shaking a watch that has stopped.*)

CATHERINE: Confound this watch! It's stopped again. And the nearest watchmaker is a day's ride into Savannah.

ELI: Here, let me look at it.

PHINEAS (*laughing*): Well, I see what you mean, Eli. You can't pass up a chance to tinker, can you?

(ELI *wanders out of the room, ignoring both* PHINEAS *and* CATHERINE.)

Scene two: The next morning in the same sitting room.

ELI (*entering*): Good morning! Good morning! It's so bright and cheerful! And here's a little gift for you (*handing* CATHERINE *her watch*).

CATHERINE (*listening to the watch tick*): Eli, you've fixed it!

PHINEAS: He fixed it all right. I saw his lamp burning into the night.

(*Enter a servant,* GEORGE GREENE.)

GEORGE: Master Miller, a seller of fine cloth is here to see you.

PHINEAS: Oh, send him away, George. I don't want to see anyone today.

CATHERINE: Phineas! Don't be that way. Let's look at his cloth. (*Enter the cloth* SALESMAN.)

CATHERINE: What have you to show me in fine cloth, sir? Do you have cotton?

SALESMAN: Not much. Only this. (*He hands a bolt of beautiful cotton cloth to* CATHERINE.)

PHINEAS and CATHERINE: How beautiful!

CATHERINE: I wish you had more of this cotton cloth.

SALESMAN: I'm sorry, Ma'am. But cotton's scarce. If only someone could invent a machine that would get those pesky cotton seeds out of the lint. He'd make a fortune, that's certain. I travel from plantation to plantation, and that's all I hear, "Do you have more cotton?" I've got to say "no" every time.

ELI: Invent a machine?

PHINEAS: You see, Eli, cotton can grow all over these parts. And we could pick all we need, what with our slaves and all. But in every cotton plant, there are seeds in the lint. They're sticky as maple syrup. We've got to get a slave to pick the seeds out one by one. You can't make money that way. I'd have to have an army of slaves.

CATHERINE: You're the very man.

ELI: Pardon me, Ma'am?

CATHERINE: You're the very man! You fixed my watch so well. I'll bet you could make such a machine.

SALESMAN: There's a fortune in it! (ELI *begins to stare out the window, thinking.*)

PHINEAS: No, Eli! You're not at it again, are you? What about reading the law? (ELI *ignores* PHINEAS *and walks from the room, staring ahead, deep in his thoughts.*)

Scene three: Some weeks later in the same sitting room. PHINEAS *and* CATHERINE *are sitting sipping tea.*

ELI (*rushing into the room carrying a large boxlike machine*): I've done it! I know I have. (ELI *dumps a bundle of raw cotton on the floor.*)

CATHERINE: Eli, my floor!

ELI (*ignoring* CATHERINE'S *words*): I've done it. I think I've made a little engine that will get you all the raw cotton you want. Without the seeds!

PHINEAS (*showing a great amount of interest*): Show me!

ELI: Here! This is how it works. You put the cotton in this box. Then you turn the handle. The wire fingers pull the cotton through the screen. The cotton lint goes through. But see what happens to the seeds. They're caught in the screen.

PHINEAS: This is amazing. If you've really done it, you're a rich man!

ELI: There's only one problem. I haven't found a way to get the lint out of the machine.

CATHERINE: You inventors! Can't see the forest for the trees. (*She goes to a drawer and takes out a clothes brush.*) Just brush the stuff off. (*She wipes the lint from the wire fingers with one sweep of the brush.*)

ELI: You've done it! My problem is solved! My model is complete!

PHINEAS: I have a feeling that this funny little machine is going to cause quite a stir.

A drawing of Whitney's cotton gin.

Cotton Becomes "King"

Eli Whitney's funny little machine did cause a stir. He and Phineas Miller formed a company to make bigger cotton engines, or "gins."

In much of the South, farmers gave up planting tobacco and other crops and started to grow cotton. In time, cotton became the South's most important crop. Look at the bar graph. The amount of raw cotton produced in the United States grew from 1800 to 1859.

The switch to cotton came at just the right time for southern planters. The War for Independence caused them to lose England as their biggest customer. By 1840, factories in the North and in England wanted as much southern cotton as they could get.

The switch to cotton meant that southern planters needed thousands of people to plant and pick the crops. The planters believed that they couldn't make money unless they had thousands of people who worked for only their food, housing, and clothing. The only people who fit this description were, of course, the slaves.

The planters in Georgia, North Carolina, and South Carolina made a lot of money growing cotton. Even so, they found it hard to give the cotton factories all the cotton they wanted.

More land, thought the planters, was needed. If they had more land, they could grow more cotton. If they had more cotton, they could sell more to the factories.

Some planters decided to move west. As the chart shows, a number of southern and western states came into the Union by 1845. In each of these states, planters forced black people to work as slaves.

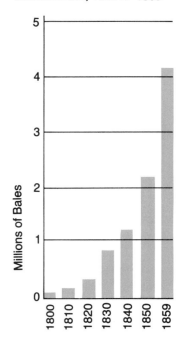

Cotton Produced in the United States, 1800 to 1859

(y-axis: Millions of Bales; x-axis: 1800, 1810, 1820, 1830, 1840, 1850, 1859)

New States, Southern Region, 1812 to 1845

State	Year entered the Union
Louisiana	1812
Mississippi	1817
Alabama	1819
Florida	1845
Texas	1845

Checking Up

1. The switch to cotton was good for white southern farmers. Why was it bad for slaves?

2. Why might the switch to cotton be good for New Englanders?

Building Social Studies Skills

Using a Line Graph

You have already seen how statistics, or number facts, can give you information on many things. Usually, a single statistic gives you a single idea.

> There were 2,060,000
> male farm workers in 1820.

This type of statistic is fine if you just want to know about farm workers in 1820. Perhaps you want to compare farm workers from 1820 to 1860. You might see the statistics this way:

American Male Farm Workers (1820 to 1860)	
Number	**Year**
2,060,000	1820
2,700,000	1830
3,700,000	1840
4,900,000	1850
6,200,000	1860

What is the important information in this small chart? To answer that, you will have to look at five numbers and five years.

You probably figured out that the number of male farm workers goes up over the forty years. You could have quickly seen this idea if the numbers had been on a line **graph**. A graph is a picture that shows how statistics change over time.

Look at the graph below. It uses the same statistics as the chart. What's the difference, then?

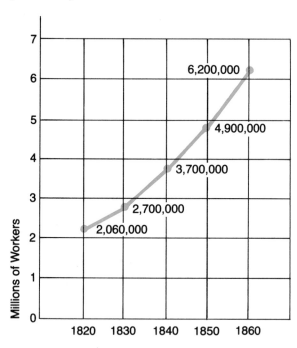

American Male Farm Workers
(1820-1860)

What's important in the chart are the individual numbers of farm workers. But you must read all the numbers to see how the number of workers changed over time. In the graph, the individual numbers have been joined by a blue line. The graph quickly shows how the number of workers changed over time. Reading from left to right, the blue line goes up. The number of farm workers increased over forty years.

How a Line Graph Is Made

The squares formed by lines crossing is called a grid. At the left edge of the grid is a column of numbers. They show the number of male farm workers. Each square stands for one million male farm workers.

Below the grid is another set of numbers. These numbers stand for the ten-year periods between 1820 and 1860. A dot is placed on the line that stands for 1820. That dot also stands for the number of men who worked on farms in that year. In 1820, it was a little more than two million. The same steps are followed for the years 1830, 1840, 1850, and 1860.

To make the graph even easier to read, a line is drawn from dot to dot. The line shows at a glance how the number of male farm workers changed over time.

If we want to compare one set of statistics with another, we can put two sets of dots on the same graph. Copy the graph "American Male Farm Workers" on a separate sheet of paper. Trace the line in one color.

Add the following statistics to the graph.

American Nonfarm Workers (1820 to 1860)

Number	Year
800,000	1820
1,100,000	1830
1,700,000	1840
2,700,000	1850
4,300,000	1860

Connect the dots with a different color than you used to show "American Male Farm Workers." Give your graph with two lines a title. Call it:

American Workers, Farm and Nonfarm (1820 to 1860)

Use your new graph to answer the following questions.

1. Were there more people who worked on farms or off farms in 1840?

2. Did the number of nonfarm workers increase or decrease over time?

3. The change in the number of nonfarm workers from 1820 to 1860 was _____.

4. There were _____ million more farm workers than nonfarm workers in 1850.

Reviewing Chapter 13

Write your answers on paper. Do not write in the book.

Using Key Words

technology   capital   graph
industrial   factory

Number your paper 1 to 5. Write a short meaning for each of the above key words.

Reviewing Main Ideas

Number your paper 1 to 5. Next to each number write the letter of the phrase which correctly completes the sentence.

1. Samuel Slater brought the Industrial Revolution to America when he
   a. invented the cotton gin.
   b. founded the city of Lowell.
   c. started a cotton factory.

2. The Lowell Girls were   **a.** founders of the city of Lowell.   **b.** women who worked in the early factories.   **c.** people who came to America from other countries.

3. In order to expand their cotton business, southern planters thought they needed   **a.** cheap slave labor.   **b.** more land in the North.   **c.** western factories to buy cotton.

4. In many southern states cotton got the name "King Cotton" because
   a. American cotton was so soft.   **b.** it was the South's main source of in-

come.   **c.** the king of England ordered it planted in colonial days.

5. The cotton gin was important because it   **a.** planted cotton seeds faster.
   b. helped pick cotton faster.   **c.** separated cotton lint from its seeds.

Thinking Things Over

Pretend that you are a young man or woman growing up on a large farm in South Carolina. You have gone on vacation to the North. Write a letter home describing how the people live their daily lives.

Practicing Skills

Draw a line graph that shows:

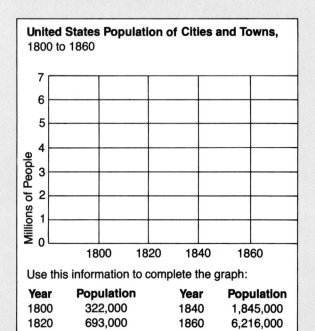

United States Population of Cities and Towns, 1800 to 1860

Use this information to complete the graph:

Year	Population	Year	Population
1800	322,000	1840	1,845,000
1820	693,000	1860	6,216,000

Transportation and Communication

In 1800, the main means of **transportation** on land were walking, riding on animals, or riding in carriages or wagons pulled by animals. On water, people traveled in boats or on rafts that were pushed with poles, pulled by ropes, paddled by oars, or blown along by the wind.

In 1800, the main means of **communication** were speaking to each other in person or writing letters to each other. People sometimes got information from newspapers and broadsides. **Broadsides** are single sheets of paper on which information is printed. They can be sold, handed out to people, or nailed to posts and walls.

Up through 1860, people used the old means of transportation and communication. After that they began using a few new ones as well. They traveled in trains and steamboats. They also found a way to communicate with each other across the United States in seconds instead of in days.

Lesson 1 Changes in Transportation

In the early 1800s, it was not easy to travel west. People had to make their own trails in the wilderness. But the urge to go west was strong. Between 1800 and 1825, Americans built thousands of miles of roads.

The major road built during the 1800s was the National, or Cumberland, Road. It began in Cumberland, Maryland, and went through parts of West Virginia, Pennsylvania, Ohio, and Indiana. The building went on for years. By 1850, the National Road went all the way to Vandalia in southern Illinois. See the map on page 227.

The National Road made travel west much easier than ever before. People rode in wagons that bumped along on a

Facts and Figures

Do you remember the last time your parents paid a toll on the highway? It is not a new habit for Americans. They have been paying tolls for over a hundred years. Like today, the money collected was used to keep up the road. Here are some charges you might have paid in 1809 along a toll road in New York.

20 sheep	8¢
20 hogs	8¢
20 cattle	18¢
20 horses	18¢
Horse and rider	5¢
Two-horse stage	12$\frac{1}{2}$¢
Four-horse stage	18$\frac{1}{2}$¢
Four-horse wagon	75¢
Six-horse wagon	$1.00

Why are there different tolls for different things? Is this still done on toll roads today?

narrow path. The path had been leveled by pick and shovel. Then pieces of stone were scattered on the road.

People who traveled to the United States from England and France wondered how Americans could call this bumpy path a road. But they had not seen the forest that covered the land before the road was built. If they had, they might have thought of the National Road as a smooth highway to the West.

Between 1825 and 1860, Americans tested another means of transportation on the land. It was the railroad train. Americans liked the railroads. The strength and speed of the steam engine seemed to say something about the people that built and used them.

By 1860, Americans had put down over thirty thousand miles of track. Most of those miles were in the part of the country to the north of the Ohio River. One railroad line even went as far west as Independence, Missouri.

Americans also traveled west by water. They floated on rafts or keelboats. But they had to go down rivers that happened to flow in the direction they wanted to go.

Americans also built **canals** to connect natural waterways. Canals are waterways that are dug across land. Canals often did away with the need to travel on land for hundreds of miles at a time.

The most famous of these canals opened in 1825. It was the Erie Canal. Its 363 miles connected Albany and Buffalo, New York. See the map on page 227. The Erie Canal

By the Way

By 1860, America's loco-motives were steaming along over thirty-thousand miles of track. Thirty years before that, many people thought railroads wouldn't even have enough steam to beat a horse.

The *Tom Thumb* was one of the nation's first locomo-tives. It traveled at a speed of about ten miles an hour. In 1830, the *Tom Thumb* was matched against a horse-drawn car.

The "iron-horse" seemed a sure winner for most of the nine-mile race. But it broke down! The horse trotted across the finish line to the cheers of the crowd.

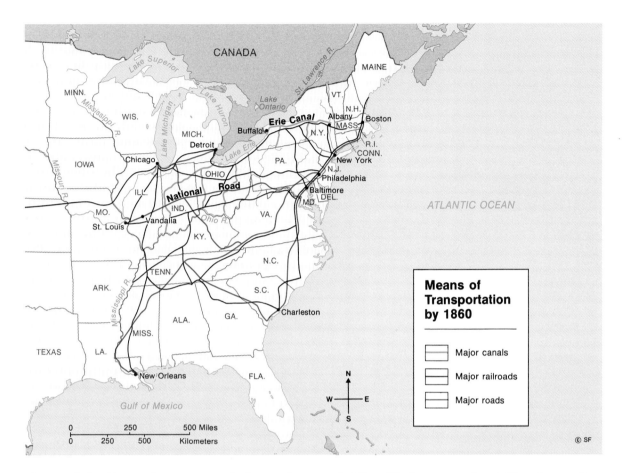

Means of
Transportation
by 1860

Major canals

Major railroads

Major roads

changed the lives of many people in, and around, New York. Passengers could travel between Buffalo and New York City in six days instead of twenty. Two thousand pounds of grain could be shipped the same distance for $5 instead of $100.

Robert Fulton helped make another giant improvement in water transportation. He found a way to use a machine to push a boat upstream, against the flow of a river. In 1807, Fulton made a test run up the Hudson River in a steam-powered boat called the *Clermont*. The trip was a success.

These boats carried passengers and goods up and down the rivers of America. By 1860, steamboats chugged along the Mississippi, Ohio, and Missouri rivers. They could be found on many smaller rivers as well.

The changes in transportation made it easier for people to move west. In 1810, only one out of every seven Americans lived west of the Appalachian Mountains. By 1860 about one out of every three did.

(above) How far was Boston from Charleston?

Rafts like this were used on the Ohio and Mississippi rivers.

227

A keelboat was a large boat with a covered deck and a V-shaped bottom. The keelboats shown above are carrying goods along the Erie Canal. What appears to be the boats' source of power?

The changes also made it easier to trade goods and to visit people living far away. Tools made in New England factories could be sent cheaply and quickly to other areas of the nation. In turn, it was easier and less costly for farmers to ship their crops to the urban areas in the East. Changes in transportation helped tie a growing nation together.

Checking Up

1. What are some different ways Americans improved their transportation from 1800 to 1860?

2. How could changes in transportation also change the way people lived?

3. How did changes in transportation help the United States grow?

Lesson 2   Changes in Communication

Americans of the early 1800s continued to use the same means of communication that people had used for thousands of years. But they also wanted to speed up their means of communication. At first, this meant trying to get the mail from one place to another faster than before.

In the East, some mail was carried quickly by railroads. However, there were no railroads joining the East and West until 1869. One way to get mail to the new settlements in the West was by stagecoach.

John Butterfield started the first stagecoach line between the Mississippi River and the West Coast. In 1858, Butterfield's Overland Mail Company was carrying mail from St. Louis to San Francisco. The distance was almost 2,800 miles. The trip took almost twenty-four days.

Twenty-four days for mail delivery was fast in the 1850s. But some people wanted to deliver the mail faster. In 1860, the Pony Express was started with this in mind. The Pony Express delivered mail between St. Joseph, Missouri, and San Francisco, California, in ten and a half days.

The Thomas Gilcrease Institute of American History and Art, Tulsa, Oklahoma

NOTICE
to Stage Coach Riders:

In cold weather don't ride with tight-fitting boots

Don't growl at the food at the station

Don't point out where murders have been committed

Don't grease your hair, because travel is dusty

Don't imagine for a moment that you are going on a picnic

(above) A broadside for stagecoach riders. (below) The transfer of mail at a Pony Express station.

The Pony Express was faster for two reasons. As the map below shows, the Pony Express route was almost eight hundred miles shorter than the stagecoach route. The Pony Express also didn't need heavy stagecoaches. It just needed ponies.

The Pony Express company set up stations every ten miles along its route. It hired hundreds of young men to ride as fast as they could from station to station carrying the mail. At each station the riders changed horses in seconds. Then they were off again at top speed. After three or four changes of horses, new riders took over.

Most of the riders were in their teens or early twenties. One of the most famous riders was William Cody. Also known as "Buffalo Bill," he was only fifteen when he rode for the Pony Express. Cody once set a record by riding 320 miles in less than twenty-two hours.

What symbols did the artist use to represent the three means of communication? What colors?

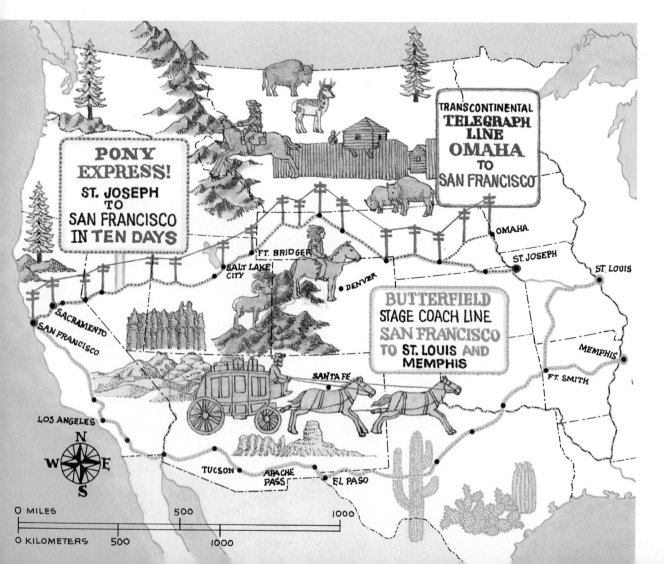

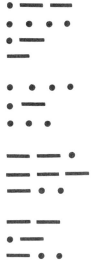

Like the Overland Mail Company, the Pony Express did not last very long. After eighteen months, the Pony Express was replaced by the telegraph. The telegraph cut the time of communication between Missouri and California from ten days to a few seconds.

The telegraph was first shown to be useful over a long distance in 1844. In that year, the inventor of the telegraph, Samuel Morse, tapped out a message in a code he had made up. The message traveled along a wire as a group of long and short bursts of electricity. The wire was hung from hundreds of poles that went from Washington, D.C., to Baltimore, Maryland. That was a distance of about forty miles. By 1861, telegraph wires stretched from New York City to San Francisco. Locate the telegraph line on the map on page 230.

Newspapers also helped improve communications. The number of newspapers in the nation greatly increased in the first half of the nineteenth century. In 1790, there were only ninety-two papers printed regularly. By 1860, there were almost four thousand.

New printing presses helped produce better newspapers faster and for less money. More and more people were able to have their own copy of at least one daily paper. This included people in the West. By 1853, San Francisco had twelve daily papers. By 1860, Denver had three.

How did Samuel Morse send a message through a thin wire? He did it by putting the message in code. Each letter of the alphabet was changed into a dot, dash, or combination of the two. The code could be sent through the wire as bursts of electricity. A very short burst was a dot. A longer burst was a dash.

What did Morse's first message say? Above is the message in Morse's code. You can probably find the entire code in an encyclopedia. Then you'll be able to figure out the message. The message is four words long.

New Yorkers discuss the discovery of gold in California. What means of communication do you see in this painting? (A detail of *California News* by William Sidney Mount, 1850.)

Like transportation, communication was going through a revolution in the 1800s. People could send and receive news faster and for less money than ever before. Changes in communication helped tie the growing nation together.

Checking Up

1. What are some of the ways that people of the 1800s sent information to one another?

2. How was the telegraph a revolution in communication?

3. Why is it important for a large nation to have fast means of communication?

KIDS IN COMMUNICATION

Communication is the sharing and understanding of ideas. By communicating, people learn about friends, neighbors, and the world. They also learn about themselves. Newspapers, television, and computers are machines, or the products of machines, that help people communicate.

These means of communication are not just for adults, though. Today, young people produce their own newspapers, TV shows, and computer programs. Sometimes they do this to make money. Sometimes they do it to help others communicate. Sometimes young people just want to learn skills for a future job.

Kids in Newspapers

Gretchen Haber, of Arroyo Grande, California, runs her own newspaper called *Pike Press*. She feels it's a great way to bring her neighborhood together. The people who buy her newspaper like to know what's new in the neighborhood. They like to see stories about themselves and their families.

For Gretchen, *Pike Press* is also a good way to learn about writing. She knows her writing must be fair and truthful. "This is important because you have to be sensitive to other people's feelings," says Gretchen.

Pike Press has also taught Gretchen a lot about business. Right now, it takes about

twenty hours and $23 to produce an issue. From her subscribers and the sale of ads, Gretchen only earns about $23. Breaking-even doesn't bother her, though. "Running my own newspaper has taught me a lot of things that I'll need to know when I begin my adult career in journalism [working for a newspaper or a magazine]."

Kids in Television

More people watch television today than ever before. But in Sun Prairie, Wisconsin, young people do more than watch. Since 1978, young people aged nine to thirteen have produced their own news show called KIDS–4. The show is "dedicated to—and for the use of—children, and children only."

233

KIDS–4 has taught these young people what goes into the making of a good TV news show. First, they study the news. Then they decide what is interesting and important. Finally, this young news staff plans the best way to present the news to Sun Prairie viewers.

The news program does not always run smoothly on KIDS–4. But the young people are still proud of their work. They know that the triumphs and goofs are theirs alone. They also know that they are providing a service to their community. By using cameras, film, and sound, the KIDS–4 news staff communicates with a large number of people.

Kids in Computers

What exactly is a computer? Very simply, a computer is a tool that solves problems. But computers can't solve anything by themselves. They need to be programmed. That is, computers have to be told what to do, and how to do it. Today, many computers are being told what to do and how to do it by young people.

Two of the youngest "programmers" are Steve Grimm and Nikolai Weaver. They were only twelve when they wrote "Filewriter." "Filewriter" is a computer program. It is a set of orders for a computer to follow. "Filewriter" tells the computer how to help people take care of their money. "Filewriter" sells for around $25.

All of these young people are helping other people to communicate. And, what they learn now may help them have a career in communications later.

Reviewing Chapter 14

Write your answers on paper. Do not write in the book.

Using Key Words

transportation   **broadside**
communication   **canal**

Number your paper 1 to 4. Write a short meaning for each of the above key words.

Reviewing Main Ideas

Some of the sentences below are true and some are false. Number your paper from 1 to 7 and write *true* or *false* by each statement.

1. The National Road began in Vandalia, Illinois, and ended in California.

2. Most of the early railroads in America were built north of the Ohio River.

3. Improvements in transportation helped many Americans move west of the Appalachian Mountains.

4. In the 1850s the fastest way to send a letter from Missouri to California was by railroad.

5. Pony Express riders rode the same routes used by stagecoaches.

6. The Pony Express was put out of business by the Butterfield Overland Mail Company.

7. Changes in transportation and communication helped unite the country.

Thinking Things Over

Pretend you are a newspaper printer in the 1800s. Write a broadside that describes one of the following events. You may draw a picture or map on the broadside.

a. First use of the steamboat

b. Beginning of the Pony Express

c. First use of the telegraph

Practicing Skills

Below are drawings of several means of transportation used from 1800 to 1860. Number your paper 1 to 7. Next to the number, write the name of the means of transportation you see here.

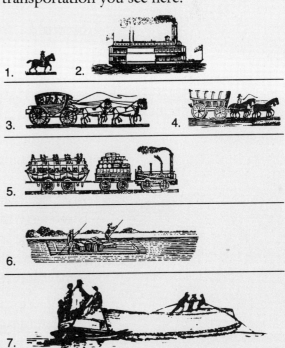

15

Conflict Between North and South

Imagine that you are living back around 1860. How would you describe the United States at that time?

You might say that the nation was going through many changes. The nation was growing as it gained new lands in the West. It was also becoming more industrial. The nation was using more and more machines to manufacture products. The nation was also becoming smaller in one way. Improved means of communication and transportation were helping to tie the people together.

You would be right if you described the nation this way. But you would be telling only half the story. For just as the nation was being tied together, it was also being torn apart. By 1860, the United States was split between northern and southern states. And **slavery** was a major cause of that split.

slavery, the condition of being a slave; the custom of owning slaves.

Lesson 1 What Was Slavery Like?

Before you read what it was like to live as a slave, study the following information. The line graphs will show you the number of free blacks and slaves in the North and South. The statistics will show you the number of southern slaveowners. The map will show where most slaves lived. Which of the following statements are true or false for the year 1860?

• Most free blacks lived in the North.
• There were more slaves in the South than in the North.
• Most white southern families owned slaves.
• There were no slaves in the North.
• Some states had more slaves than others.

This information is important because it shows the number of free blacks and slaves in the North and South. It also

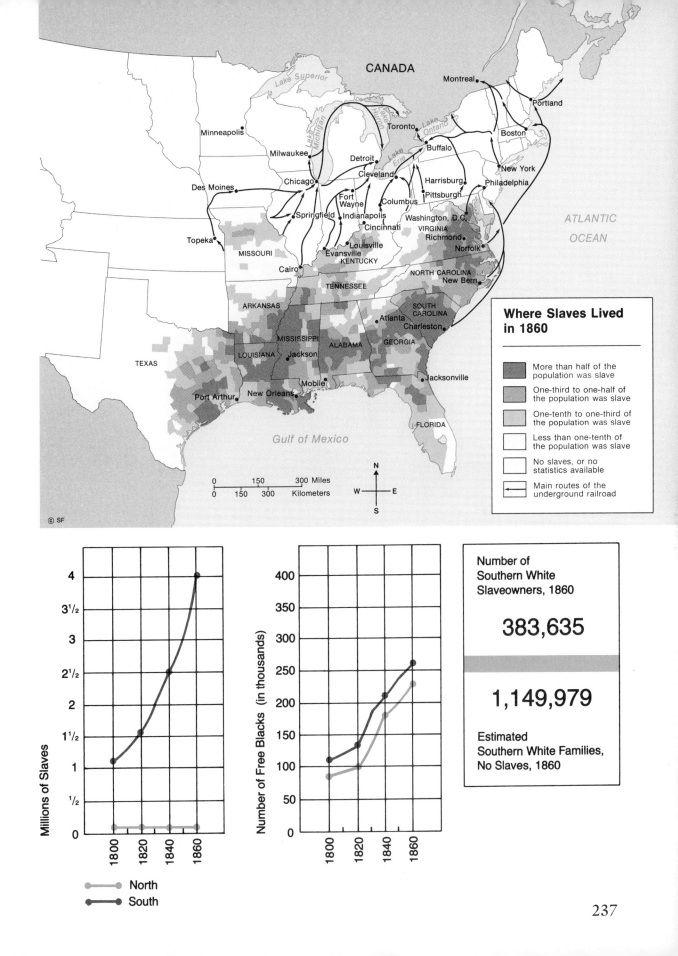

CANADA

Montreal

Portland

Lake Superior

Minneapolis

Milwaukee

Detroit

Toronto

Lake Ontario

Buffalo

Boston

Lake Michigan

Chicago

Cleveland

Lake Erie

New York

Des Moines

Fort Wayne

Columbus

Harrisburg

Philadelphia

Springfield

Indianapolis

Pittsburgh

Topeka

Cincinnati

Washington, D.C.

ATLANTIC OCEAN

MISSOURI

Evansville

Louisville

VIRGINIA

Richmond

Norfolk

Cairo

KENTUCKY

TENNESSEE

NORTH CAROLINA

New Bern

ARKANSAS

SOUTH CAROLINA

Atlanta

Charleston

MISSISSIPPI

ALABAMA

GEORGIA

LOUISIANA

Jackson

TEXAS

Mobile

Jacksonville

Port Arthur

New Orleans

FLORIDA

Gulf of Mexico

0   150   300 Miles
0   150   300   Kilometers

N
W — E
S

© SF

Where Slaves Lived in 1860

- More than half of the population was slave
- One-third to one-half of the population was slave
- One-tenth to one-third of the population was slave
- Less than one-tenth of the population was slave
- No slaves, or no statistics available
- Main routes of the underground railroad

Millions of Slaves

4
3½
3
2½
2
1½
1
½
0

1800 1820 1840 1860

Number of Free Blacks (in thousands)

400
350
300
250
200
150
100
50
0

1800 1820 1840 1860

North
South

Number of Southern White Slaveowners, 1860

383,635

1,149,979

Estimated Southern White Families, No Slaves, 1860

237

shows where most of the slaves lived. It does not, however, explain how slaves lived and worked, or how they were treated.

A Slave's Life

From 1800 to 1860, most slaves worked on cotton plantations in the South. They did every kind of job except manage the plantation. Some of the slaves worked in the homes of white slaveholders. There they cooked, cleaned, and raised the slaveholder's children. Others worked as carpenters, blacksmiths, and at other skilled jobs.

Most slaves worked all day planting, raising, or harvesting cotton. They bundled the cotton for shipment to the mills in the northern United States or in England.

Southern slaves did many of the same jobs as whites in both the North and South. Yet there was a difference. Slaves rarely got paid for their work. They received whatever food, clothing, and housing their owners decided to give them.

Sometimes slaves lived in the same houses as their owners. But usually, they lived in cabins away from the homes of the slaveholders.

The lives of slaves and free people differed in other ways, too. Slaves could not marry without their owner's approval. Even with that approval, slaves could not be sure their families would be kept together. Husbands, wives, and children could be sold separately to new owners.

Slaves needed passes to travel from place to place. They usually were not allowed to gather together in groups larger than five. Slaves were not even supposed to be taught how to read or write.

How did slaves feel about their treatment? Here is how two people who had been slaves answered this question:

"I never knew what it was to rest. I just worked all the time from morning till late at night. I had to do everything there was to do on the outside. Work in the field, chop wood, hoe corn, till sometime I felt like my back surely would break. . . .

Old Master would whip us good if we did anything he didn't like. . . . I've took a thousand lashings in my day. Sometimes my poor old body was sore for a week."

—*Sarah Gudger*

"Black folks had to go through thick and thin in slavery time, with little food most of the time, with just enough clothing to make out with. Our houses were built of logs and covered with slabs. . . .

We worked from sun to sun. . . . We ate frozen meat and bread many times in cold weather. After the day's work in the fields was over we had a task of picking the seed from cotton till we had two ounces of lint or spin two ounces of cotton on a spinning wheel."

—*Andrew Boone*

Checking Up

1. List at least three states which seemed to have more slaves than other states.

2. Describe the way of life of most slaves.

3. Why would slaves need to learn to keep their ideas about slavery to themselves?

Lesson 2   The Fight to End Slavery

Thomas Jefferson once said about slavery: "I tremble [shake] when I remember that God is just [fair]." Even though Jefferson owned slaves, he knew that slavery was wrong. He feared that the United States would be hurt someday because it allowed some of its people to own others. Many Americans in the North and South agreed with Jefferson. They tried to **abolish**, or end slavery.

The Antislavery Movement

From the 1820s to the 1860s, many blacks and whites worked together. They spoke, wrote, and acted against slavery. They wanted the United States government to abolish slavery. These people were called abolitionists. By 1850, the movement had about 200,000 members.

The abolitionists were led by a number of people. Some, such as David Walker, William Lloyd Garrison, and Frederick Douglass wanted immediate change. They wanted slavery ended at once.

Walker, a black abolitionist, told slaves to strike violently if they were not freed. Garrison printed a newspaper called the *Liberator*. In it, he spoke out against northerners who did not try to help free the slaves. Douglass, an ex-slave, told crowds what it was like to be freed from slavery.

A number of women were leaders of the abolitionist movement. Angelina and Sarah Grimké were daughters of a southern slaveholder. They left their home in South Carolina to speak out against slavery. Harriet Tubman, a runaway slave, helped over three hundred slaves escape. She was a

(far left) William Lloyd Garrison, (center) Frederick Douglass, (below) Harriet Tubman.

"conductor" on the "underground railroad." This really wasn't a railroad. And it wasn't underground. It was abolitionists who secretly hid runaways in their "stations," their homes and barns. Harriet Beecher Stowe, a writer, also worked to abolish slavery. She wrote a book called *Uncle Tom's Cabin*. Her characters made the horrors of slavery come alive for many people who had never seen it.

Rebellion and Resistance

Many slaves did what they could to fight against slavery. Some openly rebelled. In 1801, a few Virginia slaves fought to gain their freedom. Again in 1822, a group of slaves led by Denmark Vesey rebelled in South Carolina. Finally, in 1831, Nat Turner of Virginia led another rebellion.

Most slaves were not in a position to rebel or run away. But they still found ways to **resist**, or fight, their owners. Many resisted by doing as little work as possible. This would cause the slaveowner to lose money. Some slaves broke tools

or damaged crops in "accidents." Others pretended not to understand directions.

Naturally, most slaves tried to avoid making their owners angry. After all, owners had life or death power over slaves.

Instead of speaking out against their owners, most slaves expressed their feelings in stories and songs. Some of these stories were serious. Others, such as this song, made fun of their owners.

(top left) A runaway's brief freedom is about to end. (lower left) The underground railroad at work.

THE BLUE-TAIL FLY

Jim crack corn, I don't care,
Jim crack corn, I don't care,
Jim crack corn, I don't care,
Ole Master's gone away.

When I was young I used to wait
On Master and hand him the plate,
And pass the bottle when he get dry
And brush away the blue-tail fly.
Jim crack corn, I don't care, etc.

And when he ride in the afternoon,
I follow with a hickory broom;
The pony being very shy,
When bitten by the blue-tail fly.
Jim crack corn, I don't care, etc.

One day he ride around the farm;
The flies so numerous they did swarm;
One chance to bite him on the thigh,

The devil take that blue-tail fly.
Jim crack corn, I don't care, etc.

The pony run, he jump and pitch,
And tumble Master in the ditch.
He died, and the jury wondered why;
The verdict was the blue-tail fly.
Jim crack corn, I don't care, etc.

They laid him under a persimmon tree;
His epitaph is there to see:
"Beneath this stone I'm forced to lie,
All by the means of a blue-tail fly.
Jim crack corn, I don't care, etc.

Ole Master gone, now let him rest;
They say all things are for the best.
I never forget till the day I die,
Ole Master and that blue-tail fly.
Jim crack corn, I don't care, etc.

Checking Up

1. What were the abolitionists trying to do?

2. Why might people be likely to listen when Frederick Douglass and Harriet Tubman spoke against slavery?

3. How did slaves resist their owners?

Lesson 3 "A house divided against itself . . ."

Slavery–the word itself divided the people and the country. But in the 1800s, other things also divided the nation. The northern part of the country was becoming industrial. Cities and factories were changing the look of the land. The southern part of the country, however, stayed agricultural. It came to place greater importance on a single crop, cotton.

The North and the South were also divided over a special tax called a **tariff**. A tariff is a tax on imported products. People who buy products made in other countries pay an extra amount caused by the tax.

Manufacturers in the North wanted the tariff. The tax would keep people from buying goods made outside the United States. The tariff would help northern manufacturers sell their goods.

The South disliked the tariff. It had few factories of its own. The South had to import manufactured goods or buy the goods from the North. If the South bought goods from the North, the North would become rich and powerful. If the South bought goods made outside the United States, it would have to pay the tariff.

The South disliked the tax for another reason, too. If other nations did not sell their products in the United States, they might get angry. The other nations might refuse to buy southern cotton. Northerners didn't have to worry about other nations, said the South. They had plenty of **markets**, or places to sell their goods, right in the United States.

States' Rights

Southern leaders tried to defend the rights of their states. They argued that the national government should not have the power to pass laws that favored the North over the South. They said that each state should have the right to decide whether or not to obey certain laws passed by the national government.

Many northern leaders said the **states' rights** idea would weaken or destroy the nation. They felt that the Union would fall apart if each state could decide to obey or disobey national laws.

Burning and "Bleeding Kansas."

Problems in the West

The settling of the new land in the West also divided the nation. Northerners wanted the West to be settled by farmers and other free workers. Southerners wanted to start more plantations in the West. They wanted to use slave labor there.

In 1820, Congress settled the debate for a time. Missouri wanted to enter the Union as a slave state. This would have given the South twelve slave states to the North's eleven free states. This would also have given the South more voting power in Congress. The North agreed to let Missouri become a slave state. They agreed to this with the understanding that Maine would enter the Union as a free state.

Congress also decided to divide the West to avoid future problems. Above a certain line of latitude, people could not own slaves. Below the line they could.

Between 1820 and 1848, six new states entered the Union. Three were slave states and three were free. The nation seemed to have solved its problem in the West.

Let the People Decide

In 1848, however, the United States defeated Mexico in a war. New land was added to the United States. See the map on page 201. The question was asked, what should be done with this new land?

Some said that the latitude line should be followed. It had worked for twenty-eight years, they pointed out. Why not use it again? Another group said that slavery should not be allowed *anywhere* in this new land. A third group said that it should be allowed *everywhere*. A fourth group suggested that people in new states, wherever they were located, should make up their own minds about slavery.

Congress passed a law that put this last idea to work. For a number of years it seemed to help. Then, in 1854, the idea was tested in Kansas. The people of Kansas asked to vote on whether Kansas would be a free or slave state.

People against slavery moved to Kansas in large numbers. Others, from slave states such as Missouri, also entered Kansas. Fights broke out. People were killed. Before long, people did not just speak of Kansas. They called it "Bleeding Kansas."

The problem of slavery in the West seemed to tear the nation apart. A young lawyer from Illinois expressed the fears of many people when he said,

66A house divided against itself cannot stand. I believe this government cannot endure [last], . . . half slave and half free. . . . It will become all one thing, or all the other.99

The speaker, Abraham Lincoln, ran for President in 1860 and won. But all Americans did not want Lincoln to be their leader. Many whites in the South felt Lincoln would take away their power in government and their slaves, too. They prepared to fight for what they believed in.

Abraham Lincoln and Stephen Douglas debate the issue of slavery during the 1858 Illinois Senate race. Douglas is sitting to the left of Lincoln. Lincoln lost the election, but gained attention across the country for his views. This helped him get elected President in 1860.

Checking Up

1. How did the idea of a tariff divide the country?

2. How did the North and South disagree over how the West should be settled?

3. What did Lincoln mean when he said, "A house divided against itself cannot stand"?

Write your answers on paper. Do not write in the book.

Using Key Words

market   **abolish**   **states' rights**
resist   **tariff**   **slavery**

Number your paper 1 to 6. Write a short meaning for each of the above key words.

Reviewing Main Ideas

Some of the sentences below are true and some are false. Number your paper 1 to 5 and write either *true* or *false* by each number.

1. There were no slaves in the North.

2. Most white families in the South did not own slaves.

3. Some slaves managed plantations for white owners.

4. The abolitionists wanted slavery to end immediately.

5. The underground railroad was an organized escape plan for runaway slaves.

Thinking Things Over

Listed below are ideas held by people who lived in the South or in the North in the 1850s. Number your paper 1 to 5. Write an "S" if it is a southern idea or an "N" if it is a northern idea.

1. There should be high taxes on manufactured goods that came to America.

2. In order to make money, we must have markets throughout the world to sell crops.

3. Each state has a right to agree or disagree with national laws.

4. Slavery should be expanded into new western states.

5. The nation can grow strong if more factories are built.

Practicing Skills

Write 5 *true-false* questions which can be answered using the bar graph below.

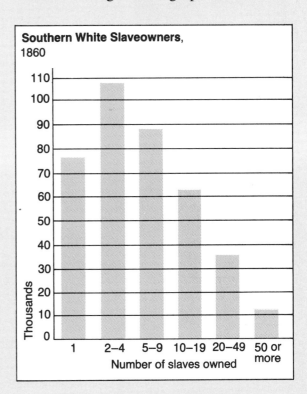

Southern White Slaveowners, 1860

Thousands (y-axis: 0 to 110)
Number of slaves owned (x-axis: 1, 2–4, 5–9, 10–19, 20–49, 50 or more)

16   Lesson 1   The North and South at War
      Lesson 2   People in the Civil War

The Civil War

After Abraham Lincoln won the presidential election of 1860, the country moved steadily towards war. The list of events below shows how the North and South became even more divided.

(top) Abraham Lincoln.
(bottom) Jefferson Davis.

- **November 6, 1860**   Abraham Lincoln elected President of the United States
- **December 20, 1860**   South Carolina legislature voted to leave the Union
- **January 9 to February 1, 1861**   Mississippi, Florida, Alabama, Georgia, Louisiana, and Texas joined South Carolina. They soon set up a new nation called the Confederate States of America
- **February 18, 1861**   Jefferson Davis became President of the Confederate States (also called the Confederacy)
- **March 4, 1861**   Abraham Lincoln sworn in as President of the United States

During these months, the country seemed to simmer like a pot on a hot stove. Everyone knew it would not take much to make the pot boil over. People wondered whether the North or the South would begin the fight.

Lesson 1   The North and South at War

At first light on the morning of April 12, 1861, the American **Civil War** began. A civil war is a struggle between people of the same country. What was it that made the pot boil over?

It can be said that both the North and the South started the Civil War. On that morning in 1861, the Confederacy opened fire on Fort Sumter, a Union fort. The Confederacy attacked because President Lincoln tried to send supplies to

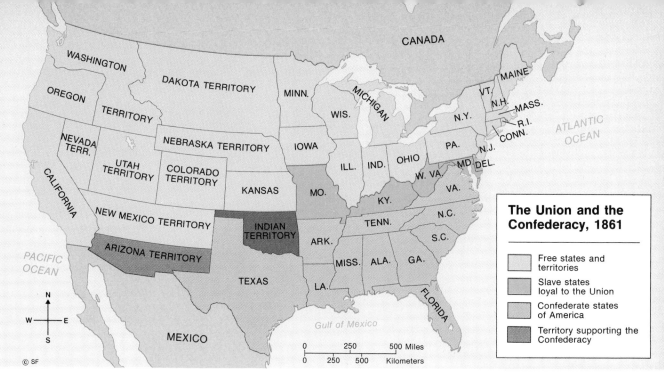

Refer to the map above to name the Confederate and Union states. Did most of the western territories support the Union or the Confederacy?

the fort. The Confederacy could not allow this to happen. They felt the fort was on Confederate land. The fort was located in the harbor of Charleston, South Carolina.

Over the next month, Virginia, Tennessee, North Carolina, and Arkansas joined the Confederacy. Some slave states located between the free states and the cotton states remained in the Union. These were Delaware, Maryland, Kentucky, and Missouri. Part of Virginia also stayed with the Union. It became a separate state called West Virginia. Look at the map above to see how the nation was divided.

Advantages and Disadvantages

For four years, the Union and Confederate armies fought each other. The map on page 250 shows some of the major battles. During the early years of the war, the Confederate armies often beat the Union armies. This seems to have happened for two reasons. The first reason was that the Confederacy had great military leaders. Robert E. Lee, Jeb Stuart, and "Stonewall" Jackson were such leaders. The second reason had to do with why the South was fighting. The South was fighting for its freedom. It wanted to be independent of the North. This made the South fight hard.

Great military leaders and a strong reason for fighting couldn't stop the South's real enemy, though. And that enemy was time. As the war dragged on, the South grew

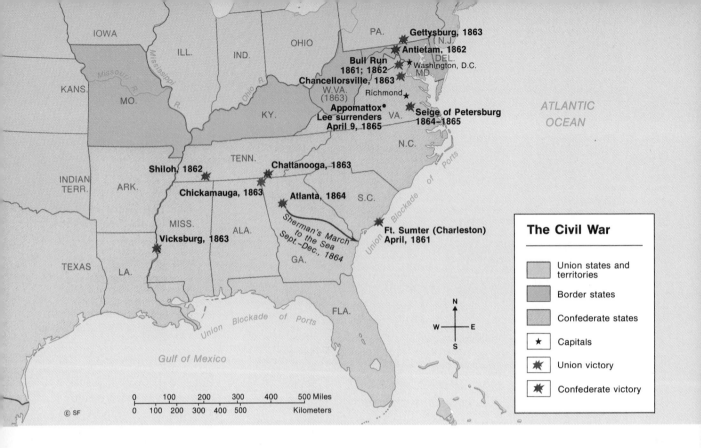

The map above shows some of the major battles of the war. In which state did the Battle of Gettysburg take place? Locate Appomattox where the war ended.

weaker. The North, however, had many things needed to win a long war. The North's factories, food supplies, railroads, and large population all helped defeat the South.

A major change in the war in 1864 also helped defeat the South. General Ulysses S. Grant was placed in charge of the Union armies. Grant had won many important battles earlier in the war. That is why President Lincoln put him in charge. Lincoln felt that Grant was the general who could beat the important Confederate leader, General Robert E. Lee.

The War Ends

Grant's army did not always beat Lee's. But Grant's army slowly wore down Lee's forces. At last, on April 9, 1865, Lee surrendered his army in Virginia. Lee turned over his sword to Grant at a place called Appomattox Courthouse.

The war was over. Americans on both sides breathed a sigh of relief. The war had cost the North and the South so much. Over 600,000 Americans were killed. Another 200,000 were wounded. Cities were destroyed. Farms were burned. Families were broken. And worst of all, the nation was torn in two.

(far right) General George E. Pickett's Confederate forces charge Union troops during the Battle of Gettysburg in July, 1863. Pretend for a moment that you are a newspaper reporter. How would you describe this type of fighting?

250

The destruction in Richmond, Virginia.

Checking Up

1. What did the South do that brought the nation close to war in 1860? What did President Lincoln do that forced the South to attack Fort Sumter?

2. What reason did the Confederacy have for fighting? What reason do you think the Union had for fighting?

3. How did the North's advantages help them?

4. What are your feelings on this statement? "No one ever really wins a civil war. Both sides are losers."

Lesson 2   People in the Civil War

In all, more than one and a half million men joined the
Union army. A little over one million joined the Confederate
army. On both sides, most soldiers were men, white, and under twenty-one years of age. Over a hundred thousand were
under sixteen years of age. Of these, there were hundreds of
drummer boys below the age of thirteen. The following song
is about one such drummer boy.

The Drummer Boy of Shiloh

Slowly

Words and Music by Will Shakespeare Hays

1. On Shi - loh's dark and blood-y ground The dead and wound - ed lay; A - mongst them was a drum-mer boy, Who beat the drum that day. A wound - ed sol - dier held him up His drum was by his side; He clasp'd his hands, then rais'd his eyes, And prayed be-fore he died. He clasp'd his hands, then rais'd his eyes, And prayed be - fore he died. 2. Look died!

2.
"Look down upon the battle field,
  Oh, Thou, our Heavenly Friend!
Have mercy on our sinful souls!"
  The soldiers cried "A-men!"
For gathered 'round a little group,

Each brave man knelt and cried;
They listened to the drummer boy,
  Who prayed before he died.
(Repeat last two lines)

253

The black 54th Massachusetts Regiment leads an attack against Confederate troops in July 1863.

The Battle of Shiloh was fought for two days in April of 1862. Over twenty thousand men were killed or wounded there. The battle made people realize something about the Civil War. It was not going to be an easy war to fight. A few people began to think that it would probably last a long time. This was a shock for many people. When the war started, most people thought it would be over quickly.

There were other things about the war that shocked people. More soldiers were dying in hospitals and in prisons than in battle. And for the battlefield soldier, life was very hard. Most soldiers lived out-of-doors. They had to deal with the heat, cold, rain, and snow. Often they did this with poor clothing and few supplies. Usually, the soldiers' biggest complaints were about food.

Oh, hard crackers come again no more!
'Tis the song and the sigh of the hungry,
Hard crackers, hard crackers, come again no more!
Many days have you lingered stayed upon our stomachs sore.

Texas steers are no longer in view.
Mule steaks are now "done up brown,"
While peabread, mule roast and mule stew,
Are our fare meal in Vicksburg town.

Women and Blacks in the War

A few women dressed as men and fought in the front lines. Others, like Pauline Cushman for the North and Belle Boyd for the South, served as spies. Several thousand women on both sides worked in hospitals as nurses. Clara Barton served as a nurse on the Union side. Sally Tompkins worked in hospitals for the Confederacy. Most women stayed at home during the Civil War. They ran farms and worked in factories and in offices.

Black people fought and worked for the Union during the war. White northerners usually did not want to fight next to black men. So, black soldiers fought in separate units like the 54th Regiment of Massachusetts.

The black soldiers fought bravely. Some were foot soldiers. Others rode in the cavalry. Still others served in the navy. By the end of the war, nearly 200,000 black people had fought for the Union. Many of these won the highest honor the United States government can give a soldier, the Medal of Honor.

Black women helped the Union, too. Harriet Tubman served as a spy. She went behind the Confederate lines and learned about the enemy's plans. In addition, Tubman continued to do what she had done before the war and led hundreds of slaves to the North.

(above) Harriet Tubman. (below) Clara Barton supervises nurses in a Washington Red Cross Hospital.

255

(far right) General Ulysses S. Grant. (near right) General Robert E. Lee.

Black slaves worked for the Confederate States whether they wanted to or not. Some went off to war along with their owners. They dug trenches, built forts, and repaired roads. Other slaves stayed home and cared for plantations. They grew food to feed armies that fought to keep them slaves.

Black people did all this with the hope of some day winning their freedom. The first step in this direction came in 1863. In that year, Abraham Lincoln signed an order called the Emancipation Proclamation. It **emancipated**, or freed, the slaves in all states at war against the Union.

This meant that slaves in Missouri, Kentucky, West Virginia, Maryland, and Delaware still were not free. It wasn't much of a reward for black people in states that remained in the Union. But it was a start.

The last death in the Civil War may have been the most costly. On April 14, 1865, just five days after General Lee surrendered to General Grant, Abraham Lincoln decided to go to a play. At the play, Lincoln sat laughing at a few funny lines. John Wilkes Booth, a person loyal to the South, crept up behind the President and shot him in the head. On the next day, Lincoln died.

Checking Up

1. Why would blacks want to fight for the Union?

2. How did women help the two armies?

3. What was the Emancipation Proclamation?

4. What changes did the Civil War bring about?

Reviewing Chapter 16

Write your answers on paper. Do not write in the book.

Using Key Words

emancipate   civil war

Number your paper to 2. Write a short meaning for each of the above key words.

Reviewing Main Ideas

Number your paper from 1 to 8. Match the names in List 1 with their correct description in List 2.

List 1

1. Fort Sumter

2. Robert E. Lee

3. Belle Boyd

4. John Wilkes Booth

5. Abraham Lincoln

6. Harriet Tubman

7. Ulysses S. Grant

8. Appomattox Courthouse

List 2

a. place where the southern army surrendered

b. important southern general

c. black woman who spied for the North

d. shot President Lincoln

e. place where first shots of war were fired

f. leading northern general

g. woman who spied for the South

h. wrote the Emancipation Proclamation

Thinking Things Over

The following statements describe the Union or the Confederacy or both during the Civil War. Number your paper 1 to 10. Place a "U" or "C" or "U&C" next to each number.

1. Had better military leaders.

2. Had more railroads.

3. Had a better chance to win, the longer the war lasted.

4. Had more soldiers in their army.

5. Had black soldiers in their army.

6. Had a bigger population.

7. Had cities destroyed and farms burned.

8. Had women help support the war.

9. Had forced black labor to support the war.

10. Had wanted to become a separate nation.

Practicing Skills

Use the map on page 249 to help you make a partial list of those states that joined the Confederacy and of those that stayed in the Union.

Pennsylvania   Massachusetts
North Carolina   Kentucky
Mississippi   Michigan
Texas   California
Ohio   Alabama

CITIZENSHIP

Memorial to a Great American

Every year, millions of Americans visit a beautiful and important monument in Washington, D.C. They walk inside and this is what they see.

This building near the Potomac River is called the Lincoln Memorial. It was built to honor a great President who believed in freedom and forgiveness, Abraham Lincoln.

We remember Abraham Lincoln as the President who freed the slaves. He also believed in the right of all citizens to vote and help make their own laws.

Lincoln often spoke about the importance of the rights and freedoms of all Americans. This was the subject of his famous speech given at Gettysburg, Pennsylvania, in 1863. Gettysburg was the site of a terrible battle during the Civil War. Over seven thousand Americans were killed and 44,000 were wounded there.

IN THIS TEMPLE
AS IN THE HEARTS OF THE PEOPLE
FOR WHOM HE SAVED THE UNION
THE MEMORY OF ABRAHAM LINCOLN
IS ENSHRINED FOREVER

A 1963 Civil Rights demonstration outside the Lincoln Memorial.

Lincoln wanted to make sure that ". . . these dead shall not have died in vain [for nothing], that this nation under God shall have a new birth of freedom, and that government of the people, by the people, for the people shall not perish [die] from the earth." These words remind us that Americans have been ready and willing to die while defending their rights and freedoms.

As the Civil War was ending, Lincoln asked northerners to forgive the defeated South. "With malice [hatred] toward none; with charity [help and kindness] for all . . . let us strive [work] to bind up the nation's wounds . . ."

At first, many northerners only wanted to punish the South. After hearing the news of General Grant's final victory, a large crowd came to the White House to cheer for President Lincoln. Someone in the crowd asked what should be done with the defeated leaders. "Hang them!" shouted the crowd.

Lincoln's young son Tad was standing next to him. He is supposed to have said: "No, no, Papa. Don't hang them. Hang on to them!"

"That's it," cried Lincoln. "Tad has got it. We must hang on to them!"

No one knows if the story is really true. But President Lincoln wanted to quickly end the bad feelings between the North and South.

A few moments after Lincoln died, a friend said: "Now he belongs to the ages." He meant that Americans would always remember and respect the ideas and deeds of this great American.

259

What Do You Know?

Write your answers on paper. Do not write in the book.

Words to Know

frontier	technology
industrial	tariff
civil war	pioneer
abolish	transportation
annex	communication

Number your paper 1 to 10. Write a short meaning for each of the above words.

Ideas to Know

Some of the sentences below are true and some are false. Number your paper 1 to 15 and write either true or false by each number.

1. The Indians and white settlers learned to live peacefully with each other on the frontier.

2. All the land west of the Mississippi River that became part of the United States was gained through war.

3. The discovery of gold in California attracted thousands of people to the West.

4. Improvements in transportation and communication brought the people in the country closer together.

5. The North's economy was built upon the plantation system.

6. The development of factories caused large cities to grow.

7. Cotton was "King" before the invention of the cotton gin.

8. Abolitionists thought slavery was good for blacks.

9. In 1860 there were approximately 4 million slaves in America.

10. Both the North and the South agreed that slavery should not expand into new western lands.

11. The North was fighting the Civil War to gain its independence.

12. The Emancipation Proclamation freed all slaves in the United States.

13. A graph is a picture that shows how statistics can change over time.

14. When you communicate with other people, you learn about yourself.

15. Joseph Reddeford Walker created the Oregon Trail.

2. Write several paragraphs to answer the following question. Who do you think are greater American heroes, the trailblazers of the early 1800's or the astronauts of the late 1900's? Explain your choice carefully.

3. You are a great newspaper writer for the *Liberator*. Write an editorial, a story expressing your personal opinion, on why slavery should not be allowed into new western lands.

Using What You Know

1. The time line below shows some of the events that led up to or were part of the Civil War. The events are not in correct order. Copy the time line. Place the events on the time line in correct order.

2. Look at the map below. It shows the large areas of land that the United States gained from 1789 to 1848. Match the letter for each piece of land to the year the land was gained.
1. 1789   3. 1845   5. 1848
2. 1803   4. 1846

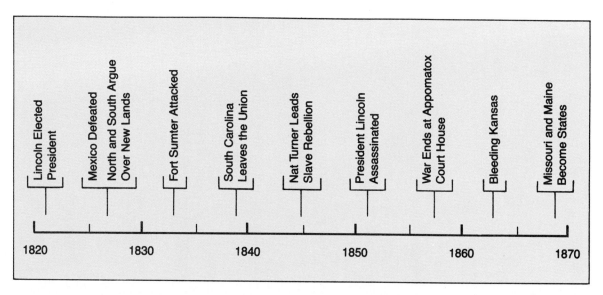

Lincoln Elected President

Mexico Defeated

North and South Argue Over New Lands

Fort Sumter Attacked

South Carolina Leaves the Union

Nat Turner Leads Slave Rebellion

President Lincoln Assassinated

War Ends at Appomatox Court House

Bleeding Kansas

Missouri and Maine Become States

1820   1830   1840   1850   1860   1870

Every once in a while—perhaps every year or every other year—most students take a special test called a standardized achievement test. Some people call these tests by another name, like "the Iowas," "the Metro," "the Stanford," "the SRA tests," etc. The tests are printed in separate booklets. The teacher reads special directions from a teacher's manual. Usually you "color" in ovals or circles to show your answer choices. Sometimes you do this right in your test booklet, but often you show your answer choices on a separate answer sheet. And sometimes even the whole school schedule is rearranged so that tests can be given to everyone at the same time.

No matter how these tests are given in your school, it is important for you to do the best on them that you can. Here are several suggestions that may help you:

1. Work through each section of the test as quickly as you can. Do not spend a lot of time on a question that you cannot answer. If there is time left over, then you can go back and try to answer those questions you skipped.

2. Always be sure that the question number and the number of your answer are the same. If you get mixed up, quickly go back to straighten it out. Erase completely, and mark your answers in the proper place.

3. Do not be concerned if you cannot answer all questions. The tests are made difficult on purpose. Just do the best you can in the time you have.

4. If you are not sure of an answer, it is wise to guess. Often your hunch is correct.

5. Above all, try not to be nervous or upset by the standardized tests. You will probably take many of them throughout your school years. They are a good way to find out what you already know and what you still need to learn.

On the next few pages are several varieties of sample tests made to look like the real ones. The questions are taken from the material in this book, however. You can use them to get acquainted with standardized tests, and to practice taking them. Write your answers on paper. Do not write in the book.

TIME OUT

for Standardized Tests

This is a test of your ability to read maps and globes. For each exercise decide which answer is correct. Then mark the proper answer space on your answer sheet. Mark only one answer space for each exercise.

Level 10 Begins Here

The map shows the routes pioneers used to travel west. Use the map to help you answer questions 1–6.

1. Which two places are the greatest distance apart?
   a. Boston and New York
   b. Chicago and Nauvoo
   c. Santa Fe and Independence
   d. Salt Lake City and Portland

2. Which city was settled by a religious group?
   a. Sacramento   c. Santa Fe
   b. Portland   d. Salt Lake City

3. Which trail went across the Sierra Nevada?
   a. Santa Fe   c. Oregon
   b. California   d. Mormon

4. Fort Bridger is _____ of San Francisco.
   a. North   c. East
   b. South   d. West

5. Salt Lake City is about _____ miles from Council Bluffs.
   a. 800 miles   c. 250 miles
   b. 1000 miles   d. 500 miles

6. Which trail went across a desert?
   a. Santa Fe   c. Oregon
   b. California   d. Mormon

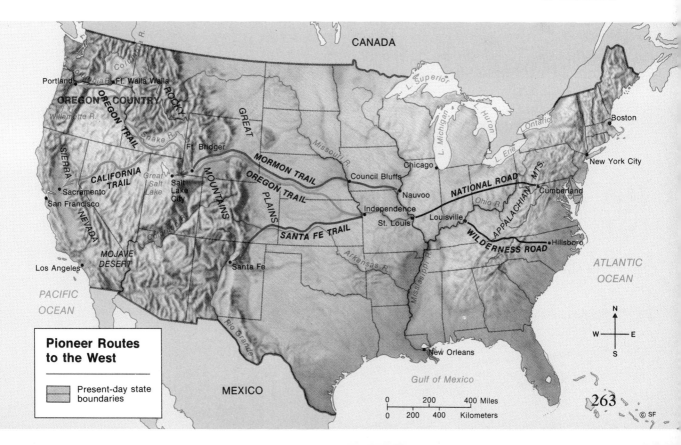

Pioneer Routes to the West

Present-day state boundaries

CANADA

Portland · Ft. Walla Walla
OREGON COUNTRY
ROCKY
Willamette R.
OREGON TRAIL
Snake R.
SIERRA
Ft. Bridger
GREAT
MORMON TRAIL
Missouri R.
CALIFORNIA TRAIL
Great Salt Lake
Salt Lake City
MOUNTAINS
OREGON TRAIL
Sacramento
San Francisco
NEVADA
PLAINS
SANTA FE TRAIL
Council Bluffs
Chicago
L. Superior
L. Michigan
Huron
L. Erie
Ontario
Boston
New York City
NATIONAL ROAD
APPALACHIAN MTS.
Cumberland
Nauvoo
Independence
Ohio R.
Louisville
St. Louis
WILDERNESS ROAD
Hillsboro
MOJAVE DESERT
Los Angeles ·
Santa Fe
Arkansas R.
ATLANTIC OCEAN
PACIFIC OCEAN
Rio Grande
Mississippi R.
New Orleans
Gulf of Mexico
MEXICO

0 200 400 Miles
0 200 400 Kilometers

263

© SF

TIME OUT for Standardized Tests

This is a test of your ability to read maps and globes. For each exercise decide which answer is correct. Then mark the proper answer space on your answer sheet. Mark only one answer for each exercise.

Level 13 Begins Here

1. The lines running north and south on these globes connect areas of the same
   1) longitude
   2) latitude
   3) attitude
   4) hemisphere

2. The lines running east and west on the globe connect areas of the same
   1) longitude
   2) latitude
   3) continent
   4) hemisphere

3. Another name for 90S latitude is
   1) North Pole
   2) Equator
   3) North America
   4) South Pole

4. Another name for the 0 east-west line is
   1) North Pole
   2) Equator
   3) North America
   4) South Pole

5. What two places shown on the globe are farthest apart?
   1) South America and North Pole
   2) Equator and South Pole
   3) North Pole and South Pole
   4) South Pole and North America

A. Parallels

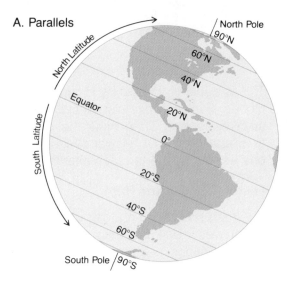

B. Meridians

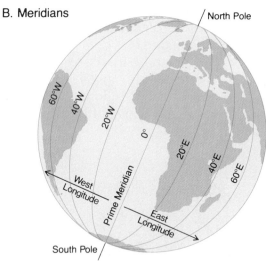

C. Global Grid

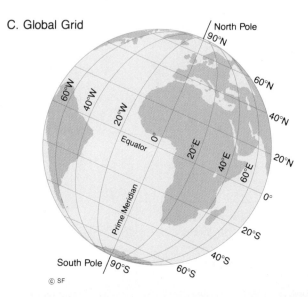

© SF

TEST 5 *Special directions:* Choose the best answer for questions 1-9. Remember to blacken only one space on your answer sheet for each question. Make sure you blacken the correct space for each answer. If you wish to change an answer, carefully erase your first answer and then blacken the space for your new answer.

1. In the 1770's a little more than half of the colonists or their ancestors were from

   A. Africa
   B. France
   C. Germany
   D. England

2. In 1800, the people in the United States who had the right to vote were

   A. white, land-owning women
   B. white, land-owning men
   C. freed black slaves
   D. black, land-owning women

3. The peace treaty of 1763 gave Canada and the lands between the Appalachian Mountains and the Mississippi River to

   A. the English
   B. the French
   C. the Indians
   D. the Dutch

4. Which of the following laws was passed first?

   A. The Tea Act
   B. The Stamp Act
   C. The Constitution
   D. The Townshend Acts

5. Which of the following is an example of "taxation without representation"?

   A. Boston Massacre C. Parliament
   B. The Stamp Act   D. Sons of Liberty

6. One of the secret groups in the colonies that fought to end the English laws and taxes was

   A. The Sons of New England
   B. The Daughters of Liberty
   C. militia
   D. Continental Mothers

7. Which of the following did the 13 colonies *not* gain from England in the peace treaty of 1783?

   A. end of war
   B. independence
   C. The Constitution
   D. right to rule themselves

8. Which of these things is true about the government set up by the Articles of Confederation?

   A. the national government had all the powers
   B. the state governments had no powers
   C. the President had strong powers
   D. the national government was very weak

9. The Bill of Rights, added to the Constitution in 1791, is

   A. a state law
   B. a list of rights of Americans
   C. a list of rights of all peoples
   D. a new plan of government

265

TIME OUT for Standardized Tests

TEST 9: Social Science

STEPS TO FOLLOW
I. Read each question.
II. Choose the *best* answer.
III. Look at the answer spaces at the right or on your answer sheet.
IV. Fill in the space which has the same number as the answer you have chosen.

Questions 1-5 are based on the chart below.

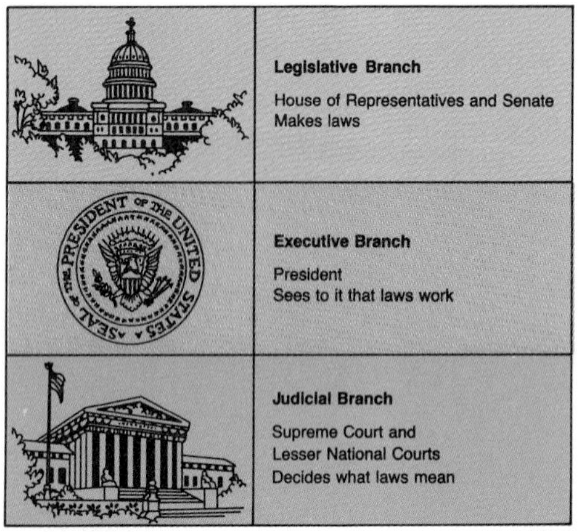

Legislative Branch

House of Representatives and Senate
Makes laws

Executive Branch

President
Sees to it that laws work

Judicial Branch

Supreme Court and
Lesser National Courts
Decides what laws mean

SAMPLE

A The Constitution of the United States was ratified in
1 1879
2 1789
3 1701
4 1941   A ① ② ③ ④

1 The chart shows the government of the United States set up by
1 the Executive Branch
2 the Constitution
3 the Judicial Branch
4 the Legislative Branch   1 ① ② ③ ④

2 In which branch of government do your Senators serve?
1 Legislative
2 Judicial
3 national
4 local   2 ① ② ③ ④

3 The First U.S. Circuit Court of Appeals is part of which branch of government?
1 Legislature
2 Executive
3 Local
4 Judical   3 ① ② ③ ④

4 You could use this chart to find out
1 the names of members of the Supreme Court
2 the term of members of the Senate
3 what the President does
4 what the laws mean   4 ① ② ③ ④

5 What would you read if you needed to know more about the national government?
1 a book on state laws
2 The Declaration of Independence
3 a book on the United Nations
4 The constitution   5 ① ② ③ ④

266

Each question in this test is followed by four suggested answers. Read each question and then decide which one of the four answers is best.

Find the row of spaces on your answer sheet which has the same number as your question. In this row, mark the space having the same letter as the answer you have chosen.

Question 1-4 are about the graph below.

Number of Men and Women Workers in the United States 1950–1980

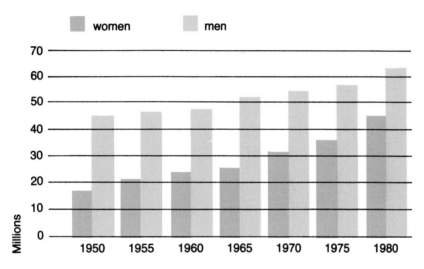

Source: Handbook of Labor Statistics Dec. 1980

1 How many women were workers in 1975?
A Over 40 million
B Over 30 million
C Over 20 million
D Over 10 million

2 How many years are covered in this graph?
A 17   C 30
B 27   D 47

3 What percentage of workers were women in 1950?
A 31%
B 39%
C 29%
D 92%

4 How many more women were workers in 1975 than were workers in 1950?
A 20 million
B 12 million
C   2 million
D   1 million

Unit 5

New Beginnings

Satori Kato came to the United States from Japan. He learned to speak English and enjoy American habits. Kato became successful in business. He invented and sold instant coffee.

Booker T. Washington was born a slave in West Virginia. After the Civil War, he went to school and learned to read and write. Washington started the Tuskegee Institute. This became an important school for the education of blacks.

Susan La Flesche Picotte was an American Indian. She learned to speak and write English on a reservation in Nebraska. Later, she became a doctor and spokesperson for her people. After the Civil War, these and other Americans learned new ways of living. They changed just as their country changed.

An Indian leans against the "singing wire"; the telegraph.

268

Chapter

17

Lesson 1 New Freedoms and New Problems
Lesson 2 Southern Whites After the Civil War
Lesson 3 Blacks Lose Their Rights

The New South

The Civil War tore the United States apart. After the war, Americans had to **reconstruct**, or put the nation back together again. Great changes took place during the four years of war. It took many years for people to learn to live with the changes.

Lesson 1 New Freedoms and New Problems

In December of 1865, the Thirteenth Amendment was added to the Constitution. An **amendment** to the Constitution means a change. In this case, the change meant that slavery was abolished in the United States.

The slaves were now free. However, many of them no longer had places to live and work. Few of them had any money. They had to get used to a new way of life.

Sharecropping in the South

Mingo White had been a slave as a child in Alabama. He described his first years of freedom this way:

66The day that we got news that we were free, Mr. White called us to the house. He said: "You are all free, just as free as I am. Now go and get yourself somewhere to stick your heads."

Just as soon as he said that, my mammy went across the field to Mr. Lee Osborn's to get a place for me and her to stay. He paid us seventy-five cents a day, fifty cents to her and two bits for me. He gave us our dinner along with the pay. After the crop was gathered for that year, me and my mammy cut and hauled wood for Mr. Osborn.

We left Mr. Osborn that fall and went to Mr. John Rawlins. We made a sharecrop with him. We'd pick two rows of

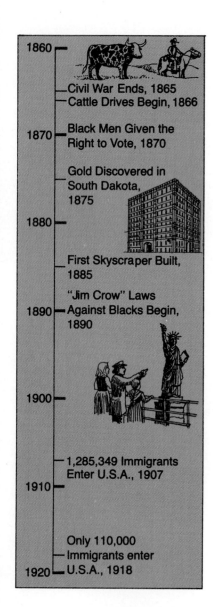

1860
— Civil War Ends, 1865
— Cattle Drives Begin, 1866

1870 — Black Men Given the Right to Vote, 1870

— Gold Discovered in South Dakota, 1875

1880 —

— First Skyscraper Built, 1885

— "Jim Crow" Laws
1890 — Against Blacks Begin, 1890

1900 —

— 1,285,349 Immigrants Enter U.S.A., 1907
1910 —

Only 110,000
— Immigrants enter
1920 — U.S.A., 1918

270

cotton and he'd pick two rows. We'd pull two rows of corn and he'd pull two rows of corn. He made sure we had food and a place to stay. We'd sell our cotton and corn and pay Mr. John Rawlins for feeding us. 99

These farmers began share-cropping after the Civil War. The kind of work they did was not much different from the days before the war, but now they were free!

Many former slaves were not as lucky as Mingo White and his mother. After their owners told them they were free, the former slaves found they had no homes. Some went off looking for family members separated when they had been slaves. Others were just left on the countryside with nowhere to go, nothing to do, no money, and no education.

Many former slaves became **sharecroppers** after the Civil War. Sharecroppers did not own land. They rented it from someone else. Usually, the sharecropper paid the rent by giving the landowner a "share" of the "crop."

The landowners also made money by selling tools, seeds, and other goods to the sharecroppers. They were usually charged very high prices for these goods. But they had no-where else to go to buy the things they needed. Slowly,

271

After the war, southern blacks had their first chance to go to school and learn to read and write.

many sharecroppers went into debt. Many felt they were not much better off being free than they had been as slaves.

The United States government tried to help the freed slaves get used to their new lives. To do this, it set up the Freedman's Bureau. The Bureau gave food, clothing, and medicine to those most in need of help. It helped people rent land and find jobs.

There were some improvements. Another amendment to the Constitution allowed black men to vote. Soon blacks were elected to government offices. These black officials worked to rebuild the South in a new way. They voted to set up public schools for both black and white children. They also used tax money to build railroads, bridges, and streets.

The United States government kept soldiers in the South for several years after the war. This was in part because it had taken a long time for blacks to get some rights. The soldiers tried to make sure that those rights were not taken away.

Checking Up

1. What problems did blacks face after the Civil War?

2. List some improvements in the lives of blacks after the war.

3. Imagine that you are a freed black after the Civil War. What would be the hardest thing for you to learn about your new life?

Lesson 2   Southern Whites After the Civil War

The Civil War greatly changed life for southern whites too. Most of them were poorer than before the war. Many of their fields and homes had been burned by soldiers. Farm animals had been stolen or killed for food. Although southern whites still had land, they no longer had slaves to work the land. Many businesses had been destroyed. Their owners had gone broke. Great numbers of young men had been killed or wounded. Almost every family had suffered a loss.

The first problem southerners faced was finding a way to put the land to good use again. Most of the owners of large farms divided their land into smaller pieces. They sold or rented pieces of land to white or black farmers. Other owners sharecropped with black or white farmers. Southern farms were soon back in business.

Still, whites in the South were always being reminded that they had lost the war. Large parts of cities like Atlanta, Georgia, had been destroyed. Soldiers camped near cities and towns. Black people were free from slavery, and there were large groups of them wandering about the countryside. Southern whites had a hard time getting used to the soldiers. And they found it hard to change their attitudes and actions toward the people who had been slaves.

The year is 1865. Reconstruction has already begun in Charleston, South Carolina.

Black men register to vote in Richmond, Virginia, after the Civil War.

Also, leaders in the United States Congress blamed southern whites for starting the war. They decided to punish them. Congress forced the southern states to agree to several changes in the Constitution. Some of the changes seemed to finish business the Constitution of 1789 had left undone. For example, slavery was outlawed. Black men could vote. Blacks and whites had to be treated equally under the law.

To white southerners, other changes seemed unfair. For example, Confederate leaders could not vote or hold office in government. This meant the southern states lost some of their best, most experienced leaders.

In addition, large numbers of northern whites moved to the South. Many of them hoped to start businesses or farms. Others saw a chance to take part in government. Southern whites believed these people had come south to take advantage of them.

Checking Up

1. In what ways were many southern whites poorer after the war than before the war?

2. How and why did Congress punish the South?

3. Imagine that you are a southern white after the Civil War. What would be the hardest change for you to get used to?

Lesson 3   Blacks Lose Their Rights

Many southern whites were upset by the changes going on around them. Some decided to return to the old ways of the South. They wanted to take away the new rights blacks had gained. They also wanted northern whites to leave the South. Secret groups were formed to bring about these changes. One of these groups was the Ku Klux Klan.

Members of the Ku Klux Klan rode around at night dressed like ghosts. Many southern blacks and northern whites were beaten, shot, or hanged by the Ku Klux Klan. The Ku Klux Klan also attacked southern whites who did not agree with them.

Lorenzo Ezell was a child when he became free in South Carolina. He described how the Ku Klux Klan worked:

66We left the plantation in 1865 or 1866 and by 1868 we were having an awful time with the Ku Klux. First time they came to my mamma's house at midnight and said they were soldiers come back from the dead. They were all dressed up in sheets and acted like spirits. They groaned around and said they had been killed wrongly and had come back for justice. One man looked just like any other man, but he sprang up about eighteen feet high all of a sudden. Another said he was so thirsty because he hadn't had any water since he was killed at Manassas Junction. He asked for water and he just

The hooded members of the Ku Klux Klan.

275

kept pouring it in. We thought sure he must be a spirit to drink that much water. Of course, he wasn't drinking it. He was pouring it into a bag under his sheet. My mamma never believed in spirits, so she knew it was just a man. They told us what they would do if we didn't go back to our masters and we all agreed and then they all disappeared.**99**

The Ku Klux Klan and other groups wanted southern white men to be back in power. They got their wish after 1877. In that year, the United States government removed its soldiers from the South. Without soldiers to protect them, most black men stopped voting. Northern whites returned home. In just a few years' time, black officials lost their offices in government.

Segregation: Keeping Blacks and Whites Apart

After 1890, southern white leaders passed new laws. They were called "Jim Crow" laws. The purpose of these laws was to **segregate**, or separate, whites and blacks. Blacks had to use separate drinking fountains and washrooms. They had to sit apart from whites in restaurants, parks, and on buses and trains. Blacks were even buried in separate cemeteries.

Segregation meant that blacks did not have the same rights or opportunities as whites. For example, southern state governments spent more money educating whites than blacks. Blacks were also stopped from gaining better jobs and voting in elections.

Blacks in the North

These conditions in the South caused many blacks to move to the North. There, they felt they would have a better chance to get a good education and a job. Blacks believed that there were no "Jim Crow" laws in the North. They felt their rights would be safe.

But reality did not match the dream. Blacks found that northerners wanted little to do with them. Most northern whites did not want blacks in their neighborhoods. Blacks usually had to live in separate areas of Detroit, Chicago, New York, and other big cities.

Read how one black, Langston Hughes, described life in the North. Hughes moved to Cleveland in 1916.

How did segregation laws come to be called "Jim Crow" laws? Jim Crow was a character mentioned in a song. The character was based on a real slave named Jim Crow. The person in the song was supposed to represent the "typical" or average slave. By 1838, the term "Jim Crow" was used just as people would use "Negro." Thus, by the 1890s anything "Jim Crow" also referred to "Negro" or black. As the above picture shows, "Jim Crow" laws lasted a long time in the United States.

&&Rents were very high for colored people in Cleveland, and the Negro district was [very] crowded, because of the great migration. It was [hard] to find a place to live.

White people on the east side of the city were moving out of their frame houses and renting them to Negroes at double and triple the rents they could receive from others. An eight-room house with one bath would be cut up into apartments and five or six families crowded into it, each two-room kitchenette apartment renting for what the whole house had rented for before.

But Negroes were coming in in a great dark tide from the South, and they had to have some place to live.&&

(top) A black family at home in their northern apartment. (bottom) Getting around in New York City in the early 1900s.

Checking Up

1. What were the goals of secret groups like the Ku Klux Klan?

2. How did "Jim Crow" laws change life for blacks?

3. Why did blacks migrate north?

4. Imagine that you are black living in the late 1800s. You have just arrived in a northern city. What would your life be like?

277

Write your answers on paper. Do not write in the book.

Using Key Words

sharecropper   segregate
amendment   reconstruct

Number your paper 1 to 4. Write a short meaning for each of the above key words.

Reviewing Main Ideas

Number your paper 1 to 7. Next to each number write the letter of the phrase which correctly completes the sentence.

1. The job of the Freedman's Bureau was to: **a.** give free southern land to freed slaves. **b.** rebuild southern cities. **c.** help freed slaves get used to their new lives.

2. What problem(s) did freed blacks find as sharecroppers? **a.** They kept only a small part of their crop. **b.** They were charged high prices for equipment. **c.** Both of the above.

3. The government kept soldiers in the South to **a.** help blacks keep their rights. **b.** protect the United States from Mexico. **c.** stop the South from starting a second Civil War.

4. Which of the following changes were made to the Constitution after the Civil War? **a.** Black men could no longer vote. **b.** Laws had to treat blacks and whites differently. **c.** Slavery was forbidden.

5. How did the war affect southern farms? **a.** The number of farm animals increased. **b.** Small farms were joined together to form large farms. **c.** Large farms were divided and sold or rented in smaller parts.

6. How were southern whites punished by Congress? **a.** Congress took their land and gave it to freed blacks. **b.** Southern cities were not allowed to rebuild. **c.** Some could not vote or hold office in government.

7. The purpose of the Ku Klux Klan was to **a.** prevent freed blacks from using their new rights to vote or go to school, etc. **b.** rebuild southern cities. **c.** keep freed blacks out of the northern states.

Thinking Things Over

Pretend you were a slave and are now free living in the South just after the Civil War. Write a letter to a friend telling the things you like and dislike about your new life.

Practicing Skills

Examine the photo on page 273. Tell how you would have felt if you had been a southerner faced with rebuilding the South.

The Last Western Frontier

For almost three hundred years, Americans who wanted to make a fresh start in life headed west. The West was the land of opportunity. New chances waited on the other side of the next hill.

To American colonists, the West was the land just past their settlements. To Americans of 1776, the West was the land between the Appalachian Mountains and the Mississippi River. To Americans of the 1840s, the West was the land on the Pacific Coast.

After the Civil War, Americans settled the last West. This West lay between the Great Plains and the Rocky Mountains.

Lesson 1 Miners and Ranchers

The hope of finding gold, silver, or copper brought many settlers to the last West. Thousands of people hurried to California during the gold rush of 1849. Others rushed to Colorado, Montana, South Dakota, and Nevada in the 1860s and 1870s.

Boom Towns!

When one person made a strike, more followed to search for ore. Mining camps, or towns, grew up almost overnight. Because of this, the mining camps were nicknamed "**boom towns.**" One such boom town was Central City, Colorado. Gold was discovered there in 1859. The quiet town of three thousand almost exploded to thirty thousand in one month. Other boom towns are shown on the map on page 281.

Not everyone moving to a boom town went to mine for ore. Many people went to provide the miners with services. General stores, barbershops, bathhouses, saloons, hotels, and

Black and Chinese workers are shoveling rocks and earth into a "sluice box." How did this device help them find gold?

279

blacksmith shops sprang up on both sides of a boom town's muddy streets. One witness to a boom town wrote:

66The streets are lined with freight of every description; heavy teams are constantly coming in with more; buildings are going up everywhere . . . men are rushing about in every direction . . . all is life, bustle and excitement . . . . There is [business] here, and money enough to build it up rapidly, and when the season becomes more moderate, carpenters and masons need not be idle an hour; there will be work enough for all 99

It seemed that almost everyone in the boom towns wanted to get rich quick. Not everyone, however, wanted to obey the law while doing it. Boom towns were often centers of lawlessness. Gamblers, thieves, murderers, and gunslingers were almost as common as the miner's pickax and mule.

The boom town of "Last Chance Gulch" in Montana. This boom town survived and grew into a major city. See if you can find out the name of that city.

CANADA

WASHINGTON
Molson • Old
Toroda

Orofino
Florence

Columbia

MONTANA
Last Chance
Gulch

Missouri R.

NORTH DAKOTA

OREGON

IDAHO
Gilmore
De Lamar
Idaho City
Silver
City

Snake R.

SOUTH DAKOTA
Deadwood
Rochford • Galena
Rockerville

WYOMING

PACIFIC
OCEAN

Tuscarora
Jarbridge

Humbug
NEVADA
Unionville

Coloma
Town Talk
Sonora
Placerville
Hornitos
Bodie
Belmont
Goldfield
Mariposa

Virginia City

Park City

UTAH

Silver
Reef

Colorado R.

NEBRASKA

Kokomo
Aspen
COLORADO
Telluride
Silverton

Central City
Fairplay
Cripple Creek

KANSAS

Arkansas R.

CALIFORNIA

ARIZONA
Oatman
Jerome
Crown King
Vulture City

Ehrenberg

Quijotoa
Greaterville

NEW MEXICO

Dos Cabezas
Tombstone

OKLAHOMA

TEXAS

N
W E
S

Rio Grande

MEXICO

0   200   400 Miles
0 200 400   Kilometers

© SF

Mining Towns

• Towns that people still live in

• Ghost towns

Which western states had the most mining towns? Compare this map to the physical map on page 36. Where are mining towns likely to be found?

Few towns or camps had a judge or sheriff to fight crime. Often these law officers had to ride from town to town. When they arrived in a new town, they found a lot of crime to fight. One townsperson said, "The justice courts are kept hot and our jail is overcrowded."

Many townspeople didn't wait for the law to come to them. They found it quicker and cheaper to fight crime with ropes than with jails. If people were accused of crimes, they would be tried. If necessary, they would be hanged from the nearest tree, all in a matter of hours. This was known as "miner's law."

Boom-town residents were always ready to show visitors their "hanging tree." But they were also willing to show their culture. Many mining camps had churches, opera houses, theaters, and music halls. If the camps grew into communities, they showed off other things as well. Schools, street lights, sewer systems, churches, and public transportation became common in the boom towns that survived.

Most boom towns didn't survive, though. If gold or silver was found elsewhere, the townspeople went after it. Today,

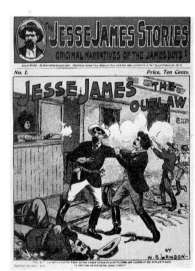

Those who broke the law were called *outlaws*. And one of the West's most famous outlaws was Jesse James. At one time, he was the most wanted outlaw in the West. Many books, not always containing the truth, were written about him.

281

The ghost town of Rhyolite, Nevada.

It's four long years since I reached this land,
In search of gold among the rocks and sand;
And yet I'm poor when the truth is told,
I'm a lousy miner,
I'm a lousy miner in search of shining gold.
Oh, land of gold, you did me deceive,
And I intend in thee my bones to leave;
So farewell, home, now my friends grow cold,
I'm a lousy miner,
I'm a lousy miner in search of shining gold.
        from *I'm a Lousy Miner*

the West is the final resting place for hundreds of ghost towns. You Bet, Town Talk, Rough and Ready, Humbug, Gouge Eye, and Vulture City are only a few of the West's ghost towns. All that remain now are some weathered buildings and memories.

Cowboys and Cattle

A few gold seekers struck it rich. As the above song says, most did not. Many tired of the long, back-breaking hours spent looking or mining for ore. Some looked for work with companies that made a business of mining. Some opened stores or businesses to serve the miners. Many became ranchers or farmers.

Ranching, or cattle farming, became a popular business after the Civil War. This happened for two reasons. One, millions of buffalo were killed on the Great Plains. This opened up new lands for cattle. Two, railroads were built over the western lands.

The Long Drive

The cattle were raised on the grassy plains of Texas, Colorado, Arizona, and Montana. When the cattle were ready for market, they were shipped east by train. However, first the cattle had to be brought to the railroads. This was done by means of a cattle drive. A cattle drive was not really a drive at all. It was a very long walk. Cowboys on horses forced the cattle to walk hundreds of miles over dusty trails. Their goal, as the map below shows, was to reach the cattle pens next to the railroad tracks in Sedalia, Missouri, or Abilene, Kansas, or some other "cow town."

After 1885, cattle drives became less and less common. One reason is shown on this map. Before 1880, cattle were driven along the trails to the towns of Sedalia, Kansas City, Abilene, and Dodge City. By 1883, both the Northern and Southern Pacific Railroads had been completed. How did the completion of these railroads help bring an end to the long cattle drives?

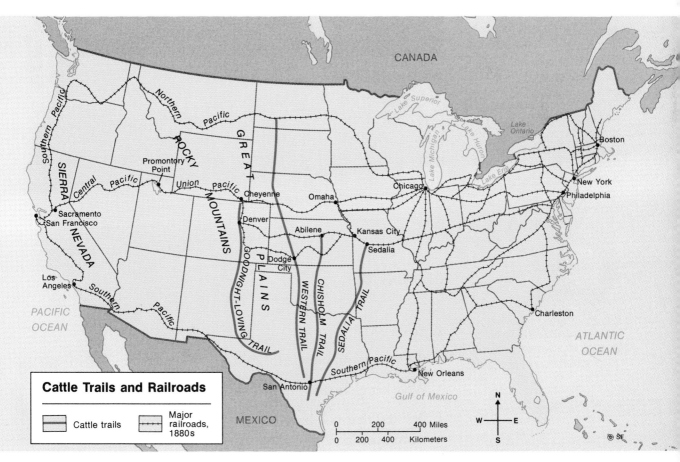

Cattle Trails and Railroads

Cattle trails

Major railroads, 1880s

283

For $30 a month, a cowboy put up with dust, mosquitoes, saddle sores, angry steers, red bean pie, and "sleepin' under the stars."

What's in a Name?

Before barbed-wire fences were used to keep herds of cattle apart, ranchers branded their cattle with hot irons. It was important for the ranchers to try and make their brands very different. That way, the ranchers could identify their own cattle.

But cattle could be stolen. It was possible to place a second brand over the first to make a new brand. If this was done well, the first rancher might not be able to prove ownership. The trick was to make the first brand hard to mark over.

One rancher thought he had discovered the best brand. But as it turned out, he didn't. He soon noticed that many of his cattle were disappearing. His brand was the famous "Ten in Texas," or

Can you figure out what mark was placed over his to make a new mark? You will get a *star* if you figure it out.

The Thomas Gilcrease Institute of American History and Art, Tulsa, Oklahoma

A cattle drive was hard on both the cows and the cowboys. Each day they had to travel far enough to get to the next watering hole. At night the cowboys camped out next to a fire. They were served their meals off the back of a chuck wagon.

Checking Up

1. What did miners do when their luck ran out?

2. Why were mining camps called boom towns?

3. What dangers do you think a cowboy faced?

4. Pretend that you have just arrived in a mining camp. How would you go about learning the customs or habits of the camp?

Lesson 2 The Great Railroads

By the 1850s, many Americans wanted a railroad that would connect the settled East and the Pacific Coast. Few thought it would be easy. As one congressman said, it would be just as easy "to build a railroad to the moon."

In 1862, Congress passed a law to build the first **transcontinental** railroad. The Central Pacific and Union Pacific railroad companies were formed to do the work. From the start in 1867, the two companies were in a race across the country. Each railroad had been promised a bonus from the government. For every mile of track laid, the railroads received land and money. The company that put down the most track would get the biggest bonus.

East from California

The Central Pacific's line headed east from Sacramento, California. Workers laid track through the high Sierra Nevada. They built bridges across rivers. They hauled dirt to make a level roadbed. They blasted tunnels through solid rock. Once across the mountains, they worked in the heat of the deserts. In all, the Central Pacific's workers put down 689 miles of track. Locate the Central Pacific on the map on page 283.

Most of the Central Pacific's workers were Chinese. Some had lived in California for years. Others were hired in China, and then took ships to California. The Chinese were skillful and hard working. One railroad manager said of them:

66Wherever we put them we found them good . . . if we found we were in a hurry for a job of work, it was better to put on Chinese at once.99

West from Omaha

The Union Pacific's 1,086 miles of track headed west from Omaha, Nebraska. The Union Pacific had a great advantage in the race. Its workers had to lay track across the flat Great Plains.

But the workers faced attacks by Indians who knew that the railroads would bring millions of white people to their lands. The builders also had trouble with herds of buffalo

The building of the first transcontinental railroad required a great deal of material. Over 720,000 rails were needed for the 1800-mile railroad. Each of these rails weighed about 500 pounds. The rails were attached to over 4,500,000 ties. More than 21,000,000 spikes were needed to hold the rails in place.

that tore up the track. The Union Pacific hired hunters to kill the buffalo. Armed guards fought the Indians.

A majority of the Union Pacific's workers were Irish. But blacks, Swedes, Norwegians, and Mexicans also worked on the road. Many of the workers were Civil War veterans. All worked hard to bring the East and West together. Locate the Union Pacific on the map on page 283.

On May 10, 1869, the two lines met at Promontory, Utah. Five days later, a golden spike was hammered to hold the last rail in place. One worker described what happened:

66When they came to drive the last spike, Governor Stanford, president of the Central Pacific, took the hammer. The first time he struck he missed the spike and hit the rail.

What a howl went up! Irish, Chinese, Mexicans, and everybody yelled with delight. "He missed it. Yee." The engineers blew the whistles and rang their bells. Then Stanford tried it again and tapped the spike. The tap was reported by telegraph in all the offices east and west. It set bells to tapping in hundreds of towns and cities.99

Facts and Figures

In its first year of operation, the railroad carried over 150,000 passengers. Some went first class for about $100. They sat on soft seats that could be turned into sleepers at night. Second-class passengers paid about $80. For that they sat on covered wooden seats. Third-class passengers paid about $40. Immigrants heading west usually purchased this type of ticket. For that price they rode on uncovered wooden benches.

The Central Pacific's "Jupiter" engine and the Union Pacific's "No. 119" gently touched. The Promontory telegraph tapped out "Dot. Dot. Dot. Done." The nation was joined together.

Later, other transcontinental lines were built. All helped tie the country together. People and goods traveled from coast to coast.

With the railroads finished, the companies collected their bonuses of money and land. They sent agents to the East and Europe to attract settlers. "Go West," they said, "and you will earn more, spend less, and live better."

Checking Up

---

1. What dangers and problems did the workers for each company face?

2. Why were the transcontinental railroads important?

3. What different kinds of workers helped build the Union and Central Pacific railroads.

(top left) A broadside announcing the opening of the first transcontinental railroad. (bottom left) The two railroads meet at Promontory Point.

287

Building Social Studies Skills

Using Scales on Maps

Many people use scales to measure their weight. Each birthday, as you step on a scale, you might see that you have gained some weight. Your mom or dad will use the scale, if they're on a diet, to measure the weight they've lost.

Maps have scales, too. They are called **bar scales**. A bar scale does not, however, measure a map's weight. Scale on a map measures distance. Maps are not drawn full size. The places and distances shown on maps must be smaller than their real size on earth. A map of a country, state, city, or even a room would be much too large to use if it were drawn the same size as the real place. A map scale compares size on a map to size in real life.

For example, the map scale might show that the distance of one inch on a map is equal to a distance of one hundred miles on earth. On another map an inch might be equal to ten miles, or even one mile. The size of these maps could be the same. But their scales will be different. They are showing different distances on earth.

Look at the three maps of the building of America's first transcontinental railroad. **Map 1** shows the entire route of the railroad. It goes from Omaha, Nebraska, to San Francisco, California. Check the scale on this map. One inch on the map equals 500 miles on earth.

Map 2 shows the route of the railroad within Utah. This map is just as large as Map 1. But it shows a *smaller* area of the earth. What has happened to the scale? On Map 2, one inch equals 150 miles on earth.

Now look at **Map 3**. It shows the area around Promontory Point within Utah. This map is the same size as the first two maps. But, like Map 2, the third map shows a *smaller* area of the earth. Because it shows a smaller area, what has happened to the scale? Now one inch on the map equals 25 miles on earth.

Exploring with Maps

1. About how far is it from Promontory to Ogden on Map 3?   **a.** 40–50 miles   **b.** 80–100 miles   **c.** 120–150 miles

2. How far is it on Map 2?

3. How far is it on Map 1?

4. How far is it from Promontory to Utah's *western* border on Map 1? Do not measure along the tracks. Measure *directly* west.   **a.** about 50 miles   **b.** about 75 miles   **c.** about 100 miles

5. About how far is it on Map 2?

6. About how far is it on Map 3?

7. Explain what happens to scale on a map as the area that the map shows gets smaller.

8. What does Map 1 show that Map 3 cannot? What does Map 3 show that Map 1 cannot?

288

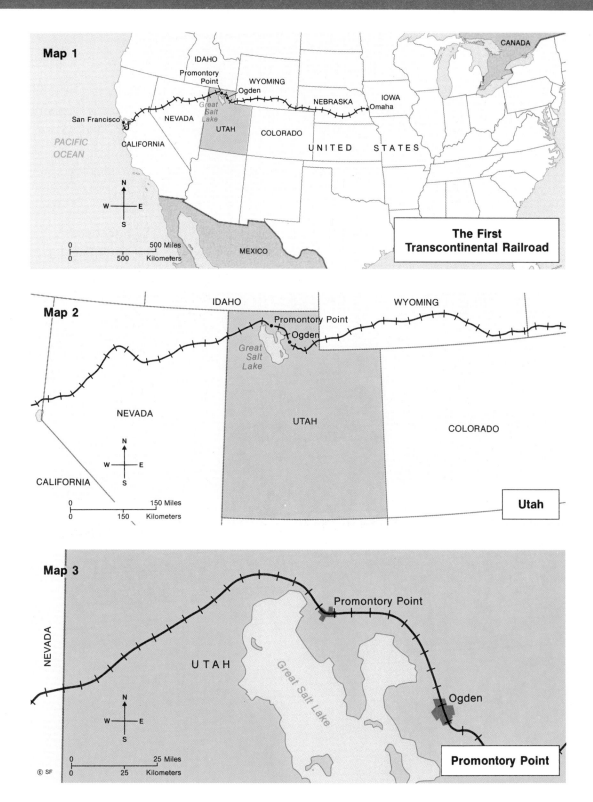

Map 1

IDAHO

Promontory
Point

WYOMING

Ogden

NEBRASKA

IOWA

Omaha

San Francisco

NEVADA

Great
Salt
Lake

CANADA

PACIFIC
OCEAN

CALIFORNIA

UTAH

COLORADO

UNITED   STATES

N
W   E
S

0   500 Miles
0   500   Kilometers

MEXICO

The First
Transcontinental Railroad

IDAHO

WYOMING

Map 2

Promontory Point

Ogden

Great
Salt
Lake

NEVADA

UTAH

COLORADO

N
W   E
S

CALIFORNIA

0   150 Miles
0   150   Kilometers

Utah

Map 3

Promontory Point

NEVADA

UTAH

Great Salt Lake

Ogden

N
W   E
S

0   25 Miles
0   25   Kilometers

© SF

Promontory Point

289

Lesson 3   The Homesteaders

The pioneers of the 1840s and 1850s called it the "Great American Desert." They shook their heads in disbelief. "Godforsaken," they said as they headed past this territory for Oregon and California.

By the 1860s, a new group of pioneers looked at the Great Plains differently. They saw the land between the Missouri River and the Rocky Mountains as a garden. They saw it as their promised land.

As they migrated west, many of these new pioneers sang a song:

> **"**O, come to this country and don't you feel alarm
> For Uncle Sam is rich enough to give us all a farm!**"**

As the song said, Uncle Sam, meaning the United States, was giving land away. Anyone, according to the Homestead Act of 1862, could claim 160 acres of land. The land was free. Free, that is, if one crop was produced within five years.

It didn't matter if the land was free or selling at $2.50 an acre. People rushed to get it. All kinds of Americans, black and white, rich and poor, settled on the **homesteads**. And

(top) A broadside announcing the sale of railroad land. (bottom) A Nebraska couple outside their sod house. What crop are they growing?

the pioneers came from Europe, too. There were Russians, Norwegians, Swedes, Irish, and Germans. If they spoke one word of English, it was "land!"

The first thing the settlers noticed about their land was that it had few trees. Wood for building houses had to be brought in by rail. But that was costly. Many settlers chose to build their homes with the natural resource that was available—sod. They cut blocks of grass and dirt and stacked them up as walls. Branches covered with more sod served as a roof. Because of this, the pioneers were called sodbusters.

What a land they chose to live on! In the summer, the land was baked by 100 degree temperatures. In the winter, the land was frozen at 40 degrees below zero. The surface was so hard that most plows, at first, just bounced off it.

The pioneers, however, found that the soil below the surface was rich. In many years, the crops were good. Some years, however, they were bad.

Sometimes insects were the problem. Millions of grasshoppers flew:

(top) Sod being cut for a new house. An acre of sod was needed for the average house. (bottom) The inside of a sod house.

66. . . in clouds upon clouds, until their fluttering wings looked like a sweeping snowstorm in the heavens, until their dark bodies covered everything green upon the earth. 99

They ate all the green plants and then laid eggs. The next year, even more grasshoppers appeared. No crops could grow then.

The real enemy of the pioneer though, was water. In most years, it was the lack of water that caused problems. Dust storms and prairie fires were common. Too much water was just as dangerous. Floods could quickly wash away a sod house and fields of corn and wheat.

Many things helped the pioneer survive on the Great Plains. Windmills brought water up from wells. Steel plows cut through the stone-hard ground. Barbed-wire fences helped keep cattle and cowboys off the fields. But none of these were as important as the people themselves.

The only thing tougher than the Great Plains was the pioneers' spirit. Many prairie settlers looked failure in the eye every day. They felt that the only way to succeed was to work hard. One pioneer showed this feeling in a letter to a friend. "Tired?" he wrote after spending three days cutting wheat. "You better believe it!"

Checking Up

1. What two ways could people get land on the Great Plains?

2. List the problems sodbusters faced.

3. How did the prairie settlers learn to live in their new surroundings?

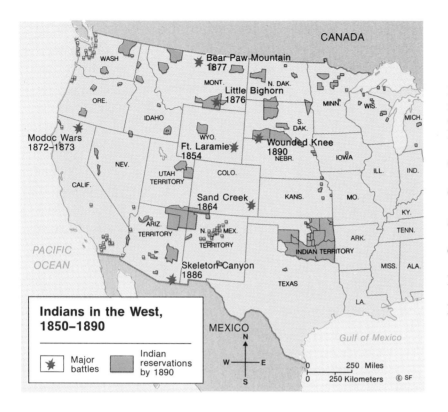

Indians in the West, 1850–1890

Major battles ★

Indian reservations by 1890

In 1979, the populations for some of the largest Indian reservations were:

Navaho (Ariz., N.M., Utah)	159,124
Creek (Okla.)	28,224
Cherokee (Okla.)	25,300
Southern Pueblos (N.M.)	21,433
Choctaw (Okla.)	18,171
Papago (Ariz.)	16,033
Pine Ridge (So. Dakota)	16,000

Lesson 4   The Indians' Last Stand

The West after 1860 was a land filled with exciting sounds. There was the sharp "clink" of the miners' pickax from deep in the earth. There was the joyful shout when someone found gold or silver. There was the heavy "thud" as a hammer drove a spike into a railroad tie and the shrill whistle from a locomotive as it raced across the plains. There was the deep ripping sound of the steel plow as it cut through prairie sod. And there was the soft whisper as a pioneer said thanks for a good harvest.

But there were also sounds of sadness, loss, and anger. They came from the American Indians. Chief Crazy Horse of the Sioux said as white settlers moved onto Indian land: "We preferred our own way of living . . . all we wanted was peace and to be left alone." Sounds such as this grew louder as miners, ranchers, and homesteaders moved west.

Before the Civil War, many Indians were moved onto reservations west of the Mississippi River. There, on the Great Plains, they joined other Indians such as the Sioux, Cheyenne,

(opposite)
Former slaves have found their promised land on the plains of Nebraska.

and Crow. The United States government made treaties, or agreements, with the Indians. The government promised that the land on the reservations was to be the Indians' "as long as grass grows or water runs."

Not all whites followed the treaties. After the war, settlers slowly began to move onto the Indians' land. Other treaties were made. These took even more land from the Indians.

The pioneers and Indians wanted to use the same land. But they wanted to use it in different ways. The homesteader wanted to plow and fence the land. The rancher wanted to let the cattle feed on the best grass. The miner wanted to dig deep holes in the earth.

The Indians wanted to be free to move across the open plains. They wanted to camp, hunt, or perhaps, raise a few crops. Their people had done that for centuries.

Nothing Left to Do but Fight

Spoken words and written words failed to stop the settlers. The Indians soon believed they had to fight to defend their land and way of life. Red Cloud, a great chief of the Sioux, explained why his people finally went to war.

      66If the Great Father kept white men out of my country, peace would last forever . . . . The Great Spirit raised me in this land, and has raised you in another land . . . I mean to keep this land.99

The Indians and the settlers fought for almost thirty-five years after the Civil War. Some of their battles are shown on the map on page 293. The Indians fought hard, and they won some important battles.

The Indians, though, never had a chance to win the long war. They had too few warriors and weapons. In the end, the Indians were almost without food and shelter. White hunters had reduced the buffalo herds from sixty million to about one thousand.

By the 1890s, most Indians lived on reservations. Their way of life changed greatly. They could no longer hunt and follow the buffalo. They were told to live as farmers. But the land on the reservations was usually poor. Soon, the Indians depended on the government for food and shelter.

(top) *"Custer's Last Stand."* This painting is considered to be an accurate reconstructions of the battle. The artist researched the battle for over twenty years before painting the picture. Custer is shown below the yellow battle flag.
Custer's brothers, Tom and Boston also died in this battle which some think might have been avoided. Custer's attack was carried out *against* the orders of his superiors. (bottom) The battlefield as it appears today. One Indian said after the battle: "It was hard fighting; very hard all the time. I have been in many hard fights, but I never saw such brave men."

Detail Courtesy of The Buffalo Bill Historical Center, Cody, Wyoming

By the Way

June 25, 1876 will always be remembered as a historic day. It was the day of the American Indians' greatest victory and the U.S. Cavalry's worst defeat. It was the day of the Battle of the Little Bighorn, or "Custer's Last Stand."

General George A. Custer had been sent to the Black Hills of South Dakota to remove the Indians to a reservation. But the Black Hills were a sacred area to the Indians. They would not give up without a fight.

On that day in June, Custer's force of 264 men was out-flanked by Chief Crazy Horse's 1,000 warriors. In less than 20 minutes, Custer's force was wiped-out on a small hill overlooking the Little Bighorn River in Montana.

295

This walled compound in Minnesota held 1,700 Sioux Indians before they were placed on a reservation farther west.

Chief Ten Bears of the Comanche told how his people felt about the loss of their way of life:

66I was born upon the prairie, where the wind blew free, and there was nothing to break the light of the sun. I was born where there were no enclosures and where everything drew a free breath. I want to die there . . . and not within walls.99

Checking Up

1. How did the Indians and whites disagree over the land?

2. After the Civil War, what did the United States government do to Indian lands?

3. What did the loss of the buffalo have to do with the defeat of the Indians?

4. Imagine that you have been placed on a reservation. What new way of life would you have to learn?

Chief Joseph

He was known to his people as In-mut-too-yah-lat-kat: Thunder Traveling over the Mountains. To the whites, he was known as Chief Joseph of the Nez Percé (nez′ pėrs′) Indians of Oregon and Idaho.

Joseph became the leader of his people in 1871. This was a difficult time for the Nez Percé. The government had taken most of their land. The Nez Percé were told to move to a reservation.

Chief Joseph did not believe in war. His people had always been at peace with whites. But settlers and the government were determined to push the Nez Percé onto a reservation. Chief Joseph was forced to act. He decided to take his people to safety in Canada.

In June of 1877, the Nez Percé began a four-month march. The United States Army followed and attacked them. The Indians' twelve-hundred-mile march is shown on the map.

Chief Joseph led his people to within forty miles of Canada. Winter was settling in by this time. The Nez Percé were starving and freezing. Chief Joseph made the only decision he felt he could make. He surrendered to save the rest of his people.

"I am tired," he said; "my heart is sick and sad. From where the sun stands now, I will fight no more forever."

Before he died in 1904, Chief Joseph explained what he had tried to do for his people. "Let me be a free man—free to travel, free to stop, free to work . . . to think and talk and act for myself—and I will obey every law . . ."

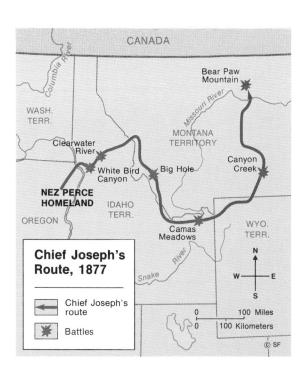

CANADA

Columbia River

Bear Paw
Mountain

Missouri River

WASH.
TERR.

MONTANA
TERRITORY

Clearwater
River

Big Hole

Canyon
Creek

White Bird
Canyon

NEZ PERCE
HOMELAND

IDAHO
TERR.

OREGON

Camas
Meadows

WYO.
TERR.

Snake River

N
W — E
S

**Chief Joseph's
Route, 1877**

← Chief Joseph's
route

✳ Battles

0   100 Miles
0   100 Kilometers

© SF

297

Write your answers on paper. Do not write in the book.

Using Key Words

transcontinental   boom town
homestead   bar scale

Number your paper from 1 to 4. Write a short meaning for each of the above key words.

Reviewing Main Ideas

Number your paper 1 to 8. Match the words with their correct description below. Write the letter of the correct description next to the number.

1. "last West"   5. Homestead Act 1862
2. boom town   6. Sioux/Cheyenne
3. cattle drive   7. Promontory Point
4. "cow town"   8. Central Pacific

a. railroad built largely by Chinese, started from Sacramento

b. free land to people who farmed and lived on it for five years

c. towns that grew along railroad lines where cattle were loaded

d. Indian tribes of the northern Great Plains

e. place where transcontinental railroad was completed in 1869

f. land between Great Plains and the mountains of the Pacific coast

g. cattle forced to walk to railroad towns for shipping

h. towns that grew where gold and silver were discovered

Thinking Things Over

As the West was settled the settlers' and Indians' lives crashed together. Each had a different idea of how people should live. Explain what you think the settlers and Indians thought about:

1. buffalo   3. reservations
2. railroads   4. land

Practicing Skills

The land called "the West" changed location in American history. Examine the map below. Match each area with the time when it was called "the West." Number your paper 1 to 4 and place the correct letter next to it.

a. 1840s and 1850s   c. the Great Plains
b. Colonial West   d. 1783–1840

Chapter

19

The Growth of Business and Labor

The use of machines to do work and make goods had started long before the Civil War. But the war was a turning point. During the war, machines were used in new ways. Americans saw that they could do much more work and many more kinds of work than anyone had ever thought. From 1865 to 1900, big businesses grew up to make machines and to produce the energy to run them. They caused many changes in people's lives.

Lesson 1 Inventions, Inventions, Inventions!

Machines. Everywhere Americans looked after the Civil War, there seemed to be new kinds of machines. Some people joked that if the number of machines kept growing, there would be nothing for people to do.

Americans had good reasons for making machines to do work. One was that Americans had more work than they could do. One person using a good machine could do the same amount of work as ten, twenty, or even fifty persons. Some machines could even do work that people could not do at all.

Inventions and Inventors That Changed the World

1867	Pullman Sleeping Car George M. Pullman
1868	Typewriter Christopher L. Sholes
1868	Airbrake George Westinghouse
1873	Barbed Wire Joseph Glidden
1876	Telephone Alexander G. Bell
1879	Cash Register James Ritty
1884	Fountain Pen Lewis E. Waterman
1885	Adding Machine William S. Burroughs
1889	Roll Film George Eastman
1899	Vacuum Cleaner John Thurman

An "automatic washing machine" used on an Indiana farm in 1914.

299

Thomas A. Edison is shown here with his phonograph. In school, Edison had been called a "slow learner."

By the Way

Some inventions of the years around 1900, such as the electric light, changed the world. Others did not. Here are a few inventions that did not "make it."

- The above invention undressed a man if he fell asleep with his clothes on.
- The self-tipping hat (1896) allowed men with their arms full to say hello to people passing by.
- The personal fire-escape (1879) was a parachute attached to a head band.
- Chicken glasses (1903) were used to keep the birds from harming each other as they pecked for food.

For fun, draw what you think the last three inventions looked like?

Americans **invented** thousands of machines every year. Benjamin Franklin's lightning rod, stove, and bifocals; Eli Whitney's cotton gin; Robert Fulton's steamboat; Samuel Morse's telegraph; Elias Howe's sewing machine. They were always creating a new world to live in.

And if there was one person who created more new worlds than any other, it was Thomas A. Edison. During his lifetime, he made over one thousand inventions. Edison is most famous for his invention of the incandescent [glows with heat] light bulb. With it, he opened up a whole new world for many people: night life! Gas and oil lamps soon began to disappear after 1879. People could do just about anything after dark in greater safety and comfort.

Even before the light bulb, though, Edison had made a name for himself. By 1877, he had invented a copying machine, a microphone, and the phonograph. After the light bulb, Edison's success continued. In the soft glow of his lamp, Edison worked late into the night. By 1902, he had invented a telegraph that worked without wires, a motion picture camera, and a battery.

Checking Up

1. Imagine that you lived during the years 1865–1900. How would some of the inventions on page 299 have changed your life?

2. If you could invent something, what would it be?

Lesson 2 From Rags to Riches

It was something that most Americans dreamed of. Even from the earliest days of the country's history, it was true. All that anyone asked for was a chance at it. It was what America was all about: success!

Success came in many ways. For some, success was wealth. For others, it was fame. For a few, it was power. For all it meant the same thing. In America, *anyone* could rise "from rags to riches."

During the 1860s and 1870s, Horatio Alger wrote about this idea. In all, he produced more than one hundred "rags to riches" stories. Only the characters and details changed from story to story.

Alger's heroes succeeded because of hard work, honesty, education, and clean living. There was always another idea behind each success story, too. People could control and change their lives for the better.

One Success Story

There were many people in the United States who were living examples of the rags to riches stories. One of them was Andrew Carnegie. Carnegie came to the United States from Scotland at the age of twelve. He was a poor boy, so he had to find work. First he labored in a cotton mill. Later, he worked in the telegraph office of the Pennsylvania Railroad.

One day there was an accident on the railroad. Traffic was blocked. Something needed to be done right away. But Carnegie's manager was not there. So, young Carnegie took matters into his own hands. He began to send messages out on the telegraph. Soon the trains were rerouted and moving again.

Carnegie was rewarded with a promotion. He became an assistant to the head of the Pennsylvania Railroad Company. This was the start of his rapid rise to wealth and power.

Carnegie worked hard to learn how businesses ran. He also saved his money. Soon, he took his savings and started his own company that produced steel. By 1890, his company controlled more than two-thirds of the nation's steel production. In 1900 alone, his company's **profits** were $40 million.

One of Horatio Alger's books. Some of his other titles were *Bound to Rise, Frank and Fearless, The Young Adventurer,* and *Strive and Succeed.* What scene is shown on *Brave and Bold?*

profit, what is left when the cost of goods and of carrying on the business is subtracted from the amount of money taken in.

THE LADDER OF FORTUNE.

Industry and Morality bring solid rewards.   Idle schemes and speculations yield poverty and ruin.

The scene: New York City—a tough, competitive, and rapidly growing metropolis. Dick Hunter is an orphaned teenager, trying to make his own way in the world. He is discussing his future with a Mr. Whitney.

You know in this free country poverty in early life is no bar to a man's advancement. I haven't risen very high myself," he added, with a smile, "but have met with moderate success in life; yet there was a time when I was as poor as you."

"Were you, sir?" asked Dick, eagerly.

"Yes, my boy, I have known the time when I have been obliged to go without my dinner because I didn't have enough money to pay for it."

"How did you get up in the world?" asked Dick, anxiously.

"I entered a printing-office as an apprentice, and worked for some years. Then my eyes gave out and I was obliged to give that up. Not knowing what else to do, I went into the country, and worked on a farm. After a while I was lucky enough to invent a machine, which has brought me in a great deal of money. But there was one thing I got while I was in the printing-office which I value more than money."

"What was that, sir?"

"A taste for reading and study. During my leisure hours I improved myself by study, and acquired a large part of the knowledge which I now possess. Indeed, it was one of my books that first put me on the track of the invention, which I afterwards made. So you see, my lad, that my studious habits paid me in money, as well as in another way."

Carnegie believed that his success was the result of hard work. He also believed that successful people had a duty to help others succeed. "The man who dies rich dies disgraced," he said. He gave millions of dollars to build libraries, hospitals, and schools.

(above) A page from one of Horatio Alger's books. What message is Mr. Whitney trying to give Dick Hunter? (left) This drawing appeared in 1875. According to the picture, what qualities do people need to become successful? How will people be rewarded if they have those qualities? Does it appear that a woman could climb the ladder of success?

Checking Up

1. What was it that most Americans believed they could achieve?

2. How did Horatio Alger help Americans learn about the "rags to riches" idea?

3. How was Andrew Carnegie's life an example of "rags to riches"?

4. Do most Americans still believe that the way to get ahead is through hard work, honesty, education, and clean living? Explain your answer.

Lesson 3   Hard Times for Workers

Some inventions made the average person's life easier and more enjoyable. Other inventions helped businesses grow. These inventions were often in the form of new machines. These helped manufacturers produce goods faster and for less.

For example, after 1860, new machines helped the shoe industry. These machines quickly sewed the upper part of the shoe to the sole. More shoes were made in less time and for less money. But such machines also made work boring and dull for the factory worker.

Most of the workers in factories came from farms. They were used to long hours of work that never seemed to end. But working in a factory was different. Farm workers did many different jobs every day. A shoe factory worker, though, usually did the same job over and over again, day after day, week after week, and year after year.

Factory workers in other businesses had similar experiences. A woman who worked in a canning factory in the 1890s described one day's work in this way:

66Side by side in rows of tens or twenties we stand before our tables waiting for the seven o'clock whistle to blow. My first job is an easy one. Anybody could do it. I place a lid of paper in a tin jar-top, over it a cork. This I press down with both hands, tossing the cover, when done, into a pan.

Over in one corner machinery groans and roars. I move in time with the sounds of the machines filling, washing, wiping, packing. Every part of me is offering some of its energy. One hour passes, two, three hours. I fit ten, twenty, fifty dozen caps, and still my energy keeps up.

When the twelve o'clock whistle blows, we herd down to a big dining room and take our places. The lunch bundles are unfolded. In ten minutes the meal is over. There are twenty minutes spent in dancing, singing, resting, and talking.

At 12:30 sharp the whistle draws back the life it has given. I return to my job. My shoulders are beginning to ache. My hands are stiff. My thumbs almost blistered. I am beginning to feel tired. Oh! the monotony [sameness] of it, the never-

The Homestead Steel Works in Pennsylvania. What do you think life would have been like in such a steel town?

ending supply of work to be begun and finished, begun and finished, begun and finished! Would the whistle never blow?**99**

Shoe factory workers, canning factory workers, steel workers—they experienced the same thing. Twelve or fourteen hour work days were common. And they were common six days a week.

Long hours weren't the only complaint. Most factories in the late 1800s were dark, dirty, and dangerous. Many workers were killed or injured on the job every year. Most workers got very little pay for working so long and hard in unsafe places. They would not have agreed so quickly with Horatio Alger or Andrew Carnegie that hard work would bring success.

Rise of Labor Unions

One worker had little power to make changes. What if a worker asked the boss for more pay or better working conditions? The boss could say, "You can quit and find another job, if you don't want to work here." Most workers tried to keep their jobs and make the best of a poor situation.

After 1870, many workers grew tired of feeling that they had no power to change their lives. They also feared the power their bosses had over them. A boss might pay little attention to one worker's complaints. But the boss could not as easily overlook the complaints of many.

To gain power, workers began to form **labor unions**. Union members promised to help each other when times were bad. They also worked together to get better pay, shorter hours, and better working conditions. Unions did help many workers. But not without a struggle.

Employers would usually listen to their workers' complaints. But they didn't always do something about them. Workers and unions had to be willing to do more than talk.

In the 1880s and 1890s, workers tried to solve their problems by striking. A labor **strike** is a stopping of work. An employer could not make money if the workers went on strike. The workers hoped this would force the employer to meet their demands.

A young boy working in a Georgia cotton mill about 1910. Is it legal for children to do such work today?

305

There were over one thousand strikes during these years. Some of them were settled peacefully. Others became violent struggles. One such struggle was between the American Railway Union and the country's railroad owners.

The union workers refused to go back to work. Instead, they gathered outside the company factory. The Illinois state militia was then sent in. The strikers responded by burning a number of railroad cars. A Chicago newspaper reported on what happened next:

66The command to charge was given. . . . From that moment only bayonets were used. . . . A dozen men in the front line of rioters received bayonet wounds. . . .

Tearing up cobble stones, the mob made a determined charge. . . . One by one . . . they [the militia] fired point blank into the crowd. . . .

The police followed with their clubs.

The ground over which the fight occurred was like a battlefield. The men shot by the troops and police lay about like logs.99

This painting is entitled "The Strike." What might the workers be discussing with the owners? How has the artist shown that some workers were willing to do more than talk about their poor working conditions?

Women Fight for Their Rights

Life for many American women changed greatly with the growth of factories. Growing numbers of women took paying jobs. Some went to work in factories. A few went to work in offices. A large number began sewing clothes in their homes to make money.

Women often found **discrimination**, or unfair treatment. Sometimes they were not allowed to do certain kinds of work. Most of the time they were not given the same pay as men. Rarely were women promoted before men.

Beginning in the 1840s, women formed groups to gain more rights. These groups grew much larger after the Civil War, as more and more women took paying jobs. One woman, who wanted her rights as a worker, explained:

66We women did more than keep house, cook, sew, wash, spin and weave, and garden. Many of us had to earn money besides. We worked secretly, because everyone had the idea that men, not women, earned money, and that men alone supported the family. Most women accepted this as normal. I can say that I rebelled, although silently . . . I wanted to work, but I wanted to choose my job and I wanted to collect my wages.99

Soon, women would not be happy to rebel silently. Soon they would not be happy with just changes at work. Soon they would fight for another right they felt all citizens should have: the right to vote. They would, as one worker said, "Rise like lions after slumber!"

Demonstrating for the right to vote.

Checking Up

1. How did factory work differ from work that was done on farms?

2. Why did factory workers form unions?

3. How did American women's lives change with the growth of factories?

Reviewing Chapter 19

Write your answers on paper. Do not write in the book.

Using Key Words

invent   discrimination   strike
labor union   profit

Number your paper 1 to 5. Write a short meaning for each of the above key words.

Reviewing Main Ideas

Number your paper 1 to 4. Next to each number write the letter of the phrase which correctly completes the sentence.

1. American businesses used more and more machines because **a**. there were too few people to do the work. **b**. machines could produce much more than people. **c**. unions wanted machines to replace people.

2. Thomas Edison's most famous invention was **a**. electricity. **b**. the typewriter. **c**. the electric light bulb.

3. The main ideas of Horatio Alger's stories were always **a**. that women should have equal rights. **b**. workers need unions. **c**. people succeed through hard work, education, and honesty.

4. One problem that many workers were not used to when they began to work in a factory was **a**. hard work. **b**. long hours. **c**. monotony.

Thinking Things Over

Take a clean sheet of paper. Make a poster or handout announcing a women's rights meeting or a union membership drive. Your poster or handout should be creative and attractive. Make sure it reflects the important ideas behind the women's rights or union movement.

Practicing Skills

Study the line graph below. Then answer the questions that follow.

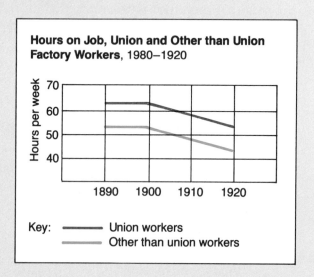

Hours on Job, Union and Other than Union Factory Workers, 1980–1920

1. How many hours per week did the average union worker spend on the job in 1890? How many in 1920?

2. How many hours did the average factory worker who did not belong to a union spend on the job in 1890? How many in 1920?

Chapter

20

Lesson 1 Newcomers
Lesson 2 Learning to Be Americans
Lesson 3 Life in the Growing Cities

Immigration and the Growth of Cities

About seven out of every ten Americans now live in cities. This was not always so. The United States did not become an urban nation until about 1920. Up until then, most Americans lived in small towns or on farms. How did the United States change from a rural nation to an urban nation?

Lesson 1   Newcomers

The bar graph at the right shows how the number of large cities in the United States grew between 1860 and 1920. Cities were growing for several reasons. Many Americans left their farms to look for jobs in the cities. However, the main reason was that more and more **immigrants** came to the United States. Immigrants are people who move from one country and settle in another. The graph at the right shows how many immigrants came to the United States between 1870 and 1920. The map on page 310 shows where they came from.

Where They Came From

Cities such as New York, Philadelphia, Boston, and Chicago grew with each passing day. Before 1890, they grew with immigrants from countries in northern and western Europe. These immigrants were from Germany and Ireland. There were also thousands from England, France, Holland, and Sweden.

After 1890, most immigrants came from countries in eastern and southern Europe. These were newcomers from Poland, Russia, Hungary, Italy, and Greece.

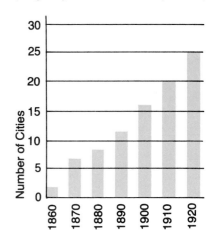

Large Cities in the United States, 1860-1920

(Large city: 250,000 or more persons)

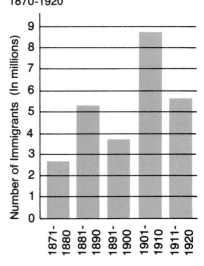

Immigration to the United States, 1870-1920

309

Immigrants also came from the continent of Asia. But by 1920, only about 500,000 Chinese and Japanese immigrants had settled in the United States. In comparison, over eight million immigrants came from Germany and England. Why was there such a difference?

Most Asians settled in California. They found work on the railroad lines and in the gold fields. For years they were welcome because they were hard workers. But by the 1880s, many gold mines had shut down. And the railroads had been built.

To get jobs, Asians were willing to work for less. This angered whites who were out of work. Soon, Americans were discriminating against Asian immigrants. Laws were passed to keep the number of Asian immigrants low.

Why They Came

"He who is well off doesn't move," goes an old Italian saying. Those who are happy, stay where they are. Like the American pioneer, the immigrant moved to find a better life. Like the pioneer, the immigrant saw America as a "promised land."

One such immigrant was Mary Antin. In the early 1880s, she and her family still lived in Russia. But they found it harder and harder to live there in peace. The Antins were Jewish. And in Russia, Jews were persecuted, or treated badly. Finally, her father left Russia to find a home for the family in America.

On this map, the size of the arrows helps show where most immigrants came from. Did more immigrants come from Canada or Asia between 1890 and 1917? About how many immigrants came from Central and South America during that time? Why might more immigrants come from certain areas than others? Why might the United States allow more immigrants from certain areas than others?

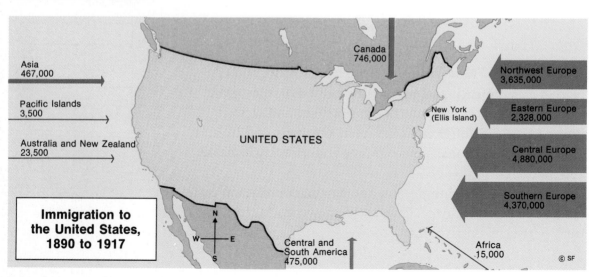

Immigration to the United States, 1890 to 1917

Asia 467,000
Pacific Islands 3,500
Australia and New Zealand 23,500
UNITED STATES
Canada 746,000
New York (Ellis Island)
Northwest Europe 3,635,000
Eastern Europe 2,328,000
Central Europe 4,880,000
Southern Europe 4,370,000
Central and South America 475,000
Africa 15,000
© SF

"... "Next year—in America!" So there was our promised land.... My father was ... glad of his own deliverance
but sore at heart for us whom he left behind.... My father
was inspired by a vision. He saw something—he promised
us something. It was this "America." And "America" became
my dream....

With the children, he argued, every year in Russia was a
year lost. They should be spending the precious years in
school, in learning English, in becoming Americans. United
in America, there were ten chances of our getting to our feet
again to one chance in our scattered, aimless state in Russia.

So at last I was going to America! Really, really going, at
last! The winds rushed in from outer space, roaring in my
ears, "America! America!" "

Immigrants arriving in New York in 1906. What did "the better life" include? Most immigrants needed only a few words to explain: "To practice my own religion." "To work." "To plow my own field." "To be free." "To eat 'till my sides ache." "To own a new pair of shoes."

Checking Up

1. Where did most immigrants to America come from before 1890? After 1890?

2. Why do you think most immigrants settled in cities?

Lesson 2   Learning to Be Americans

For as little as ten dollars, an immigrant could try to find "the better life" in America. That amount paid for the two-week ride aboard a crowded steamship. Crowded? Uncomfortable? It didn't matter. The promised land was big enough for everyone.

Or so the immigrant thought. But by the early 1900s, as many as fifteen thousand immigrants arrived daily. And most entered the United States at the same place. It was a small piece of land in New York Bay called Ellis Island. The immigrants, however, renamed it. It became known as the "island of tears."

Here, the immigrants had their first contact with Americans. "What is your name?" the American official asked. "Where do you come from?" "What work can you do?" "How much money do you have?" "Have you ever been in jail?" Most immigrants were understandably confused. Most could speak only the language they learned at home. Even with an interpreter's help, Ellis Island was a frightening place.

The immigrants were also given a medical exam. Those with serious illnesses could not enter the country. Others

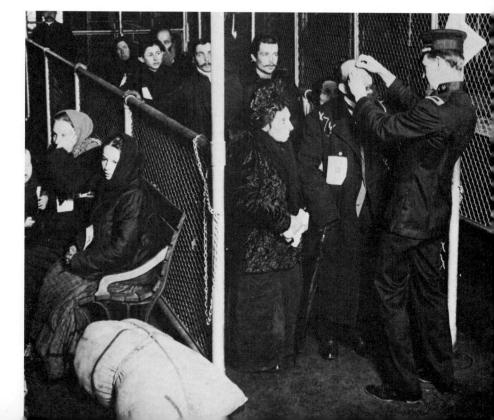

Immigrants being checked at Ellis Island.

might have letters drawn on their backs. Each letter stood for a particular illness. "H" for heart disease. "F" for facial rash. "L" for limp. "E" for an eye disease.

Eight out of every ten immigrants were allowed to stay. But many of them found they now had new last names. This happened for two reasons. The immigrants did not know how to read or write English. And secondly, the immigration officials were too busy. They didn't have the time to carefully record each name. Thus, a Yugoslavian name such as Luchich became Lucas. The Polish name Marciszewski became Muskie. The Russian named Ouspenska became Spensky. It was all part of learning to be an American.

After Ellis Island

After passing through Ellis Island, the immigrants found themselves in New York City. Many stayed. Others went west to Cleveland, Detroit, Chicago, or beyond. Wherever they went, immigrants from the same country usually tried to live near one another. Living near people who spoke the same language made life less confusing.

In each large city, neighborhoods of immigrants grew. In one, everyone might be Greek. In another there might be Czechs, Italians, Chinese, or Russian Jews. Often, the only thing dividing neighborhoods was a single street.

Life was usually difficult for the immigrants. Many of them had little money. Jobs were sometimes hard to get. Immigrants often had to live in rundown housing. Other Americans sometimes called the newcomers names and tried to make them feel unwelcome.

At first, no one helped the immigrants but their families and friends. Then an idea was born. In 1889, Jane Addams and Ellen Starr opened a **settlement house** in the poorest part of Chicago. Hull House, as it was called, gave help to the poor immigrants who lived nearby. They came to Hull House for food, medical care, and education. Soon, most large cities had at least one settlement house.

Immigrants also learned about the American way of life by going to public schools. In the classrooms, hallways, and on the playgrounds, immigrant children learned the rules and customs of their new home. They learned about freedoms and rights that they had never had before.

We, the People

When immigrants arrived in the United States, they were quick to learn the culture of their new home. Just as quickly, many immigrants contributed to the American culture. Many of their contributions came in the form of what we eat.

Ernest A. Hamwi, an immigrant from Syria, invented the first ice cream cone. He was selling zalabias, a wafer-thin pastry, at the St. Louis World's Fair in 1904. The booth next to his was selling ice cream. During a busy period, the booth ran out of clean bowls. Hamwi quickly rolled one of his zalabias into the shape of a cone and scooped a ball of ice cream into the center.

Also introduced at the St. Louis World's fair was the hamburger on a bun. A vendor began selling the ground beef patties on buns after he, too, ran out of dishes.

The hamburger as a meal was born in Germany. There, in the city of Hamburg, cooks tried to improve upon the Russian custom of serving *uncooked* ground meat. In the 1880s German immigrants brought the idea of *cooked* ground meat with them.

313

An Italian neighborhood in New York City about 1900. What activity is taking place on this street? What sounds and smells would greet you on this street?

As Mary Antin explained, the immigrant learned about America in another way, too.

“Our learning about American ways began with the first step on the new soil. My father instructed us even on the way from the pier to Wall Street.

The first meal was a lesson. My father produced food, ready to eat, without any cooking, from little tin cans. After the meal, he showed us a piece of furniture, which he called a "rocking-chair." There were five of us newcomers, and we found five different ways of getting into the American chair.

In our flat there was no bathtub. So in the evening my father took us to the public baths. As we moved along, I was delighted with the lights of the streets. People did not need to carry lanterns. In America, then, everything was free, as we had heard in Russia.”

Checking Up

1. Why do you think the immigrants renamed Ellis Island?

2. How did immigrants learn about life in America?

Beacon of Freedom

A large ship steamed into New York harbor on a chilly morning in 1910. Hundreds of excited immigrants were on deck. They spoke many different languages: Polish, Greek, Hungarian, Russian. The word "America," though, was the same in all languages.

Mothers and fathers lifted their small children to view the harbor and the skyline of New York City. And then they saw it. Suddenly, there was silence on deck. A small boy whispered, "Look Mama, there it is!"

None of the people had seen the Statue of Liberty before. But all knew it like a friend. To these immigrants, and millions of others, it was a sign of freedom.

At the statue's feet lay broken chains. In its left arm was a copy of the Declaration of Independence. And in its right hand, high above the harbor, was the torch.

A young girl who had been on the ship said that "the torch was a beacon [light] of freedom. I felt like a new person as I looked at it. From that moment, I knew that whatever I became would be up to me. In America I would have a fair chance to make the most of myself."

In 1884, France gave the statue to the United States. France said the United States was a symbol of liberty all over the world.

Many Americans quickly started to raise money to pay for the pedestal on which the statue stands. One, Joseph Pulitzer, was an immigrant from Hungary. He had found freedom and opportunity in the United States. He wrote articles in his newspaper asking Americans to give money.

Soon, other newspapers around the nation were helping raise money. Even schoolchildren gave their savings to the cause. By 1886, the pedestal was built. The Statue of Liberty was put in place.

The words of Emma Lazarus, an immigrant, appear on a metal tablet inside the pedestal. She wanted to tell the world about the freedom and hope that could be found in America.

Give me your tired, your poor, Your huddled masses yearning to breathe free, The wretched refuse of your teeming shore, Send them, the homeless, tempest-tost to me, I lift my lamp beside the golden door!

Lesson 3   Life in the Growing Cities

On October 8 and 9, 1871, a large fire swept the city of Chicago. The fire was later traced to the barn of Mrs. Catherine O'Leary, on the city's west side. A story began that Mrs. O'Leary's cow had kicked over a lantern, which started the fire. Whether the cow really started the fire isn't important. What is important is that the Great Chicago Fire killed 200 persons and left 200,000 without homes. Almost all of the stores and offices in downtown Chicago were destroyed.

Improvements in the Cities

The Great Chicago Fire caused leaders of big cities all over the country to think hard about safety. City governments began writing tougher laws about building. Some said that wooden buildings and sidewalks could no longer be built. Others said how much space there must be between buildings.

In the twenty years that followed, other changes appeared. New street lights made it possible for people to stay out late at night. Better ways were found to carry water to homes.

Downtown Chicago in 1910. What different methods of transportation do you see in this picture? How was the road made? Photograph courtesy of *The Chicago Historical Society*.

316

A skyscraper under construction in New York City.

History Update

City-dwellers have always had to put up with a variety of problems. About 1900, they thought the worst problem was pollution. But it wasn't the kind of pollution that billowed out of factory smoke stacks, or bubbled up from lakes and streams. No, it was the kind that came from horses.

This carrier of goods and people, this four-legged friend of sport could leave up to twenty-five pounds of manure daily on the city streets. In a city such as New York, it represented more than just eye and nose pollution. When it rained, carriages and people had to wade through almost a sea of manure. When it dried, the manure turned into a fine dust that crept onto and into everything.

What was the solution? "The car!" said many people thankfully. Surely, they thought, cities would become quieter, cleaner, and healthier places to live now that the car was replacing the horse.

Cities also put in sewers. Some city governments no longer allowed people to have cows or chickens in their backyards.

Cities grew upward and outward. They grew upward when a new kind of building, the **skyscraper**, appeared in the 1880s. The first skyscraper had ten stories. As time passed, buildings went even higher. Cities grew outward as streetcar lines were built. The streetcars made it possible for people to live far from their work.

The cities also became centers for entertainment. Concerts, shows, and plays brought people from their homes into theaters. Traveling shows opened and closed nightly in small theaters. Large circuses got their start. Parks were built as places to enjoy the outdoors.

Learning and ideas bloomed. Colleges and universities drew students from all parts of the country. Magazines from the cities reached people in small towns and on farms. Public libraries opened and grew.

The Other Side of City Life

There was an ugly side to city life, too. There simply was not enough good housing for everyone. Immigrants were packed into dirty, dark **tenements**. These were cheap apartment buildings with small rooms, few windows, and few bathrooms. Trash could often be found everywhere.

Jacob Riis, an immigrant from Denmark, wanted to change life in the tenements. He wrote magazine articles about life in the tenements. Stories, like the following one, influenced the government to try and fix up the tenements.

317

(top) Clothes lines bring a neighborhood together. (bottom) A tenement in New York City about 1910. This room served as bedroom, living room, and kitchen.

66The hall is dark and you might stumble over the children pitching pennies back there. Not that it would hurt them; kicks and cuffs [slaps] are their daily diet. . . . All the fresh air that ever enters those stairs comes from the hall door that is forever slamming and from the windows of dark bedrooms. . . . The sinks are in the hallways, that all the tenants may have access. . . . The tenement is much like the one in front we just left, only fouler, closer, darker . . .99

The future of the cities lay with the people they drew to them. And the city drew all kinds of people. The city—it was, for many, the only place where a fortune could be made. If you failed one day, the next would surely be better. And if you failed again, maybe your children would do better. The people—they did not easily give up their dreams.

Checking Up

1. How did the Great Chicago Fire help change the look of some American cities?

2. How did cities grow upward and outward?

3. What was the "ugly side" of city life?

GOOD FOR WHAT AILS YOU

Good for what ails man, woman, or beast. FIX-IT-ALL cures broken bones, poor eyesight, colds, chicken pox, aching feet, and flea bites. Keeps bugs off plants. Stops cars from rusting. Stock up now.

Chances are, you will never see an advertisement like this one. But 100 years ago, claims as wild as this were often made about patent medicines. Patent medicines were liquids and pills that a person could buy without a doctor's advice. Many of them were sold by traveling shows. Most of these medicines had no value in curing illness. In fact, some of them were drugs that made healthy people sick. The drugs killed pain but didn't kill germs.

Most Americans did not then have ways to find out whether a medicine was good or bad. They had to trust the person who made it or sold it.

The same was true of food. Many Americans did not know whether the food they were eating was good or bad. As more and more Americans lived in cities, fewer of them were growing crops and raising animals. They had to trust the person who sold or packaged food.

In 1906, a book called *The Jungle* was written. It was a story, but it was also based on real events. *The Jungle* was about the meat-packing business. Here is a short description of what went on in one factory.

WOLCOTT'S INSTANT PAIN ANNIHILATOR.

Fig 1. Demon of Catarrh. Fig 2. Demon of Neuralgia. Fig 3. Demon of Headache. Fig 4. Demon of Weak Nerves. Fig 5. Demon of Toothache.

66There would be meat stored in great piles in rooms; and the water from leaky roofs would drip over it, and thousands of rats would race about on it. These rats were nuisances [troublesome], and the

319

A sausage-making plant in Chicago.

packers would put poisoned bread out for them, they would die, and then the rats, bread, and meat would go into the hoppers [grinders] together.**"**

The Jungle shocked America. Congress rapidly passed the Pure Food and Drug Act of 1906. This law set up rules for food packers. It said they could not prepare or sell spoiled or dirty foods. It also set up rules for drug makers. It said that they could not sell drugs with labels that told lies. This law tried to make sure that foods and medicines were pure.

Other laws were passed after 1906 that made even more rules about food and drugs. All of these laws try to keep Americans from being cheated when they buy foods or medicines.

Write your answers on paper. Do not write in the book.

Using Key Words

immigrant   **tenement**
settlement house   **skyscraper**

Number your paper from 1 to 4. Write a short meaning for each of the above key words.

Reviewing Main Ideas

Number your paper 1 to 4. Next to each number write the letter of the phrase which correctly completes the sentence.

1. The United States became an urban country about   **a.** 1865.   **b.** 1880.
   c. 1920.

2. The main reason that American cities grew in the period after the Civil War was because   **a.** many southern farms were destroyed during the Civil War.   **b.** of the large number of immigrants that entered the United States.   **c.** people wanted to live close to schools and universities.

3. From 1880 to 1920 most immigrants to the United States came from
   a. Europe.   **b.** Africa.   **c.** Asia.

4. Immigrants came to America to
   a. find better jobs.   **b.** find more freedom.   **c.** find better jobs and more freedom.

Thinking Things Over

You are on the immigrant ship shown on page 311. What worries and hopes do you have about living in a new country?

Practicing Skills

Carefully examine the bar graph below.

1. In what decade did the largest number of immigrants arrive from England, Ireland, and Germany?

2. In what decade did the largest number of immigrants arrive from Italy, Austria-Hungary, and Russia?

3. When did the immigrant population change from the first group to the second?

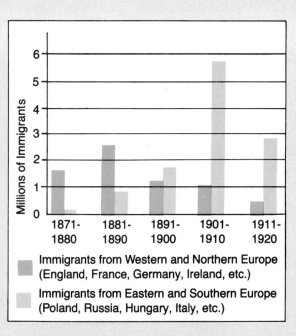

Immigrants from Western and Northern Europe (England, France, Germany, Ireland, etc.)

Immigrants from Eastern and Southern Europe (Poland, Russia, Hungary, Italy, etc.)

UNIT 5 TEST

What Do You Know?

Write your answers on paper. Do not write in the book.

Words to Know

amendment	union
sharecropper	discrimination
segregate	immigrant
boom town	settlement house
transcontinental	tenement
homestead	strike
invent	

Number your paper from 1 to 13. Write the definition for each of the words above.

Ideas to Know

Some of the sentences below are true and some are false. Number your paper 1 to 20. Write either *true* or *false* by each number. If you think an answer is false, explain why on your paper.

1. Slavery continued in the northern states for many years after the Civil War.

2. The government helped freed slaves by setting up schools.

3. Once the southern armies were defeated, southern whites accepted freed blacks as equals.

4. The southern way of life changed because of the destruction during the Civil War.

5. Black men gained the right to vote after the Civil War.

6. "Jim Crow" laws were passed to end segregation.

7. Large numbers of Americans moved west because of the discovery of gold, silver, and other metals.

8. Boom towns and cattle towns helped organize life in the West.

9. Asians, whites, and blacks all worked together to build the first transcontinental railroad.

10. More Americans moved west after the opening of the transcontinental railroad.

11. Barbed wire was used to keep Indians off settlers' property.

12. One cause of the Indian wars was that Indians and settlers wanted to use the land in different ways.

13. The increased use of machines after the Civil War helped American businesses grow.

14. Machines were used in factories because they helped workers produce more.

15. People believed that, in America, anyone could succeed by working hard.

16. Unions grew in the late 1800s because most factory jobs were dangerous and paid little.

17. Strikes in America were always peaceful.

18. The greatest number of immigrants to America came from Europe.

19. Once they arrived, immigrants had little to learn about living as Americans.

20. Many people were attracted to live in the city because life in the tenements was so comfortable.

Using What You Know

1. You are the director of education for Hull House in 1895. Name two classes you would teach to newly arrived immigrants. What ideas or skills would you teach to help the immigrant learn to live in America?

Hull House Immigrant Education Program

	Title	Ideas/Skills taught	Reason class is useful
Class 1			
Class 2			

2. Use the map on page 283 to answer the following questions.
   1. What two railroads were built between San Francisco and Omaha?
   2. Abilene and San Antonio were two cities on the _____ trail.
   3. The Goodnight-Loving Trail connected the cities of _____ and _____.

3. Look at the picture on page 305. Pretend you are one of the children working in the picture. Write a paragraph explaining what you must do every day for your job. How do you feel about your job?

4. Look at the graph below. Use it to answer the following questions.
   a. What was America's population in 1860? In 1900?
   b. How much did America's population grow from 1860 to 1900?

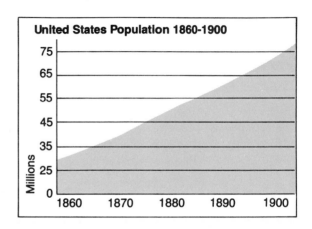

United States Population 1860-1900

323

Unit 6 New Directions

10 . . . 9 . . . 8 . . . It was July 16, 1969. The spaceship *Apollo 11* was about to roar off the launch pad at Cape Kennedy, Florida. 7 . . . 6 . . . 5 . . . It had started eight years before. On May 25, 1961, President John F. Kennedy asked the nation to meet the challenge ". . . of landing a man on the moon and returning him safely to earth." 4 . . . 3 . . . 2 . . . This was not the first important decision or challenge Americans would face in their history. Space was a new frontier. And new frontiers had been crossed before.

1 . . . "We have lift-off!"

Chapter
21

Lesson 1 Gaining New Lands
Lesson 2 The World at War

America Becomes a World Power

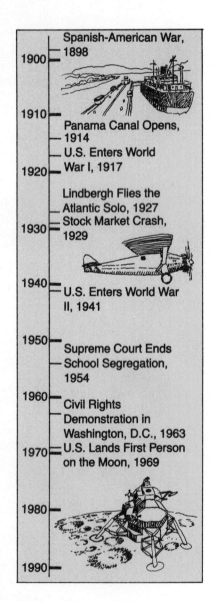

Spanish-American War, 1898

1900

1910

Panama Canal Opens, 1914

U.S. Enters World War I, 1917

1920

Lindbergh Flies the Atlantic Solo, 1927

Stock Market Crash, 1929

1930

1940

U.S. Enters World War II, 1941

1950

Supreme Court Ends School Segregation, 1954

1960

Civil Rights Demonstration in Washington, D.C., 1963

1970

U.S. Lands First Person on the Moon, 1969

1980

1990

Until the 1890s, Americans were busy with things at home. They were settling the West. They were also starting new businesses and farming new lands.

By the 1890s, however, much of the West had been settled. American farms and factories were producing more than ever before. Because of this, some Americans began to look outside their own borders. They became interested in gaining markets in other countries. There, they could sell **surplus**, or extra, farm and factory goods. Americans could also buy more raw materials for their factories.

Americans wanted to show other countries that the United States was a strong nation with world-wide interests. But Americans also remembered President Washington's advice about not getting too involved with other countries. In this chapter you will read about America's new world interests. You will also see how this led to a greater involvement with other countries.

Lesson 1   Gaining New Lands

Having overseas markets and becoming a world power may have been new ideas for the United States. But they were not to Europeans. Spain, France, and England had had those goals for many years. They had been setting up colonies in Latin America, Africa, and Asia since the 1500s.

It was easy for European countries to trade in these areas. Africa and Latin America were within range of their shipping companies and large navies. And by 1869, Asia was, too. The Suez Canal had opened shipping between the Mediterranean and the Red Sea. This meant that ships from Europe no longer had to go around Africa to get to Asia.

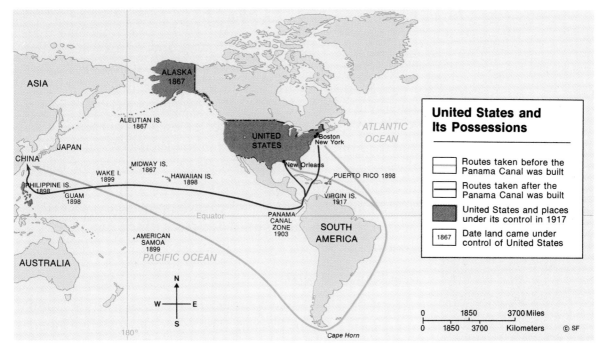

United States and Its Possessions

Routes taken before the Panama Canal was built
Routes taken after the Panama Canal was built
United States and places under its control in 1917
1867 Date land came under control of United States

The United States did not want to be left out of this growing trade. The first place the United States naturally looked to for trade was Latin America and the Caribbean. You can see why by looking at the map above.

By the 1890s, most of Africa was already divided up among European nations. So the other place the United States looked to for trade was Asia. The problem with Asia, however, was distance. As the above map shows, most ships left the ports of New York, Boston, or New Orleans. They had to sail all the way around South America and across the Pacific Ocean.

Such a trip to Asia was long and dangerous. A ship had to carry enough food, water, and fuel to last six to nine months. Ship captains could not count on finding an island where they could take on supplies. Also, storms sunk many ships as they went around Cape Horn. To have more trade with Asia, the United States had to meet two needs.

- Islands had to be found along the shipping routes in the Pacific Ocean. American ships could stop at these islands for supplies.
- Another route had to be found to avoid the trip around South America.

An inch represents how many miles on this map's scale? About how far would a ship have to travel from New York to China *before* the building of the Panama Canal? How far would it travel after?

327

The Spanish-American War

In 1898, the United States fought and won a war with Spain. There were many causes of what has become known as the Spanish-American War. The results, however, meant one thing. Under the treaty that ended the war, the United States gained some of Spain's colonies. Two of them, Guam and the Philippine Islands, are in the Pacific Ocean. Find these islands on the map on page 327. Gaining these islands helped the United States trade with Asia. American ships began stopping at these islands to pick up fuel and other supplies. The islands also served as a place to sell American goods.

The Panama Canal

In 1903, the United States signed a treaty with the Latin American nation of Panama. The treaty allowed the United States to build a canal through Panama. The Panama Canal is shown on the map on page 327. Americans spent almost ten years building the canal. Its opening in 1914 also helped increase trade with Asia. The trip from eastern ports was now much shorter. Instead of going around Cape Horn, American ships passed through Central America. Soon, American trade with Asia was eight times more than what it had been before the canal was built.

By 1914, the United States was on its way to meeting its new goals. It was trading with countries all over the world. And it was becoming a world power.

The Panama Canal under construction. The project took ten years to complete and cost approximately $400 million. The canal is a little over forty miles long. Ships pass through three locks that raise them about eighty-five feet above sea level. For a look at the canal today, turn to page 427.

Checking Up

1. How did European nations and the United States try to find raw materials and sell surplus goods?

2. Why was it important for the United States to gain islands in the Pacific Ocean?

3. How did the opening of the Panama Canal help the United States trade with Asia?

4. What do you think it means to be a "world power"?

Lesson 2   The World at War

In Flanders fields the poppies blow
Between the crosses, row on row,
   That mark our place; and in the sky
   The larks, still bravely singing, fly
Scarce heard amid the guns below.

          —from *In Flanders Fields*

I have a rendezvous with Death
On some scarred slope of battered hill,
   When Spring comes round again this year
   And the first meadow flowers appear.

          —from *I Have a Rendezvous with Death*

The poets speak of crosses and soldiers. They speak of guns and waiting for Spring and Death. They speak of the world at war in 1914.

"Flanders" is an area in France. That was the scene of some of the heaviest fighting in World War I. The poet, John McCrae, was an English soldier during the war.

The second poet speaks about a rendezvous, or meeting with Death. Does he have much hope that he will live through the war?

Both poets do have hope that the world will return to normal. What lines in the poems tell you that?

Today, we know the war these poets speak of as World War I. Like many wars, no one expected World War I to last very long. No one expected many people to die. Yet, this war was unlike any other in history. In past European wars, hired soldiers had done the fighting. World War I was fought by ordinary people. One day they were at work in an office or factory. The next, they were learning how to be soldiers.

Some weapons were used for the first time. Tanks rumbled across the battlefields. Airplanes sputtered through the sky. Submarines crept below the ocean surface. And all destroyed far more than in past wars. In one battle in 1916, for example, 700,000 men were killed or wounded.

Historians do not agree on what caused the war. But some results were clear when it ended in 1918. Millions of people had died. Hundreds of cities and towns had been destroyed. And flowers would not bloom in some fields for many years to come.

historian, a person who studies how people lived and what they did in the past.

World War I started as a fight between two **alliances** in Europe. The map on page 330 shows the countries in each alliance. It was felt that the alliances would make it harder to go to war. No country would want to fight if the sides were equal. But the alliances actually made it easier to go to war. The countries in each alliance agreed to fight for their partners if one was attacked. When one country from each alliance went to war, all the countries went to war.

alliance, people or nations that have joined together for a special purpose.

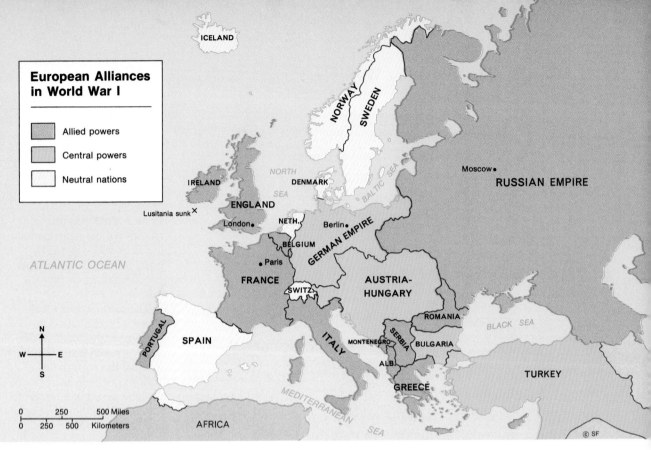

European Alliances in World War I

- Allied powers
- Central powers
- Neutral nations

ICELAND

NORWAY

SWEDEN

NORTH SEA

BALTIC SEA

Moscow•

RUSSIAN EMPIRE

IRELAND

DENMARK

ENGLAND

Lusitania sunk ✕

London•

NETH.

Berlin•

GERMAN EMPIRE

BELGIUM

• Paris

ATLANTIC OCEAN

FRANCE

SWITZ.

AUSTRIA-HUNGARY

ROMANIA

BLACK SEA

N
W—E
S

PORTUGAL

SPAIN

ITALY

MONTENEGRO

SERBIA

BULGARIA

ALB.

GREECE

TURKEY

MEDITERRANEAN SEA

AFRICA

0   250   500 Miles
0   250   500   Kilometers

© SF

Which countries were members of the Allied powers alliance? Which were members of the Central powers alliance? Name three countries which remained neutral during the war.

The War and the United States

Going to war for another country is what the United States had tried to avoid. It did not want to be "dragged into" anybody else's war. When the war began in 1914, most Americans said "This is Europe's problem, not ours!" President Wilson told the country that the United States would remain neutral.

The United States almost entered the war in 1915. On May 7, a German submarine sank an English ship, the *Lusitania*. See the map on page 330. Over one hundred Americans were on board. President Wilson quickly protested. Eventually, Germany apologized. It promised not to sink other passenger ships without first protecting the passengers.

Germany would break and make the same promise twice again. By 1917, many Americans were asking for war. At that time, they were feeling closer to England and France than to Germany. President Wilson had learned that Germany was trying to talk Mexico into attacking the United States. This knowledge made many Americans even angrier.

In 1917, President Wilson asked Congress to declare war on Germany. Submarine warfare was one of the causes he mentioned. But he raised another issue as well.

> 66The challenge is to mankind. . . . We will not choose the path of submission [giving in] . . . . We are glad . . . to fight thus for the ultimate peace of the world, and for the liberation of its people . . . for the rights of nations great and small . . . to choose their way of life. . .99

The war caused some changes in the United States even before Americans joined the fight. Factories did well because the fighting countries bought supplies in the United States. Since the war stopped immigrants from coming to America, factories looked elsewhere for workers. They sent agents to the South to persuade black Americans to move to northern cities and work in factories. The agents promised high pay and free train passes to the North. Thousands of blacks moved north. This is often called The Great Northern Drive. One black man in Alabama wrote this letter to a newspaper, the *Chicago Defender:*

(top) United States troops advance against German forces in World War I. (bottom) An all black regiment ships off to the war in France. In all, over 116,000 American soldiers died during the war.

Posters such as this encouraged people to buy war bonds. The money from the sale of war bonds was used to pay for the cost of the war. People who bought the war bonds felt that they were helping win the war, just like soldiers.

66Sir: I am writing to let you know that there are 15 or 20 families that want to come up there at once but can't because they have no money. If you send 20 passes, there is no doubt that every one of us will come at once. We can't get a living out of what we do now. Some of these people are farmers, and some are cooks, barbers, and blacksmiths. The greater part are farmers, good workers, and honest people. We work but can't get much for it, and they don't want us to go away.

I am a reader of the *Defender* and am delighted to know how times are there. I was glad to know we could get some one to pass us away from here to a better land.99

American women also began working in factories in growing numbers. When the war removed men from their jobs, women stepped in to replace them. They held many jobs that had been closed to them before.

The war ended in November, 1918, with an Allied Powers' victory. The fighting had destroyed people, buildings, land. France, Germany, and Russia each lost over one million soldiers. England lost about 900,000 soldiers. Some governments of Europe were unable to govern. Many countries had lost their colonies. The United States, however, came out of the war as one of the five strongest countries in the world.

Checking Up

1. List the countries in each of the two alliances.

2. Why weren't alliances such a good idea after all?

3. How was World War I different from earlier wars?

4. Why did the United States want to stay out of the war? According to President Wilson, what challenges faced the world?

5. What changes took place in the United States because of World War I?

Write your answers on paper. Do not write in the book.

Using Key Words

surplus   alliance   historian

Number your paper 1 to 3. Write a short meaning for each of the above key words.

Reviewing Main Ideas

Number your paper 1 to 4. Next to each number write the letter of the phrase which correctly completes the sentence.

1. By the 1890s, American factories were producing so many goods that some businesses wanted to start selling to   **a.** Americans living in the West.   **b.** Americans living in the cities.   **c.** people in other countries.

2. In the 1890s, America first tried to set up trade markets in   **a.** Africa.   **b.** Europe.   **c.** Asia.

3. The Panama Canal and the Philippine Islands were important to the United States because they shortened the trade routes to   **a.** Africa.   **b.** South America.   **c.** Asia.

4. Some Americans wanted to enter World War I against Germany because   **a.** Germany asked England to attack the United States.   **b.** German submarines attacked American ships.   **c.** Germany closed the Panama Canal.

Thinking Things Over

World War I was fought by ordinary people. Design a poster for the army or navy that encourages American men and women to enlist, or join voluntarily, during World War I. Posters such as this usually had slogans that gave reasons for joining. One of the posters on page 332 had a slogan that encouraged people to buy war bonds. It was "Weapons For Liberty." What slogan will your poster have?

Practicing Skills

With the map below, correctly match the location of each of the following places.

a. Germany   1. _____

b. England   2. _____

c. Philippine Islands 3. _____

d. Panama Canal   4. _____

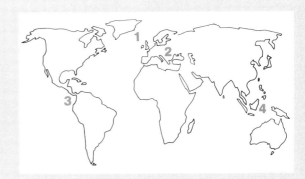

Chapter

22

Lesson 1 Prosperity and
the New Production
Lesson 2 New Roles for Women
Lesson 3 Good Times, Bad Times

The 1920s: The Great Promise

"Every day in every way, things are getting better and better." This was an important idea in the 1920s. Many people then thought the future looked rosy. But like roses, futures can fade.

Lesson 1   Prosperity and the New Production

prosperity, a time of good fortune, success; good economic times.

"This country believes in **prosperity**," said President Calvin Coolidge. He meant that Americans wanted to live well. Never before had so many Americans lived as well as they did during the 1920s.

Americans gazed longingly at store windows and advertisements. There they saw the many new products of American technology–electric refrigerators and vacuum cleaners, radios, washing machines, and cars. All of these products made life easier and more enjoyable.

During the 1920s, American workers produced more goods in a shorter time than ever before. There were at least two reasons for this. Americans were happy that World War I was over. They wanted their lives to return to normal. Because of this, they worked very hard at their jobs. But just as important, they worked with new tools and machines. The result was an increase in the amount of goods workers made.

Farmers, for example, worked with new tractors, reapers, and combines. As a result, farmers produced more crops in less time. In 1929, American farmers produced three times as much as they had in 1865.

The Automobile Industry

No greater increase in production was seen than in the automobile business. Automobiles had been produced since the 1890s. They weren't affordable, though, until the 1920s.

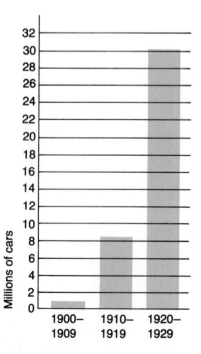

Automobiles Made
1900–1929

The assembly line helped build cars quickly and inexpensively. In the 1920s, the Ford Motor Company assembly lines produced as many as 20,000 cars a day.

The reason for this was **mass production**. Mass production means making goods in large amounts with the help of machines and standard parts. Goods that are made this way cost less than goods produced one by one.

In 1913, Henry Ford began to mass produce cars. He divided the work of making a car into small steps. Each of his workers was responsible for a single job. As a car was being made, it was pulled along an **assembly line** past each worker. By the time the car reached the end of the assembly line, all the jobs had been done.

Before Henry Ford used mass production, only the rich could buy cars. The cars cost a lot because the workers could only make a few. With mass production, great numbers of cars were produced. The cost of buying them went down. Ford's cars sold for around $400. That price was well within many people's pocketbooks.

assembly line, a row of workers and machines along which work is passed until the final product is made.

A Ride in the "Horseless Carriage"

One writer described her family's first car this way:

❝Dad had seen the car in the factory and fallen in love with it. He named it Foolish Carriage because, he said, it was foolish for any man with twelve children to think he could afford a horseless carriage.

(top right) *Real* horsepower at work! The horse proved that it was still an important worker in the 1920s.
(above) This ad appeared in the *Saturday Evening Post* magazine in 1908. This car was built before assembly lines were used and cost $850 dollars. When the assembly lines started in 1914, the cost of a car went down to about $400 or $500. How did the assembly line help reduce the cost of making a car?

The car kicked when he cranked and spat oil in his face when he looked into the engine. It squealed when he put on the brakes and rumbled when he changed speed. Sometimes Dad would spit, squeal, and rumble back. But he never won a single fight with the car.

As in many cars then, the driver sat on the right side. Whoever sat to the left of Mother and the babies on the front seat had to be on the lookout. That person would tell Dad when he could pass the car ahead.

"You can make it," the lookout would shout.

"Put out your hand," Dad would holler.

Eleven hands would come out from both sides of the car. We had seen Dad nick fenders, hit chickens, and knock down trees, and we weren't taking any chances.

The growth of the car business caused other industries to grow. They had to make all the things a car uses. Service stations sprang up. New and better ways of paving roads were found. People began opening motels (motor hotels) to serve traveling drivers.

Checking Up

---

1. What is prosperity? What were some examples of American prosperity in the 1920s?

2. Why were American workers producing more in the 1920s?

3. Explain how the cost of an item goes down as more of the item is produced.

Lesson 2 New Roles for Women

Women's **suffrage**, or the right to vote, had long been a cause for women. Many had hoped to gain the right to vote after the Civil War. But it was not to be. The Fifteenth Amendment to the Constitution gave black men the right to vote. Women were not included.

Between 1890 and 1919 the women's rights movement grew very strong. Women gained the right to vote in many states. Montana was one of the first states where women could vote. In 1916, the voters in Montana elected Jeannette Rankin to Congress. She was the first woman to serve in the House of Representatives.

Jeannette Rankin worked with other leaders such as Harriot Stanton Blatch, Carrie Chapman Catt, and Alice Paul. Together they worked for national suffrage. They wanted women in *every* state to be able to vote.

These women could have gone from state to state trying to get the right to vote. But this would have been a slow process. The quickest way for all women to gain the right to vote was by amending the Constitution.

Women demonstrating for the right to vote.

337

Many men had long believed that women should not take part in government. They also felt that women could not do certain kinds of work or understand certain ideas. The work that women did during World War I helped change the minds of many men. They saw that women could contribute much in government and at work.

In 1919, Congress passed an amendment to the Constitution. It said that women could not be kept from voting. The amendment went to the states for **ratification**, meaning approval. Enough states gave their approval by August 26, 1920.

"Is the women's rights movement done? Will they stop parading about in protest?" many people asked. "No!" shouted the women. Carrie Chapman Catt further explained:

66. . . What is the women's movement and what is its aim? It is a demand for equality of opportunity between the sexes. It means that when and if a woman is as well qualified as a man to fill a position, she shall have an equal and un-prejudiced [fair] chance to secure it 99

Carrie Chapman Catt speaks on the rights of all women. The speech was made from a boat near the Statue of Liberty.

Many women wanted the same opportunities as men. They wanted to work outside the home. Some wanted to go to college and have a career.

During the 1920s, many women moved into the business world or attended college. There, many met other forms of discrimination. They often received different treatment and lower pay. The struggle against these practices continues today.

Checking Up

1. Why do you think women wanted the right to vote? Why do you think it was denied them?

2. How did their work in World War I help women get the vote?

3. What happened to the women's rights movement after the amendment was ratified? What rights do women still want?

Lesson 3 Good Times, Bad Times

"Hurry! Hurry! Hurry! Step right up and try a ride in an aer-o-plane. See your house from the air." With shouts like these, airplane pilots urged Americans at country fairs to try something new. In the 1920s, airplanes were very small. They could not fly fast or far. But riding in one was an adventure. And adventure was one thing Americans wanted in the 1920s.

Americans wanted to forget the horrors of World War I. They wanted to relax and enjoy themselves. The new methods of production gave them time to do that. People were producing more goods in less time. That is one reason why they did not have to work as long as workers did in the past. By 1929, many American workers were on the job for only 48 hours a week. In 1865, most Americans had worked 60 or more hours a week.

The Roaring Twenties

Americans chose to use their spare time having fun. For many, fun came in the form of **fads**. Fads are things that people are interested in for a short time. In the 1920s, it was common to see people in a goldfish-swallowing contest. A few people even chose to sit atop flagpoles. Thousands attended marathon-dance contests. Americans also fell in love with cross-word puzzles and a Chinese game called mahjongg (mä'jong'). And speaking of love, the "true romance" magazines sold by the millions!

Many new words and sayings were heard during the 1920s. Below is a partial list.

ALL WET—wrong
APPLESAUCE—nonsense; same as baloney, bunk, banana oil, hokum, and horsefeathers.
BEE'S KNEES—a great person or thing; same as berries, darb, and the cat's meow.
BIG CHEESE—an important person
CHEATERS—eyeglasses
DOGS—human feet
FLAT TIRE—a dumb, boring person
GOOFY—silly
JAKE—okay
KEEN—attractive
SCRAM—leave in a hurry
SWELL—great; marvelous
TIN LIZZIE—an old car

A goldfish-swallowing contest. One contestant claimed to have swallowed thirty goldfish. What fads do Americans have today?

339

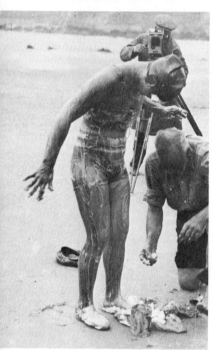

(top)
Carroll Dickerson's jazz band in Chicago in 1924. (above) Gertrude Ederle being rubbed with grease before her channel crossing in 1926. Why was it necessary to rub long-distance swimmers with grease?

These fads all made the 1920s a time of new sights. But the 1920s were also a time of new sounds. People discovered the music of "jazz" and "the blues." Millions stared at movie screens and listened to the first "talkie" films. Also heard for the first time was radio. Radio brought news, sports, and comedy right into a family's living room.

Radio, movies, and sports took up more and more time in people's lives. The stars in these businesses became heroes to the whole country. Babe Ruth was baseball's greatest hero. He drew so many fans to New York's Yankee Stadium that it was called the "house that Ruth built." In 1926, swimming champion, Gertrude Ederle, achieved a long-dreamed-of goal. She broke the men's record by swimming the 35 miles across the English Channel in 14 hours and 31 minutes.

The cheers for other sports heroes still echo in stadiums across the United States. Gene Tunney and Jack Dempsey in boxing. Helen Wills and Bill Tilden in tennis. Red Grange and Jim Thorpe in football.

In movies, women fell for the romantic Rudolph Valentino. Men came to see Mary Pickford and the "Modern Girl," Clara Bow. These women did more than just make films popular, however. They opened up a new career for other women. And one of the greatest stars in movies was not a man or woman. It was a mouse. Mickey Mouse, the cartoon character, was born in 1928.

Of all the heroes, though, none was greater than Charles A. Lindbergh. In 1927 he became the first person to fly alone nonstop from New York to Paris. He had to stay awake and fly for 33½ hours. A "ticker-tape" parade greeted him when he returned to New York.

Lindbergh's flight helped interest people in flying. But as one person put it, Lindbergh gave America so much more.

66He is the modern 'perfect knight . . .' He has all that we want for ourselves: youth, honor, romance, victory. He is the dream that is in our hearts. He has shown us that we are not rotten to the core . . .99

Even after Lindbergh's flight, a few people remained worried about the United States in the 1920s. They saw too much nonsense—too much fun. No one seemed to take life seriously. As you will read next they had reason to be worried. The country had more than just a roaring, or fun side. It had a troubled side, too.

The Other Side of the 1920s

Not everyone shared in the prosperity of the roaring twenties. One group that didn't was the farmers. One reason for their bad times had to do with changes in farming. Farming was no longer just a family business. Farmers grew crops

(above left) Rudolph Valentino and Vilma Banky starring in *Son of the Sheik.* (above) Mickey Mouse in 1928. Name some current movie "stars."

Facts and Figures

The *Spirit of St. Louis* that Charles Lindbergh flew to Paris had no front window. In its place, Lindbergh installed an extra gas tank. This tank held some of the 450 gallons of fuel carried on the trip. The fuel weighed about 4,000 pounds. By comparison, Space Shuttle burns about 8,000 pounds of fuel *every second* on liftoff.

341

In the 1930s, farm prices fell so low that farmers protested by "dumping" their products. These farmers hoped to raise the price of milk by cutting down on the supply available to people.

riot, wild, violent behavior in public by many people.

mainly to sell them. Many farms became little more than food factories. As in any other factory, machines did most of the work. Fewer farm workers were needed.

During World War I, farm owners made quite a bit of money. The prices of crops almost doubled, because so many people wanted to buy them. When the war began, American farmers had several choices. Should they grow more crops or not? If so, how much should they grow?

Many American farmers decided to grow much more. They bought more land and machines so that they could grow more. They had to borrow money from banks to buy the land and machines. The farmers never thought they would have trouble paying the banks back. People all over the world wanted their crops.

American farmers did fairly well until about 1925. By then European farmers had recovered from World War I. They were planting their own crops. They no longer needed to buy so much from the United States. American farmers were stuck with more land and machines than they needed. And they still owed money to the banks. When they could not pay off their loans, the farmers had to give up their machines. Worse yet, many had to give up their farms.

In the early 1920s, the weather also hurt the farm business. A drought began on the Great Plains. For several years, not enough rain fell. Crops grew poorly. All of these things added up to cause bad times for farmers. Many families moved to the cities for work.

Blacks in the 1920s

The cities did not prove to be the answer, though. Many were packed with the homeless and the jobless. They were also the scene of numerous labor strikes. Worst of all, cities like Chicago, Detroit, and Cleveland became battlegrounds between blacks and whites.

Over 400,000 blacks had moved North during World War I. There, they filled jobs left by white servicemen. Many also moved into areas once reserved for whites. When the white servicemen returned after the war, the trouble began. Whites wanted their old jobs and apartments back. Many blacks were not willing to just step aside. The result was **rioting**, bloodshed, and many deaths.

342

A meeting of the Ku Klux Klan.

Prejudice also greeted blacks in the small towns of the West, Midwest, and the South. The Ku Klux Klan once again grew strong. "Colored only" and "Whites only" signs signaled the return of Jim Crow laws. Blacks experienced discrimination in jobs, schools, and housing.

Good times, bad times. Was America headed for trouble? The poet Edna St. Vincent Millay wrote:

> My Candle burns at both ends;
>   It will not last the night;
> But ah, my foes, and oh, my friends—
>   It gives a lovely light!

How long would the light burn?

prejudice, an unfair opinion or judgment about someone or something.

Checking Up

1. Why did Americans have more leisure time in the 1920s?

2. How did many Americans choose to spend their leisure time?

3. Who were some of the heroes of the 1920s? Who are some heroes that Americans have today?

4. What problems did farmers and blacks have during the 1920s?

Write your answers on paper. Do not write in the book.

Using Key Words

mass production	assembly line
suffrage	ratification
fad	riot
prejudice	prosperity

Number your paper 1 to 8. Write a short meaning for each of the above key words.

Reviewing Main Ideas

Number your paper 1 to 6. Next to each number write the letter which correctly matches each person with his or her accomplishment.

1. Henry Ford
2. Red Grange
3. Gertrude Ederle
4. Jeannette Rankin
5. Rudolph Valentino
6. Charles Lindbergh

a. first woman elected to Congress.
b. football star of the 1920s.
c. movie star of the 1920s.
d. inventor of the assembly line.
e. first solo flight from New York to Paris.
f. set record for English Channel swim.

Some of the sentences below are true and some are false. Number your paper from 1 to 5. Write either *true* or *false* by each.

1. After World War I America suffered the same problems as Europe.

2. Mass production reduced the cost of making many products.

3. The women's rights movement ended after women received the right to vote.

4. Many American farmers began to go broke in the middle of the 1920s.

5. Prejudice began to increase as blacks moved into northern cities.

Thinking Things Over

Write a paragraph or two telling how the growing amount of spare time for Americans changed their lives during the 1920s.

Practicing Skills

Make a line graph showing how airplane production grew from 1913 to 1929. Use this information:

Year	Number of planes*	Year	Number of planes*
1913	29	1922	37
1914	32	1923	56
1915	152	1924	60
1916	269	1925	344
1917	135	1926	708
1918	29	1927	1,386
1919	98	1928	3,499
1920	72	1929	5,414
1921	48		

*Does not include airplanes made for fighting in wars.

After making the graph, answer these questions:

1. During what three-year period was the biggest jump in aircraft production?

2. When did Lindbergh make his flight across the Atlantic? How did his flight affect aircraft production in 1928 and 1929?

The 1930s: The Great Depression

Many Americans thought that the good times of the 1920s would never end. President Herbert Hoover, for example, believed that poverty was disappearing. "The poorhouse is vanishing from among us," was his comment.

Hoover and most Americans were shocked when prosperity turned sour in 1929. Many businesses started to hang new signs on their doors and windows. But the signs did not announce "Grand Openings." They announced failure: "Closed," "Out of business," "Gone to Florida . . . forever!"

In the 1930s, there were other signs that things were not as good as everyone thought. Hundreds of banks would close their doors as usual at 5:00 P.M. Then they failed to open again the next morning. Millions of workers were told that "this paycheck was your last." Soon, many people did not have enough money to pay for food, clothing, or housing. What had happened? How had the country gone from prosperity to **depression**?

depression, a time when people are out of work, prices are falling, businesses are not selling, and people have little income to spend or save.

Banks closed in the 1930s because they used their savers' money unwisely. Bank accounts were not insured at this time. If a bank misspent money, it could be gone forever. In this photo, people have lined up outside a New York City bank. They hoped to take their money out of the bank before it closed.

Lesson 1 The Great Crash

There were many causes of the depression. One important cause had to do with the **stock market**. The stock market is the place where shares of stock are bought and sold. Buying stock is the same as becoming part owner of a company. When people buy shares of a company's stock, the company uses the money to buy machines, tools, land, or buildings. If the company does well, it makes money. The company then gives part of this money back to the stock owners.

Up until 1928, most people wanted to buy the stocks that paid them the most every year. They bought stocks and owned them for years on end. However, early in 1928, many people began to "play" the stock market. Players did not want to wait years to get rich. Instead, they wanted to get rich overnight.

Playing the Stock Market

Here's how they played the market. They watched the prices of stocks that were being sold in the stock market. They tried to buy stocks when their prices were low. They tried to sell after the price had gone up.

The price of any stock depends on **supply** and **demand**. This means the amount of a stock for sale and how many people want to buy it. In 1928 and 1929, many people wanted to buy. This caused the prices to go up for almost every stock. For example, a person bought 1,000 shares of stock in XYZ Company at $10 a share. But other people wanted XYZ, too. This forced the price up to $35 a share. The person had originally paid $10,000 for the 1,000 shares. Now the shares were worth $35,000. When the shares were sold, the person made $25,000 for doing nothing more than buying and selling stock at the right time.

For eighteen months in 1928 and 1929, prices were like a rollercoaster on its way upward. Each day a new millionaire appeared who "bought low and sold high." The key, of course, was to find a buyer.

In October, 1929, the rollercoaster began to go downward. Stock prices started to fall. People tried to sell their stocks before the prices went down too far. But with everyone trying to sell, the prices fell rapidly. There were no buyers. Many people's fortunes faded like a dying rose.

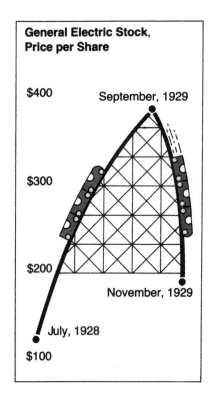

General Electric Stock, Price per Share

$400 — September, 1929

$300

$200 — November, 1929

$100 — July, 1928

Causes of the Great Depression

For the next ten years, the country was in a depression. The Great Depression, it has been called. The country had seen other depressions. None lasted so long or were so hard as this one, though.

Was it all caused by people "playing" in the stock market? No, the Great Depression had other causes, too.

Industry produced too much. Throughout the 1920s, American industry produced new and wonderful products. Americans had many products that helped them in the home and made their life more enjoyable. But Americans could only buy so many radios, vacuum cleaners, washers, and cars. By the end of the 1920s, many warehouses were filled with a surplus of these and other goods.

Laying off workers. When businesses did not sell their products, they began to lay off their workers. By 1930, over four million people were out of work. These unemployed people bought little more than the necessities of life.

Mystery in History

Most Americans could tell you that Charles Lindbergh was the first man to fly solo across the Atlantic Ocean. But who was the first woman? Her name was Amelia Earhart. She made her historic flight in 1932. Later, she became the first woman to fly from Honolulu to the mainland of the United States. Her next feat was to fly across the United States in both directions.

In 1937, she tried to fly around the world. Her plane was reported lost near Howland Island in the Pacific Ocean. No trace of her, or her plane, was ever found.

Unemployed workers sell apples along 42nd Street in New York City. The apples sold for about a nickel a piece. During the depression, the apple became a symbol for those people who were out of work.

347

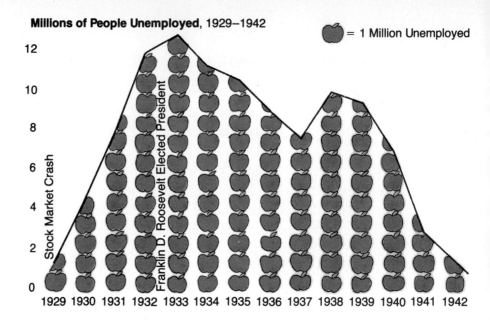

Millions of People Unemployed, 1929–1942

= 1 Million Unemployed

Stock Market Crash

Franklin D. Roosevelt Elected President

12
10
8
6
4
2
0

1929 1930 1931 1932 1933 1934 1935 1936 1937 1938 1939 1940 1941 1942

This picture graph shows the number of unemployed people from 1929 to 1942. What picture is used to represent unemployed people? How many people are represented by each symbol? When was Franklin D. Roosevelt elected President? Did unemployment go up or down after his election?

insure, arrange payment of money in case of loss, accident, or death.

Credit buying. "Buy now, pay later" and "Pay as you go" were new ways to buy for most American shoppers in the early 1920s. Millions bought products this way. Few paid for them later. Thousands of businesses closed when their customers failed to pay their bills.

Banking practices. Banks were excited about the stock market game, too. Banks used their customers' savings to play. When the stock market crashed, these savings accounts went with it. Since accounts were not **insured**, people could do little more than complain.

Banks lost money in another way, too. Millions of Americans borrowed money to buy goods or stocks. When workers began to get laid off, they failed to make loan payments. When the stock market crashed, stock owners could not repay their loans, either.

Over-stocked warehouses. Banks closing. Workers losing their jobs. Unwise credit buying. These all weakened the country. Only a few people paid any attention. Most people were too busy with marathon dances, getting rich quick, and their heroes to see what was happening.

Checking Up

1. What were some of the causes of the Great Depression?

2. Which cause do you think was the most important? Why?

Lesson 2   Living Through a Depression

❝They're always tellin' us that we should be glad we got food and all that, 'cause back in the Thirties they used to tell us people were starving and got no jobs and all that stuff.❞

—a sixteen-year-old in the 1970s

"No one knows," said one man about the depression of the 1930s. "No one knows unless they've been there." By 1932, over twelve million people were *really* "there." In that year, one out of every four workers was unemployed.

From boom to bust. From prosperity to depression. It happened so quickly. One man explained:

❝I remember my Uncle Harry. He had a beautiful home on Long Island during the boom years—the '20s. He made his pile in the stock market. I can still see him in his chauffeured Pierce-Arrow. After the '29 crash, he lost everything. He was grateful to get a job as a waiter in a restaurant.❞

Uncle Harry was lucky. Others were less fortunate. They couldn't find jobs. Many of the unemployed found themselves in long lines. Long lines that wound around city blocks. These "bread lines," as they were called, moved slowly toward "soup kitchens." Inside these kitchens were free food and warmth in winter. Even yesterday's richest people stood in line for bread and soup. Hunger makes everyone equal.

People who lived through the Great Depression remembered it this way:

"There was no complaining because everyone suffered equally."

"A person who had a job—even a part-time job felt . . . lucky."

"There was a great deal of sharing what you had, no matter how little that was."

"I remember a hungry stranger in my mother's kitchen, repeating after every sip of the bowl of vegetable soup she gave him, 'Oh, God bless you!'"

(below) Many who did not have a friend's kitchen to eat in waited in bread lines.

PAID FOR TO THIS POINT
Every Dollar PAYS FOR 20 More Meals

People who lost their homes or could not pay the rent often settled in vacant lots or parks. There, they built "Hoover Towns" or "Hoovervilles." The places were called this because many people believed that President Herbert Hoover had not done enough for the needy people in the United States. This Hooverville was built outside Marysville, California. What do you think the man in the photo is thinking?

The poor gave American cities and towns a new look. As one man remembers, the look was anything but pleasing. He was speaking about Chicago. But his words tell the story of a thousand cities across America.

66Downtown I saw strange sights. In Garland Court back of the library, special garbage cans were set out by the thoughtful kitchen help of a restaurant. The garbage cans contained bread heels, and hundreds of starving men gratefully helped themselves. At other cans, people did their own sorting, stopping to chew on bones and bits of meat.

In warm weather, Grant Park was full with thousands of men (and women) sleeping atop newspapers on the wet grass. When it turned cold, a thousand shanties [shacks] went up overnight along the lakefront . . . . The shacks were made of tin signs and ancient boards, but they had chimneys and primitive heating systems.

On the lower level of Wacker Drive, men burrowed under the concrete loading docks, wrapping themselves in newspapers as a defense against the cold. At least the rain and snow

Sharing potatoes. Try to find someone who has lived through the Great Depression. Ask what they remember the most about those times.

couldn't reach them there. But death did; frequently, a terrible smell would be the signal for police to explore the burrows and remove a body to the morgue.

God knows what people lived on. At the Pixley and Ehlers cafeteria . . . I'd see a shabbily dressed man sit down with a 5-cent cup of coffee and put 10 spoons of sugar into it for nourishment. Then he might pour a fourth of a bottle of catsup into a glass of water and stir it until it became free "tomato juice." **"**

For many Americans, the depression did not mean going from good times to bad. It meant going from bad to worse. Farmers had been in a depression since the mid-1920s. For many, it continued into the 1930s. Prices continued to fall. But the rain didn't. By the early 1930s, the topsoil was so dry it began to blow away. The Great Plains states became a sea of swirling dust storms. Tens of thousands of farmers simply packed up and moved from the Dust Bowl.

A woman who lived in Kansas and Oklahoma in the 1930s remembers:

"It wasn't just the depression, it was the eternal [longlasting] drought and the infernal dust that every puff of wind raised. The farmers could not work the land to keep the dust from blowing because they had no fuel, the tractors were worn out, there was no seed for crops. The topsoil blew off the fields and into great hills of dust against the fences and buildings."

The farmers weren't alone. They were joined in this deep poverty by blacks. If blacks were the "last hired" for a job in the 1920s, they were the "first fired" from a job in the 1930s. Out of every 100 male black workers, 36 were unemployed in 1936. For white males, the figure was 21 out of 100.

Many blacks weren't surprised by this. One, Clifford Burke, commented:

66The Negro was born in depression. It didn't mean too much to him, The Great Depression, as you call it. There was no such thing. The best he could be is a janitor or a porter or shoeshine boy. It only became official when it hit the white man.99

Checking Up

1. What is a depression?

2. What was a "bread line"? a "soup kitchen"?

3. If you had lived during the thirties, what would have been the hardest thing for you to get used to?

Lesson 3   New Deal, New Hope

> They used to tell me I was building a dream,
> And so I followed the mob—
> When there was earth to plough or guns to bear
> I was always there—right there on the job.
> They used to tell me I was building a dream,
> With peace and glory ahead—
> Why should I be standing in line
> Just waiting for bread?

—from a popular song of the 1930s

Except for the bread line, suffering Americans did not know where to turn for help. **Charities** helped as much as they could, but many ran out of money. State and city governments also helped, but they, too, began to run out of money. The bread and soup kitchens soon began to close.

In the past, the United States government had stayed out of matters like these. It was not in the habit of giving aid to people who had lost their jobs. In fact, many Americans believed the Constitution did not give the federal government the power to care for the needy.

President Herbert Hoover was torn by the people's unhappiness. But he felt his hands were tied. He felt that it was dangerous to help people too much. They might forget how to help themselves. He also wondered if there was anything the federal government could ever do to make the depression end. Most of his advisers felt that the depression would end on its own as others had.

In 1932, the depression reached its lowest point. It seemed that Hoover's popularity had, too. Hoover ran against Franklin Delano Roosevelt in the 1932 presidential election. Roosevelt, who was governor of New York, promised the American people "a new deal." Roosevelt easily won the election.

Many Americans thought that Roosevelt understood them. He, too, had seen hard times. His hard times had nothing to do with money, however. His hard times had to do with his health. In 1921, Roosevelt was stricken with polio. The disease left him unable to walk. He had to get around in a wheelchair or by wearing leg braces.

charity, a group of people who collect money to help the poor, sick, or helpless.

An unemployed worker in the early 30s. How did he feel about charity?

Roosevelt's courage and strength spread across the nation. He was winning his war against one disease. The nation, under his leadership, felt it could win a war against another disease—the depression.

Roosevelt's years as President were full of new ideas. He believed the government should not wait for hard times to end. Roosevelt tried to find ways the government could help the needy and end the depression.

Right after he took office, Roosevelt asked Congress to pass new laws to help end hard times. And Congress quickly answered. It passed laws to help farmers, bankers, workers, the elderly, and the poor. Some laws made it harder to repeat the errors of the 1920s. Some laws made it harder to borrow money to buy stock. Another law set up a government agency to insure savings accounts.

Other laws set up government departments. These departments either tried to end the depression or help those hurt by it. Together, Roosevelt's work and his years in office are called the New Deal.

Was the New Deal a success or a failure? Historians do not agree. Most say it was a little of both. Many feel that the federal government spent too much money trying to help the needy. Millions of dollars were spent, they point out, on programs that had little success. And worst of all, unemploy-

(above) Eleanor Roosevelt distributes food to the needy. After becoming President, Franklin D. Roosevelt depended on his wife to visit with Americans. She found out what they needed and wanted. (below) President Roosevelt greets a crowd near his home in Warm Springs, Georgia.

CCC workers plant seedlings in Montana in 1938. The CCC was important because its workers reforested many areas. How else was this organization important? For a look at a modern CCC, turn to page 392.

ment stayed high. In 1940, it was still at 6 million. Other historians emphasize the good side of the New Deal. Many programs were successful. Some continue today. The New Deal, they say, gave Americans hope.

Many people had become afraid of what the next day might bring. The New Deal gave them the feeling that good times were coming. A popular song of the late 1930s was "Happy Days Are Here Again."

Perhaps the most important thing the New Deal did was to ask a question. "Should the federal government try to keep hard times from ever returning?" Should it always be trying to solve the problems of the needy? Such an effort is expensive. It is a choice that Americans must still make.

Checking Up

1. Why did many Americans feel that Roosevelt understood them?

2. What was President Roosevelt's New Deal?

3. How can the New Deal be both a success and a failure?

SOME NEW DEAL AGENCIES

Reconstruction Finance Corporation (RFC)
loaned money to banks, life insurance companies, railroads, and the like to keep them from going out of business.

Civilian Conservation Corps (CCC)
put young men to work planting trees, building roads, and the like.

Federal Emergency Relief Administration (FERA)
gave money to state and local governments to put needy people to work.

Agricultural Adjustment Administration (AAA)
paid farmers money to make up the difference between what they could sell their crops for and what they needed to live on.

Home Owners Loan Corporation (HOLC)
loaned money to people in danger of losing their homes because of debts.

Federal Bank Deposit Insurance Corporation (FDIC)
insured some of the savings people had in banks in case banks closed.

National Recovery Administration (NRA)
tried to limit the amount of goods made by businesses to increase jobs and prices.

355

Building Social Studies Skills

Judging the Mass Media

"Here are today's top stories. Congress still can't agree on the military spending budget. Governor Morris wants more money for highway construction. And, of course, our baseball team loses again! More about these and other stories in just a minute," announces the reporter.

Most people find out about what's going on in the world with the help of the **mass media**. Newspapers, magazines, radio and television stations are parts of the mass media. They communicate information to large numbers of people.

The medium that most people turn to is television. In a 30- or 60-minute program, Americans can learn about a protest at city hall or a war ten thousand miles away.

But how much news do you actually get by watching television? To find out, fill in the Television Viewing Record. It will show you about how much time a TV station gives to news.

It will also show the time given to sports, weather, and features. Features are interesting stories that don't have to have anything to do with the day's events. One feature might give a movie or concert review. Another feature might describe interesting places in town. A third might show the new toys available during the holiday season.

After you have filled in your chart, compare your results with a classmate who viewed a different station.

When you have completed your chart, answer the following questions.

1. How much time was used for news stories?

2. How much time was given to sports, weather, and feature stories?

3. How much time was given to lead-ins [the time spent introducing the news show] and outs [the time spent closing and running the credits]?

4. Did the station present all the news that happened in the day? How do you think the station decided what news items to show?

Pick up a newspaper the day after you complete the chart. Find a story in the paper that was also on TV. Which seems to have more details? Write down any details found in one, but not the other.

5. Can you think of some reasons why television news has become so popular?

TELEVISION VIEWING RECORD

Station_____ Channel_____ Time_____

(News item, feature, sports, weather, commercials)

Time given to each

1._____ _____
2._____ _____
3._____ _____
4._____ _____
5._____ _____
6._____ _____

Write your answers on paper. Do not write in the book.

Using Key Words

depression   **stock market**   **supply**
demand   **insure**
charities   **mass media**

Number your paper 1 to 7. Write a short meaning for each of the above key words.

Reviewing Main Ideas

Number your paper from 1 to 7. Select the letter of the phrase which best completes the sentence.

1. The prices for stock being sold on the stock market increase when **a.** the country is in a depression. **b.** more people want to buy the stock. **c.** fewer people want to buy the stock.

2. When American factories produced too many products to sell, they were forced to **a.** lay off workers. **b.** give extra goods to charities.

3. One reason banks were forced to close was that they **a.** had too much money to lend to people. **b.** owed too much money to factories. **c.** lost their customers' money in the stock market.

4. The first group of people to suffer the depression was the **a.** bankers. **b.** farmers. **c.** factory workers.

5. The lack of rain on the farmland of the Great Plains in the 1930s was so bad that the area was called **a.** the great depression. **b.** the crash of 1929. **c.** the dust bowl.

6. President Hoover's feelings about people suffering in the depression were that **a.** charities were doing such a fine job that the central government did not need to help. **b.** no depression really existed, therefore the central government needed to do nothing. **c.** it was dangerous for the central government to do too much, because people would forget how to help themselves.

7. President Roosevelt's "New Deal" refers to **a.** Roosevelt's work to have the central government help the people during the depression. **b.** Roosevelt's attempt to fight polio. **c.** Roosevelt's guidelines for buying and selling stock.

Thinking Things Over

Farm families caught in the dust bowl often had to pack up their car, leave most of their possessions behind, and move west. Pretend you are living in the dust bowl in the 1930s. What things would you leave behind? What would you take with you?

Practicing Skills

How do the pictures on pages 347–352 show the people's suffering during the depression?

357

Chapter

24

Choices About War and Peace

World War I was called "The War to End All Wars." People all over the world hoped that it would be the last. "A lasting peace; that's what we want," said the world's leaders.

But by 1939, the ground again shook with the rumble of tanks and bombs. How did the Second World War begin? What part did the United States play in it?

Lesson 1   The World at War–Again

The depression that hit America in the 1930s was hard on other countries, too. Life in Germany, for example, was worse than in the United States. But Germany had had problems even before the depression came.

Germany's problems began as early as the end of World War I. At that time, Germany was officially blamed for starting World War I. Because of this, Germany had to help pay the cost of the war for such nations as England and France. This was hard to do. The German government had little money of its own. And it could not borrow from Germany's businesses and industries. Most were ruined because of the war.

The German people were told they would no longer be ruled by a king. Instead, Germany was to become a democracy. Germany was also not allowed to have a large military.

These things were hard for the Germans to bear. They were willing to listen to anyone who talked of solving their problems. One who talked very loud was Adolf Hitler.

Adolf Hitler wanted to be **dictator** of Germany. That is, he wanted to have complete control over the people. He wanted to make all the decisions in government. Hitler knew that one way to get people to follow him was to blame someone else for everything that was going wrong.

The dictators Benito Mussolini (left) and Adolf Hitler (right).

dictator, a person who has complete power or authority over others.

358

"Germany was never beaten by outside enemies," Hitler claimed. England, France, and the United States had never clearly won World War I, he said. Instead, Germany had been beaten by inside enemies, by **traitors**. Germany had been "stabbed in the back," he concluded. He accused Jewish people in Germany of betraying their country.

The Jews of Germany had not caused Germany's problems. But, as one of Hitler's followers said, "People will listen to a big lie rather than a small one." Many of the German people listened. By 1934, Adolf Hitler had reached his goal. He was dictator of Germany.

traitor, a person who betrays his or her country or ruler.

Other Dictators

Italy had some of the same problems as Germany. Unemployment was high. And many of the workers who did have jobs were often on strike. Like the Germans, millions of Italians listened to one man "with all the answers." His name was Benito Mussolini. Mussolini said that the cure for Italy's problems was to have the government control business. To do this, people would have to give up some of their freedoms. The need for change was so great that many Italians went along with Mussolini's ideas.

Hitler and Mussolini decided to help each other. In 1936 they signed a treaty called the Axis Pact. They agreed to support each other in case of a military attack by another country. Later, they were joined by General Hideki Tojo (hē'de-kē' tō'jō) of Japan. He was part of a military group that had taken control of Japan's government.

The Germans, Italians, and Japanese wanted to take control of land outside their borders. They felt this would help them become strong powers. During the 1930s, Japan invaded part of China. The Italians conquered Ethiopia and Albania. Germany took over Austria and Czechoslovakia.

Why No One Stopped the Dictators

When World War I ended in 1918, the whole world looked forward to peace. To prevent future wars, many countries joined together to form the League of Nations. In the **league**, representatives from each country could talk things over. Problems could be worked out across a table instead of a battlefield.

German soldiers take Jews from their homes in Warsaw, Poland. Why did Hitler and his followers blame all of Germany's problems on the Jewish people? Hitler believed that the German people were the best people in the world. He called them the "master race." The Jews, he said, were not part of the race. The Jews were continually persecuted while Hitler was dictator of Germany. By 1945, over six million European Jews had been killed.

359

German troops advance through Yugoslavia in April 1941. The German army moved very quickly at the start of the war. So quickly, that their attacks were called the *Blitzkreig* or lightning war.

It was a good idea. But it didn't work. Hitler, Mussolini, and Tojo were not about to listen to just talk. The League didn't have an army to enforce its rules.

Some of the world's leaders did not believe that these three countries were a real problem. England, for example, felt that Germany had been punished too hard. Some leaders in England felt that Hitler would be satisfied once Germany was on its feet again. But Hitler was not satisfied.

On September 1, 1939, German troops, planes, and tanks attacked Poland. Years earlier, France and England had signed a treaty with Poland. In that treaty, the two countries agreed to protect Poland in case it was attacked. For that reason, on September 3, France and England declared war on Germany. In a short time, most of Europe was at war, again.

Checking Up

1. What is a dictatorship?

2. Who were the dictators of Germany, Italy, and Japan?

3. Why were many Germans and Italians willing to listen to someone who wanted to be a dictator?

Lesson 2   The United States Enters the War

It was a calm December morning in 1941. Americans were just waking up all across the nation. They sat on the edge of their beds. They yawned and stretched. It was the beginning of a lazy Sunday, a day of rest. A day of peace and quiet, or so Americans thought.

The country was much like its people on that day. It was waking up from a horrible depression. It was once again starting to stretch. Production was up. Unemployment was down, though not yet beaten.

Most families were preparing their Sunday supper. It was a supper Americans might remember. It was a day they could never forget. Late in the day, Americans began to get the news. Japanese planes had bombed the American military base at Pearl Harbor in the Hawaiian Islands. Find Pearl Harbor on the map on page 374. A day later, December 8, 1941, the United States was at war with Japan.

By December 11, the United States was also at war with Germany and Italy. Because of their treaty with Japan, both had declared war on the United States.

Up to this time, many Americans were **isolationists**. They wanted to stay out of Europe's problems. World War I was still clear in their minds. "Let Europe fight its own battles. Why should we be dragged into their war?" These were common sayings among Americans after war began in 1939.

Why Did Japan Attack Pearl Harbor?

If America was not too concerned with Europe, the opposite was true with Asia. It wanted Asia to be free so that all nations could trade there.

Japan had other ideas in the 1930s. It attacked and took over part of China. The United States sent a strong warning to Japan. Any more attacks or take-overs and the United States would stop trading with Japan. Japan's answer came in early 1940. It took over Northern Indo-China. As promised, the United States cut off all trade with Japan. Soon after, Japan took over Southern Indo-China. Locate Indo-China on the map on page 374. The United States response came just as quickly. All Japanese money in United States banks was locked away.

Facts and Figures

In 1941, the average family's yearly income was between $2,000 and $2,500. The family could expect the following expenses:

food	$733
clothing	$267
rent	$461
electricity	$134
home furnishings	$97
miscellaneous	$808
savings	$000
total	$2,500

What would a "typical" Sunday dinner have cost? In 1941, a four-pound roasting chicken was about $1.20. A loaf of white bread was 9¢. A pound of butter was 44¢. One can of corn was 12¢. An apple pie for dessert could be made for about 35¢.

No historian is completely sure of what happened next. There seems to have been a lot of confusion inside Japan. Some of Japan's leaders wanted to make peace with the United States. Others felt that Japan was being bullied by the United States. By December 7, 1941, someone in Japan had decided what to do.

"Where Were You When . . . ?"

"Do you remember where you were and what you were doing the day Pearl Harbor was attacked?" Most Americans begin their answers the same way. "Of course I do!"

❝I was listening to the Redskins football game. I was twelve or thirteen years old. I didn't pay too much mind. But every time the news came on about it, I knew it was something kind of mean. Even a twelve-year-old kid knew it had to be pretty bad.❞

❝. . . I was scared. I guess I had heard about the First World War. I knew that war meant people got killed. . . .❞

❝I didn't know where Pearl Harbor was. But every ten minutes after that, there was more on it. So it wasn't very long before we realized it wasn't just a little bombing somewhere.❞

❝We just finished dinner when the news came over the radio. I was stunned. . . . [One] son, at that time, was about fifteen. . . . The other [son] was two years younger. I thought both of them would escape. Even up till he was a senior in high school, I kept thinking he wouldn't have to go, because it was getting near the end of the war. He was killed just six weeks before the war ended.❞

❝I remember thinking: "Oh, what a thrilling experience this is going to be to live through a war!"❞

❝. . . I was shocked like everyone else, . . . and it flashed through my mind, "What's going to happen to me? What's going to happen to the family?"❞

❝I was driving home . . . and the news . . . came over the radio—and I said: "Here we go again."❞

President Franklin Roosevelt asking Congress to declare war on Japan after the attack on Pearl Harbor.

❝It was a Sunday. It was quiet. I remember the sunshine, of all things, because it seemed [strange] that the sun was shining when we heard this news. Someone telephoned. They said: "Did you hear? The Japanese have attacked Pearl Harbor!" We immediately turned on the radio—that was before television—and we didn't ever stop listening. Of course, I thought it was the end of the world. Shock! Horror! We were on the West Coast, and we thought surely they would be along here.**❞**

After the Attack on Pearl Harbor

Most Americans were shocked and angered over the attack. The feelings of people living in the states of Washington, Oregon, and California, however, went beyond that. They felt they might be attacked next.

Some believed the attack could come from outside the United States. The Japanese might attack the West Coast as they had attacked Pearl Harbor. Others felt the attack could come from the inside. "After all," they said, "there were a lot of people of Japanese descent living on the West Coast. Maybe they would take sides with Japan."

A fever spread along the West Coast. Were the Japanese Americans to be trusted? Were they loyal to the United States or to Japan? Within two months after Pearl Harbor, these questions were answered.

". . . I saw the attack, I saw the bombs that were dropped in the ocean very, very [clearly]. I still thought that it must be the Army Air Force. Then, when I heard over the radio that Hawaii was under attack, I ran up the side of my property and there I saw the most dreadful thing I ever saw in my life. The fire, the blasting of the ships, just one after the other, in flames!"

This is the Manzanar Relocation Camp in California. It was one of ten camps located in the western deserts and the swamplands of Alabama and Arkansas. It was felt that moving the Japanese Americans to these camps would prevent them from bringing harm to the United States during the war.

By late 1944, the government felt that the Japanese Americans were no longer a threat. They were not allowed to move back to their homes, but they could leave the camps. Many young men chose to enter the army. They formed the 442nd Battle Team. The 442nd Battle Team fought in Italy. The Japanese American soldiers proved they had always been loyal to the United States. When the war ended, they were among the most decorated soldiers in the army.

In February, 1942, President Roosevelt made an important decision. He decided that the 112,000 Japanese Americans living on the West Coast had to be moved. They were forced to sell their homes and businesses. Then, they had to move to relocation camps.

Most of these Japanese Americans were United States citizens. They, or their parents and grandparents, had lived in the United States for years. They had built successful businesses. They had helped their communities grow. Many of the families had sons in the army or navy. But it did not matter. They were considered a threat to the country.

Checking Up

1. Why were many Americans isolationists in 1941?

2. Why did Japan attack the United States in 1941?

3. Most Americans had a similar reaction to the news about Pearl Harbor. What do you think it was?

4. Why were the Japanese Americans forced to move into relocation camps during the early part of the war?

Lesson 3   Soldiers Without Guns

World War II was a total war. It involved everyone in the countries that were fighting. Men, women, and children all had a part to play in the war.

In the United States, about 15 million men joined the fighting services. About 200,000 women also joined the services, but the major help that women gave was in factories and hospitals. Millions of women built ships, tanks, trucks, planes, and other machines of war. Women did most of the work of caring for the wounded.

The help that children gave was of a different kind. One person remembered the times in this way:

66One of the worst things about the war was that we all wanted our country to win, but there wasn't much that we, as kids, could do to help it win. We had paper drives and scrap-metal drives. Every kid tried to buy a savings stamp

Without the thousands of factory workers in the United States, World War II could never have been won. Here, workers at the Boeing Aircraft Company in Seattle, Washington, roll out the 5,000 B-17 bomber from their assembly line. Planes like this were used to bomb German factories and cities. One B-17 at work is pictured on page 372.

ration, allow only certain amounts of food, gasoline, and other goods to each person.

(top) Children tend to their "Victory Garden."
(bottom) These ration stamps allowed people to buy only a limited amount of certain things.

[stamp sold by the United States government to help pay for the war] a week. The money from the stamps went to the government, to help pay for the war. We pasted the stamps into little folders, and if you collected a certain number you could turn them in for a war bond [a bond sold by the government to pay the costs of war].

We had a victory garden. Every family that lived in an apartment was assigned a plot alongside the railroad tracks. We grew corn, tomatoes, beans, and other vegetables right there in the city, next to the tracks.

Shoes and soap were **rationed**. We were told in school that soaping people's windows at Halloween was **unpatriotic** [not showing love and support of one's country] as well as mean. My mother and her friends saved bacon fat and other grease and used it to make lye soap. Making it was a huge mess, but the soap was better than the kind you could buy.

My folks were always telling us not to ruin our shoes because they couldn't get ration stamps for new ones. If the soles wore out, we glued on rubber soles. They didn't hold very well, and someone in class always had at least one floppy shoe.

Sugar and lots of other foods were rationed. Our big treat at Christmas was a banana in each kid's stocking. Bananas came from Central America, and ships had to go through waters full of German submarines. Needless to say, bananas were hard to get.

If we didn't want to eat everything on our plates, we were told, "There are children starving in Europe or China who would love to have what you've left. Now, finish your dinner."

I guess the biggest help children gave was in stopping waste. We all really had what we needed, and we knew we were better off than the kids in England, or France, or China. They were being bombed all the time. We had air raid drills, but we didn't really have to worry. 99

Total War, Total Effort

The government, however, was worried. It knew that many Americans thought the war was something happening hundreds of miles away. Americans with that attitude might not do all they could to help win the war. If Americans did not help out at home, the war could be lost on the battlefield.

The government, therefore, tried to bring the war closer to home. It asked all Americans to think of everything that they did as a choice. The choice could be patriotic, or of course, unpatriotic. What Americans chose to do could help the United States or hurt it.

If Americans were late for work, a poster reminded them that they were making a pilot wait for his plane. If Americans hoarded, bought more than they needed, a poster reminded them that a soldier might go hungry. If they spoke to strangers about their work, a poster reminded them that the strangers might be the enemy. If Americans complained, a poster reminded them that the enemy was laughing.

What message were posters such as these trying to give Americans during World War II?

Lend your Life copy

If your newsdealer tells you he is all out of copies of LIFE, please don't blame him. The fact is that because of Government restriction of paper we cannot print enough copies to give him all he needs for his customers.

LIFE is doing its utmost to see that newsdealers in all parts of the country get their full share of all available copies. But LIFE knows that each week many readers will not be able to find LIFE on their newsstands. To all readers who do get copies, LIFE's sincere thanks for sharing them with others.

Read the *LIFE* magazine ad above. Why was it necessary for people to share their copies? Why was B.F. Goodrich telling people how they could make their tires last longer? The young man pictured above is holding the 70 pounds of rubber bands he collected. The bands could be melted down and used to repair automobile tires. How was he being patriotic?

"There go our tires, Dad!"

TODAY millions of motorists are riding on the last set of tires they may be able to buy for a long time. Many of us may have to go without our cars entirely.

Is this a big sacrifice? Or only a little one? That depends upon how you look at it.

It's a big sacrifice if your life is wholly made up of little things. Like driving to the station, taking a Sunday afternoon spin, or motoring to the movies.

But it's very little if you focus your eyes upon the big objective—a world run for free people—a world where our children may have a normal chance for happiness.

For there are, after all, many things more important than tires. There's the right to think, and talk, and worship

as we like. There is, in fact, everything that generations before us have thought worthy of sacrifices far beyond any we are asked to make.

Your tires (the ones you might have bought) are serving you a thousand times better where they are. For rubber moves the army and sails the navy. One battleship needs the rubber of 10,545 tires. Our bombers and fighters could not fly without rubber. Tanks, trucks, scout cars, and gun mounts need it by the thousands of tons.

If you could know in detail how vitally our armed forces need rubber, you might well say, "I'm glad they took my tires in time!"

We at The B. F. Goodrich Company are not finding the going easy, either. It is not a simple thing to break the

routine of 71 years overnight.

But all these things are small in the face of the great objective. Total victory for American ideals merits the utmost any of us can give . . . to the last penny and the last pound of food, if need be.

For we of America are not in the habit of doing things halfway. We have staked everything we have, or hope for, that we can and *will* beat the dictator powers into submission.

Isn't it true that going without tires is, after all, a little thing?

Your B. F. Goodrich Silvertown Store or Dealer is "Tire Information Headquarters" for your community. Here you can get the latest information on government regulations. You can find whether or not your present tires can be repaired, recapped or retreaded. You can probably buy a good used tire. And—if you are permitted to buy new tires—you can get new Silvertowns.

How to make your tires last longer

1. Do not run a tire constantly on the same wheel.

2. Do not take corners at high speed.

3. Never slam on your brakes—except to prevent an accident.

4. Have your wheel alignment, front and rear, checked regularly.

5. Don't drive at high speed.

6. Start up gently; do not spin your wheels and grind off rubber.

7. Do not bump into curbs—no tire will stand such abuse.

Remember, every ounce of rubber you save helps your country.

In war or peace
B.F. **Goodrich**
FIRST IN RUBBER

Soon, magazine and newspaper advertisers picked up on the idea. Advertisers, of course, wanted to remind Americans of their product's name. In the process, they also reminded Americans about the war and how everyone had a part in it.

Checking Up

1. How was World War II a total war?

2. How did children help the United States war effort?

3. Why was the government worried that not all Americans would help out at home?

WOMEN ON THE HOME FRONT

From 1941 to 1945, life changed in the United States as never before. Since most young men were shipped overseas to fight, many women found new doors open to them. Women were asked to leave their "housewife" jobs and enter the "working man's world." As one woman remembers, "The war . . . only gave us the opportunity to do things we couldn't do before."

Before the war, about 13 million women worked outside the home as nurses, waitresses, secretaries, salesclerks, and teachers. That figure rose quickly after the war began. By 1943, over 18 million women were working outside the home. At least 5 million of them were working in factories that made the supplies for fighting the war.

Women also took jobs as meat packers, crane operators, cab drivers, office managers, barbers, and police officers. Suddenly, no job was for men only. Another woman recalls, " . . . jobs were so easy to find that we could be picky."

Women often found themselves working between 60 and 70 hours a week. But most women remained proud to help their country win the war. "We all had the feeling we were fighting to make the world safe for democracy," said one woman.

Other women were working just to earn more money. With husbands, brothers, and fathers gone, many women were totally in charge of their homes. The pay from wartime jobs helped out. Pre-war

Two of the millions of women that worked in wartime factories.

(below) Real "Rosie the Riveters" on the assembly line.

jobs usually paid about 35¢ an hour. During the war, many people were paid as much as 87¢ an hour. "The pay was better than anything else in town, but naturally women weren't paid as well as men," pointed out one woman.

Women did *not* usually earn as much as men, even for the same work. But working women did make another important gain. One man remembers, "We had a lot of women there. They did light construction and intricate wiring on the controls, switchboards, and control devices. The women were very adept [good] at that, and we had some who could really out-class the men. I think the men respected them—they did their part, and I think it worked out very nice."

The government had the same high opinion of the work women did. It tried to bring more women into the factories. It printed a poster of a pretty woman worker dressed in fancy overalls. The poster was supposed to show the "typical" or average woman worker. She led a hard, but fun life, the poster seemed to say. And because she was doing war work, the woman was a patriotic American. Her name was "Rosie the Riveter." (A rivet is a small metal nail that joins two pieces of

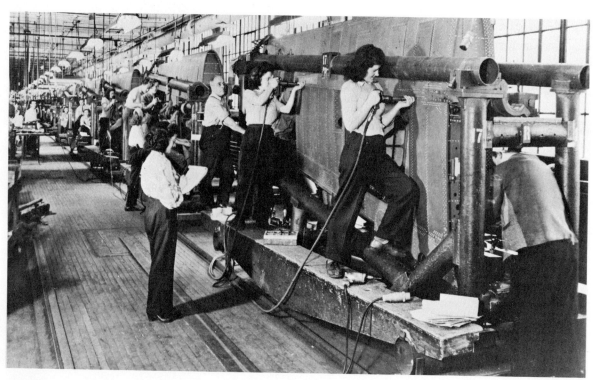

metal.) A song was even written about her. "Everyone stops to admire the scene/ Rosie the Riveter on a B-17." (A B-17 was a bomber used during the war.)

Real life did not always match the posters, though. Many women found the work to be too hard. "My first job was as an operator of a turret lathe and I was a little scrawny teenager at that time. It definitely was not women's work, so I quit after three days."

Other women had not been that interested in working at a "man's job" to begin with. "I would never have worked in a factory if there hadn't been a war on," stated one woman.

By 1945, the war appeared to be almost over. Suddenly, women were being asked to give up the jobs they had been asked to take. "Give your job to a veteran!" (A veteran is a soldier who returns home.) "Go back home!" said new government posters. Women were being asked to turn in their overalls for high heels.

Many women did not mind, either. One woman factory worker remembers, "Most of the women I knew wanted to get married and leave the factory, anyhow." Another recalls, "I didn't mind. Sure I would have liked to stay on at what I was doing, but the job didn't belong to me."

Many women did mind, though. Mozelle Watts worked in a steel mill during

the war. She also fought to keep her job after the war. "Whenever a man said I should be home washing dishes, I always replied, 'You men can have my job when I'm good and done with it!' "

Women who helped win the war also helped change the United States work force. Though some left their jobs when the war ended, many women had shown that they could do a "man's job." Women had also had the chance to find out if they *wanted* to do a "man's job."

Lesson 4   Decisions During War

Where should the United States fight first, against Japan or against Germany? This was the choice American leaders had to make in December, 1941. Most Americans wanted to fight Japan first. They were angry about the attack on Pearl Harbor. However, American leaders believed that they must help defeat Germany first. England and the Soviet Union were the only large European countries still fighting Germany. If they lost, the United States would find it very hard to beat Germany alone.

American leaders decided that the United States would aim at Europe first. It attacked Germany and Italy from the air and on the ground. For the next four years, American bombers weakened Germany by destroying important industries. In the meantime, American soldiers made a number of land invasions against German and Italian troops. These invasions are shown in red arrows on the map on page 375.

On June 6, 1944, the United States and other countries made what they hoped was a final invasion of Europe. Their goal was to defeat the German army and put an end to Hitler's dictatorship. By 1945, they had pushed into the western part of Germany.

Americans had not ignored the war against Japan. Factories had quickly gone to work to rebuild the United States Navy. The new navy and the Marine Corps fought to retake Japanese-held islands in the Pacific. Because Japan held so much territory, the struggle was long and hard. Thousands

(above)
During World War II, black pilots were not allowed to fly with other airmen. They were placed in separate units like the one above. You read about one such pilot in Unit 1. "Chappie" James was a member of one of the all-black pilot groups. Here, black fighter pilots plan for a mission over Italy. Black airmen proved that color had nothing to do with performance. During World War II, they shot down 261 enemy planes, and earned 150 medals.
(right)
B-17 bombers on a mission over Germany.
(far right)
United States Marines fighting during the battle of Iwo Jima in 1945. Find this battle site on the map on page 374.

of Americans never returned from such Pacific islands as Guadalcanal, Midway, Iwo Jima, and Okinawa. These battle sites are shown on the map on page 374.

By the middle of 1945, American forces were closing in on the home islands of Japan. Victory was a long way off but getting closer. One American who would never see victory was Franklin D. Roosevelt. The great wartime leader had died on April 12, 1945.

Almost immediately, the new President, Harry S. Truman, was faced with a difficult decision. Scientists in the United States had invented a powerful new weapon. It was called an atomic bomb. President Truman had to decide if the United States should use the bomb against Japan.

Many scientists advised against it. They had seen the bomb tested and believed that it was too deadly. They asked Truman to invite Japanese leaders to a test. Once the Japanese saw the bomb's power, they would surrender.

Truman decided against this. He feared the bomb might not work since it was so new. If the test failed, the Japanese would only laugh at the United States.

President Truman had to consider other things as well.
1. How long would the war last if the bomb were not used? American generals said that the war would last another year or two. They said 500,000 American troops and several million Japanese people could die if the war continued.
2. Should he warn the Japanese that the United States had a terrible new weapon?

We, the People

In battle, a leader must make many decisions. The Battle of Midway is a good one to study to see what choices leaders must make.

Admiral Chester Nimitz was in charge of the American navy in the Pacific. By chance, his men overheard a Japanese message. The message said the Japanese planned to attack the American airfield on Midway Island. Here is what Nimitz did.

First, he sent a false message about Midway. If the Japanese repeated his message, he would know that Midway was the target. If they ignored the message, he would know they were planning to attack somewhere else. The Japanese repeated the false information in the message.

Next, Nimitz had to decide how to fight the Japanese. All his battleships were protecting the West Coast of the United States. If he used these ships, the coast would be unprotected. He decided to attack with his three aircraft carriers. The planes aboard the carriers attacked the Japanese before they got to Midway. In this battle, American planes did as much damage to the Japanese as the attack on Pearl Harbor had done to the American navy.

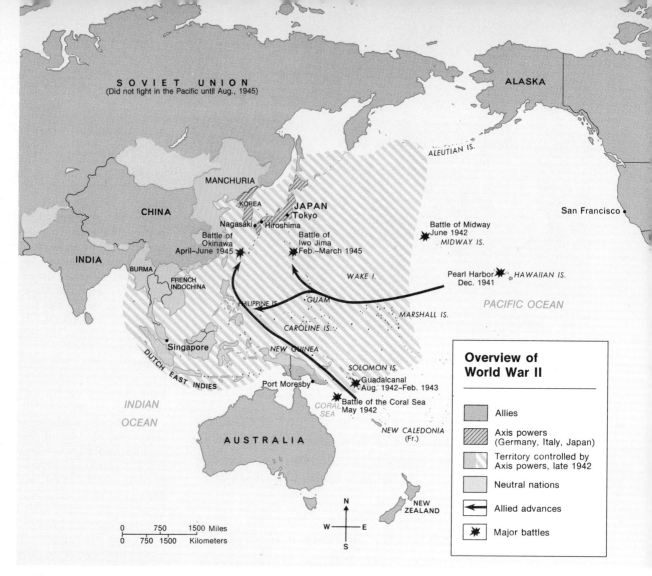

Overview of World War II

	Allies
	Axis powers (Germany, Italy, Japan)
	Territory controlled by Axis powers, late 1942
	Neutral nations
←	Allied advances
✹	Major battles

1. What color represents the territory controlled by Japan by late 1942?

2. Pearl Harbor is about _____ miles from Japan.

3. Which of the following places had Japan conquered by the end of 1942?
—Singapore
—Midway Island
—Indochina
—New Caledonia

3. How many people would be killed if the bomb were used? Scientists told him 20,000 would die, and many homes and factories would be destroyed.

Truman decided that by using the bomb, he could end the war right away. In July, he warned the Japanese to surrender or be destroyed. However, he did not tell them that a new weapon would be used on them.

On August 6, 1945, an American plane dropped an atomic bomb on Hiroshima [hir'ō shē'mə], in Japan. The bomb killed almost 80,000 persons. It destroyed over half of the city. Three days later, the United States dropped an atomic bomb on Nagasaki [nä'gə sä'kē]. Locate these two cities on the above map. It killed or injured about 100,000 Japanese. On August 14, the Japanese surrendered. World War II was over.

Checking Up

1. Why did many Americans want the United States to fight Japan first? Why did it decide to fight Germany and Italy instead?

2. Why did Truman decide to drop the atomic bomb?

3. Do you think the United States should have warned the Japanese that the atomic bomb would be used against them if they did not surrender? Explain why.

4. How do you think people of different countries can learn to live in peace?

1. What color shows the territory in Europe and Africa that was controlled by the Axis powers?

2. The Axis powers were stopped in their invasion of the Soviet Union at a line of three cities. What were those cities?

3. Using the red arrows, from which directions were Germany and Italy attacked during World War II?

National Cemeteries

It was a misty day in November, 1921. A large warship steamed slowly up the Potomac River toward Washington, D.C. Its cargo was a single coffin. Within it was the body of an American soldier.

On November 11, the coffin was carried across the river to the National Cemetery at Arlington, Virginia. The coffin was placed in a large stone tomb on top of a grassy hill. These words are carved on the side of the tomb:

**HERE RESTS IN HONORED
GLORY
AN AMERICAN SOLDIER
KNOWN BUT TO GOD**

In any war there are thousands of dead soldiers who cannot be identified. This soldier was one such "unknown" American buried in France during World War I. His final resting place at Arlington became known as the Tomb of the Unknown Soldier. He was to represent all the unknown American soldiers who died for the United States in World War I.

American soldiers have been buried at Arlington since the Civil War. General Robert E. Lee and his wife, Mary Custis, were the original owners. But Union soldiers took and held the land during the Civil War. President Lincoln asked to have the land set aside as a cemetery for Union soldiers.

Until 1967, all those who served with honor in the American armed forces could be buried at Arlington. Today, however, space is limited. Special permission is usually given to bury medal winners, disabled veterans, and some government officials.

Arlington is one of 125 national cemeteries. The United States also keeps over thirty cemeteries in other countries. These cemeteries contain the graves of almost two million Americans.

The Tomb of the Unknown Soldier

Lesson 5   America at Peace

Much had changed in the United States between 1941 and 1945. In 1941, Americans still suffered the last pains of the Great Depression. But in 1945, jobs were plentiful. People earned a lot of money. In 1941, many Americans wished to have little to do with other nations. But in 1945, the United States was strong and rich, a leader in the world.

From 1941 to 1945, Americans had fought and won the biggest war in history. They had seen 15 million people march off to war. More than 300,000 of these were killed and 800,000 were wounded, captured, or missing. The American people of 1945 were hungry for peace and all the good things peace could bring.

Most American people were hungry for something special after World War II. That something special was not food. Many Americans were hungry for certain goods.

For nearly ten years, Americans had lived through the Great Depression. During those years, most people barely had enough money to buy the things they needed, let alone the things they wanted.

Then came World War II. Many Americans who stayed home during the time from 1941 to 1945 had enough money to buy the things they wanted. But factories were busy making goods for the war.

The hunger Americans had for things after World War II caused a problem. Producers of goods had trouble making enough of the things Americans wanted. This meant that goods like food, clothing, and homes became scarce. Sellers

By the Way

In 1946, a restaurant in Madison, Wisconsin, listed the following items on its menu.

Menu

Sandwiches	
Baked Ham	25¢
Egg Salad	25¢
Tuna Fish	30¢
Potatoes	
American Fried	20¢
Hashed Brown	25¢
French Fried	20¢
Omelettes and Eggs	
Ham Omelette	50¢
Two Fried Eggs	40¢
Scrambled Eggs	60¢
Dinners	
Steak Sandwich on Toast; Grilled Onion, French Fried Potatoes, and Cole Slaw	65¢
Fried Chicken	$1.00
T-Bone Steak	$1.90

One of 2,000 drive-ins built across the country between 1947 and 1950. Now that the war was over, people could once again use their autos for recreation.

raised the prices of the few goods they had. They figured that people who really wanted to buy would pay a high price. The illustrations below show how prices rose during the last years of the 1940s.

Rising Prices, 1945 to 1950

The average family income in 1946 was $3,940. In 1950, the average family made $4,440. This may seem like a big jump in income. But if you take into account the rise in prices from 1945 to 1950, Americans could really afford to buy *fewer* things in 1950 than in 1946!

The grocery bag of food that cost $6.80 in 1945 cost $10.12 in 1950.

The house or apartment that cost $84.00 per month in 1945 cost $107.00 per month in 1950.

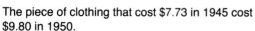

The piece of clothing that cost $7.73 in 1945 cost $9.80 in 1950.

If it cost $7.80 per week to get from place to place in 1945, it cost $9.80 in 1950.

Checking Up

1. What are some reasons the American people were "hungry for things" after World War II?

2. Income rose from 1946 to 1950. Why could Americans afford to buy less in 1950 than in 1946?

378

Reviewing Chapter 24

Write your answers on paper. Do not write in the book.

Using Key Words

dictator   traitor
league   isolationist
ration   patriotic

Number your paper 1 to 6. Write a short meaning for each of the above key words.

Reviewing Main Ideas

Number your paper 1 to 5. Pick the word or phrase which correctly completes each sentence and place its letter next to the proper number.

1. One of the main ideas in Adolf Hitler's speeches to his people was that **a.** the League of Nations would help Germany. **b.** it was good Germany surrendered in World War I. **c.** the Allied countries treated Germany very unfairly after the war.

2. The purpose of the League of Nations was to **a.** punish Germany for causing World War I. **b.** help end the worldwide depression. **c.** talk out problems and keep peace between nations.

3. During World War II, President Roosevelt signed a presidential order that forced Japanese-Americans to **a.** join the army. **b.** be sent back to Japan. **c.** sell their homes and move to relocation camps.

4. The secret weapon which President Truman used against Japan to end the war was **a.** the atomic bomb. **b.** the submarine. **c.** the bomber attack.

5. The problem that America faced after World War II was **a.** the continuing Great Depression. **b.** rebuilding the United States factories destroyed in the war. **c.** rising prices for such goods as food, clothing, and housing.

Thinking Things Over

Pretend that today the government has asked all children to save food, money, materials, energy, and resources at home, due to a national emergency. List and describe five sacrifices you would make.

Practicing Skills

Number your paper from 1 to 4. Match the place on the map with its name below.

a. Pearl Harbor   **c.** Japan

b. Germany   **d.** Soviet Union

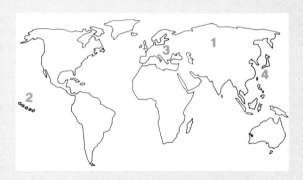

Chapter

25

Lesson 1 Working Against Discrimination
Lesson 2 Determined to Reach Their Goals

Choices About Rights and Opportunities

Strange was the land, strange were its ways

Two seeking shelter entered inside:
room for them both, yet one was denied.

Two hungry men with money to pay:
one was served food, one turned away.

Two on the bus riding in town:
only one was allowed to sit down.

Strange was the land, strange were its ways.

The "strange land" of the poem you have just read was the United States. The "strange ways" were the ways some Americans treated their neighbors whose skin was not white or whose first language was not English. In this chapter, you will learn what some of these strange ways were and what Americans did to change them.

Lesson 1 Working Against Discrimination

An important step in ending America's "strange ways" was taken in the schools. In Topeka, Kansas, an eight-year-old black girl named Linda Carol Brown wanted to go to a public school near her home. But a law said that only white children could attend that school. Linda would have to attend an all-black school.

Linda and her parents felt the law was unfair. Schools should not be segregated. They should not be closed to some children just because the children were black.

Linda's parents and a group called the National Association for the Advancement of Colored People (the NAACP)

These Little Rock, Arkansas, students had to be protected by soldiers as they went to school.

stood up for her. They took the school district of Topeka to court. In May, 1954, the Supreme Court of the United States decided that black children should be able to attend the same schools as whites.

Many schools obeyed the Court. They allowed black and white children to attend classes together. But some communities still refused to let this happen. In 1957, the schools of Little Rock, Arkansas, planned to **integrate**. But many people of Little Rock refused to allow integration. President Dwight D. Eisenhower sent soldiers to Little Rock. The soldiers brought order and protected the black children as they entered the schools.

Black Americans fought against segregation outside the schools, too. In some cities, blacks were forced to ride in separate parts of buses. In 1955, in Montgomery, Alabama, Rosa Parks refused to give up her seat on a public bus to a white person. She was arrested. The black people of Montgomery refused to ride the city buses until they could sit where they wanted.

Throughout the United States, in the North as well as in the South, black people demanded treatment equal to that given to whites. In a some places, black people led marches through town protesting segregated housing and schools. But in many northern towns, black people had a difficult problem. Segregation happened there by custom, not by law. Customs of people are sometimes more difficult to change than laws.

Black people had several leaders who worked for them, protested with them, and even went to jail for them. Some of these leaders were Roy Wilkins, Whitney Young, James Farmer, and Martin Luther King, Jr.

The hard work of these and thousands of other people paid off. In 1964, Congress and President Lyndon B. Johnson worked together to pass the Civil Rights Act of 1964. The **civil rights** law was meant to end discrimination in schools, hotels, restaurants, and unions. In 1965, the Voting Rights Act was passed. The law was aimed against special tests and taxes that had been used to stop blacks from voting.

Many black people still did not feel enough had been done to end discrimination. In the parts of the cities where blacks

integrate, to bring groups together by making schools, restaurants, and the like available to people of all races on an equal basis.

Martin Luther King, Jr., led blacks in a non-violent struggle against discrimination. People all over the world honored him as a leader in getting equal rights. In 1964, he was awarded the Nobel Peace Prize.

civil rights, the rights held by every citizen of a nation, no matter his or her color, religion, and the like.

381

lived, jobs were hard to find. People lived in run-down buildings. They had little money to buy the things they needed.

By 1966, many black people lost hope for improving their lives. In that year, some black people rioted in the Watts section of Los Angeles, California. Twenty-eight people died and hundreds of buildings burned down. In 1967, other black people rioted in Detroit. Forty people died there. Then in 1968, the black leader, Martin Luther King, Jr., was shot by a white man. Because of this, riots broke out in 125 American cities.

When the riots of the 1960s ended, not much had changed. White people had learned how deeply black people felt about discrimination. Some buildings had burned down. But black people still had trouble finding well-paying jobs. They still were among the first to be fired when times were bad.

Still, black people had come a long way since the end of World War II. They were making good the promise they made to themselves in a song they sang as they worked for their rights. The song was this:

We shall overcome,   Oh, deep in my heart,
  We shall overcome,   I do believe,
We shall overcome   We shall overcome
  someday.   someday.

TRO—© Copyright 1960 & 1963 Ludlow
Music, Inc., New York, N.Y.

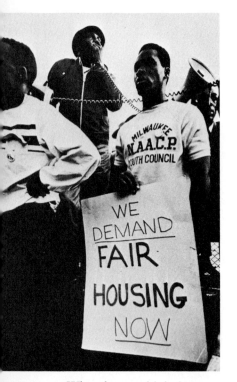

What do you think these protesters meant by "Fair Housing Now"?

Checking Up

1. What do the following words mean: segregation, integration, and discrimination?

2. How did blacks fight segregation and discrimination?

3. How did the central government help fight segregation and discrimination?

4. Why did some black people riot in the late 1960s?

Rosa Parks

She was tired. Her shoulders ached from leaning over the sewing machine. "I just have to take the bus home from work today," she might have said.

Riding the buses in Montgomery, Alabama, was something Rosa Parks did not look forward to. She was angry at having to pay at the front of the bus and then walk to the back door to get on. She was angry at having to sit in the back of the bus. She was angry at having to give up her seat to a white person if the bus was full. But it was the 1950s. Such treatment was common for blacks in the South.

Rosa Parks paid the fare and sat in the first seat of the black section. The bus quickly filled up. A white person got on and looked for a seat.

"Get up," said the bus driver to Rosa. Rosa was tired, but not just from work. She was tired of unfair treatment. She had had enough.

"No," she said softly.

Rosa Parks was arrested and fined $10. It was the usual fine for such an offense. But within 48 hours, leaflets were spread throughout the black neighborhoods. "Walk!" was the message. Walk to school, work, church, and everywhere. Just don't ride the buses until the bus company changes its policy.

But the company refused to change. And so, the blacks in Montgomery refused to ride. The strike against the company worked well since over twenty-five thousand of the company's daily riders were black. Montgomery became known as "the walking city."

The strike lasted for almost a year. Finally, in November of 1956, the Supreme Court decided that the bus company had been denying blacks equal rights. Blacks would have to be allowed to sit anywhere.

Rosa Parks had done more than just keep her seat on a bus. She started a movement that united blacks in a struggle for their civil rights. Because of this, she is known as "The Mother of the Modern Civil Rights Movement."

383

Lesson 2   Determined to Reach Their Goals

From the 1940s to the 1970s, other groups besides black people were discriminated against. Spanish speaking Americans, Asian Americans, American Indians, and American women wanted to enjoy the same rights as other Americans.

During the 1960s, these groups made gains because of civil rights laws. Yet they could improve their lives in other ways, too. Spanish speaking, Asian, and Indian Americans fought against being judged by others simply because of their looks. They pointed out that everyone is an individual. A person is not good or bad because his or her skin, hair, or eyes have a certain color. And not all people of a group are exactly alike. Here is what a Puerto Rican girl named Dorita said about this subject:

66I'd like to tell white people to stop and think and just give us people a chance. Like let's say you go somewhere and you're looking for a job, and the company is white. They don't even take a second look—they just don't give you a chance. There's a lot of Puerto Ricans who know plenty of things. They're pretty intelligent, but if you don't give them a chance, how can they prove themselves? . . .99

(top) American Indians and (bottom) Spanish speaking Americans protesting against discrimination.

Spanish speaking, Asian, and Indian Americans formed groups to work toward equality in the United States. For example, Mexican American farm workers joined together in 1962. They formed the United Farm Workers and were led by Cesar Chavez. The United Farm Workers wanted better working conditions and higher pay.

Some American Indians started the American Indian Movement (AIM). AIM protested the way some Americans treated Indians. They wanted the government to honor the treaties signed long ago in American history. And they wanted to end discrimination against Indians in housing, schooling, and jobs.

Asian Americans pointed out that they suffered from discrimination, too. Most Americans seemed to know less about the problems of Americans of Chinese, Japanese, and Korean descent than about any other group. This may have been so because many people in the United States had a wrong picture in their minds of Asian Americans. The picture showed only people who were hard working, rich, and in no need of help. The truth was that many Asian Americans had low-paying jobs, lived in run-down neighborhoods, and needed the same help from their government as anyone else.

The Women's Movement

Like Miss Beverly Jones in the verse at the right many American women in the 1960s and 1970s felt that they were "going nowhere in a hurry." For many women it was harder to get well-paying jobs than it was for men. Sometimes they couldn't even get into the schools that prepared them for good jobs. If women did get a good job, they might have a hard time getting ahead in it. And women often got less money for their work than the men who did the very same jobs.

Women often suffered other kinds of discrimination as well. They had trouble getting loans from banks. Some clubs kept women from joining. And if a woman wanted to join the United States Army, Navy, or Air Force, she often had to settle for a job that a man didn't want.

Some women joined groups like the National Organization for Women (NOW). Such groups wanted women to get the same rights, chances, and treatment as men. They worked to try to change the laws of the United States government and of the states.

Miss Beverly Jones had a
  PhD in Physics
And she went to town to
  look for some work
Every place she applied
  they said that she was
  qualified to be a
  secretary or a clerk
The word got out on the
  day she was born
But she was 20 years
  gettin' the news
And the I–don't–know–
  where–I'm–going–
  but–I'm–goin'–
  nowhere–in–a–hurry
  blues

These women were attending a national conference on women's rights. What are some rights that they want for all women?

1981 Weekly Earnings by Occupation	👤	👤
Clerical Workers	$220	$328
Computor Specialists	355	488
Editors, reporters	342	382
Engineers	371	547
Lawyers	407	574
Nurses	326	344
Physicians	401	495
Sales workers	190	366
Teachers (elementary)	311	379
Waiters	144	200

Woman's pay

Men's pay

sexist, behavior or language that favors or discriminates against men or women.

One such change was passed by Congress in March, 1972. It was known as the Equal Rights Amendment or ERA. Since it was an amendment to the Constitution, at least 38 states had to approve it before it became law. Congress gave the amendment's supporters ten years to get the necessary approval. By November, 1972, 21 states had approved the amendment.

The amendment was only one sentence long. "Equality of rights under the law shall not be denied by the United States or any state on account of sex." By 1980, though, many people openly disagreed on what that one sentence meant.

Many of those against the amendment were women. Some women felt that they already had equal rights. Others worried that women would have to serve in the military. Men and women alike wondered what would happen to families if mothers worked outside the home.

By the 1982 deadline, only thirty-five states had given their approval. The amendment failed to become part of the Constitution. Still, many people felt that the women's movement had succeeded.

The women's movement had cleared the air. It had argued for the idea that women should have the chance to do what they want in life. And, said the movement, they should be treated equal to men in whatever work they chose.

The women's movement had another effect, too. **Sexist** language began to disappear. Words such as *mailman, chairman*, and *spokesman* are not as common as they were ten years ago. They are being replaced with *mail carrier, chairperson*, and *spokesperson*.

Checking Up

1. What did Dorita mean when she said, "Everybody is an individual"?

2. What were the goals of Spanish-speaking Americans, American Indians, and Asian Americans in the 1960s and 1970s?

3. How have some women been discriminated against? What gains did women make during the 1970s?

Reviewing Chapter 25

Write your answers on paper. Do not write in the book.

Using Key Words

civil rights
integrate
sexist

Number your paper 1 to 3. Write a short meaning for each of the above key words.

Reviewing Main Ideas

Number your paper 1 to 10. Select the phrase which correctly describes the names listed below. Place the correct letter next to the number.

1. Rosa Parks
2. NAACP
3. ERA
4. Watts
5. NOW

6. Lyndon B. Johnson
7. Martin Luther King, Jr.
8. Dwight D. Eisenhower
9. Linda Carol Brown
10. Cesar Chavez

a. President who sent troops to integrate the Little Rock schools
b. black civil rights leader who was shot and killed
c. refused to sit in "black" section of the bus
d. attempted amendment to the constitution to protect women's rights
e. student who refused to attend all-black school
f. major black civil rights organization
g. place of rioting in the 1960s
h. President who signed the 1964 Civil Rights Act
i. organized Mexican farm workers
j. civil rights group for women

Thinking Things Over

Read the following paragraphs spoken by Martin Luther King, Jr., in 1963. Then tell, in your own words, what the "American dream" was for the speaker and many of his followers.

I have a dream that one day this nation will rise up and live out the true meaning of its creed [belief]: "All men are created equal." . . .

I have a dream that my four little children will one day live in a nation where they will not be judged by the color of their skin but by the content of their character [the way they think, feel, and act]. . . . .

Practicing Skills

Discrimination may happen to anyone. It may happen to you for one of the following reasons: age, height, weight, color, language, income. Write a paragraph about a time when you were discriminated against. Describe what happened and why. Tell what your feelings were at the time.

Chapter

26
Lesson 1 The World Around Us
Lesson 2 Ecology: Protecting the Environment

Choices About the Environment

❝Borman: This is *Apollo 8* coming to you live from the moon . . . . We showed you first a view of Earth as we've been watching it for the past 16 hours. Now we're switching so that we can show the moon that we've been flying over at 60 miles altitude. . . .

The moon is different to each of us. My own impression is that it's a vast, lonely, forbidding type existence . . . and it certainly would not appear to be a very inviting place to live or work. Jim, what have you thought?

Lovell: Well, Frank, my thoughts are very similar. The vast loneliness up here of the moon is awe-inspiring, and it makes you realize just what you have back there on Earth.**❞**

Lesson 1   The World Around Us

The *Apollo 8* camera focused on Earth. Over 200,000 miles away, millions of Americans switched on their TV sets. They saw their home in the universe as no person had ever seen it. A small circle of blue, white, and brown at sea in an ocean of black. A small light glowing in an endless darkness.

The Earth and Moon as seen from *Apollo 8* spacecraft. How did this moon mission help make many people aware of their environment?

388

Americans began to realize that the light could go out. They saw that their home in the universe was really a living thing. Like other living things, the earth could be killed.

Almost immediately, a new word found its way into many people's vocabulary. The word was **environment**. Simply stated, the environment is everything around us. It is the land, air, and water. It is the natural resources that help us meet our needs and wants. It is the quiet forest and mountain stream that we visit on vacation. It is the oil that runs our cars and heats our homes.

Many Americans began to realize that the environment was being changed. The air and water were being **polluted**, that is, dirtied. The natural homes of wildlife were being destroyed by new highways and growing communities. Whole forests were being cut down leaving only barren land. Another natural resource, oil, was not only being used, it was being used up! Living areas were slowly becoming noisy, crowded, and ugly. And what was causing all this change? Something that makes up a big part of the environment was causing the change. People.

Volunteer workers clean up an oil spill near San Francisco, California. (below) Air pollution from a factory.

People were changing their environment without even knowing it. Farmers used dangerous chemicals on their land to make crops grow faster and more abundantly. Drivers ran their cars on gasoline that fouled the air. Private companies and government leaders in cities and towns allowed waste to be dumped into lakes and rivers. Factory owners ran machines that poured unhealthy smoke into the air. Miners dug giant holes in the earth.

Clearly, the environment needed to be protected. By 1970, a government agency was set up to help. The Environmental Protection Agency (the EPA) was to prevent the pollution of air and water. Citizens' environmental groups such as the Sierra Club and Friends of the Earth started or grew. Another, the National Wildlife Federation clearly stated its goals:

66To create and encourage an awareness among the people of this nation of the need for wise use and proper management of those resources of the earth upon which our lives and welfare depend: the soil, the air, the water, the forests, the minerals, the plant life, and the wildlife.99

Earth Day celebrations became annual events. On such days, towns and cities held "clean-ups" or "teach-ins." At clean-ups people cleared away litter from parks, alleys, and streams. At teach-ins, people learned how to save precious resources through careful use and **recycling**. Recycling meant that bottles, cans, and newspapers could be used over and over again. All of these helped make more Americans aware of what they were doing to their environment.

(top) Earth Day in 1970. Why are such celebrations and "teach-ins" important? (above) Citizens recycling their used bottles. Why recycle? One reason is that it takes less energy to make new bottles out of used ones than it does to make new bottles out of raw materials.

Checking Up

1. Define the term *environment*.

2. What are some common examples of pollution? What might you give as examples of "ear" and "eye" pollution?

3. What are some ways the country tried to protect the environment in the late 1960s and early 1970s?

Lesson 2   Ecology: Protecting the Environment

The effort to protect the environment became known as the **ecology** movement. The ecology movement had three major goals:

ecology, the study of changes in the environment.

- to clean up polluted air and water, and prevent further pollution from wastes and harmful chemicals.
- to **conserve**, or save, the country's natural resources. This included fuels such as coal, oil, and natural gas. It also included park lands and wilderness areas used for enjoyment.
- to find alternate sources of energy in order to conserve other fuels. The country began experimenting with solar (sun), hydro (water), thermal (heat), nuclear, and wind power.

Events of the 1970s showed the country that it had to be careful in its use of natural resources. In 1973, oil became scarce. In that year, the governments of many Arab countries cut off shipments of oil to the United States. Americans had much less oil than they had the year before.

People lined up at gas stations to fill their cars' gas tanks before the stations ran out of fuel. They also turned down the heat in their homes. Company owners turned down the heat, turned off some of the lights, and even sent some workers home for a while.

The problem and the cure. (left) Americans use more energy than any other group of people on Earth. Much of their energy needs are for transportation. (above) Americans must continue to experiment with alternate sources of energy. Here, a modern windmill and a solar collector provide power for a small area of New York City.

391

History Update

Remember President Roosevelt's Civilian Conservation Corps (CCC) of the 1930s? (See page 355.) That program ended in the 1940s. But the idea stayed alive.

In 1976, California started its own conservation corps. It employs 1,900 men and women between the ages of 18 and 23.

The workers must get up at 5:30 A.M. and run two miles. Then they work all day. Common jobs are stopping forest fires, sandbagging hills during floods, clearing polluted streams, and replanting trees.

The program has been very successful. The CCC has almost a year of work ahead of it at all times. It is one of the only programs in California to get more money to operate every year.

In the winter of 1976–1977, terribly cold weather hit many parts of the United States. In some places, the temperature remained below freezing for months at a time. People had a hard time getting enough oil and natural gas to heat their homes. The winter of 1977 and 1978 was almost as cold as the one before.

During the 1970s, the ecology movement grew. Congress helped by passing a number of laws. Some of the laws tried to protect wildlife. Some made it harder for companies to pollute the air and water. Others attempted to conserve the nation's fuels. One such law set the national speed limit at 55 miles an hour.

There was only one problem. It was very expensive to clean up polluted areas and to protect the nation's wildlife and national parks. It was very expensive to try and find alternate sources of energy. It was very expensive to save the earth.

The people were in a different mood as the country entered the 1980s. They did not want the government to spend as much money as it had in the past. The leaders in government responded by cutting back on many programs. Some of the first programs cut were those that protected the environment. The ecology movement did not end, but it did slow down. It had accomplished a lot, but much remained to be done.

ECOLOGY WATCH

Ecology is the study of changes in the environment. How is the environment changing around you? Answering the questions that follow will give you an idea.

Animals
Are nearby cities, mines, or farms taking living space away from wildlife?

Pollution
Does you community have laws against litter; against eye and ear pollution?

392

Animals
Are there wild animals in your area on the endangered species list?

Air
Is your air fit to breathe according to EPA standards?

Energy
Do people you know obey posted speed limits?

Soil
Is topsoil being eroded where you live? Is farmland giving way to cities and towns?

Energy
Does your family recycle cans, bottles, and newspapers?

Water
Is there a water shortage in your area?

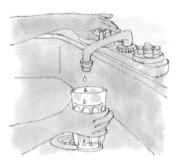

Energy
Does anyone in your area use solar or other sources of power?

Trees
Are trees being cut down where you live? Are they being replanted?

Water
Is there a water pollution clean-up program in effect near you? Are cities allowed to dump sewage into nearby waterways?

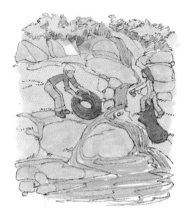

Checking Up

1. Define the words *ecology*, *conserve*, and *recycle*.

2. What are some benefits from the ecology movement?

3. Why did the ecology movement "slow down" in the early 1980s?

YOUR NATIONAL PARKS

It was a chilly September night in 1870. A group of men huddled around a flickering campfire. They were members of a government expedition to Yellowstone, an area in western Wyoming.

Excited voices echoed in the night air. The men argued about what should be done with the wilderness that surrounded them.

"I'll stake a claim and sell shares to miners. Surely they'll find gold!" said one.

Another offered, "I'll build a tourist camp in the center of all the geysers [a column of steam and water that comes from a hot spring]. I can charge people money to see the geysers blow!"

A third member was ready to build a town with hotels, saloons, and gambling halls.

All three wanted to make money off the land. Only a fourth man, Cornelius Hedges, had a different idea. He thought the land should be kept exactly as it was. The land should be made into a national park for all people to enjoy.

The members of the expedition finally agreed. Yellowstone was not to become a land that was owned. It was to remain a land that was shared by all.

Which national park is closest to your home? Which state has the most national parks?

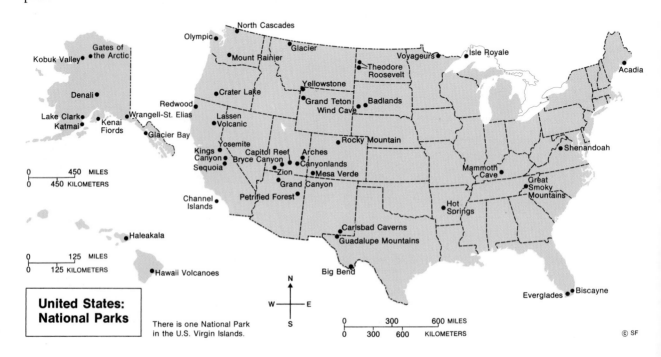

United States: National Parks

There is one National Park in the U.S. Virgin Islands.

© SF

In 1872, Congress made Yellowstone the first national park in the United States. Over the next one hundred years, Congress set up forty-seven other national parks. These national parks are shown on the map on page 394. Congress had two purposes behind these decisions. The parks were set up to make sure that the natural environment and animals in these areas would not be destroyed. Just as important, though, was that these lands should be kept forever for the pleasure of people.

Was the decision to set aside land a wise one? In 1898, the famous explorer, John Muir, thought that it was. "Thousands of nerve-shaken, overcivilized people are beginning to find out that going to the mountains is going home; that wildness is a necessity." In other words, the parks gave people a chance to breathe the open air and understand nature.

Many people, today, don't agree with John Muir, though. They see the beautiful environment as only one of the national parks' resources. Natural gas, oil, trees, and minerals are others. Some people want to use these resources, too. They ask, "If the United States has a shortage of resources, why not use what's in the national parks?"

It might be true. Using these other park resources could get rid of some shortages. But what would happen to the land? Many people feel that the land and wildlife would be changed forever. The decision to use all the parks' resources, however, is not the only one facing Americans.

(below) Campers enjoy a quiet moment around a campfire. (bottom) Visitors to Yellowstone National Park (see the map on page 394) meet one of the park's residents.

The national parks are being used by more and more people every year. Many people are just trying to escape the stress and closeness of city life. In doing so, however, these people are helping create what they are really trying to leave.

Some park entrances are lined with more cars than trees. Inside, the parks' "open spaces" are filled with campers and mobile homes. Overflowing garbage bins and other litter are common sights.

Different people have suggested different solutions to this problem. Some people want more of the parks' wilderness areas opened up. "Put paved roads into more areas of the parks," they say. "This will allow the people to spread out more."

"No!" say others. "Paved roads take away from the natural beauty. The wilderness areas of the parks should be left to the hikers. There's an easier way to cut down on overcrowding. Don't let as many people into the parks!"

"No!" says the first group. "These are *national* parks. That means they should be shared by *all* people."

The government has the difficult job of deciding the wisest way to use the parks. Is there a way to enjoy the parks without destroying them?

"I DUNNO, I THINK THE WEST WAS MORE ROMANTIC BEFORE THEY PAVED IT"

Write your answers on paper. Do not write in the book.

Using Key Words

environment   **pollute**   **recycle**
ecology   **conserve**

Number your paper 1 to 5. Write a short meaning for each of the above key words.

Reviewing Main Ideas

Number your paper 1 to 6. Select the word or phrase which correctly completes each sentence. Place the correct letter next to its number.

1. The purpose behind the first Earth Day was to **a.** celebrate America's space travels. **b.** have people think about protecting earth's environment. **c.** show Arab countries that America did not need their oil.

2. In recent years, the biggest cause of change in our environment is **a.** weather. **b.** wildlife. **c.** people.

3. In 1973, oil in the United States became scarce because **a.** America did not have enough money to buy oil from other countries. **b.** all of America's oil wells went dry. **c.** some Arab countries stopped shipping oil to America.

4. During the 1970s, the government became active in the ecology movement by **a.** passing laws to protect the environment. **b.** creating the first national park. **c.** closing America's national parks.

5. The ecology movement is slowing down because **a.** it is hopeless to try to protect the environment. **b.** people do not want to spend so much money on environmental programs. **c.** the environment is now clean and is in no danger.

6. One reason we have national parks is **a.** so people have a chance to experience and understand nature. **b.** to have natural resources to sell for a profit. **c.** to have something other countries don't have.

Thinking Things Over

The spirit behind Earth Day is to help clean up and protect our environment. List and explain two projects that your class could do to help protect and clean up your school and neighborhood.

Practicing Skills

Pretend that you are a newspaper reporter assigned to cover a debate at a local town meeting. The subject of the debate is what to do about the resources that lie within a nearby national park. Write a story that explains what was said at the meeting. What did the two sides in the debate want to do with the resources in the park?

What Do You Know?

Write your answers on paper. Do not write in the book.

Words to Know

alliance   environment
assembly line   prejudice
depression   stock market
dictator   isolationist
ration   segregate

Number your paper 1 to 10. Write the definition of each key word above.

Ideas to Know

Some of the sentences below are true and some are false. Number your paper 1 to 20 and write either *true* or *false* by each number. If you think the answer is *false*, explain why on your paper.

1. In the 1890s, America looked for new lands and markets because America had extra farm and factory goods.

2. America entered World War I because Mexico attacked American ships.

3. World War I helped make America a world power.

4. One of the causes of the Great Depression was credit buying.

5. Mass production meant fewer Americans could buy the goods they wanted.

6. Women's suffrage means women should not be discriminated against because of their sex.

7. Farmers in America did not suffer from the Great Depression.

8. The only cause of the Great Depression was the stock market crash.

9. During the Great Depression factories had to lay off millions of American workers.

10. Roosevelt's New Deal was his plan to keep America out of World War II.

11. To gain power, Hitler often spoke about the sufferings of the German people.

12. America entered World War II when Pearl Harbor was attacked.

13. Japan wanted America to trade in Asia in the late 1930s.

14. During both World War I and World War II job opportunities opened up for women.

15. President Truman decided to use the atomic bomb to end the war in Europe.

16. In the 1920s, Americans used fads to help them forget about World War I.

17. One goal of the NAACP is the segregation of the races.

18. Other group besides black Americans have been part of the civil rights movement since World War II.

19. When Congress passed the ERA, it became part of the Constitution.

20. Our government has done nothing to help protect the environment.

Using What You Know

1. Pretend your family is living on a farm in the 1920s in the Oklahoma dust bowl. Write a letter to your friend in Indiana to explain what the dust bowl is and why you have to move to California.

2. Two popular characters in posters which tell people to protect the environment are Smokey the Bear and Woodsie Owl. Take a clean sheet of paper and make your own poster reminding people to take care of the environment.

3. On your paper copy the time line below. Complete the time line by writing the following events above the correct date.

   • Astronauts land on the moon
   • Women gain right to vote
   • Stock market crash
   • Supreme Court integrates schools
   • Civil Rights Act
   • Pearl Harbor attacked
   • America enters WWI
   • Panama Canal
   • Atomic bomb dropped
   • Lindbergh crosses Atlantic
   • EPA set up

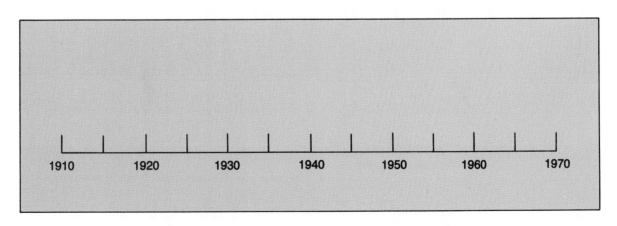

1910   1920   1930   1940   1950   1960   1970

Unit ⑦

Neighbors Near and Far

Chapter 27
Canada: Yesterday and Today

Chapter 28
Mexico: Yesterday and Today

Chapter 29
Central America and the Caribbean

Chapter 30
The Continent of South America

The United States has neighbors to the north and south. Canada, Mexico, Costa Rica, Colombia, and Barbados are but a few. With them, the United States exchanges goods, customs, and ideas. With them, the United States shares a land that is home to over 500 million people. That home is the Western Hemisphere. Turn to your atlas pages of 454 and 455. Identify these and other countries in the Western Hemisphere.

In 1979 althletes from many countries in the Western Hemisphere gathered in Puerto Rico for the Pan-American Games. Like the Olympics, this sporting event is held every four years. The site moves from country to country.

401

Chapter

27   **Lesson 1** From Colony to Nation
      Lesson 2 The People and Resources

Canada: Yesterday and Today

Imagine you are visiting Canada for the first time. One afternoon, you enter a large department store. It is the Hudson's Bay Trading Post. The store is like many department stores that you would see in the United States.

As you browse, you read labels and check prices. All the care instructions on the labels are in both French and English. The money you use to pay for your purchase is printed in both French and English. Later, you pick up some maps in a travel office. They, too, are written in both languages. Why is it that many things in Canada are printed in both French and English? The answers are found in Canada's history.

What changes has the trading post called Quebec gone through since 1608?

Lesson 1 From Colony to Nation

Canada, like the United States, was explored and settled by Europeans. In Chapter 5, you read about the English explorer, John Cabot. He explored much of the area around present-day Newfoundland in 1497. Cabot had been sent to find an all-water passage to Asia. He failed to find a passage to the riches of Asia. But he did find something of great value. The waters around Newfoundland were filled with fish. By the early 1500s, fishing was a major industry for such countries as England, France, and Spain.

The large body of land to the west of Newfoundland also interested these countries though. France sent the explorer, Jacques Cartier, to see if he could find a passage to Asia. Cartier failed to find any such passage. He also failed to find any riches or set up a lasting colony. But his voyages did keep people interested in this land he called "Kanata." Trace Cartier's route on the map on page 403.

What's in a Name?

What does the word *Canada* or *Kanata* mean? Many historians agree that Cartier's use of the word comes from the Iroquois Indian word that means village or settlement. Cartier was probably referring to the Indian settlement on the present site of Quebec.

402

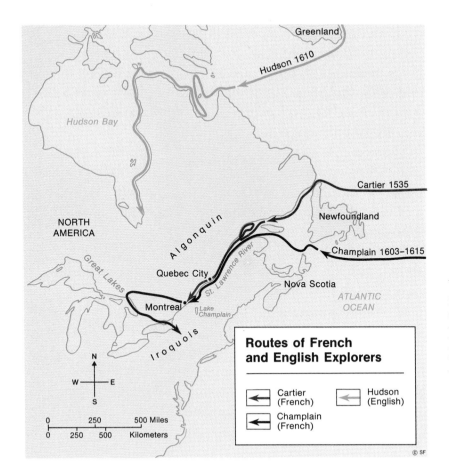

Why did Henry Hudson feel that he was sailing on an ocean when he entered what became known as Hudson Bay? How wide is the bay from its east to west coast?

New France

After Cartier's discoveries, France became less interested in finding a water route to Asia. Slowly, France realized that real riches lay in Canada. One of those riches was fur.

France sent Samuel de Champlain to Canada in 1603 to set up a trading post. With the help of Indians, he explored much of the St. Lawrence Valley and the area around the Great Lakes. In 1608, he started the trading settlement of Quebec. Soon, other traders and missionaries explored Canada. Small farming villages developed in the next fifty years. New France was now growing in the New World. Locate Quebec City on the above map.

England in Canada

In 1610, England sent Henry Hudson to try to find the passage to Asia. Hudson sailed his ship, the *Discovery*, into

By the Way

Each November, a special group of tourists pass through Churchill, Manitoba. When the tour group arrives, it heads for its favorite site, the town dump. These travelers are giant polar bears who come to snack at the friendly town of Churchill. The bears are on their annual journey across Canada and Alaska. The people of Churchill have learned that the best way to get along with the bears is to leave them alone.

Sometimes, a bear will get too nosey or unfriendly. Rather than fight with a 1700 pound polar bear, officials will put the problem guest to sleep and airlift it to a safer spot outside of town. As a result of teamwork, there have been few arguments between the people of Churchill and their uninvited guests.

what we now call the Hudson Straits. He felt certain that he had found the way to Asia. But the straits were full of icebergs. Sailing was dangerous. Hudson's crew was terrified of the "great and whirling sea" of ice. Polar bears rambled from iceberg to iceberg. Soon, there was talk of a mutiny, or a rebellion against the captain.

Hudson convinced his crew to go on with the journey. They sailed into what appeared to be a huge, calm ocean. After weeks of following a coastline, they realized they were in a closed bay. Today it is known as Hudson Bay. Follow Hudson's route on the map on page 403.

By then the bay had begun to freeze. The crew was stranded for the winter. Food ran low, and the crew suffered terrible hardships. Since Hudson would not turn back to England, the crew mutinied. They set Hudson, his son, and several loyal sailors adrift in the freezing bay. The castaways were never heard from again.

The crew made its way back to England. With them went maps and information about the Canadian wilderness. Later, based on Hudson's voyage, England claimed this part of North America. This claim led to a conflict with France.

Eskimo workers unload flour at a small village along Hudson Bay.

Conflict Between England and France

England's interests in the New World grew during the 1600s. You read in Chapters 6 and 7 how England set up colonies along the Atlantic Coast. England exported some furs from these colonies, but not as many as France. To compete with France, England had to trap for furs where France trapped–in Canada.

By 1670, England had set up the Hudson's Bay Trading Company. England slowly took away some of France's fur trade. This competition led to fighting. Besides furs, the two countries also fought over land and fishing rights in Nova Scotia, Newfoundland, and the Ohio Valley.

The fighting ended in 1763. England defeated France in the French and Indian War. One result of the war was clear. England now controlled all of New France. Canada had become an English colony.

England Rules Canada

In 1763, England ruled all of North America east of the Mississippi. The map on page 142 shows this large area of land. Twenty years later, however, England lost much of this territory. Thirteen of England's colonies fought for and won their independence.

England did not want the same thing to happen in Canada. French Canadians were, therefore, allowed to practice their own religion, vote, and follow some of their own laws. The peace was kept in another way, too. When the Americans fought for their independence, many of those who were loyal to England went to Canada. Soon, Canada was almost more English than French.

Most Canadians were happy to be in an English colony. Canada sold England a number of raw materials. In return, Canada purchased manufactured goods from England. England also provided the colony with protection.

Slowly, however, a **reform** movement grew. Some Canadians wanted more than trade and protection. They wanted to make their own laws.

reform, to make better; to improve by removing faults.

England remembered its experience with the thirteen colonies. Perhaps, some officials thought, it was better to give in a little. This was the policy England began to follow.

In 1980, Canada's population was about 24,000,000. The people live in any one of ten provinces and two territories. A **province** is a division within a country similar to a state. The list below gives the name of each province and its population.

Alberta   2,063,800
British
    Columbia   2,662,000
Manitoba   1,028,300
New Brunswick   707,100
Newfoundland   562,500
Northwest
    Territories   46,257
Nova Scotia   856,100
Ontario   8,600,000
Prince Edward
    Island   124,000
Quebec   6,301,200
Saskatchewan   966,000
Yukon Territory   26,001

Queen Elizabeth II of England greeting a crowd in Saskatchewan.

In 1867, the English **Parliament**, or law-making body, passed the British North America Act. Under this act, the Canadian **provinces** of Ontario, Quebec, Nova Scotia, and New Brunswick were united. Each province kept its own government. Each also sent representatives to a national government in the capital city of Ottawa. But England still controlled Canada's dealings with other nations.

In 1931, more reforms were granted. Canada and other colonies of England became independent nations. They were allowed to make their own laws. They could also make their own decisions concerning other countries.

But Canada was still loosely tied to England. Canada, along with other former English colonies and England, formed the Commonwealth of Nations. A **commonwealth** is a group of citizens or nations that work together for a specific purpose. Through this Commonwealth, Canada made important trade and defense treaties.

Modern Canada

Today, Canada is a strong and independent nation. Its government is much like that of the United States. Each province has control over its own taxes, health, and education. The provinces are also united in a federal system. They send representatives to the Canadian Parliament. The Parliament is made up of two houses. One is called the Senate, the other the House of Commons. Canada's government and people are led by the Prime Minister. Even though Canada is no longer an English colony, the official ruler of Canada remains the king or queen of England.

Checking Up

1. What did the first European explorers hope to find when they arrived in Canada?

2. Why did England feel it had to have a different policy towards Canada than it had had with its American colonies?

3. How is Canada independent but still tied to England?

406

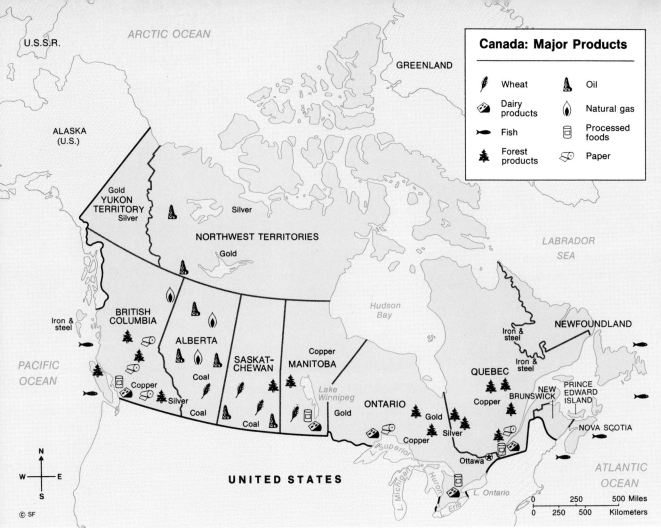

Canada: Major Products

Wheat		Oil	
Dairy products		Natural gas	
Fish		Processed foods	
Forest products		Paper	

Lesson 2   The People and Resources

The map above tells an interesting story about Canada. Canada is a large nation in terms of square miles or kilometers. In fact, it is second in size only to the Soviet Union. Though much of the land is unused, Canada has made good use of the land in certain areas.

Canada's ten provinces produce many goods, from furs and minerals in Manitoba to cheese in Ontario and fish in Nova Scotia. A lumberjack who works in the forests of British Columbia knows a different Canada than the factory worker in Montreal or the wheat farmer in Saskatchewan.

The people of these provinces have different backgrounds and practice different beliefs. The many **ethnic** groups hold on to their special cultures and add to Canada's diversity. Yet, these people have worked together to build a strong nation.

Study the above products map of Canada. Identify Canada's ten provinces and two territories. Do all the provinces produce the same products? If not, why not? You may wish to look back to the maps on pages 42, 46, and 56. How do landform, climate, and vegetation help determine what products will be produced in an area?

ethnic, belonging to a group of people with its own language and customs.

(above right) Canadians of Chinese ancestry celebrate the New Year in Vancouver, British Columbia. (above) A wheat field on the interior plains of Saskatchewan. (top) Tanks on one side of this logging ship are allowed to fill with water. This causes the boat to tilt. As it tilts, the boat's cargo of 30,000 pounds of logs slides into a bay outside of Vancouver, British Columbia.

The two largest ethnic groups in Canada are French and English. But many Canadians are also of German, Ukranian, Italian, Asian, Dutch, Scandinavian, and Polish backgrounds. In addition, there are almost 300,000 Indians and 20,000 Eskimos in Canada.

Both French and English have been spoken in Canada since colonial times. During the long years of French-English conflict, both groups were patriotic to their original countries. Neither group would learn the other's language. Their early stubbornness still affects Canada today. Many French-Canadians speak French and English. But few English Canadians speak French.

When Pierre Trudeau (pē er′ trü dō′) became Prime Minister of Canada in 1968, he encouraged all people to become **bilingual**. Bilingual is the ability to speak two languages. Trudeau believed that Canada could succeed as a nation only if its citizens united.

The United States and Canada

"This is the border," says Mrs. Bolduc. She points to the edge of a doorframe in her home. "See, over in the living room, you are in the United States. Step into the kitchen, *et voilà*, you are in Canada."

Michel and Arlette Bolduc live in a very special house. Half their house is on the Quebec side of the United States–Canada border. The other half is on the Vermont side. The brother and sister were raised in the same house by the same parents. But because of where each was born, Michel is a Canadian citizen and Arlette is American. Their home is not typical. But it gives a good idea of how close the United States and Canada are. The people of these two countries share life in many ways.

Michel and Arlette read both United States and Canadian papers daily. One story the Bolducs read was about a special gift Canada gave to the United States. When the United States invited nations to join in the space shuttle program, Canada designed a robot arm to be used by the shuttle in outer space. The Canadian government gave this invention to the United States as a gift. The United States plans to buy more Canadian robot arms for future space crafts.

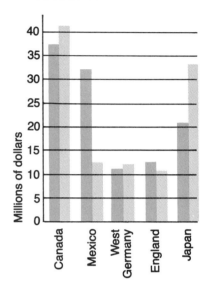

Value of Trade Between U.S. and Selected Countries

■ Goods exported to major U.S. trading partners

░ Goods imported from major U.S. trading partners

(left) A test of the Canadian-made robot arm during a recent space shuttle mission. *(above)* Competition between Canadian and United States hockey teams.

409

When Jacques Cartier explored Canada in 1535, his boats could barely squeeze through the narrow St. Lawrence River.

Today, freighters up to 730 feet long and seventy-six feet wide glide through the St. Lawrence Seaway. One such ship is seen in the photo to the right. Thanks to a joint effort between the United States and Canada, the river has been made wider and deeper. Fifteen locks were built to allow ships to travel more than 750 miles along the seaway. Thirteen locks are operated by Canada, and two by the United States. More than sixty million tons of cargo pass through the seaway each year.

Michel and Arlette are happy to see their countries cooperate. They know that cooperation goes beyond space exploration. Arlette's American newspaper was printed on Canadian paper that was carried through the St. Lawrence Seaway to New York. The seaway was built as a cooperative effort between Canada and the United States. It helps both countries communicate with other nations through trade and transportation.

Checking Up

1. According to the map on page 407, what are two of Canada's main products?

2. What are three ways in which Canada and the United States have cooperated?

3. Look at the bar graph on page 409. Which country shares the most trade with the United States?

CROSSING THE BORDER

Upon entering Mexico, the sign reads "Aduana (ä-thwä′nä)." In Canada, a similar sign reads "Douanes (dwän)." Below each sign is the English translation–"Customs Inspection."

Travelers crossing from the United States into Canada or Mexico must first pass a customs inspection. Customs laws are the rules travelers must obey when crossing borders.

To enter Mexico or Canada, you may need to show some proof of your United States citizenship. A birth certificate or driver's license is usually acceptable. Canada and Mexico do not require visitors from the United States to show a passport.

Both countries also have rules on the kinds and amounts of food, gifts, and equipment that you may bring in with you. In Canada, for example, campers may bring in only two days' worth of food. Additional food may be taxed. Gifts valued over $25 may also be taxed. Similar customs laws are enforced when you reenter the United States.

Why do countries have such laws? They are trying to protect their merchants. Let's say you have just visited Mexico. The United States customs inspector notices that you are carrying a fine Mexican leather belt. Under the law you might have to pay a tax. The government would rather you buy from, and thus help, a merchant in the United States.

But there is another reason. You would have paid sales tax on that belt if you bought it in the United States. The government wants to collect that money even if you bought outside the country.

Let's say you have twenty belts. You may not be allowed to bring them in. The inspector may feel you are going to try to sell them in the United States.

It is fun to sample different products in other countries. But smart travelers know how much they can buy without having to pay taxes at customs.

Reviewing Chapter 27

Canada
AHEAD 2 MILES
EN AVANT 2 MILLES

Write your answers on paper. Do not write in the book.

Using Key Words

reform   bilingual
province   ethnic
parliament   commonwealth

Number your paper 1 to 6. Write a short meaning for each of the above key words.

Reviewing Main Ideas

Number your paper 1 to 5. Next to each number write the letter of the phrase which correctly completes the sentence.

1. The first explorers who came to Canada were looking for   a. a passage to Asia.   b. furs.   c. new lands to establish colonies.

2. The first natural resources that attracted Europeans to Canada were   a. forests.   b. fishing waters.   c. fur animals.

3. The conflict between England and France as to who owned Canada was settled by the   a. Canadian Civil War.   b. American War of Independence.   c. the French and Indian War.

4. In 1867 the British North American Act gave   a. part of Canada back to France.   b. the Canadian people more self-government.   c. Canada its independence.

5. Canada's federal system of government means   a. Canadians can speak English or French only with government approval.   b. England and France still share control of Canada.   c. the Canadian provinces are united together in a Parliament.

Thinking Things Over

Pretend you are Henry Hudson. Write a letter to be given to your crew explaining to them why the expedition must continue despite the dangers of the voyage.

Practicing Skills

Examine the map below. Match the places with their locations on the map.

_____ 1. Newfoundland
_____ 2. Ontario
_____ 3. Quebec
_____ 4. Hudson Bay
_____ 5. Great Lakes

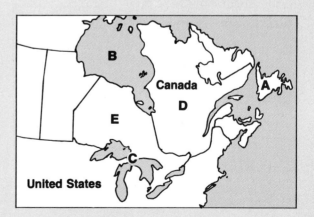

Chapter

28

Lesson 1 From Colony to Nation
Lesson 2 The People and Resources

Mexico: Yesterday and Today

There is little activity on the remains of the stone pyramid. Its once bright colors of red, blue, and yellow have long since faded. Archaeologists dig here and there trying to find its hidden secrets.

All around the pyramid are the sights, sounds, and smells of an urban area. Buildings of steel, glass, and concrete stare down at it. Automobile horns and exhaust remind it of its old age.

The pyramid looks out of place in the modern city of Mexico. But it isn't. The pyramid of the ancient Aztecs, and the skyscrapers of Mexico City go hand in hand. They tell us much of what we need to know about Mexico. A country becoming modern. A people trying to hold on to their past. The old and the new, together.

History Update

Mario Perez is a ditchdigger in Mexico City. In 1978, he was working on a new subway station when his shovel hit something hard. He stopped digging and carefully cleared away the dirt. He saw a reddish, carved rock. Though he wasn't sure what he had found, he reported it to his crew chief.

Mario had discovered the Aztecs' Great Temple. The Aztecs believed the temple was the site of the birth of one of their gods hundreds of years ago. In the 16th century, Hernando Cortez stood on top of the pyramid and looked over the city of Tenochtitlán.

Archaeologists continue to uncover the history of Mexico lying beneath modern Mexico City. Thanks to the careful digging of Mario Perez, scientists have one more link to the rich history of Mexico.

Lesson 1   From Colony to Nation

Mexico's history dates back thousands of years before the arrival of the Spanish in 1519. Scientists think that **nomadic**, or wandering, groups of Indians arrived in Mexico about 25,000 B.C. By the time Hernando Cortez arrived, the Mayan, Toltec, and Aztec Indians had already developed advanced cultures. You read about the Aztecs in Chapter 5.

Cortez had no idea of the riches he would find when he reached the Aztec capital of Tenochtitlán (te nôch′ tē tlän′). When the Aztec leader, Montezuma, welcomed Cortez to the city, he opened the doors to the Spanish army. This army captured the city and ended the last of the great Indian nations of Mexico.

Spain ruled Mexico from 1524 until 1821. Mexico's society changed greatly during that time. It was divided into at

least four **classes** of people. At the top were the Spanish landowners, government officials, and merchants. Next in importance were the **creoles** (krē′ōlz). These people also held valued jobs in Mexican society. Many were soldiers, lawyers, doctors, or merchants. But they were looked down upon by the highest class. The creoles were Spanish, but they had been born in Mexico, not Spain. Next in line were the **mestizos** (me stē′zōz). These were the offspring of marriages between people of Spanish descent and Indians. Last came the Indians and blacks.

class, a group of people who are alike in some way.

The village of Jaiapa, Mexico. The rich and poor live side-by-side in modern Mexico.

The Spanish rule of its Mexican colony was harsh in many ways. The Spanish took over all the rich farm lands and created haciendas. Indians and blacks were often forced to work as slaves on these huge farms.

The Spanish also introduced new diseases such as smallpox. Thousands of Indians died from this and other diseases.

The creoles and mestizos had many complaints against the Spanish. They felt that taxes were too high. They also believed that it was impossible to succeed in Mexican society. Creole merchants also had to trade according to Spanish laws. They were not free to export and import goods on their own.

Mexico's fight for independence from Spain began in 1810. Father Miguel Hidalgo (mē gel′ ēdh äl′gō), a creole priest, led the struggle for reform. He rang the church bell in his town of Dolores. "Viva Mexico! Death to the Spaniards!" he shouted. During the next eleven years, the Mexicans and Spaniards fought a bitter war. It finally led to Mexico's independence in 1821.

The Young Nation of Mexico

In one way, little changed after the revolution. One set of harsh rulers replaced another. The country was still divided between those that had a great deal of money and those that had little or none. Mexico also lost one-half of its territory to the United States after a war in 1848.

Many leaders took power only to be overthrown by other leaders with different ideas. This problem kept the Mexicans from ending the misery left over from Spain's rule. One leader, however, did much to reform the government. Benito Juarez (be nē′tô hwär′es), an Indian lawyer, became president in 1861. Because of his Indian background, he knew the real suffering of the people. He dedicated his life to gaining reforms for the poor of Mexico.

When Juarez died in 1872, the country again was shaken. In 1876, Porfirio Diaz (pôr fē′rēô dē′äs) took power. He kept order for the next 34 years. But Diaz was a dictator. The people lost many of their freedoms. By 1910, the people had had enough of Diaz. The Mexican Revolution began.

Benito Juarez is painted here leading Mexican troops against the French who invaded Mexico in 1860.

Traffic loops around Mexico's Independence Monument in downtown Mexico City.

Some of the heroes of the revolution were Francisco Madero (fran sis'kô ma dé rô), a lawyer, and the bandits Emiliano Zapata (e mē lē a'nô sa pa'ta) and Pancho Villa (pan'chô vē'yä). All worked to overthrow Diaz and gain land for the poor farmers. By 1917, the revolution had achieved an important goal. A new constitution was written. It included many reforms. The haciendas were divided among the people. For the first time, many Mexicans had the feeling of working their own land.

Checking Up

1. What is a *class* of people? How would you describe the classes in Mexico?

2. Who are some of the heroes of the Mexican Revolution?

3. Why do you think land reforms were important to the poor of Mexico?

416

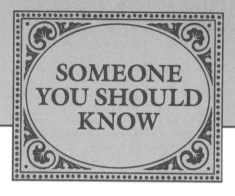
Josefa Dominguez

Father Hidalgo might never have rung the bells of Dolores had it not been for Josefa Dominguez (jō sē′fä dō ming′gwez).

At age 13, Dona Josefa married Miguel Dominguez, a government official. When Father Hidalgo began to organize Mexicans to revolt against Spanish rule, Josefa urged her husband to join the rebellion. Thereafter, the rebels held many meetings in a back room at the home of Miguel and Josefa Dominguez. Social gatherings were held in the front rooms to disguise the meetings.

Some rebels became afraid their plot would be discovered. To save themselves, they told the Spanish authorities. When officials told Miguel Dominguez of the plan, he pretended to know nothing. He locked his wife in an upstairs room of the house to keep her from getting further involved. To clear himself, he went with the Spaniards to search for the rebels.

As soon as Miguel was gone, Josefa stamped on the floor to signal Ignacio Perez a rebel who lived below the Dominguezes. She told Perez to find Captain Aldama, another rebel leader, and warn Father Hidalgo.

Perez and Aldama rode all night. They reached the town of Dolores as the peasants gathered for early mass. After hearing the message, Father Hidalgo rang the bells of Dolores, calling for everyone to join and create a free Mexico.

In 1821, when Mexico finally won independence, Josefa Dominguez was offered a government job and money. She refused any reward. When she died in 1829, the nation mourned her death. Today many streets and squares bear her name. Her face on the 5- and 20-peso notes reminds Mexicans of the spirit of the revolution.

Lesson 2 The People and Resources

Today the people of Mexico are a blend of three cultures—Spanish, Indian, and modern Mexican. Unlike the English and French Canadians who hold on to their separate backgrounds, most Mexicans have a mixed background. This mixture can be seen in the people, their life-styles, and the products they produce.

Ethnic Mexico

Most Mexicans are of mixed Spanish and Indian blood. These mestizos make up over three-fourths of Mexico's population. The rest of the people are divided between either Mexicans of pure Indian blood or pure Spanish blood.

In Mexico, most people are Roman Catholic, the religion brought by the Spanish. Many ancient Indian religious beliefs are still practiced, though. They are often combined with Catholic customs. One example is All Saints Day, also known as the Day of the Dead. This feast day combines Indian services for the dead with Catholic prayers. Another holiday that combines old and new beliefs is Corpus Christi Day. Corpus Christi Day is dedicated to the celebration of life. The high point of the day is the flying pole dance which is similar to the ancient rain dance of the Totonac (tô tô-nak′) Indians.

Mexicans celebrate their past. (above) A Conchero (kôn chā′ rō) Indian dancer. (right) Only the bravest try to re-create the flying flag pole dance.

418

(top) Modern irrigation methods are used on a small Mexican farm. (middle) A market crowded with goods and shoppers in a small village. (bottom) A modern shopping center.

Traces of ancient times can be seen not only in religious beliefs, but also in the way people make their living today. More than half of Mexico's population works at farming. The United States buys many of the crops produced on Mexican farms. Cotton, coffee, sugar, and fruits are the main Mexican export crops. Identify these and other crops on the map below. Many rugged regions are now being irrigated for farming, and hardy new crops are being grown.

Until 1934, many of Mexico's natural resources were owned by foreign traders. They were not interested in the welfare of the Mexican people. Then the government decided to **nationalize** many industries. This meant that the Mexican government took over control of these businesses. The profits they made were to be used to help the Mexican people.

Mexico has been building up new industries during the last fifty years. Minerals, gas, and oil produced in Mexico are sold worldwide. The United States buys many of these products from Mexico. Railroads, mines, and factories are also being developed. These industries help the people by giving

Look at the population distribution map on page 65. Locate the areas where most of Mexico's people live. Use the map below to list the products that come from these heavily populated areas.

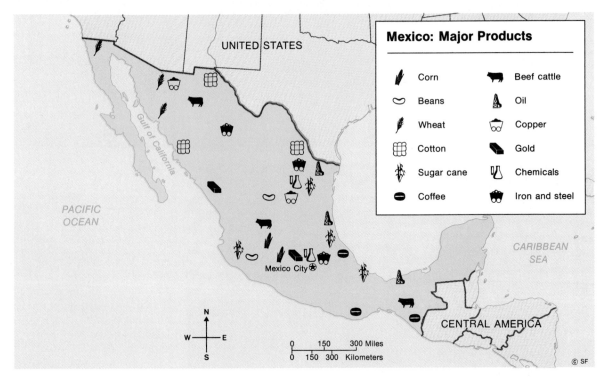

420

Mexican oil workers. Mexico now produces more oil than any other nation in the Western Hemisphere except the United States and Venezuela. (below) Mexican coffee being exported to Japan.
Fishing boats return with a large catch.

them jobs. The profits are then used to provide health care and education for Mexico's millions of people.

The United States has been helpful to Mexico in developing its new industries. However, Mexican leaders are careful not to depend too much on help from the United States. The people of Mexico are determined to become a strong nation on their own. Mexico still suffers from growing pains, such as overpopulation and unemployment. But the people are working hard to build their new nation. The country is learning to make the most of its natural resources.

Checking Up

1. Explain how Mexico is a land that mixes the old and new.

2. What are three of the major crops produced in Mexico?

3. How is Mexico making use of its resources?

Building Social Studies Skills

Understanding Time Zones

The measurement of time is very important to your daily activities. It is important that you get to school on time. Radio and television programs start at a certain time. Trains, buses, and airplanes have to be on time. Can you imagine some of the problems that would occur if every place in the United States had a different way of measuring time?

The earth rotates as it travels around the sun. This means the sun does not rise and set at the same time in every part of the United States. When it is 7:00 A.M. in New York, it is 4:00 A.M. in San Francisco.

Time zones have been set up to help keep track of the sun's progress from the East to the West. There are seven time zones in the United States. Look at the map and find the seven. What are their names? In which time zone do you live?

The time in each of these time zones is one hour different from its neighboring zones. The hours are earlier to the west of each zone and later to the east.

Each zone is centered on a line of longitude. The time at the meridian that runs through the center of the zone is used by all the places within the zone. The Central Standard Time Zone is centered on the 90°W meridian. Name the meridians for two of the other time zones in the United States.

You can see that the boundaries between these seven zones are not always straight lines. The boundaries jog in places to make it possible for neighboring towns and cities to have the same time.

The United States has not always had standard time zones. Every community once set its own time by the sun. Railroads tried to make their schedules simpler by setting up railroad time along sections of their routes. But in 1883, there were still about 100 different railroad times. That year, all the railroads divided up the United States into four time zones.

International travelers are helped by this row of clocks at O'Hare International Airport in Chicago, Illinois.

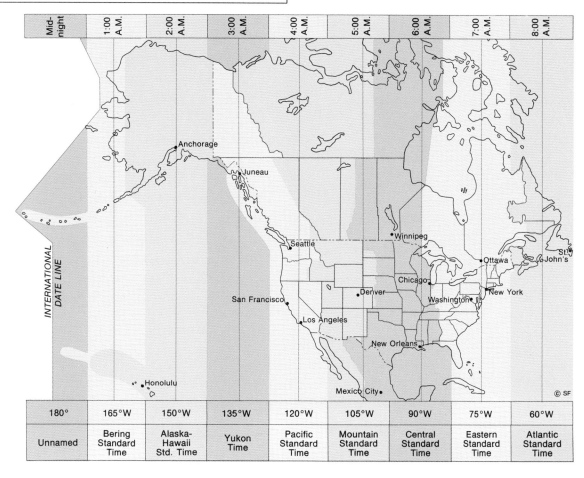

Time Zones: Canada, United States, Mexico

Midnight	1:00 A.M.	2:00 A.M.	3:00 A.M.	4:00 A.M.	5:00 A.M.	6:00 A.M.	7:00 A.M.	8:00 A.M.

180°	165°W	150°W	135°W	120°W	105°W	90°W	75°W	60°W
Unnamed	Bering Standard Time	Alaska-Hawaii Std. Time	Yukon Time	Pacific Standard Time	Mountain Standard Time	Central Standard Time	Eastern Standard Time	Atlantic Standard Time

Exploring with Maps

Look at the map to answer the following questions.

1. How many hours' difference is there between the Eastern Standard Time Zone and the Bering Standard Time Zone?

2. What state is in four different time zones?

3. In what time zone is New Orleans?

4. What other cities in North America are in this time zone?

5. When it is 9:00 A.M. in Chicago, what time is it in San Francisco?

6. When it is 8:00 P.M. in Los Angeles, what time is it in New York?

7. On which meridian is Pacific Standard Time based?

423

Write your answers on paper. Do not write in the book.

Using Key Words

nomadic	**creole**
nationalize	**mestizo**
class	**time zone**

Number your paper 1 to 6. Write a short meaning for each of the above key words.

Reviewing Main Ideas

Number your paper 1 to 9. Choose the phrase that best describes each numbered term or name. Place the correct letter next to the number on your paper.

1. Hernando Cortez

2. mestizo

3. Benito Juarez

4. Emiliano Zapata

5. Josefa Dominguez

6. Montezuma

7. creole

8. Miguel Hidalgo

9. archaeologist

a. people of Spanish ancestry who were born in Mexico

b. Aztec leader defeated by the Spanish army

c. scientists who examine ancient ruins to learn about past cultures

d. saved Mexican revolutionaries by warning rebel leaders the Spanish authorities were coming

e. Spanish explorer who conquered the Aztecs

f. priest who started the fight for Mexican independence in 1810

g. a class of people in Mexico who are the offspring of marriages between Indians and Spanairds

h. Indian president who reformed the Mexican government

i. bandit who fought for the Mexican revolution in the early 1900s

Thinking Things Over

Look at the picture of the pyramid remains on page 413. Pretend that you are an archaeologist studying Aztec artifacts. Why do you think pyramids such as this one were built? Why is it important to save them now?

Practicing Skills

Use the map on page 420 to make a list of five products that Mexico could export to the rest of the world.

Lesson 1 Central America
Lesson 2 Costa Rica
Lesson 3 The Caribbean

Central America and the Caribbean

South of Mexico is a narrow strip of land called Central America. Nearly 22 million people live within the nations of Guatemala, El Salvador, Honduras (hon dŭr′əs), Nicaragua (nik′ ə rä′ qwə), Costa Rica, Belize, and Panama.

East of Central America are the Caribbean Islands. In these islands live over 25 million people.

Both areas hold the promise of growing **economies**. But both feel the growing pains that go along with such growth.

economy, a way of deciding what goods will be made, how they will be made, how many will be made, and who will get them.

Lesson 1 Central America

Look carefully at the map below. The land in some places is only thirty miles wide. The length, however, stretches for

What are the capital cities of the seven nations of Central America?

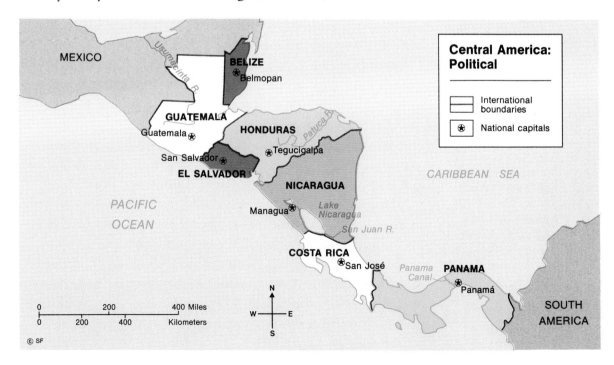

Central America: Political

| | International boundaries |
| ✪ | National capitals |

MEXICO

Usumacinta R.

BELIZE
✪ Belmopan

GUATEMALA
Guatemala ✪

HONDURAS
Patuca R.
✪ Tegucigalpa

San Salvador ✪
EL SALVADOR

CARIBBEAN SEA

NICARAGUA

PACIFIC OCEAN

Managua ✪
Lake Nicaragua

San Juan R.

COSTA RICA
✪ San José
Panama Canal

PANAMA
✪ Panamá

SOUTH AMERICA

0   200   400 Miles
0 200 400 Kilometers

N W E S

© SF

One of Central America's forty-two active volcanoes erupts. You live at least a thousand miles away. Can this far-off blast of red rock and lava affect you?

Scientists are beginning to think the answer is yes. As far back as 1783, Benjamin Franklin suspected that volcanic dust could block out sunlight. More recently, volcanoes in Mexico and Guatemala have proved him right. Huge clouds of volcanic dust have spread through the upper atmosphere. The results are cooler temperatures, more cloudy days, and extra colorful sunsets as far away as Chicago and Tokyo.

Scientists have plenty of time to learn how much the clouds will really change our weather. The dust from these volcanoes may take five or more years to settle.

interdependent, needing each other for goods and services.

over one thousand miles. In its length, is a land of diversity. Honduras is almost entirely mountainous. Guatemala has a number of active volcanoes. Belize is mostly plains. Panama is almost covered by rainforests.

Ethnically, Central America is like Mexico. El Salvador, Honduras, Nicaragua, and Panama have large mestizo populations. Guatemalans are primarily Indian in background. Many Costa Ricans are of Spanish descent. People of African descent make up most of Belize's population.

Two-thirds of all Central Americans earn their living by farming. Many work on **subsistence farms**. These farms produce just enough for their workers to eat. Corn, beans, and fruits are grown on such farms.

Another type of farm is the plantation. These produce bananas, coffee, rubber, and cacao. Many times, the plantations are owned by people living outside of Central America.

Most of the products Central America exports are agricultural. Most of the products it imports are manufactured. Central American nations have little industry of their own.

Trading this way has produced both good and bad results. On the good side, Central American nations are **interdependent** with whom they trade. They supply needed agricultural goods. In return, other countries help them learn about modern technology.

(far left)
A modern banana process-
ing plant in Guatemala.
(near left) The Panama
Canal. How does this canal
help world wide trade?

On the bad side, most Central American countries are in
debt. They usually import more than they export. The countries are spending more money than they earn. The governments have little, if any, money to help their people. Most of
the people living in the rural highlands need education and
medical help.

And the people have little money to help themselves. Central America is still a land of those that "have" and those that
"have not." As the chart to the right shows, the **per capita
income** is around $1,000 or less.

Six of the seven countries are former colonies of Spain. Independence was granted in 1821. Since then, the countries
have had many changes in their governments. This has made
it difficult to build strong economies. With so many changes,
it is hard for the people to work together.

Facts and Figures

Per capita income is the average amount of money
made by *each* person in a
country. Some people earn
much more than this. Many
earn less. The per capita income in the seven Central
American nations is:

Belize	$1,030
Costa Rica	$1,810
El Salvador	$ 610
Guatemala	$1,020
Honduras	$ 530
Nicaragua	$ 660
Panama	$1,350

Checking Up

1. What are the seven nations of Central America?

2. How are these nations interdependent with other nations?

3. Look at the land use map of Central America. What are
   major products these nations could export?

427

Lesson 2 Costa Rica

The Indians who lived there told stories of gold, diamonds, and other wealth. The Spanish believed the stories. They named the land Costa Rica, or rich coast.

No such wealth was ever found. But Costa Rica has been the jewel of Central America. Costa Rica has had a lasting government. Costa Ricans have used their resources wisely. They have had a strong, growing economy.

Find Costa Rica on the map on page 425. Most Costa Ricans live on the Central Plateau. This plateau is found in the mountain range that runs through Costa Rica. The land is made up of rich, volcanic soil. The climate stays between 75° F. and 80° F. year round. The climate and soil are perfect for growing coffee, sugar, cacao, and bananas. Identify these products on the map on the next page.

The geography, climate, and natural resources are similar to those found in other Central American countries. And like its neighbors, Costa Rica has had several political changes. What makes Costa Rica different, then?

(right)
Costa Rican coffee growers get ready to ship their crop off to the market. (above) A rainforest.

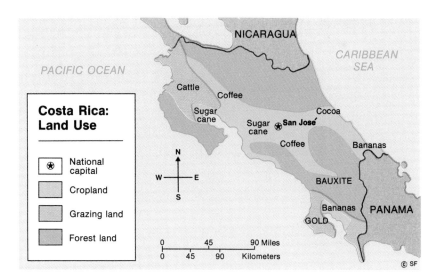

Costa Rica: Land Use

PACIFIC OCEAN

NICARAGUA

CARIBBEAN SEA

Cattle
Coffee
Sugar cane
Sugar cane ⊛ San José
Cocoa
Coffee
Bananas
BAUXITE
Bananas
GOLD
PANAMA

★ National capital

Cropland

Grazing land

Forest land

0 45 90 Miles
0 45 90 Kilometers

What is most of the land used for in Costa Rica?

Most people in other Central American countries work on large plantations. They work for someone else. They never have the feeling of working for themselves. This is not the case in Costa Rica. There are many more small landowners in Costa Rica. These small farmers have the satisfaction of working for themselves. They aren't just helping a plantation owner get wealthier.

Democracy has also been important to Costa Ricans. They gained their independence from Spain in 1821. Since then they have been proud of their democracy and racial equality. These ideals have remained strong even through great changes in their government.

Costa Ricans also feel strongly about education. Public schools were formed in 1849. Today, in Costa Rica, 87 out of every 100 people can read and write. Other Central American nations, such as Guatemala and Nicaragua, have few schools. Many of the people there do not read or write.

Other policies have helped Costa Rica avoid political problems. The government has provided low-cost hospital care. Workers are guaranteed a minimum wage. Imports are taxed to protect local businesses. The government tries to make sure that everyone who can work has a job. Costa Ricans feel that if they help themselves from within, they will have better products to sell to customers outside their country.

Costa Rica is very mountainous. Few people, though, are completely separated from the rest of the nation. They are

A fish farm in Costa Rica. The pens contain fish in various stages of growth.

(top) A busy street in downtown San José. What street signs tell you that Costa Rica trades with other countries? (above) The Pan–American Highway joins Costa Rica to other countries in Central America.

joined by an air communication system. This system includes fifty-five radio stations and eleven television stations. In addition, Costa Rica has built many roads and railways. The country is also united by the Pan–American Highway. The highway links almost all the major cities of the country and leads to other countries in North and South America.

Most of the workers in Costa Rica work on farms. There they grow coffee, bananas, and other export crops. Other workers are busy in lumbering, fishing, and mining. Only one-tenth of the people work in factories. But this figure is changing. The government is building hydroelectric plants to provide growing businesses with power.

Today the United States sells Costa Rica oil, factory-made goods, and other products they need. But Costa Rican industry is growing. This means they will produce more of what they need in their own factories.

If the economy of Costa Rica remains strong, the government will be able to provide many more social services such as schools and hospitals to its citizens.

Checking Up

1. How is Costa Rica different from other Central American countries?

2. How does a strong economy help Costa Rica build more social programs to help its people?

3. What helps keep Costa Ricans in touch with each other?

Lesson 3   The Caribbean

❝[I]. . . walked among some trees, which were the most beautiful thing to see that ever I had seen . . . .
  . . . fair and sweet smell of flowers or trees from the land
. . . sweetest in the world.
  . . . the loveliest gardens in the world.❞

These are the words Columbus used to describe the islands he saw in the New World. Columbus thought he had reached the East Indies near Asia. In reality, he had sailed to the islands off Central and South America. Because of what Columbus thought, the islands are now called the West Indies. The seven thousand islands are also called the Caribbean Islands. Three groups of islands make up the Caribbean Islands or West Indies. The three groups are the Greater Antilles, the Lesser Antilles, and the Bahamas. See the map below.

List two islands in each of the three island groups. In which group is Barbados located? the Cayman Islands?

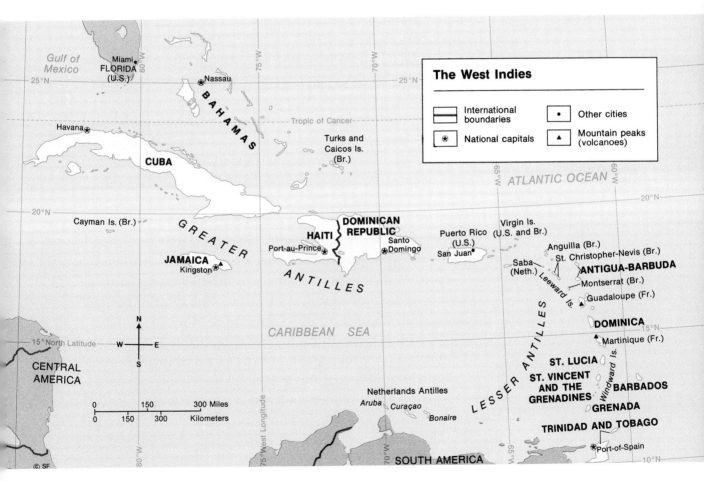

431

The Caribbean Islands are a popular vacation spot for people from all over the world. In 1981, about nine million visitors came to the islands. About one million vacationed on St. Thomas in the Virgin Islands pictured above.

Few of the islands were populated when they were first discovered. Some islands were inhabited by Indians. In Haiti, the peaceful Arawaks welcomed Columbus. These Indians were conquered by the Spanish in five years. In Martinique (märt′ n ēk′), a fierce tribe, the Caribe (kä rē′ bā) Indians, protected the island from the Spanish. They were, however, later taken over by the French. The English and Dutch also colonized in the area.

Europeans brought blacks from Africa. The blacks worked as slaves on the large sugar-cane plantations. Today, most of the people are black or mestizo. But there are also people of Chinese, Danish, Dutch, English, French, Portuguese, and Spanish descent.

Most West Indians make their livings in one of three ways. One of those is tourism. People from all over the world travel to the islands. The warm breezes, blue water, sunshine, and white sand make the islands perfect vacation spots. Some West Indians work in the many hotels and resorts. Others earn a living by selling souvenirs and crafts.

Most West Indians, though, earn their living by farming. And of all farm products, sugar cane is the most important. But the islands also produce and export other crops. Bananas, coffee, tobacco, cacao, and citrus fruits are but a few. These crops are still grown on large farms or plantations.

Industry is also beginning to develop. Mining is important in Jamaica. Oil is refined on Trinidad and Tobago. The textile industry is growing in Haiti and the Dominican Republic. The refining of sugar cane into sugar, molasses, and rum continues to be the largest industry.

A sugar refinery in Trinidad. One of the growing industries of the Caribbean.

432

Puerto Rico: Symbol of the Future?

Every year, thousands of people visit the West Indies as tourists. Every year, thousands of West Indians try to leave the islands. They are trying to escape from poverty. They are trying to find new lives. Like their neighbors in Central America, West Indians have a low per capita income. Much of their work is seasonal. The tourist trade booms during winter months, but fades in the summer. Plantation workers are needed for planting and harvesting. The rest of the year, most of these workers are idle.

One Caribbean island that is trying to change is Puerto Rico. Locate the island of Puerto Rico on the map on page 431. It is fast becoming an example for other West Indian nations. The Puerto Ricans also lived in poverty for most of their history. This was especially true while Puerto Rico remained a colony of Spain.

Part of Puerto Rico's problem was land. There was not enough good farmland for the large population. Most of the land was held by a wealthy few. Operation Bootstrap began to change all that.

Operation Bootstrap was a self-help program. The Puerto Ricans began by breaking up the large farms. The land was then sold to small farmers. These farmers were encouraged to grow crops for export.

There were other programs, too. Schools and hospitals were opened. Hydroelectric plants were built. Advisers were brought in from the United States and other countries. Factories were built. Soon, most people were doing something other than farming. Today, Puerto Ricans have the highest per capita income in Central and South America.

The old and the new are captured in this photo of San Juan, Puerto Rico. In the background is a modern hotel for tourists. In the foreground is an old Spanish fort.

Puerto Rico is a land of change. After the Spanish-American War in 1898, it became a possession of the United States. Today, it has commonwealth status. This means that its people are citizens. But they do not have the same rights and responsibilities as other United States citizens. They cannot vote in national elections. They do not pay taxes directly to the government. But they do have a strong trade agreement with the United States.

Some Puerto Ricans want independence for their land. Others want Puerto Rico to become the 51st state. The question will not be an easy one to decide.

Checking Up

---

1. How do most West Indians make a living?

2. What are two problems that West Indians face?

3. How has Puerto Rico tried to solve its problems?

Reviewing Chapter 29

Write your answers on paper. Do not write in the book.

Using Key Words

economy   **subsistence farms**
interdependent   **per capita income**

Number your paper 1 to 4. Write a short meaning for each of the above key words.

Reviewing Main Ideas

Number your paper from 1 to 7. Select the word or phrase which correctly completes each sentence. Write the letter of the correct phrase next to each number.

1. Most people in Central America make their living by   **a.** selling goods to tourists.   **b.** working in factories.   **c.** working on farms.

2. The goods that Central America exports to other countries are mainly **a.** manufactured.   **b.** agricultural.   **c.** industrial.

3. The European country that controlled most of the Central American nations as colonies was   **a.** England.   **b.** France.   **c.** Spain.

4. Despite geographic problems, Costa Rica has united its people by a system of   **a.** radio and television stations.   **b.** airplane transportation.   **c.** hydroelectric stations.

5. When Columbus landed in the Caribbean Islands, he thought he was in   **a.** Asia.   **b.** North America.   **c.** South America.

6. Puerto Rico tried to solve its land problem by   **a.** dividing large farms into smaller farms.   **b.** combining small farms into larger farms.   **c.** having the government own all the land.

7. The people of Puerto Rico have the right to   **a.** pay United States taxes.   **b.** vote in United States elections.   **c.** be United States citizens by birth.

Thinking Things Over

Why is it important for Central American countries to begin to export more than they import? (Hint: if a country imports more than it exports, is it earning more than it spends, or spending more than it earns?)

Practicing Skills

Using the data below, draw a line or bar graph showing the growth of Puerto Rico's population.

Year	Population
1900	953,000
1920	1,299,000
1940	1,869,000
1960	2,349,000

The Continent of South America

From a quiet Indian village 20,000 feet up in the Andes Mountains to the lively city of Buenos Aires, the people of South America lead lives that sometimes seem centuries apart.

Let's take a look at the land where jungles, mountains, and deserts meet. Perhaps we can better understand the people and history of South America. Examine the map and statistics below. What are the twelve nations that make up South America?

Is the map to the left a
  • political map?
  • climate map?
  • landform map?

How can you tell?

The Countries of South America

Country	Area in Square Miles	Population
Argentina	1,072,162	27,860,000
Bolivia	424,164	5,150,000
Brazil	3,286,487	123,000,000
Chile	292,258	11,100,000
Colombia	439,737	26,400,000
Ecuador	109,483	7,814,000
Guyana	83,000	824,000
Paraguay	157,048	3,000,000
Peru	496,224	17,300,000
Suriname	63,037	375,000
Uruguay	68,536	2,900,000
Venezuela	352,144	14,540,000

South America:
Political

⊛ National capitals

Lesson 1 Welcome to South America

When Spanish explorers landed on the coasts of South America in the early 1500s, they saw the jagged range of the Andes Mountains. The riches of the Inca Empire called the Spaniards into the mountains. The Spanish explorers conquered the heart of the Inca nation, the magnificent city of Cuzco (küs′ kō).

After 300 years of Spanish and Portuguese rule, the people of South America began to build their own independent nations. Today, there are twelve republics in South America.

Within South America, there are three very different landform regions. One of them is the high mountains-plateau region. Find it on the map below. The Andes stretch north and south along the western coast for over 4,400 miles and include several active volcanoes. With peaks over 22,000 feet, the Andes are the second highest mountains in the world. The higher regions are always cool.

What are the three major landform regions of South America? What are two products that Venezuela might export?

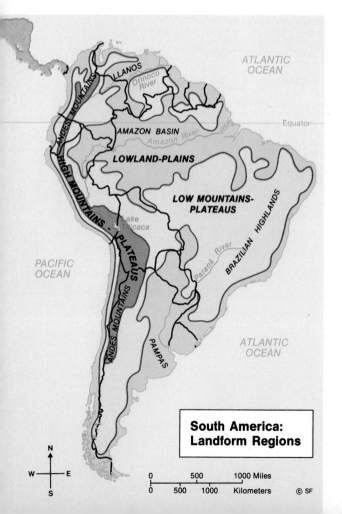

South America: Landform Regions

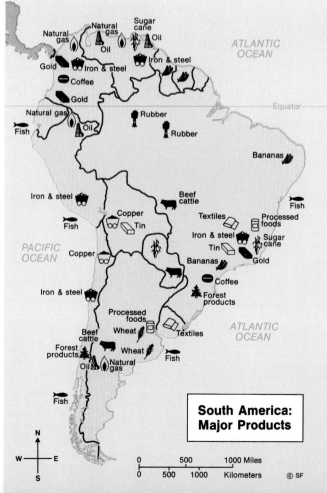

South America: Major Products

The low mountains-plateau region in the east covers much of Brazil. The Brazilian mountains rise to about 10,000 feet. Here the climate is milder, becoming very dry toward the center of the continent.

The lowland-plains region lies between the two mountain ranges. This area includes the Pampas, or fertile plains of Argentina. It also includes the Amazon River and valley. This area is low and tropical, with such dense jungles that many areas are still unexplored. Farther south lie the Llanos (lä nôs), which are plains of tall, tropical grass. Identify these three landform regions on the map on page 436.

Because the landform regions are so extreme, some people have never traveled to other areas. There are many impassable peaks in the Andes. The jungles and deserts also make travel difficult. Not until the 1930s did transportation reach into more remote areas.

High in the Andes Mountains of Peru is the lost city of Machu Picchu (mä′ chü pē′ chü). The remains of this Inca Indian city were found in 1911 by an English archaeologist. Much of the Inca's culture, like the Astecs' in Mexico, were destroyed by the Spanish in the 1530s.

adapt, adjust to change.

What's in a Name?

Though the cowboys of Montana and the gauchos (gou′chōs) of Argentina–seen above on the Pampas of Argentina–ride across two very different ranges, they share a common language. The language of ranching developed before the American Revolution, when Mexican settlers began raising cattle in present-day Texas. Many "cowboy" terms come from Spanish. The term *ranch* comes from the word *rancho* meaning farm.

Other Spanish words you might know are *lasso, rodeo, sombrero,* and *buckaroo.* Gaucho first referred to outlaws of Spanish and Indian blood. The meaning has now changed into a title that is widely honored. In Buenos Aires, when a person asks a favor of a friend, he or she says "Háceme una gauchada" (ä′sā mā ü′nä gou chä′THä) which means "Do me a good turn."

People learn to **adapt** their life-styles to the climate and landforms of their areas. A villager living high in the mountains near Lake Titicaca (tē tē ka′ ka) must adjust to the thin, cold air of higher climates. An Indian living along the Amazon River adapts to the thick vegetation and warm, humid air. Most of the people live in rural areas. Farming, mining, and ranching are the main livelihoods.

The cities of South America would be much more familiar to you than most of the rural areas. Built by the Spaniards and Portuguese, the older cities look like many European and North American cities. If you visited Bogotá (bô gô ta′), Buenos Aires (bwā′nôs aē′rēz), or Rio de Janeiro (rē′ō dā zha ner′ō), you would find high-rises, suburbs, and slums.

The ethnic make-up of South America is much like that of Mexico and Central America. Before the Spanish arrived, the population was mostly Indian. As Europeans arrived, the population grew to include whites and mestizos. Wealthy landowners imported African slaves to work the land. Today many blacks live in South America.

438

South American governments have faced many problems since independence was won in the early 1800s. Uniting the people has been difficult. Many are isolated by landform regions and language differences. In some villages the people speak their own languages. They do not understand Spanish or Portuguese. Spanish is the official language of eleven republics. Portuguese is the language of Brazil.

Checking Up

1. Think about South America's landform regions. Why is travel difficult in South America?

2. What are two reasons why governing such diverse areas might be difficult?

3. Look at the products produced by South American nations on page 436. What products do these nations export to other countries, such as the United States and Canada?

(above left)
A mixture of the old and new in Peru. Peruvians celebrate the ancient customs of their Incan ancestors as well as the traditions of the Catholic church. (above) Ecuadorians examine the growing number of imported manufactured goods.
(opposite)
The modern city of Caracas, Venezuela.

439

Lesson 2 An Andean Village

Over the past 60 years, transportation has reached more remote areas in South America. One project that has helped unite more people is the Pan–American Highway. Begun in 1925, the road reaches from Mexico to Argentina and Brazil. It also connects to United States highways and reaches up through Canada. The highway was built as a united effort by many countries in the Western Hemisphere.

Though the road still has many rough passages, it has opened up new areas that could not be reached before. The whole highway covers more than 28,000 miles. Let's take a trip along the Pan–American Highway and visit three very different parts of South America.

Our first stop as we drive south through Peru will be high in the Andes Mountains. As we drive along the brilliant blue of Lake Titicaca, we see two children herding llamas up toward their village. Though it is 1982, Nilo and Petra's job is almost the same as it was for Indian children 300 years ago. Find the children's home on the map below.

The sun is bright, but the mountain air can get very cold. Nilo wears his wool shawl slung over his back. The wool for his shawl was woven by his mother. She clipped the wool of

A small Peruvian farm in the Andes Mountains.

About how far is it from Caracas to Bogotá? from La Paz to Rio de Janeiro?

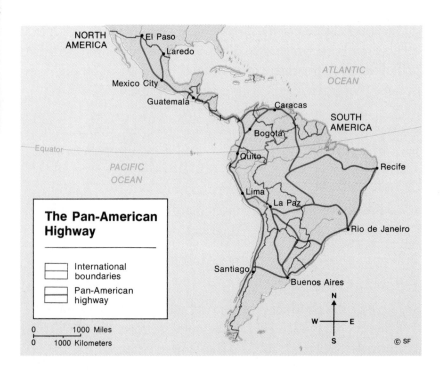

The Pan-American Highway

International boundaries

Pan-American highway

0   1000 Miles
0   1000 Kilometers

© SF

440

Llamas in the Andes Mountains.

a llama and spun the wool into yarn on an ancient spindle. After she dyed the wool, she wove it into a pattern that the family has woven for many generations.

In the folds of Petra's shawl, she carries a sheepskin water bag, some hard cheese, and a few cooked potatoes for lunch. The children have been out since early morning to bring the llamas to a good grazing ground. Usually the llamas carry produce from the family's small strip of farmland to the next village. Today, however, they are only grazing.

The Bolivian city of La Paz (la pas′) is not far from Nilo and Petra's home. But there is a world of difference between the ancient Indian farmlands and the city. Sometimes a small airplane will fly over the village heading for La Paz or Lima. Its shadow passes over the village women as they work in a highland field. Nilo's mother works in a line of women, sorting out the tiny potatoes on which the villagers base their diets.

The highland village is not as isolated as it used to be. Today, the highway comes close to the gathering of thatched huts. It leads to many trade centers that the Indians could never reach before. Steamboats chug along the lake and provide links to other villages and cities surrounding the lake. Once a week, Nilo's father climbs down to the lake, leading a llama loaded with the week's produce. He will sell the food to a trader who will sell it again at Chinchero (chēn che′rô). Chinchero is a town dating back to Inca times. Nilo's father will buy cheese made by a third village, Laja (Lī yä), while he is down by the dock. Maybe he will find a treat for his children that he could not find in his own town.

Wood is scarce around Lake Titicaca. People build their boats with a plentiful resource, reeds. Lake Titicaca is the largest lake in South America. It is also the highest lake of its size in the world; it is over 12,000 feet above sea level.

Though the village is very poor, neighbors have pooled their money to buy a radio receiver and transmitter. The radio provides a valuable connection to other villages and cities. Since there is no doctor in their village and no one owns a car or truck, the radio is an important communications link. Nilo's parents listen to the news and discuss current events with their neighbors. Though the stories they hear might be happening hundreds of miles away, they know they must keep up with the news. Technology is getting closer to their village day by day.

Although Nilo and Petra's parents cannot read or write, they hope their children will learn. Sitting in a thatched hut high in the mountains, each evening the children listen to the crackling radio. They hear about the world beyond the mountains and plateaus, beyond the blue lake. They wonder what life might be like, further along the Pan–American Highway.

Checking Up

1. What are three types of transportation used in this Andean village?

2. Use the products map on page 436 to list three products that might be grown on Nilo and Petra's farm.

3. What problem might Nilo and Petra's family have in listening to the radio?

Lesson 3   The Port City of Buenos Aires

As we follow the highway south through the Andes, we will turn east at Santiago, and leave the mountain range. The Pan–American Highway crosses the great Pampas of Argentina and goes all the way to Buenos Aires. Let's take this route, and view life in the busy capital of Argentina.

Driving through the fertile grasslands, we see few trees, and the weather can be extreme. In winter, the whole plain floods from heavy rains. In summer the dry heat reaches 115° F. (46° C.). We are likely to see gauchos (gou′chōs), or cowboys driving herds of cattle through the grasses.

As we draw near the city, we see rows of tin and wood houses close together. These homes are called *villas miserias* (bē′yas mē sé rē as) or, homes of misery. They are the homes of poor farmers who have come to the city to find work in factories or on the docks. In the distance, the people of the villas miseria can see the high-rises of the city.

Soon we pass large apartment buildings and shopping centers. Some high-rises are more than twenty stories tall, and crowd close together. Past the apartments, we ride through the suburbs of Buenos Aires. Here the streets and homes look very English in design. There are parks with green lawns and trees that were brought from England in the nineteenth century. Tall cyprus trees separate yards filled with tropical plants and flowers.

What's in a Name?

When we think about the old west, we picture rugged cowboys driving cattle across the western plains. In South America, cattle are driven across the Pampas of Argentina, Uruguay, Paraguay, and Brazil. Huge ranches cover thousands of acres of grassland. Cowboys there are called gauchos.

In Argentina, gauchos do not do all the hard work alone. They work side by side with gauchas, or women "cowboys." These skilled horsewomen help brand cattle, tame wild horses, and lead herds to fresh grazing grounds. Gauchas took their place of honor in the 1800s when they fought alongside gauchos against the Spanish. Today, gauchas still earn much respect across the wide grasslands of Argentina.

The busy port at Buenos Aires.

443

(Above and right) The busy
city of Buenos Airos.

Through the suburbs, we reach the center of the city. Buenos Aires was founded in 1536, but most buildings were not built until the late 1800s. The streets are all straight and wide. Railways lead into the city, and there are many subway lines. Buses move down the crowded streets. Near the harbor, an expressway roars with trucks bringing produce from the Pampas to the shipping docks.

A walk along the docks tells much about life in this harbor town. Since Buenos Aires's life centers on shipping, the people often call themselves porteños (pôr te′nyôs). This means "port dwellers." The port is the trade center for all of Uruguay, Paraguay, and Argentina.

One porteño who works on the docks is Tadeo Reilly. Each day he helps load freighters with the products Argentina exports to other South American nations, North America, and Europe. One day he might load leather products and refrigerated beef, bound for the United States. Or he might work on an oil freighter heading for France. The heaviest work is when he loads quebracho (ke bra′chô). The name of this hard wood means "ax breaker." Grown on the Pampas, this wood is used for railroad ties and bridge construction. Some logs weigh as much as four or five tons!

When Tadeo unloads freight coming into Buenos Aires, he handles goods that Argentina cannot produce itself. He has helped unload farm machinery from the United States.

444

Sometimes a shipload of Italian motorcycles arrives, or subway cars shipped from England. When new buildings are built, workers might use steel milled in Indiana or electrical wiring produced in Brazil. Tadeo's job is really international.

After his workday, Tadeo heads for the subway. The crowded streets look like some United States cities at rush hour. Tadeo will ride the subway past the suburbs to his small apartment.

Tadeo shares the three-room apartment with his parents and four brothers. Though their home looks like many Argentine homes, there are many reminders of Tadeo's European background. In Argentina, nine out of every ten people have European ancestors. Tadeo's grandparents came from Ireland in 1880. His neighbors have German, English, Spanish, and French backgrounds. All speak Spanish, the official language, but many old world customs mix with the new life of Buenos Aires.

As the Argentine government interacts with other nations, Tadeo's job might change. The products he unloads reflect Argentina's trade relations with other nations. For example, when Argentina fought with England over the Falkland Islands, Tadeo no longer handled goods shipped to or from England. When the United States was helping build the Pan–American Highway, Tadeo unloaded heavy road building equipment shipped from Detroit. Tadeo is only one of Buenos Aires's seven million people. But his job is an important link between Argentina and the rest of the world.

Checking Up

1. Locate Buenos Aires on the map on page 435. What in Buenos Aires serves as the major trade center between Argentina, Paraguay, and Uruguay?

2. Use the map on page 436 to list three products Tadeo might load onto a ship destined for other countries.

3. Most of Argentina's population is of European background. How is this ethnic make-up different from many other areas of South America?

We, the People

One love shared by the nations of both North and South America is baseball. Many players from Canada, Central and South America, and the Carribean have played on United States teams. You have probably heard of these names as you watch the progress of your favorite teams:

Canada
Ferguson Jenkins
   Chicago Cubs

Cuba
Bert Campaneris
   Oakland A's
Tony Perez
   Montreal Expos

Mexico
Fernando Valenzuela
   Los Angeles Dodgers

Panama
Rod Carew
   California Angels
Ben Ogilvie
   Milwaukee Brewers

Puerto Rico
Ivan De Jesus
   Philadelphia Phillies

Venezuela
Dave Concepcion
   Cincinnati Reds

445

Lesson 4   A Brazilian Plantation

Traveling north along the Pan–American Highway, we pass through Uruguay and enter the nation of Brazil. More than any nation in South America, Brazil is a land of huge frontiers. From great desert plains to steaming jungles along the Amazon River, Brazil is a land where contrasts truly live side by side. Historic Brazil blends with future dreams, from rugged western cattle ranches to the modern city of Brasília.

To really see inside Brazil, we will follow the highway past the lively city of Rio de Janeiro and head inland. We will take a backroad through the Brazilian low mountains-plateau region. Our destination is a cacao plantation in the Brazilian state of Bahia (bə ē ′ ə).

The crops grown on Brazilian plantations have brought either great wealth or great poverty to landowners, workers, and the Brazilian economy. Cacao, coffee, tobacco, and cotton are all crops that have made plantations prosper. But unless planters alternate their crops year by year, the land becomes exhausted. Brazilian farmers have learned to rotate their crops and avoid using up great tracts of land that could make them wealthy.

As we drive through Bahia, we see rows and rows of cacao trees. Workers, dressed in white homespun cotton pants and shirts, are picking ripe cacao beans. They load the beans into baskets slung over donkeys' backs. The scene could be taking place in the seventeenth, eighteenth, or nineteenth century.

Rio de Janeiro in Brazil.

(left) Plantation workers in the state of Bahia, Brazil. (below) Construction of the Pan–American Highway through a Brazillian jungle.

When the workers lead their donkeys to the main road, the twentieth century takes over. Modern trucks built by Brazil's auto industry wait to take the crops to the markets in the city of Salvador. The trading center has been Brazil's connection to the world market for over four hundred years.

As we drive past the cacao groves, we see the houses of the workers. The main house stands at the center of the cacao groves. It is built in the Portuguese style, with a red tile roof and long, whitewashed walls. The owner of this plantation is of Portuguese descent. His family has held this land since the early 1800s.

Today over half of Brazil's work force is in farming. The population is made up of blacks, whites, Indians, and mestizos. Farm workers on most plantations are very poor. Until the 1800s the fields were worked by slaves. Portuguese landowners forced African or Indian slaves to do this hard work. Although today these workers are free, their lives have not changed much. Their homes have no electricity or plumbing. Few of the workers can read or write.

The landowner is responsible for the health, education, and religious needs of the workers. So, near his house is a small church, a doctor's house, and a one-room school for the workers' children.

In Brazil, the national religion is Roman Catholicism. The religion most workers follow is a combination of Christianity and African and Indian beliefs. For almost every saint there is

447

(top) A village along the Amazon River (bottom) Brazilians fish along the Amazon River. Locate the Amazon River on the map on page 435. It is over 3,900 miles in length. Even at that, the Amazon is not the longest river in the world. But it does carry the most water. What is the longest river in the world? Where is it located?

a matching good African or Indian spirit. Exu Tiriri is a bad spirit, equal to the Christian devil. Good spirits are honored with offerings and prayers, and evil spirits are warded off with magic spells.

In the past many wars were fought over land, slaves, and guns. "Singers" carried the news of these wars and other messages from towns to plantations and back again. Today the songs remind Brazilians of the hard life that has gone into building their country. This song was sung at a fair near the plantation town of Pirangy (pi rän′ gē). It tells of a feud over a cacao grove.

> It was a pity, it was a shame,
> So many the folks that died;
> Horacio's men and the Badaros, too,
> On the ground they lay side by side.
> Oh, it was enough to break your heart,
> All the killing that was done,
> And all the folks that lost their lives
> Each day from sun to sun. . . .

Brazilian plantation workers and owners alike look forward and backward daily. Modern machines help plant and transport crops east to thriving ports and markets. To the west, plantations are backed by untamed jungles and deserts. Many areas of Brazil, especially along the Amazon, are still as mysterious to Brazilians as they were to Portuguese explorers four hundred years ago. The future of Brazil may lie in learning how the wilderness can help the nation prosper.

Checking Up

1. What does it mean when a farmer rotates his crops? How does crop rotation help the land and the farmer?

2. What produce might you see for sale in a Bahia marketplace?

3. Brazil has a population of over 129 million. Use the maps on pp. 435 and 440 to name three of Brazil's largest cities.

Reviewing Chapter 30

Write your answers on paper do not write in the book.

Using Key Words

adapt

Write a short meaning for the above key word.

Reviewing Main Ideas

Some of the sentences below are true and some are false. Number your paper 1 to 9 and write either *true* or *false* by each number.

1. French explorers landed in South America in the early 1500s and conquered the continent.

2. Most of South America is flat with one type of climate.

3. The population of South America is made up of whites, mestizos, Indians, and blacks.

4. All South Americans speak Spanish.

5. Life in some isolated South American villages has not changed much in hundreds of years.

6. The *villas miserias* are the homes of the wealthy plantation owners.

7. Bueno Aires is a very modern city.

8. Many South Americans hold religious beliefs that are a mix of Christian, Indian, and African traditions.

9. The Andes are the level plains of Argentina.

Thinking Things Over

Pretend that Petra and Nilos come to visit you. Think about what their life was like in Peru. What would you like them to see in your hometown? What would you like them to learn about your life-style and how Americans live? What else would you like to learn about them? Answer the questions by completing the chart below.

I would take my guests to visit. . .	I hope that they would learn. . .	Things I would like to learn about them. . .
1.		
2.		
3.		

Practicing Skills

Using the map of South America on page 435, complete the following sentences.

The only two countries in South America that do not border an ocean are 1. _____ and 2. _____ .

The largest country in South America is 3. _____ .

The South American country that borders Central America is 4. _____ .

The capital of Bolivia is 5. _____ .

What Do You Know?

Write your answers on paper. Do not write in the book.

Words to Know

reform	parliament
province	ethnic
bilingual	class
nomadic	economy
subsistence farm	interdependent
per capita income	adapt

Number your paper from 1 to 12. Write the definition of each of the above key words.

Ideas to Know

1. Some of the sentences below are true and some are false. Number your paper 1 to 20 and write either *true* or *false* by each number. If you think an answer is false, explain why on your paper.

   1. Canada was first explored by England and Spain.

   2. England gained control of Canada by winning the French and Indian War.

   3. Today Canada makes its own laws but is still a member of the British Commonwealth.

   4. The issue of language still divides many Canadians.

5. Canada is divided into ten provinces and two territories.

6. The first cities in Mexico were built by Spanish explorers.

7. Mexico has always been made up of many ethnic groups.

8. Mexico fought a war with Spain for its independence.

9. President Benito Juarez started many reforms to end the misery left by Spain's rule in Mexico.

10. The Mexican Revolution of 1910 gave power back to Spain.

11. Most of all Central Americans earn their livings by farming.

12. Most Central American countries are economically independent. They do not have to trade with other countries.

13. Costa Rica is the poorest nation in South America.

14. Another name for the Caribbean Islands is the West Indies.

15. Puerto Ricans are United States citizens.

16. Puerto Ricans can vote for the President of the United States.

17. The mountain range which runs through South America is the Andes.

18. Climate and geography help shape the life-styles of South Americans.

19. Most South Americans make their living by working in factories.

20. Plantations play an important role in Brazil's economy.

2. Number your paper 1 to 5. Match each of the historical figures with their accomplishment by writing the correct letter next to each number.

1. Christopher Columbus

2. Jacques Cartier

3. Samuel de Champlain

4. Hernando Cortez

5. Benito Juarez

   a. explored the United States and Canada and founded Quebec.

   b. discovered the West Indies

   c. was the "reform" president of Mexico

   d. conquered the Aztec Indians

   e. early French explorer searching for an all-water route to Asia.

Using What You Know

1. Think about all the countries that you have read about in Unit Seven (Chapters 27-30). Select one of these countries as a place that you would like to visit. In one or two paragraphs answer these questions. Why would you like to visit that country? What would you enjoy seeing in that country? What would you hope to learn from your trip?

2. Using the information below, make a bar graph that compares the number of immigrants who came to the United States in 1979 from:

Canada 20, 181
Mexico 52, 479
West Indies 71, 029
South America 35, 715

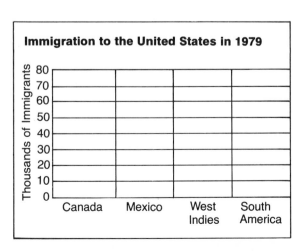

Immigration to the United States in 1979

(Thousands of Immigrants: 0, 10, 20, 30, 40, 50, 60, 70, 80)

Canada   Mexico   West Indies   South America

The World: Political

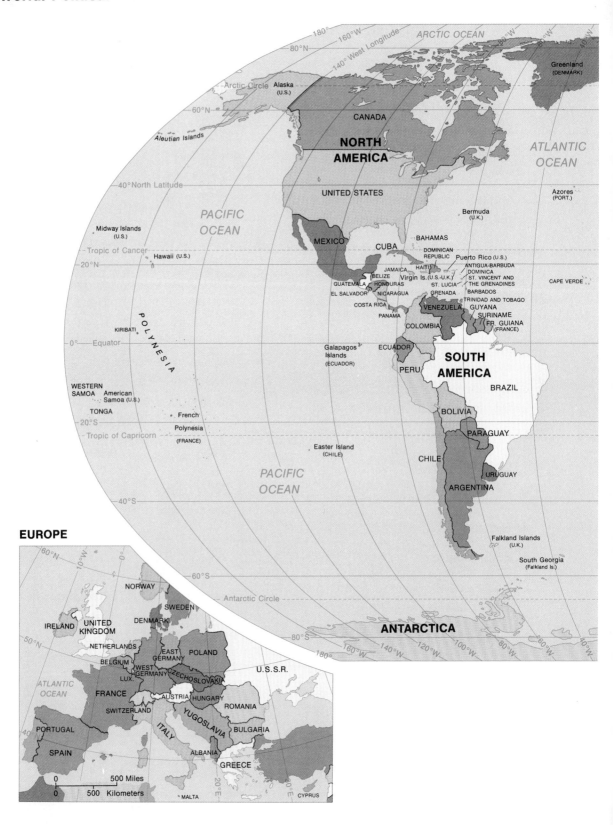

EUROPE

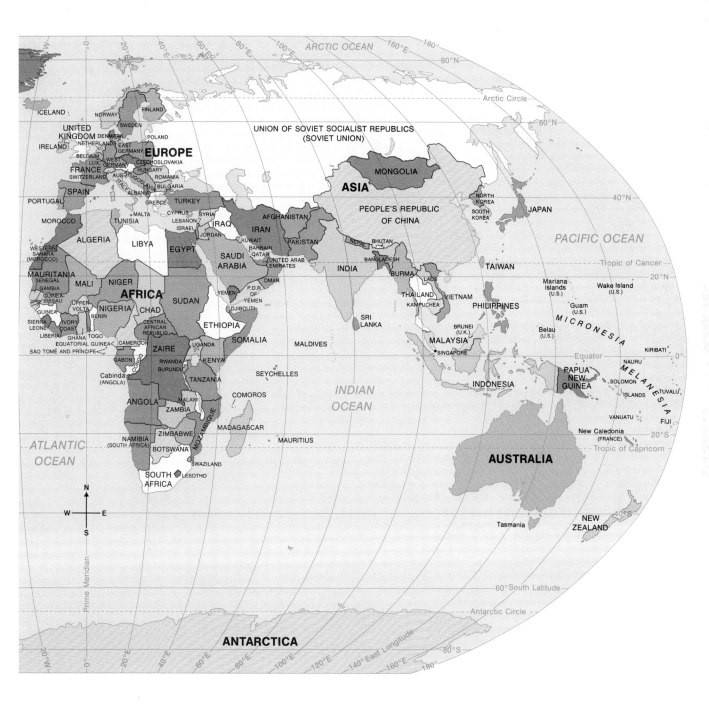

The World: Physical

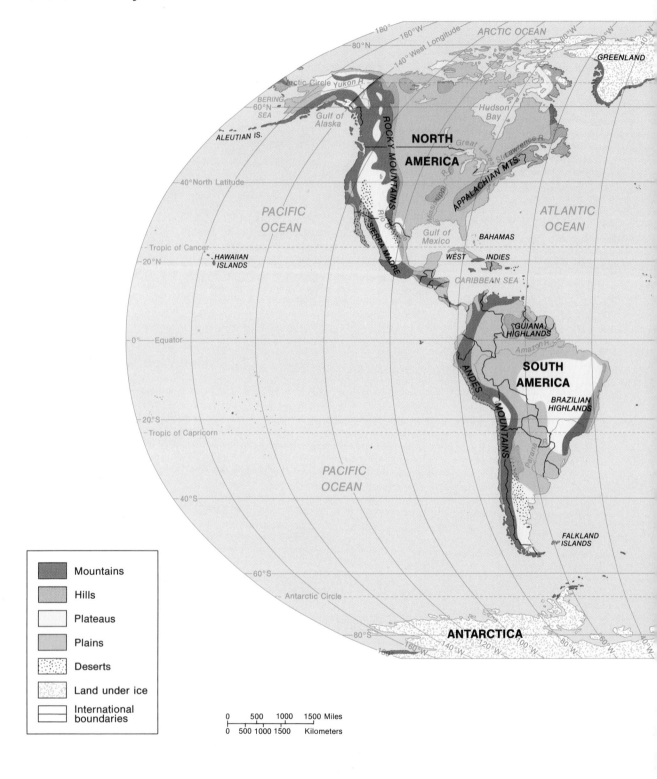

ARCTIC OCEAN
180°
160°W
140° West Longitude
80°W
60°W
80°N
GREENLAND
Arctic Circle Yukon R.
BERING
60°N
SEA
Hudson
Bay
ALEUTIAN IS.
Gulf of
Alaska
ROCKY MOUNTAINS
NORTH
AMERICA
Great Lakes
St. Lawrence R.
APPALACHIAN MTS.
40° North Latitude
PACIFIC
OCEAN
Rio Grande
Mississippi
ATLANTIC
OCEAN
Tropic of Cancer
20°N
HAWAIIAN
ISLANDS
SIERRA MADRE
Gulf of
Mexico
BAHAMAS
WEST INDIES
CARIBBEAN SEA
0° Equator
GUIANA
HIGHLANDS
Amazon R.
SOUTH
AMERICA
ANDES
BRAZILIAN
HIGHLANDS
20°S
MOUNTAINS
Tropic of Capricorn
Paraná
PACIFIC
OCEAN
40°S
FALKLAND
ISLANDS
60°S
Antarctic Circle
80°S
ANTARCTICA
160°W
140°W
120°W
100°W
80°W
40°W

Legend:

- Mountains
- Hills
- Plateaus
- Plains
- Deserts
- Land under ice
- International boundaries

0   500   1000   1500 Miles
0   500 1000 1500   Kilometers

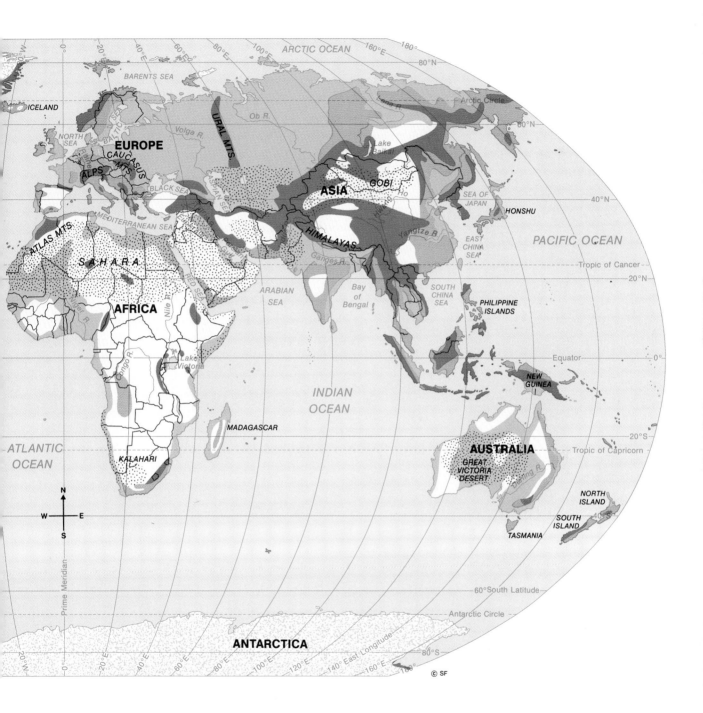

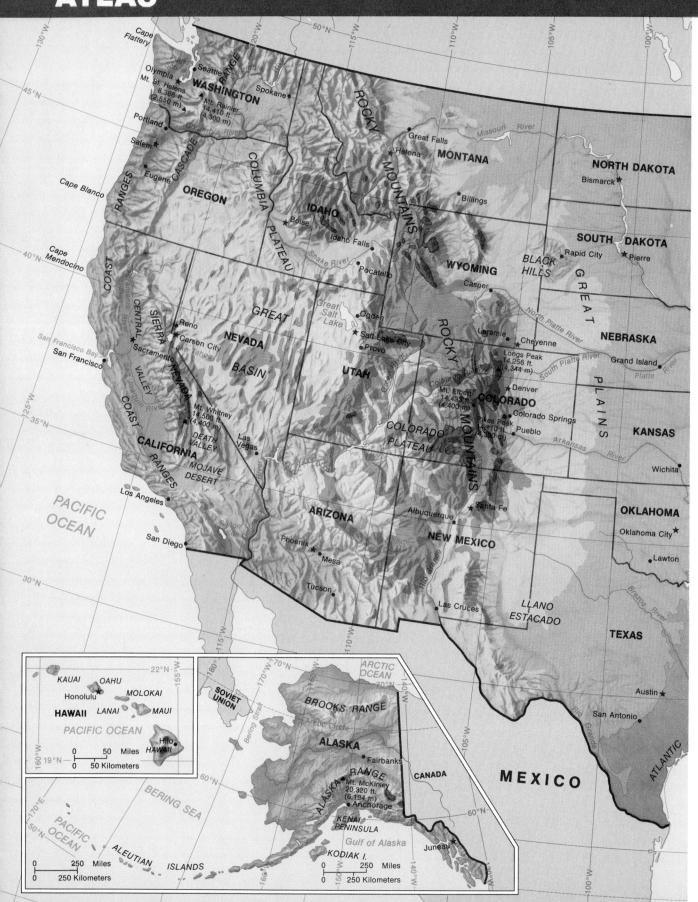

CANADA

Grand Forks
Fargo
MINNESOTA
Duluth
Lake Superior
St. Paul
Minneapolis
Sioux Falls
WISCONSIN
Green Bay
Madison
Milwaukee
MICHIGAN
Lake Michigan
Grand Rapids
Lansing
IOWA
Cedar Rapids
Davenport
Rockford
Chicago
Gary
Detroit
Lake Huron
Lake Erie
Toledo
Cleveland
Lake Ontario
Rochester
Buffalo
St. Lawrence River
Bay of Fundy
MAINE
Augusta
Lewiston
Portland
Burlington
Montpelier
VT. N.H.
Concord
Manchester
Boston
Cape Cod
ADIRONDACK MTS
Albany
Worcester
MASS.
CONN.
Hartford
R.I.
Providence
Bridgeport
NEW YORK
Des Moines
Omaha
Lincoln
CENTRAL
ILLINOIS
INDIANA
Springfield
Indianapolis
Ft. Wayne
Peoria
OHIO
Columbus
PENNSYLVANIA
Pittsburgh
Harrisburg
Philadelphia
Wilmington
Jersey City
Newark
LONG ISLAND
Trenton
New York City
NEW JERSEY
Kansas City
Topeka
Kansas City
St. Louis
Jefferson City
PLAINS
Cincinnati
Frankfort
Louisville
Lexington
Wheeling
WEST VIRGINIA
Huntington
Charleston
WASHINGTON D.C.
VIRGINIA
Baltimore
Annapolis
DELAWARE
Dover
MARYLAND
DELMARVA PENINSULA
Chesapeake Bay
ATLANTIC OCEAN
40°N
MISSOURI
KENTUCKY
Nashville
Knoxville
Richmond
Newport News
Norfolk
OZARK PLATEAU
APPALACHIAN MTS
BLUE RIDGE MTS
Mt. Mitchell 6,684 ft. (2,030 m)
PIEDMONT
Greensboro
Raleigh
NORTH CAROLINA
Charlotte
Cape Hatteras
35° North Latitude
Tulsa
ARKANSAS
Fort Smith
Little Rock
Pine Bluff
Memphis
TENNESSEE
Greenville
SOUTH CAROLINA
Columbia
COASTAL
PLAIN
Cape Fear
Charleston
Savannah
Dallas
Shreveport
MISSISSIPPI
ALABAMA
Jackson
Meridian
Birmingham
Montgomery
Columbus
GEORGIA
Atlanta
ATLANTIC
Jacksonville
LOUISIANA
Houston
COASTAL
PLAIN
Baton Rouge
New Orleans
Biloxi
Mobile
Tallahasse
Mississippi Delta
Cape Canaveral
FLORIDA PENINSULA
FLORIDA
Tampa
Lake Okeechobe
Miami
Gulf of Mexico
20°N
Florida Keys
Straits of Florida
CUBA
Tropic of Cancer

95°W
90°W
85°W
80°W
75°W
70°W
65°W
50°N
70° West Longitude

| 0 | 100 | 200 Miles |
| 0 | 100 | 200 | Kilometers |

The United States: Physical–Political

Land Elevation

Feet	Meters
10,000	3,000
7,000	2,000
3,000	1,000
700	200
(Sea Level) 0	0 (Sea Level)
Below Sea Level	Below Sea Level

International boundaries

State boundaries

National capital

State capitals

ATLANTIC OCEAN

PUERTO RICO (U.S.)
San Juan

20°N

N
W E
S

| 0 | 100 Miles |
| 0 | 100 Kilometers |

© SF

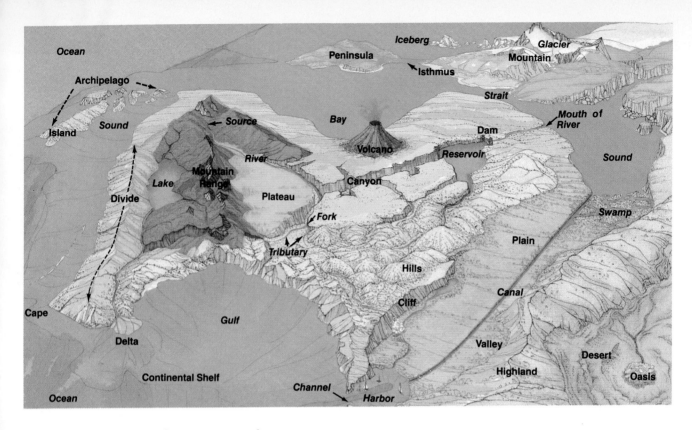

Geography Words

archipelago, a group of many islands.

bay, part of an ocean or lake extending into the land; usually smaller than a gulf.

canal, a waterway dug across land for ships to pass through.

canyon, a deep, narrow valley with steep sides.

cape, a point of land extending into a body of water.

channel, a narrow, deep waterway connecting two bodies of water; the deepest part of a river or waterway.

cliff, a steep slope of rock or soil.

continental shelf, a plateau beneath the ocean from which the continents rise.

dam, a wall built across a stream or river to hold back water.

delta, a triangular deposit of sand and soil that collects at the mouth of some rivers.

desert, a dry, barren region that is usually sandy and without trees.

divide, a ridge of land between two regions drained by different river systems.

fork, the place where a stream or tributary joins a river.

glacier, a huge mass of ice that moves slowly down a mountain.

gulf, part of an ocean extending into the land; usually larger than a bay.

harbor, a sheltered area of water where ships can anchor safely.

highland, an area of mountains, hills, or plateaus.

hills, raised parts of the earth's surface, with sloping sides; smaller than mountains.

iceberg, a large mass of ice floating in the ocean.

island, an area of land completely surrounded by water.

isthmus, a narrow strip of land with water on both sides, connecting two larger areas of land.

lake, a large body of water surrounded by land.

mountain, a landform with high elevation and a pointed or rounded top; higher than a hill.

mountain range, a row of connected mountains.

mouth (of a river), the part of a river where its waters flow into another body of water.

oasis, a fertile place in the desert where there is water and some vegetation.

ocean, the great body of salt water that covers almost three fourths of the earth's surface; the sea.

peninsula, land surrounded by water on all sides but one.

plateau, a broad and flat or gently rolling area high above sea level.

plain, a broad and flat or gently rolling area usuallly low in elevation.

reservoir, a place where water is collected and stored.

river, a large stream of water that flows into a lake, ocean or other body of water.

sound, a body of water separating a large island from the mainland; an inlet of the ocean.

source (of a river), the place where a river or stream begins.

strait, a narrow waterway connecting two large bodies of water.

swamp, low, wet land supports grass and trees.

tributary, a stream or river that flows into a larger stream or river.

valley, low land between hills or mountains.

volcano, an opening in the earth's crust through which steam, ashes, and lava are forced out.

458

Glossary

Full Pronunciation Key

The pronunciation of each word is shown just after the word, in this way:
ab bre vi ate (ə brē′vē āt). The letters and signs used are pronounced as in the words below. The mark ′ is placed after a syllable with a primary, or heavy, accent, as in the example above. The mark ′ after a syllable shows a secondary, or lighter, accent, as in **ab bre vi a tion** (ə brē′vē ā′shən).

a	hat, cap	i	it, pin	p	paper, cup	z	zero, breeze
ā	age, face	ī	ice, five	r	run, try	zh	measure,
ä	father, far			s	say, yes		seizure
		j	jam, enjoy	sh	she, rush	ə	represents:
b	bad, rob	k	kind, seek	t	tell, it		a in about
ch	child, much	l	land, coal	th	thin, both		e in taken
d	did, red	m	me, am	ŦH	then, smooth		i in pencil
		n	no, in				o in lemon
e	let, best	ng	long, bring	u	cup, butter		u in circus
ē	equal, be			u̇	full, put		
ėr	term, learn	o	hot, rock	ü	rule, move		
		ō	open, go				
f	fat, if	ô	order, all	v	very, save		
g	go, bag	oi	oil, voice	w	will, woman		
h	he, how	ou	house, out	y	young, yet		

The pronunciation key is from the *Thorndike-Barnhart* Dictionary Series.

---

abolish (ə bol′ish), *verb,* do away with completely; put an end to.

A.D. and **B.C.,** the letters A.D. stand for *anno domini* in Latin. They are used to indicate the years on a calendar after the birth of Jesus, almost 2,000 years ago. B.C. stands for the years before Jesus' birth.

adapt (ə dapt′), *verb,* adjust to change.

agriculture (ag′rə kul′chər), *noun,* the production of crops and the raising of livestock; farming.

alliance (ə lī′əns), *noun,* a union of persons, groups, or nations formed by agreement for some special purpose.

amendment (ə mend′mənt), *noun,* change made in a law; a change for the better; an improvement.

ancestor (an′ses′tər), *noun,* a person from whom one is descended; a grandparent or great-grandparent.

annex (ə neks′), *verb,* join or add a smaller thing to a larger thing.

459

archaeologist (är′kē ol′ə jist), *noun*, a scientist who studies the objects left by earlier people to find out how they lived.

artifact (är′tə fakt), *noun*, an object made and used by people.

assembly line, a row of workers and machines along which work is passed until the final product is made.

bar scale, a series of marks made along a line at regular intervals to measure distance on a map.

bilingual (bī ling′gwəl), *adjective*, containing or written in two languages. Canada is a bilingual nation because both English and French are official languages.

boom town, mining or cattle towns that grew quickly; a town that has a sudden increase in business and activity.

boundary (boun′dər ē), *noun*, a limiting line or thing; a border.

broadside (brôd′sīd′), *noun*, a large sheet of paper on which information is printed and which is publicly displayed.

cabinet (kab′ə nit), *noun*, a group of advisors chosen by the head of a nation to help in the running of the government.

canal (kə nal′), *noun*, a waterway dug across land for ships or small boats to go through.

capital (kap′ə təl), *noun*, money that is used to build new machines, tools, and factories.

cede (sēd), *verb*, hand over; give up.

charity (char′ə tē), *noun*, generous giving to the poor or to organizations that look after the sick, the poor, and the helpless.

checks and balances, a system in the Constitution where the power of each of the three branches is checked or limited by the other two branches.

civil rights, the rights of a citizen, especially the rights guaranteed to all United States citizens regardless of race, color, religion, or sex.

civil war, a struggle between people of the same country.

class (klas), *noun*, group of people or things alike in some way; the rank or division in a society.

climate (klī′mit), *noun*, the usual kind of weather found in a place over a period of years.

colony (kol′ə nē), *noun*, a group who leave their own country and settle in another land. The colony is ruled by the country from which the settlers came.

commonwealth (kom′ən welth′), *noun*, the people who make up a nation; citizens of a state; an association of nations, as in the British Commonwealth of Nations.

communication (kə myü′nə kā′shən), *noun*, an exchange of news, ideas, and information by writing, speaking, etc.

compromise (kom′prə mīz), *verb*, settle differences of opinion by agreeing that each side will give up part of what is demanded.

confederation (kən fed′ə rā′shən), *noun*, joining together in a loose alliance.

congress (kong′gris), *noun*, a meeting; a group that meets to discuss ideas and make decisions.

conquer (kong′kər), *verb*, overcome by force.

conserve (kən serv′), *verb*, keep from loss or from being used up; preserve.

constitution (kon′stə tü′shən), *noun*, a written plan for government; a set of rules that explains what a government can and cannot do.

creole (krē′ōl), *noun*, a person of Spanish descent who was born in a Latin American country.

culture (kul′chər), *noun*, the way of life of a people.

currency (ker′ən sē), *noun*, money in use in a country.

custom (kus′təm), *noun*, a common way of doing something among a group of people.

demand (di mand′), *noun*, the desire and ability to buy something.

democracy (di mok′rə sē), *noun*, government that is run by the people who live under it.

depression (di presh′ən), *noun*, bad economic times; people are out of work, prices are falling, businesses are not selling goods, and people have little income to spend or save.

descent (di sent′), *noun*, family line; ancestors; parentage; heritage.

dictator (dik′tā tər), *noun*, a person who wants to have all the power to make governmental decisions.

discrimination (dis krim′ə nā′shən), *noun*, treating someone differently because of their race, religion, or sex.

ecology (ē kol′ə jē), *noun*, the study of how living things relate to each other in the environment; the study of changes in the environment.

economy (i kon′ə mē), *noun*, a way of deciding what goods will be made, how they will be made, how many will be made and who will get them.

emancipate (i man′sə pāt), *verb*, set free from slavery; release.

embargo (em bär′gō), *noun*, an order by a government that does not allow ships to enter or leave its ports.

environment (en vī′rən mənt), *noun*, the world around someone; the surrounding land, air, water, etc.

ethnic (eth′nik), *adjective*, belonging to a group of people with its own language and customs.

Executive Branch, the branch of government that carries out, or enforces, the nation's laws.

explore (ek splôr′), *verb*, travel over little-known lands or seas for the purpose of discovery.

export (ek spôrt′), *verb*, send goods out of a country for sale and use in another; *noun*, the article sent out. *Cotton is an important export of the United States.*

factory (fak′tər ē), *noun*, building or group of buildings where goods are made with machines, or by hand.

fad (fad), *noun*, something that everybody is interested in for a short time.

federalism (fed′ər ə liz′əm), a system of government where a central government handles common affairs, and state governments handle local affairs.

fork (fôrk), *noun*, the place where a stream or tributary joins a river.

frontier (frun tir′), *noun*, the farthest part of a settled country, where the wilderness begins.

goods (gùdz), *noun*, personal property, belongings; thing or things for sale.

graph (graf), *noun*, a line or diagram showing how one quantity depends or changes with another.

historian (hi stôr′ē ən), *noun*, one who studies how people lived and what they did in the past.

homestead (hōm′sted′), *noun*, piece of land that a settler could get free by living and working on it.

immigrant (im′ə grənt), *noun*, one who leaves his or her homeland and comes to another country.

import (im pôrt′), *verb*, bring in from another country for sale or use; *noun*, the article imported; *Rubber is a useful import.*

income (in′kum′), *noun*, money earned for providing labor or a service, from the selling or renting of property, or from investments.

indentured servant, a person who agrees to work for a certain amount of time to pay off a debt.

independent (in′di pen′dənt), *noun*, being able to make one's own decisions and laws.

industrial (in dus'trē əl), *adjective*, resulting from the production of goods by machines instead of by hand.

insure (in shür'), *verb*, arrange payment of money in case of loss, accident, or death.

integrate (in'tə grāt), *verb*, bring groups together by having the same schools, restaurants, etc.

interdependent (in'tər di pen'dənt), *adjective*, needing each other.

invent (in vent'), *verb*, make up something new.

isolationist (ī'sə lā'shə nist), *noun*, one who wants to avoid making alliances or becoming involved with other nations' affairs.

Judicial Branch, the branch of government that decides if laws are working fairly.

labor union, a group of workers joined together to protect and promote their interests by dealing as a group with their employers.

landform (land'fôrm'), *noun*, one of the many different surface features that cover the earth both on land and on the ocean floor.

league (lēg), *noun*, union of countries joined together to help each other.

legend (lej'ənd), *noun*, a story coming down from the past based on actual people and events.

Legislative Branch, the branch of government that makes the laws; Congress.

loyalist (loi'ə list), *noun*, a person who supports the existing government during times of change. During the American War for Independence, loyalists supported the king.

market (mär'kit), *noun*, center of trade; an area where goods may be sold.

mass media, means of communication such as TV, radio, and newspapers that reach large numbers of people.

mass production, making of goods in large amounts.

mestizo (me stē'zō), *noun*, a person of mixed ancestry, especially the child of a Spaniard and an American Indian.

merchant (mėr'chənt), *noun*, one who buys and sells products for a living.

metropolitan area, place made up of a large central city and surrounding suburbs.

migrate (mī'grāt), *verb*, move from one place to another.

minutemen (min'it mən'), *noun*, members of American army just before and during the American War for Independence. They kept themselves ready for military service at a minute's notice.

mission (mish'ən), *noun*, group of persons sent by a religious organization into other parts of the world to spread its religious beliefs; the church or headquarters of such a group.

mouth (mouth), *noun*, the part of a river where its waters flow into another body of water.

nationalize (nash'ə nə līz), *verb*, bring land or industries under the control or ownership of a nation.

natural resource, anything in or on the earth that can be used to satisfy people's wants and needs.

natural vegetation, plants that grow in a region without the help of people.

naturalize (nach'ər ə līz), *verb*, admit a foreigner to citizenship. After living in the United States for a certain number of years, an immigrant can be naturalized after passing a test.

neutral (nü'trəl), *adjective*, on neither side in a quarrel or war.

nomadic (nō mad'ik), *adjective*, wandering.

nonfiction (non fik'shan), *noun*, writing that deals with real people and events.

parliament (pär′lə mənt), *noun,* a lawmaking body.

patriot (pā′trē ət), *noun,* a person who loves and supports his or her country. During the American War for Independence, a patriot was one in favor of independence.

patriotic (pā′trē ot′ik), *adjective,* showing love and loyalty to one's own country.

per capita income, the average income earned by each person.

pilgrim (pil′grəm), *noun,* a person who goes on a journey to a place as an act of religious devotion.

pioneer (pī′ə nir′), *noun,* a person who goes first or does something first, and so prepares a way for others.

plantation (plan tā′shən), *noun,* a large farm on which tobacco, rice, cotton, and other crops were grown for sale.

political party, a group of people with similar ideas about what government is supposed to do.

pollute (pə lüt′), *verb,* changing a place for the worse; to dirty.

population density, the average number of people living within an area of land, usually a square mile or kilometer.

population distribution, the way in which people are spread out over a part of the earth's surface.

precipitation (pri sip′ə tā′shən), *noun,* the depositing of moisture in the form of rain, snow, dew, etc.

prejudice (prej′ə dis), *noun,* an unfair opinion or judgment about someone or something.

profit (prof′it), *noun,* what is left when the cost of goods and of carrying on the business is subtracted from the amount of money taken in.

prosperity (pro spər′ə tē), *noun,* good economic times.

province (prov′əns), *noun,* one of the main divisions of a country. Canada is made up of provinces instead of states.

pueblo (pweb′lō), *noun,* a village built of adobe and stone.

ratification (rat′ə fə kā′shən), *noun,* approval that makes a law go into effect.

ration (rash′ən), *verb,* distribute in limited amounts; allow only certain amounts of certain goods to each person.

raw materials, anything that can be manufactured, treated, or prepared to make it more useful or to increase its value.

rebellion (ri bel′yən), *noun,* fight against one's own government.

reconstruct (rē′kən strukt′), *verb,* rebuild; make over.

recycle (rē sī′kəl), verb, treating or fixing something in order that it may be used again.

reform (ri fôrm′), *adjective,* a movement that wants to make things better; *verb,* improve by removing faults.

region (rē′jən), *noun,* an area of land that has some common features that make it different from other areas.

representation (rep′ri zen tā′shən), *noun,* an act of electing someone to speak or act for others.

republic (ri pub′lik), *noun,* a nation or state in which the citizens elect representatives to manage the government.

reservation (rez′ər vā′shən), *noun,* land set aside for a reason, especially for Indians to live on.

reservoir (rez′ər vwär), *noun,* a place where water is collected and stored.

resist (ri zist′), *verb,* to act or fight against; oppose.

revolution (rev′ə lü′shən), *noun,* big change that makes a difference in the lives of many people.

riot (rī′ət), *noun,* wild, violent behavior in public by many people.

segregate (seg′rə gāt), *verb,* separate one group from others.

services (ser′vis ez), *noun,* a performance of duties; work done in the service of others.

settlement house, a place in a poor neighbor-hood where the people who live nearby can meet to get help and plan how to help themselves.

sexist (sek′sist), *adjective,* attitudes resulting from discrimination or prejudice against a sex or member of a sex.

sharecropper (sher′krop′ər), *noun,* person who farms land for an owner in return for part of the crops.

skyscraper (skī′skrā′pər), *noun,* a very tall building that is supported by an iron or steel skeleton instead of by the walls.

slave (slāv), *noun,* a person who is owned by another.

slavery (slā′vər ē), *noun,* the condition of being a slave; the custom of owning slaves.

smuggle (smug′əl), *verb,* bring in or take out of a country secretly and against the law.

source (sôrs), *noun,* the place where a river or stream begins.

states' rights, the rights belonging to the states; the belief that states have the right to decide whether or not to obey federal laws.

stock market, place where shares of stock are bought and sold.

strike (strīk), *noun,* stopping work to get bet-ter pay, shorter hours, or better working conditions.

subsistence farm, a farm that produces only enough food for the farmer and his or her family.

suburb (sub′ėrb′), *noun,* a district, town, or village just outside or near a city.

suffrage (suf′ rij), *noun,* the right to vote.

supply (sə plī′), *noun,* quantity of an item ready for purchase.

surplus (sėr′pləs), *noun,* an amount over and above what is needed.

tariff (tar′if), *noun,* a tax on imports or ex-ports.

tax (taks), *noun,* money paid by people for the support of the government and the cost of public works and services.

technology (tek nol′ə jē), *noun,* the tools and knowledge that people use to help them meet their needs and wants.

tenement (ten′ə mənt), *noun,* a building in a poor section of a city, divided into several rooms and occupied by separate families.

time line, a line that represents a certain length of time; a line that shows the order in which events occur.

time zone, a region in which the same stan-dard time is being used.

traitor (trā′tər), *noun,* a person who turns against his or her country or ruler.

transcontinental (tran′skon tə nen′tl), *adjec-tive,* crossing a continent.

transportation (tran′spər tā′shən), *noun,* way of traveling from one place to another.

treaty (trē′tē), *noun,* an agreement between nations usually to end a war.

tributary (trib′yə ter′ē), *noun,* a stream or river that flows into a larger stream or river.

urban (ėr′bən), *adjective,* in or belonging to a city; having to do with a city.

weather (we ∓ H′ər), *noun,* the daily condi-tion of the air around us at a given time; includes moisture, temperature, winds, and cloudiness.

Facts About the United States

1980	
New York	7,071,000
Chicago	3,572,000
Los Angeles	2,967,000
Philadelphia	1,688,000
Houston	1,554,000
Detroit	1,203,000
Dallas	904,000
San Diego	876,000
Phoenix	790,000
Baltimore	787,000

Largest American Cities

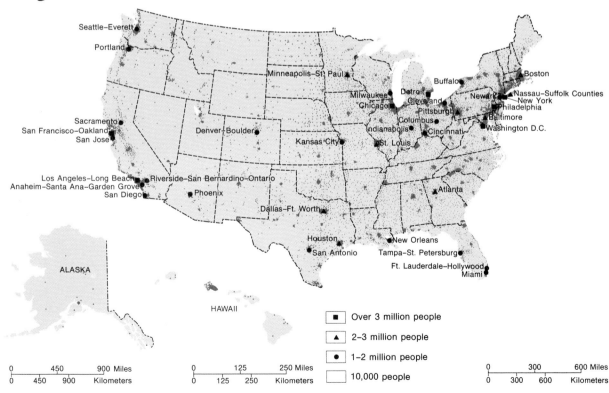

Seattle-Everett
Portland
Minneapolis-St. Paul
Milwaukee
Detroit
Buffalo
Boston
Chicago
Cleveland
Newark
Nassau-Suffolk Counties
New York
Pittsburgh
Philadelphia
Sacramento
Columbus
Baltimore
San Francisco-Oakland
Indianapolis
Cincinnati
Washington D.C.
San Jose
Denver-Boulder
Kansas City
St. Louis
Los Angeles-Long Beach
Riverside-San Bernardino-Ontario
Anaheim-Santa Ana-Garden Grove
San Diego
Phoenix
Atlanta
Dallas-Ft. Worth
Houston
New Orleans
San Antonio
Tampa-St. Petersburg
Ft. Lauderdale-Hollywood
Miami

ALASKA

HAWAII

- ■ Over 3 million people
- ▲ 2–3 million people
- ● 1–2 million people
- □ 10,000 people

0	450	900 Miles
0	450	900 Kilometers

0	125	250 Miles
0	125	250 Kilometers

0	300	600 Miles
0	300	600 Kilometers

Facts About the Northeastern States

Northeast States

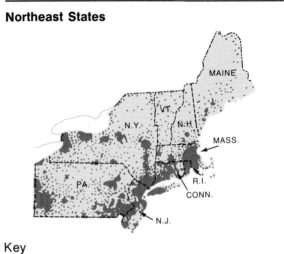

Key

•	10,000 people

The Northeast is densely populated. Most of the people earn their living by manufacturing. The Northeast is a good place for manufacturing because it has a large supply of workers, many customers, raw materials, and good transportation.

State	State Nickname	State Capital	Year Admitted to Union	Area in Square Miles	Population	Population per Square Mile	Number of Representatives in Congress*
Connecticut	Nutmeg State	Hartford	1788	5,009	3,108,000	639	6
Maine	Pine Tree State	Augusta	1820	33,215	1,125,000	36	2
Massachusetts	Bay State	Boston	1788	8,257	5,737,000	733	11 (−1)
New Hampshire	Granite State	Concord	1788	9,304	921,000	102	2
New Jersey	Garden State	Trenton	1787	7,836	7,364,000	979	15 (−1)
New York	Empire State	Albany	1788	49,576	17,557,000	367	34 (−5)
Pennsylvania	Keystone State	Harrisburg	1787	45,333	11,867,000	264	23 (−2)
Rhode Island	Ocean State	Providence	1790	1,214	947,000	903	2
Vermont	Green Mountain State	Montpelier	1791	9,609	511,000	55	1

*Figure in parentheses shows number of representatives gained or lost after 1980 census.

Facts About the North Central States

North Central States

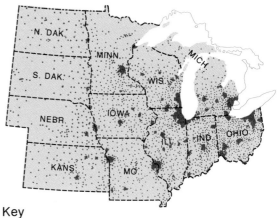

Key

█ · 10,000 people

Some of the best farmland in the world lies within the North Central Region. Many kinds of animals and crops are raised.

State	State Nickname	State Capital	Year Admitted to Union	Area in Square Miles	Population	Population per Square Mile	Number of Representatives in Congress
Illinois	Prairie State	Springfield	1818	56,400	11,418,000	205	22 (−2)
Indiana	Hoosier State	Indianapolis	1816	36,291	5,490,000	152	10
Iowa	Hawkeye State	Des Moines	1846	56,290	2,913,000	52	6
Kansas	Sunflower State	Topeka	1861	82,264	2,363,000	29	5
Michigan	Wolverine State	Lansing	1837	58,216	9,258,000	163	18 (−1)
Minnesota	North Star State	St. Paul	1858	84,068	4,077,000	51	8
Missouri	Show Me State	Jefferson City	1821	69,686	4,917,000	71	9 (−1)
Nebraska	Cornhusker State	Lincoln	1867	77,227	1,570,000	21	3
North Dakota	Sioux State	Bismarck	1889	70,665	653,000	9	1
Ohio	Buckeye State	Columbus	1803	41,222	10,797,000	264	21 (−2)
South Dakota	Sunshine State	Pierre	1889	77,047	690,000	9	1 (−1)
Wisconsin	Badger State	Madison	1848	56,154	4,705,000	86	9

Facts About the Southern States (including District of Columbia)

In the past, the South was a land mostly made up of farms. Today, the farms are still there, but many cities are growing rapidly.

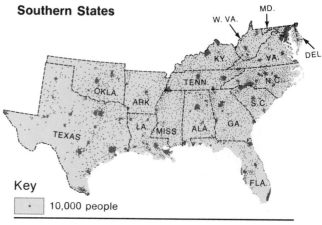

Southern States

Key

• 10,000 people

State	State Nickname	State Capital	Year Admitted to Union	Area in Square Miles	Population	Population per Square Mile	Number of Representatives in Congress
Alabama	Yellowhammer State	Montgomery	1819	51,609	3,890,000	77	7
Arkansas	Land of Opportunity	Little Rock	1836	53,104	2,286,000	44	4
Delaware	Diamond State	Dover	1787	2,057	595,000	300	1
District of Columbia	—	—	—	69	638,000	10,453	—
Florida	Sunshine State	Tallahassee	1845	58,560	9,740,000	177	19 (+4)
Georgia	Peach State	Atlanta	1788	58,876	5,464,000	94	10
Kentucky	Bluegrass State	Frankfort	1792	40,395	3,661,000	92	7
Louisiana	Pelican State	Baton Rouge	1812	48,523	4,204,000	94	8
Maryland	Free State	Annapolis	1788	10,577	4,216,000	426	8
Mississippi	Magnolia State	Jackson	1817	47,716	2,521,000	53	5
North Carolina	Tar Heel State	Raleigh	1789	52,712	5,874,000	120	11
Oklahoma	Sooner State	Oklahoma City	1907	69,919	3,025,000	44	6
South Carolina	Palmetto State	Columbia	1788	31,055	3,119,000	103	6
Tennessee	Volunteer State	Nashville	1796	42,244	4,591,000	111	9 (+1)
Texas	Lone Star State	Austin	1845	267,339	14,228,000	54	27 (+3)
Virginia	The Old Dominion	Richmond	1788	40,815	5,346,000	134	10
West Virginia	Mountain State	Charleston	1863	24,181	1,950,000	81	4

Facts About the Western States

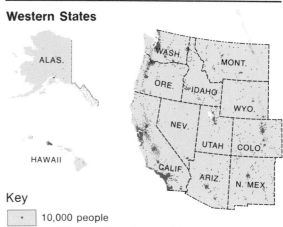

Western States

ALAS.

HAWAII

WASH.
ORE.
NEV.
CALIF.
MONT.
IDAHO
WYO.
UTAH COLO.
ARIZ. N. MEX.

Key

· 10,000 people

The West is a region of many contrasts. Most of the land is mountainous. But, some is very flat. Some places receive plenty of rain to grow crops. In other places, farmers must irrigate the land.

State	State Nickname	State Capital	Year Admitted to Union	Area in Square Miles	Population	Population per Square Mile	Number of Representatives in Congress
Alaska	The Last Frontier	Juneau	1959	589,757	400,000	1	7
Arizona	Grand Canyon State	Phoenix	1912	113,909	2,718,000	24	5 (+1)
California	Golden State	Sacramento	1850	158,693	23,669,000	151	45 (+2)
Colorado	Centennial State	Denver	1876	104,247	2,889,000	28	6 (+1)
Hawaii	Aloha State	Honolulu	1959	6,450	965,000	150	2
Idaho	Gem State	Boise	1890	83,557	944,000	11	2
Montana	Treasure State	Helena	1889	147,138	787,000	5	2
Nevada	Silver State	Carson City	1864	110,540	799,000	7	2 (+1)
New Mexico	Land of Enchantment	Santa Fe	1912	121,666	1,300,000	11	3 (+1)
Oregon	Beaver State	Salem	1859	96,981	2,633,000	27	5 (+1)
Utah	Beehive State	Salt Lake City	1896	84,916	1,461,000	18	3 (+1)
Washington	Evergreen State	Olympia	1889	68,192	4,130,000	62	8 (+1)
Wyoming	Equality State	Cheyenne	1890	97,914	471,000	5	1

Facts About the Presidents of the United States of America

Name	Date of Birth	Place of Birth	Political Party	Term of Office	Occupation after Presidency
George Washington	Feb. 22, 1732	Pope's Creek, Westmoreland County, Va.	Federalist	1789–1797	planter
John Adams	Oct. 30, 1735	Braintree (now Quincy), Mass.	Federalist	1797–1801	writer
Thomas Jefferson	Apr. 13, 1743	Albemarle County, Va.	Democratic-Republican	1801–1809	retired
James Madison	Mar. 16, 1751	Port Conway, Va.	Democratic-Republican	1809–1817	retired
James Monroe	Apr. 28, 1758	Westmoreland County, Va.	Democratic-Republican	1817–1825	writer
John Quincy Adams	July 11, 1767	Braintree (now Quincy), Mass.	Democratic-Republican	1825–1829	United States representative
Andrew Jackson	Mar. 15, 1767	Waxhaw Settlement, S.C.	Democratic	1829–1837	retired
Martin Van Buren	Dec. 5, 1782	Kinderhook, N.Y.	Democratic	1837–1841	retired
William Henry Harrison	Feb. 9, 1773	Charles City County, Va.	Whig	1841	died in office
John Tyler	Mar. 29, 1790	Charles City County, Va.	Whig	1841–1845**	lawyer
James K. Polk	Nov. 2, 1795	near Pineville, N.C.	Democratic	1845–1849	retired
Zachary Taylor	Nov. 24, 1784	near Barboursville, Va.	Whig	1849–1850	died in office
Millard Fillmore	Jan. 7, 1800	Locke, N.Y.	Whig	1850–1853**	university chancellor
Franklin Pierce	Nov. 23, 1804	Hillsboro, N.H.	Democratic	1853–1857	retired
James Buchanan	Apr. 23, 1791	Stony Batter, Pa.	Democratic	1857–1861	writer
Abraham Lincoln	Feb. 12, 1809	near present-day Hodgenville, Ky.	Republican	1861–1865*	died in office
Andrew Johnson	Dec. 29, 1808	Raleigh, N.C.	National Union	1865–1869**	United States senator
Ulysses S. Grant	Apr. 27, 1822	Point Pleasant, Ohio	Republican	1869–1877	writer

*assassinated   **succeeded to the Presidency because of the President's death

Name	Date of Birth	Place of Birth	Political Party	Term of Office	Occupation after Presidency
Rutherford B. Hayes	Oct. 4, 1822	Delaware, Ohio	Republican	1877–1881	retired
James A. Garfield	Nov. 19, 1831	Orange, Ohio	Republican	1881*	died in office
Chester A. Arthur	Oct. 5, 1830	Fairfield, Vt.	Republican	1881–1885**	lawyer
Grover Cleveland	Mar. 18, 1837	Caldwell, N.J.	Democratic	1885–1889 1893–1897	retired
Benjamin Harrison	Aug. 20, 1833	North Bend, Ohio	Republican	1889–1893	lawyer
William McKinley	Jan. 29, 1843	Niles, Ohio	Republican	1897–1901*	died in office
Theodore Roosevelt	Oct. 27, 1858	New York, N.Y.	Republican	1901–1909**	writer
William H. Taft	Sept. 15, 1857	Cincinnati, Ohio	Republican	1909–1913	United States Supreme Court chief justice
Woodrow Wilson	Dec. 28, 1856	Staunton, Va.	Democratic	1913–1921	lawyer
Warren G. Harding	Nov. 2, 1865	Corsica (now Blooming Grove), Ohio	Republican	1921–1923	died in office
Calvin Coolidge	July 4, 1872	Plymouth Notch, Vt.	Republican	1923–1929**	writer
Herbert C. Hoover	Aug. 10, 1874	West Branch, Iowa	Republican	1929–1933	writer
Franklin D. Roosevelt	Jan. 30, 1882	Hyde Park, N.Y.	Democratic	1933–1945	died in office
Harry S. Truman	May 8, 1884	Lamar, Mo.	Democratic	1945–1953**	writer
Dwight D. Eisenhower	Oct. 14, 1890	Denison, Tex.	Republican	1953–1961	writer
John F. Kennedy	May 29, 1917	Brookline, Mass.	Democratic	1961–1963*	died in office
Lyndon B. Johnson	Aug. 27, 1908	near Stonewall, Tex.	Democratic	1963–1969**	writer
Richard M. Nixon	Jan. 9, 1913	Yorba Linda, Calif.	Republican	1969–1974	writer
Gerald R. Ford	July 14, 1913	Omaha, Nebr.	Republican	1974–1977	lawyer
James E. Carter	Oct. 1, 1924	Plains, Ga.	Democratic	1977–1981	writer
Ronald W. Reagan	Feb. 6, 1911	Tampico, Ill.	Republican	1981–	

*assassinated   **succeeded to the Presidency because of the President's death

Index

Index: * = glossary word; *d.* = chart, diagram,
table; *g.* = graph; *m.* = map; *p.* = picture

Acknowledgments

Quoted Material

UNIT 1 21 from THE PEOPLE, YES by Carl Sandburg. Copyright 1936 by Harcourt Brace Jovanovich, Inc., renewed 1964 by Carl Sandburg. Reprinted by permission of the publisher. **64** excerpt from "Night Journey" copyright 1940 by Theodore Roethke from the book THE COLLECTED POEMS OF THEODORE ROETHKE. Reprinted by permission of Doubleday & Company, Inc. and Faber and Faber Ltd.

UNIT 2 84 from "Children of the Desert" from THE DESERT IS THEIRS by Byrd Baylor. Copyright © 1975 by Byrd Baylor. Reprinted with the permission of Charles Scribner's Sons and Toni Strassman, Agent. **85** from James Willard Schultz, MY LIFE AS AN INDIAN. New York: Fawcett Columbine, 1981, p. 44. **87** from EYES OF DISCOVERY by John Bakeless. New York: Dover, 1961, pp. 92–93. Reprinted by permission. **88** from AMERICAN FOLKLORE AND LEGEND. Pleasantville, New York: The Reader's Digest Association, Inc., p. 205. **96** from "The Saga Tale" from WESTVIKING by Farley Mowat. Copyright © 1965 by Farley Mowat. Reprinted by permission of Little, Brown and Company in association with the Atlantic Monthly Press and the Canadian Publishers, McClelland and Stewart Limited, Toronto. **99** from "The Voyages of Columbus and John Cabot," in Edward Gaylord Bourne, THE NORTHMEN, Columbus and Cabot (New York, 1906), 90–91, 106–10, 113. Cited in THE AMERICAN READER by Paul M. Angle. Published by Rand McNally & Company, 1958. **104–105** from Miguel Leon-Protilla (ed), THE BROKEN SPEARS: *The Aztec Account of the Conquest of Mexico.* Trans. by Lysander Kemp. Boston: Beacon Press, 1962.

UNIT 3 147 Charles Francis Adams, Ed., THE WORKS OF JOHN ADAMS (Boston, 1850), II. Cited in THE AMERICAN READER by Paul M. Angle. Published by Rand McNally & Company, 1958. **150** from the BOSTON GAZETTE, March 12, 1770. Cited in 1776: JOURNALS OF AMERICAN INDEPENDENCE by George Sanderlin. Published by Harper & Row, 1968. **154** from "British Lamentation" from LIVING DOCUMENTS IN AMERICAN HISTORY. Edited and with Introductions by John A. Scott. Published by Washington Square Press, Inc. Copyright © 1963 by John A. Scott. Reprinted by permission of the author. **155** from "Diary of a British Officer," ATLANTIC MONTHLY, Vol. XXXIX. Cited in 1776: JOURNALS OF AMERICAN INDEPENDENCE by George Sanderlin. Published by Harper & Row, 1968.

UNIT 4 195 "Moses Austin: Exploring the Ohio Valley," AMERICAN HISTORICAL REVIEW, Vol. V, pp. 523–542. **199** Black Hawk. Cited in A PEOPLE'S HISTORY OF THE UNITED STATES by Howard Zinn. New York: Harper & Row, 1980. **201** from ORIGINAL JOURNALS OF THE LEWIS AND CLARK EXPEDITION. Edited by Reuben Gold Thwaites, 8 Vols. Dodd, Mead & Co., **1904–05.** Cited in AMERICAN ODYSSEY: The Journey of Lewis and Clark. Rand McNally & Company, 1969. **208** "Jesse Applegate: A Day on the Oregon Trail," TRANSACTIONS OF THE FOURTH ANNUAL RE-UNION OF THE OREGON PIONEER ASSOCIATION: FOR 1876, Salem, Ore., pp. 57–65. **209** from "A Prairie Schooner's Varied Cargo" by Huston Horn, THE PIONEERS, Time-Life, 1974, pp. 102–103. **210** from "Overland to the Gold Fields of California in 1852" edited by Louise Barry from KANSAS HISTORICAL QUARTERLY, Vol. 11 (August 1942), pp. 227 ff. Reprinted by permission of the Kansas State Historical Society. **233** from "Make Your Own Neighborhood Newspaper" by Gretchen Haber, from THE MOTHER EARTH NEWS^R, Sept./Oct. 1981. Copyright © 1981

by The Mother Earth News, Inc., P.O. Box 70, Hendersonville, NC 28791. Adapted with permission. **233** from "Kids Channel Efforts Into TV News Show" by Mary Elson, from CHICAGO TRIBUNE, November 15, 1981. Copyright © 1981, Chicago Tribune. Reprinted with permission. **240** excerpts from "Sarah Gudger" and "Andrew Boone." From Federal Writers' Project, SLAVE NARRATIVES, A FOLK HISTORY OF SLAVERY IN THE UNITED STATES FROM INTERVIEWS WITH FORMER SLAVES. (Typewritten Records Prepared by the Federal Writers' Project, Washington, D.C., 1941). Originals are in the Library of Congress, Call Number E444.F27. **243** "The Blue-tail Fly" from ON THE TRAIL OF NEGRO FOLK-SONGS by Dorothy Scarborough. Copyright 1925 by Harvard University Press; © 1953 by Mary McDaniel Parker. Reprinted by permission of Harvard University Press. **254** "Soupy, soupy, soupy, without any bean, . . ." from THE LIFE OF BILLY YANK by Bell I. Wiley (Bobbs-Merrill Company). Reprinted by permission of Mary Frances Harrison Wiley, executrix of the Bell Irvin Wiley estate.

UNIT 5 270, 275 Excerpts from "Mingo White" and "Lorenzo Ezell." From Federal Writers' Project, SLAVE NARRATIVES, A FOLK HISTORY OF SLAVERY IN THE UNITED STATES FROM INTERVIEWS WITH FORMER SLAVES. (Typewritten Records Prepared by the Federal Writers' Project, Washington, D.C., 1941). Originals are in the Library of Congress, Call Number E444.F27. **277** From "My Soul is Full of Color . . ." by Langston Hughes, THE BIG SEA, Hill and Wang, 1940, pp. 164–165. **280–281** Taken from GOLD AND SILVER IN THE AMERICAN WEST by T.H. Watkins. Copyright © 1971 by American West Publishing Company. Used by permission of Crown Publishers, Inc. **282** Rodman W. Paul, CALIFORNIA GOLD: THE BEGINNING OF MINING IN THE FAR WEST. Lincoln, Nebraska: University of Nebraska Press (A Bison Book), 1947. **286** taken from A TREASURY OF RAILROAD FOLKLORE edited by B. A. Botkin and Alvin F. Harlow. Copyright, 1953, by B. A. Botkin and Alvin F. Harlow. Used by permission of Crown Publishers, Inc. **293** from THE TIME OF THE INDIAN by Kenneth Ulyatt, Puffin Books, 1975, p. 48 (and title page). Reprinted by permission. **303** Horatio Alger, Jr. RAGGED DICK AND MARK, THE MATCH BOY. Ragged Dick Series, 1867. **304** Adapted from Bessie Van Vorst and Marie Van Vorst, THE WOMAN WHO TOILS. (Doubleday, Page & Company, 1903.) **306** Cited in A PEOPLE'S HISTORY OF THE UNITED STATES by Howard Zinn. New York: Harper & Row, 1980, pp. 274–275. **311, 314** Mary Antin, THE PROMISED LAND. Boston and New York: Houghton Mifflin Company, 1912. Reprinted by permission. **318** Jacob Riis, HOW THE OTHER HALF LIVES. New York: Charles Scribner's Sons, 1890. **319–320** Upton Sinclair, THE JUNGLE. New York: Doubleday, Doran & Company, Inc., 1906.

UNIT 6 329 Abridged from "I Have a Rendezvous With Death" by Alan Seeger, POEMS BY ALAN SEEGER, Charles Scribner's and Sons, 1916. **329** Abridged from "In Flanders Fields" by John McCrae, THE BOOK OF CANADIAN POETRY, ed. A.J.M. Smith, W.J. Gage Limited, 1957. Reprinted by permission. **332** Excerpt from "Letters of Negro Migrants 1916–1918" by E.J. Scott, JOURNAL OF NEGRO HISTORY: Vol. 4, July 1919. Reprinted by permission of The Associated Publishers, Inc. **335–336** Abridged and adapted from p. 12 in CHEAPER BY THE DOZEN by Frank B. Gilbreth, Jr., and Ernestine Gilbreth Carey. Copyright © 1963, 1948 by Frank B. Gilbreth, Jr., and Ernestine Gilbreth Carey. By permission of Thomas Y. Crowell Company and William Heinemann Ltd. **338**

"Is Woman Suffrage Failing?" A Symposium of THE WOMAN CITIZEN, April 19, 1924. **341** Mary B. Mullett. From "The Biggest Thing That Lindbergh Has Done" in THE AMERICAN MAGAZINE, October 1927. Reprinted by permission. **350** Adapted from "When the Depression Came to 16th Street" by Jack Star, CHICAGO TRIBUNE MAGAZINE, April 27, 1975, p. 22. **349, 350, 351** From "What a Depression is Really Like," U.S. NEWS & WORLD REPORT, November 11, 1974. Copyright © 1974, U.S. News & World Report, Inc. Reprinted by permission. **353** From "Brother Can You Spare a Dime?" By permission of Harms, Inc. **362–363** from AMERICANS: REMEMBER THE HOME FRONT: *An Oral Narrative* by Roy Hoopes. Copyright © 1977 by Roy Hoopes. Reprinted by permission of the author. **369** Excerpts from "Rosie the Riveter won a war, started a revolt" by Richard Phillips, CHICAGO TRIBUNE, February 21, 1982. Reprinted by permission. **380** from I AM A MAN: ODE TO MARTIN LUTHER KING, JR. by Eve Merriam. Copyright © 1971 by Eve Merriam. Reprinted by permission of Eve Merriam, c/o International Creative Management. **382** WE SHALL OVERCOME. New words and musical arrangement by Zilphia Horton, Frank Hamilton, Guy Carawan & Pete Seeger. Used by permission of Ludlow Music Inc., The Essex Music Group, London and Australia, and the Essex Music Group (PTY) Ltd. Royalties derived from this composition are being contributed to the Freedom Movement under the trusteeship of the writers. **384** From GROWING UP PUERTO RICAN by Paulette Cooper. Copyright © 1972 by Paulette Cooper. Reprinted by permission of the author and the author's agents, Scott Meredith Literary Agency, Inc. 845 Third Avenue, New York, New York 10022. **385** From "The I Don't Know Where I'm Goin' But I'm Goin' Nowhere In a Hurry Blues" by Steve Goodman. Copyright © 1971 Kama Rippa Music, Inc. All rights administered by United Artists Music Co., Inc. Reprinted by permission. **388** From "Genesis Revisited" by Richard S. Lewis, APPOINTMENT ON THE MOON, Ballantine Books, 1969, p. 460. **390** The "Editorial Creed" by Dr. Jay D. Hair, Chairman, Editorial Board, NATIONAL WILDLIFE. **391** From "Bt and the CCC" by Mark Wexler from NATIONAL WILDLIFE, February–March 1982. Copyright © 1982 by the National Wildlife Federation. Reprinted by permission.

Illustrations

The abbreviations indicate position of pictures on a page. *Bk* is background, *t* is top, *b* is bottom, *c* is center, *m* is margin, *l* is left, and *r* is right. **14–15** (+ detail p.74) Dennis Brack/Black Star. **16–17** Scott, Foresman. **20** Doug Wilson/West Stock. **23**(t) Gscheidle/Peter Arnold; **23**(b) Scott, Foresman. **24**(r) Martin Rogers/Woodfin Camp & Associates; **24**(tl) Harald Sund, Seattle; **24** (b) Selig/Peter Arnold. **25** (+ detail p.32) Nathan Benn/Woodfin Camp. **26** Susan Dean. **28–30** Scott, Foresman. **29** Cartoon by Mike Peters, United Features Syndicate. **31** Johnson Publishing. **44** Cary Wolinsky/Stock, Boston. **45**(t) Milton Feinberg/Stock, Boston; **45**(b) Jodi Cobb/Woodfin Camp. **47**(t) Jode Cobb/Woodfin Camp; **47**(t) Tom Stack & Associates. **48**(t) Annie Griffith/Woodfin Camp. **49**(t) Harald Sund; **49**(b) David Muench. **50** Owen Franken/Stock, Boston. **51** David Muench. **57**(b) David Muench. **58**(t) Harald Sund. **59** Josef Muench. **60** Chuck O'Rear/Woodfin Camp. **61** Lowell J. Georgia/Photo Researchers. **64** Geoffrey Gove/Photo Researchers. **67** Jan Lukas/Photo Researchers. **68** (+ detail p.73) Mike Mazzaschi/Stock, Boston. **69** David Muench. **72** Grant Heilman.

UNIT 2 76–77 (+ detail p. 136) David Muench. 78 Stewart M Green. 80 National Museums of Canada, Ottawa. 81 Elliot Erwitt/Magnum Photos. 82 David Muench. 83 Arizona State Museum, University of Arizona, Helga Teiwes, Photographer. 84 Chuck O'Rear/West Light. 87 (+ detail p.93) "Laramie's Fort Exterior" (detail) by A. J. Miller, Courtesy the Walters Art Gallery, Baltimore. 89(t) Photography courtesy of Museum of the American Indian, Heye Foundation; 89(b) "The Manner of Their Fishing" by John White. Courtesy of the Trustees, The British Museum. 90 "Secoton Village" by John White. Courtesy of the Trustees, The British Museum. 94 from "Historia de Gentibus Septentrionalibus" by Olas Magnus. Printed by J. M. de Vottio, Bologna, 155. 95 Swedish Travel Information Bureau, Inc. 96 Universitetcts Oldsaksamling, Oslo. 97 National Historic Parks & Sites Branch, Parks Canada. 98 (+ detail p.107) "Nina, Pinta & Santa Maria" by Edward Moran. U.S. Naval Academy Museum. 100 Photographie Giraudon. 103 National Film Board of Canada. 106 Colliers, December 9, 1905. 110 (+ detail p.117) Jeffrey M. Ikler. 111 "Setting Traps for Beaver" by A. J. Miller. 113 Schoenfeld/Three Lions. 114 John Lewis Stage. 116 John Lewis Stage. 117 Courtesy of the National Park Service, Jamestown, Va. 120 Courtesy of American Heritage. 121(r) The Bettmann Archive; 121(l) John Lewis Stage. 124(all) Farrell Grehan/Photo Researchers. 125 "Tontine Coffee House." Courtesy The New-York Historical Society.

UNIT 3 138–139 (+ detail p. 190) "Dawn of Liberty." Lexington Historical Society. 143 Manuscript Division, New York Public Library, Astor, Lenox & Tilden Foundations. 144(all) Library of Congress. 146 Council of Arts & Humanities, Boston. George M. Cushing Photography. 147 Library of Congress. 148 Massachusetts Historical Society. 149 Museum of the City of New York. 150–151 Library of Congress. 151(r) Culver Pictures 152 Consumers Union of the United States, Inc. 154–155 Library of Congress. 156 Family Album for Americans, Ridge Press; 156(t) Scott, Foresman Collection. 157 George Washington (detail) by C. W. Peale, 1780, Colonial Williamsburg. 158 H. Armstrong Roberts. 159(t) The Franklin Institute. 159(b) Library of Congress. 160(b) The Bettmann Archive. 162(t) Library of Congress; 162(b) Watercolor by de Verger of the Royal Deux-Ponts Regiment. The Anne S. K. Brown Military Collection, Brown University Library. 163 National Park Service, G. R. Clark National Historical Park, Vincennes. 164 "Mercy Otis Warren" (detail), by John S. Copeley, Bequest of Winslow Warren. Courtesy, Museum of Fine Arts, Boston. 166–167 Detail from drawing in Scripner's Popular History of the U.S., 1897. 168 The New Public Library. 169 (+ detail p.179) Painting by Christy. U.S. Capitol Historical Society. 173 Ken Regan/Camera Five. 176 Andy Levin/Black Star. 177–178(all) Scott, Foresman. 180 Painting by A. Rivey, 1789. The New-York Historical Society. 182(t) Penn Mutual Life Insurance Co., Philadelphia. 182(m) & (b) American Historical & Literary Curiosities J. Jay Smith, New York, 1852. 183 (detail) Art Commission of New York; 183 (detail) White House Collection. 184 Andy Levin/Black Star. 185 Cartoon by Dick Locher. Copyrighted, 1980. Chicago Tribune. Used with permission. 187(t) Anne S. K. Brown Military Collection. Brown University Library. 187(b) Uniphoto © 1979 Les Moore.

UNIT 4 192–193 (+ detail p.258) "The Oregon Trail" (detail) by Albert Bierstadt. The Butler Institute of American Art. 196 American History Division, The New York Public Library, Astor, Lenox & Tilden Foundations. 198 "Trail of Tears" by Robert Lindneux. Woolaroc Museum, Bartlesville, Oklahoma. 200 Trail of Lewis & Clark by Olin D. Wheeler, 1904. 202(all) The Bettmann Archive. 203(t) The Bettmann Archive; 203(r) Texas Memorial Museum, Austin. 204 The Society of California Pioneers. 205 Harald Sund; 205(t) Larry Nielsen/Peter Arnold. 208 Jeffrey M. Ikler. 209(l) Historical Pictures Service. 209(r) Courtesy Minnesota Historical Society. 210 "Dead Mule" sketch by Bruff. Collection of Western Americana, Beinecke Rare Book & Manuscript Library Yale University. 216 "Forging the Shaft: A Welding Heat" by J. F. Weir. The Metropolitan Museum of Art. Gift of Lyman G. Bloomingdale, 1901. 218 Courtesy The Chicago Historical Society. 220 The Bettmann Archive. 223 Harper's Weekly, August 29, 1861. 226 W. C. Brown: The History of the First Locomotive in America, 1871. 227 William A. Crafts: Pioneers in the Settlement of America, 1876. 228 The New-York Historical Society. 229 "The Coming & Going of the Pony Express" by F. Remington. Thomas Gilcrease Institute, Tulsa, Oklahoma. 231 The Bettmann Archive. 232 The Museums at Stonybrook; Gift of Mr. & Mrs. Ward Melville, 1955. 233 Mother Earth News, Inc. 234(l) Chicago Tribune Photo by Val Mazzenga. Used by permission; 234(b) Alfred C. Bonanno/Time Inc. 238–239 (+ detail p.247) The Harry T. Peters Collection, Museum of the City of New York. 241(l) Metropolitan Museum of Art, New York, Gift of I. N. Phelps Stokes, Edward S. Hawes, Alice Mary Hawes, Marion Augusta Hawes, 1937; 241(m) The New York Public Library, Astor, Lenox and Tilden Foundations; 241(r) Library of Congress. 242(t) Culver Pictures; 242(b) Engraving from The Underground Railroad, W. Sill, 1872. 245 The Kansas State Historical Society, Topeka 246 Illinois State Capital. 248(t) Library of Congress; 248(b) Historical Pictures. 251 "Pickett's Charge," Battle of Gettysburg. Gettysburg National Military Park. 252 Library of Congress. 254 Library of Congress. 255(t) The Schaumberg Collection, New York Public Library; 255(b) Bettmann Archive. 256(all) Library of Congress.

UNIT 5 268–269 (+ detail 322) "Song of the Talking Wire." Courtesy Taft Museum, Cincinnati. 271 National Archives #86-G-1B-1. 272 (+ detail p.278) The Bettmann Archive. 273 National Archives #165-C-776. 274 Harper's Weekly, Jan. 27, 1872. 276 Leonard Freed/Magnum. 277(both) Brown Brothers. 279(both) California State Library. 280 from the collection of L. H. Jorud, Helena, Montana. 281 Rare Book Division, New York Public Library, Astor, Lenox and Tilden Foundations. 282 David Muench. 284 "Jerked Down" by C. M. Russell (detail). The Thomas Gilcrease Institute, Tulsa, Oklahoma. 285 A. A. Hart, reproduced with permission of the Huntington library, San Marino, CA. 286(both) Union Pacific Railroad Museum Collection. 287 Frank Leslie's Illustrated, Feb. 8, 1878. 290(t) Courtesy Baker Library, Harvard Business School; 290(b) Solomon D. Butcher Collection, Nebraska State Historical Society. 291(t) Courtesy Nebraska State Historical Society; 291(b) The Kansas State Historical Society, Topeka. 292 Solomon D. Butcher Collection, Nebraska State Historical Society. 295(t) "Custer's Last Stand" (detail) by Edgar Paxson Courtesy of the Buffalo Bill Historical Center, Cody, Wyoming; 295(b) Jeffrey M. Ikler. 296 Minnesota Historical Society. 297 Photo courtesy of the Museum of the American Indian, Heye Foundation, Neg. No. 33738. 299(l) J. C. Allen & Son, W. Lafayette, Indiana; 299(r) (+ detail p.308) General Electric. 300(l) Courtesy The American Antiquarian Society; 300(r) Library of Congress. 301 From the Collection of Landon Risteen. 302 Museum of the City of New York. 304 Keystone Mast Collection, University of California, Riverside. 305 Library of Congress. 306 "The Strike" by Robert Koehler. Courtesy of District 1199, National Union of Hospital & Health Care Employees, RWDSW/AFL-CIO and Lee Baxandall. 307 Brown Brothers. 311 (+ detail p.321) Culver Pictures. 312 Library of Congress. 314 Library of Congress. 315 Joseph Viesti; 315 Courtesy The Chicago Historical Society. 317 Brown Brothers. 318(t) Library of Congress; 318(b) International Museum of Photography, George Eastman House. 319 Library of Congress. 320 Brown Brothers.

UNIT 6 324–325 (+ detail p.398) NASA. 328 Library of Congress. 331(t) (+ detail p.333) National Archives #111-SC-94980; 331(b) Brown Brothers. 332(t) Museum of Modern Art, New York. 332(b) U.P.I. 335 Henry Ford Museum, Edison Institute No. 198. 336(l) Saturday Evening Post, Oct. 3, 1908; 336(r) (+ detail p.344) Culver Pictures. 337 Culver Pictures. 338 U.P.I. 339(t) Bettmann Archives; 339(b) Brown Brothers. 340(b) Jazzman Photo/Ramsey Archive; 340(b) U.P.I. 341(l) Brown Brothers; 341(tr) © Walt Disney Productions; 341(b) Library of Congress. 342 FPG-Photoworld. 343 Culver Pictures. 345 Brown Brothers. 347(l) (+ detail p.357) Brown Brothers. 349 Brown Brothers. 350 Library of Congress. 351 U.P.I. 352 ESSA. 353 The Detroit News. 354(t) Brown Brothers 354 U.P.I. 355 U.S. Forest Service. 358 Brown Brothers. 359 Information Center Services. 360 Ullstein Birnback. 362 Wide World Photos. 363 U.S. Navy Photo. 364 Eliot Elisofon, Life Magazine, © Time Inc. 365 Vernon T. Manion. Courtesy Boeing Aircraft Corporation, Seattle. 366(t) Victor de Palma/Black Star. 366(b) Scott, Foresman Collection. 367(tr) Wide World. 367(bl & br) Scott, Foresman Collection. 368(tl) Courtesy Life Magazine; 368(l) Clifford R. Yeich, Courtesy Reading (PA) Times; 368(r) Courtesy B. F. Goodrich. 369 (+ detail p.379) Library of Congress. 370 Baker Library, Harvard Business School. 371 Courtesy Swifts Premium. 372(t) Toni Frissell. Courtesy Frissell Collection, Library of Congress; 372(b) U.S. Air Force. 373 W. Eugene Smith, Life Magazine, © 1945 Time Inc. 376 David Holman/West Stock. 377 Allan Grant. 380 Burt Glinn/Magnum. 381, (+ detail p.387) Johnson Publishing Co. 382 Benedict Fernandez. 383 U.P.I. 384(both) Paul Fusco/Magnum. 385 Abigail Heyman/Archive. 388 (+ detail p.397) NASA. 389 (+ detail p.397) Paul Fusco/Magnum; 389(b) Scott, Foresman. 390(l) Benyas Kaufman/Black Star; 390(b) Michael Sullivan. 391(l) Ed Pieratt/Black Star; 391(b) Craig Aurness/West Light. 392 Mark Wexler. 395(t) Bill Ross/West Light; 395(b) Charles Moore/Black Star. 396 Cartoon by Jim Borgman, King Features Syndicate.

UNIT 7 400–401 (+ detail p.451) Focus on SPORT. 402(t) Elisa Leonelli/Bruce Coleman; 402(b) (+ detail p.412) Owen Franken/Stock, Boston. 404(t) Jen & Des Bartlett/Bruce Coleman; 404(b) Fred Breummer. 406 Craig Aurness/West Light. 408(t) Earl Roberge/Photo Researchers; 408(bl) Craig Aurness/West Light; 408(r) Bill Staley/West Stock. 409(bl) NASA; 409(br) MASTERFILE: Terry Hancey. 410 MASTERFILE: Peter Christopher. 411 U.S. Customs Service. 413 Mark Godfrey/Archive. 414 Jeannine F. Henebry. 415 Robert Frerk/Odyssey. 416 Peter Menzel/Stock, Boston. 418(l) (+ detail p.424) Andrew Rakoczy/Bruce Coleman; 418(r) Joseph Viesti/Alpha-F.P.G. 419(l) Robert Frerk/Woodfin Camp; 419(m) John Henebry, Jr.; 419(b) Andrew Rakoczy/Bruce Coleman. 421(l) Tom Nebbia/Woodfin Camp; 421(rt) John Henebry, Jr.; 421(rb) Bruce Coleman Inc. 422 Jay Wolke. 426(l) John Henebry, Jr.; 426(r) Alon Reininger/Contact. 427 Bruce Coleman. 428 Peter Ward/Bruce Coleman; 428(b) (+ detail p.434) Nicholas Devore III/Bruce Coleman. 429 Stephanie Maze/Woodfin Camp. 430(r) Lillian Bolstad/Photo Researchers; 430(l) Nicholas Devore III/Bruce Coleman. 432(t) Dan Lehman/West Light; 432(b) John Running/Stock, Boston. 433 Timothy O'Keefe/Bruce Coleman. 437 William Boehm/West Stock. 438(t) Loren McIntyre/Woodfin Camp; 438(b) Joachim Messerschmidt/Bruce Coleman. 439(l) Don Normark/West Stock; 439(r) John Henebry, Jr. 440(l) Sullivan & Rogers/Bruce Coleman. 441 William Boehm/West Stock. 442 (+ detail p.449) John Henebry, Jr. 443 Rick Ergenbright/West Light. 444(l) Bruce Coleman; 444(r) Joachim Messerschmidt/Bruce Coleman. 445 Thomas Nebbia/Woodfin Camp. 446 Staley/West Stock. 447(t) Carl Frank/Photo Researchers; 447(b) Toby Molenaar/Woodfin Camp. 448(t) Strong/West Stock; 448(t) Rick Merron/Magnum. 465 Scott, Foresman, 466 Peter Vandermark/Stock, Boston. 467 Fred Ragsdale/FPG. 468 Donato Leo/DPI. 469 Lester Tinker/Taurus. 470 Bettman Archives; 470 Joel Gordon/DPI.